PROMISED LAND

ALSO BY CARLETON MABEE

Bridging the Hudson:
The Poughkeepsie Railroad Bridge and Its Connecting Rail Lines,
A Many-Faceted History

The American Leonardo:
A Life of Samuel F. B. Morse
(Pulitzer Prize)

The Seaway Story
(A History of the Great Lakes-St. Lawrence Canals)

Black Freedom:
The Nonviolent Abolitionists from 1830 through the Civil War
(Anisfield-Wolf Award)

Black Education in New York State:
From Colonial to Modern Times
(John Ben Snow Prize)

WITH JAMES A. FLETCHER:
A Quaker Speaks from the Black Experience:
The Life and Selected Writings of Barrington Dunbar

WITH SUSAN MABEE NEWHOUSE:
Sojourner Truth: Slave, Prophet, Legend
(Outstanding Book Award of the
Gustavus Myers Center
for the Study of Human Rights)

EDITED BY JOHN K. JACOBS:
Listen to the Whistle:
An Anecdotal History of the Wallkill Valley Railroad
in Ulster and Orange Counties, New York

PROMISED LAND

FATHER DIVINE'S INTERRACIAL COMMUNITIES IN ULSTER COUNTY, NEW YORK

Carleton Mabee

PURPLE MOUNTAIN PRESS
Fleischmanns, New York

PROMISED LAND:
Father Divine's Interracial Communities in Ulster County, New York

First Edition
2008

Published by Purple Mountain Press, Ltd.
P.O. Box 309, Fleischmanns, New York 12430-0309
845-254-4062, 845-254-4476 (fax)
purple@catskill.net
http://www.catskill.net/purple

Library of Congress Control Number: 2008939278

ISBN-13: 978-1-930098-93-0
ISBN: 1-930098-93-6

Cover:
Divinite property on the Hudson River at Krum Elbow from *New Day*, August 14, 1941.

Back cover:
Portrait of Father Divine courtesy of the
Manuscript, Archives, and Rare Book Library, Emory University

5 4 3 2 1
Manufactured in the United States of America on acid-free paper.

To

NORMA DIERKING MABEE
(1914-2004)

who encouraged my beginning this project
but missed seeing it to completion

CONTENTS

C. PERSONAL STORIES

D. OPERATIONS

E. TEACHING AGAINST WAR

F. SLOWING DOWN

PREFACE

FATHER DIVINE lifted the despairing from the gutter to self-respect, but his methods troubled many observers. He commanded substantial wealth, but he mystified much of the world as to how he acquired it. He had charismatic power, but his talk of his supernatural abilities was difficult for the public to accept. His movement constituted one of the most completely interracial groups in America in its time, yet large numbers of Americans found this to be offensive. One of Divine's associates claimed that Divine probably met "more opposition than anyone upon the face of the earth."

This book deals with Father Divine's movement beginning in the 1930s during the Great Depression. At that time, when the movement was providing free food to thousands of the unemployed, journalist George Sokolsky, writing in the *Atlantic Monthly*, called it the nation's "most successful religious movement." This book also deals with Divine's movement during World War II, when he continued to teach, as he long had, that his true followers would not fight. This book also deals with Divine's movement soon after the war, when a newspaper prominent among blacks, the Pittsburgh *Courier*, called Divine's Peace Mission "the only organization in America" that has achieved "racial integration." This book also deals with Divine's impact after his death when the political scientist Leo Rosten declared that while Divine was "adorable," and taught "a sweet and beneficent faith," he was also a fraud, a "mountebank."[1]

Divine was long based in Harlem, and, to use a term he himself favored, he was an "Afro-American." This book, however, focuses on him as he led in creating interracial, utopian communities in overwhelmingly white Ulster County, New York, a hundred miles north of Harlem, up the Hudson River. By 1939, Divine had led in creating some thirty such communities in the county—they were experimental, cooperative, and nonviolent, and about 2,300 people were living in them. While the settled population of the county was disturbed by the arrival of these communities, Divine had high hopes for them as models for the world. Divine and his followers called them a Promised Land to which God was now leading his followers as God had once led the ancient Hebrews to their Promised Land.

This book concentrates on Divine's movement in the period from 1935, when it established its first community in Ulster County, in New Paltz, until 1985, when it sold off its last community in the county, in Kingston. This book tells how the Ulster County communities were founded and what they did. It tells the stories of selected individuals related to these communities as helping to illuminate the whole movement. It follows interconnections between Divine's movement in Ulster County and elsewhere, especially in the two metropolitan areas where Divine had his headquarters, first New York City, later Philadelphia. It spotlights the movement's nonviolent character, as has seldom been done, including how the movement applied nonviolence to World War II.

I have been drawn to this topic for several reasons. Intentional, utopian communities fascinate me. I am attracted to their idealism. I want to understand their successes and their failures. Moreover, Divine is not well enough known, I believe, in our time. His communities in Ulster County have been little written about. What participants remember about these communities needs to be recorded while the participants still survive. I myself have long lived in Ulster County, and have already written considerably on its history, as well as on themes related to the Divine movement such as the struggle for racial integration and the application of non-violence to social change.

Moreover, Divine touched me and my family,

albeit in limited ways. When I was a student at Columbia University, despite the prevailing segregation, I occasionally joined friends in visiting Harlem, including eating the inexpensive food at Divine Peace Mission restaurants. The service was courteous and the diners sang fervently as they waited at length for Divine to appear. When at last he suddenly arrived, what I recall is not what he said, but that the crowd greeted hm with frenzy. During World War II, because Divine taught nonviolence, many of his followers were conscientious objectors, and since I was one myself, I did alternate service alongside them. In the 1950s, my niece, while she was a student in a Quaker school near Philadelphia, participated in Quaker work camps rehabilitating slum housing in Philadelphia; when the students took meals at nearby Divine sites, they were impressed by the interracial brotherhood they found there. In the early 1970s, when my son and his girl friend, who later became his wife, were both students at the University of Pennsylvania, they frequented an inexpensive nearby restaurant run by Divine followers at the Tracy Hotel. They recall that once when they held hands there, a restaurant worker interrupted them, saying that they did not allow such displays of affection.

While it has been difficult to deal with the many controversies surrounding this subject, the difficulties have made the subject more compelling. They have led me to seek help, which I have abundantly received. They have led me to invite readers to make their own judgments about many issues.

In the 1930s a Divine movement periodical declared that when the story of Divine's communities in Ulster County comes to be told, "it must have a book all by itself."[2] Here is the first one.

Carleton Mabee
Gardiner, Ulster County, NY

A. ESTABLISHING COMMUNITIES

1. DIVINE AND THE RISE OF HIS MOVEMENT

FATHER DIVINE, stressing spiritual life as he did, maintained that his early mortal life was irrelevant to understanding him. When Divine was pressed about his birth, he declined to explain where or when he was born, or what his birth name was, making it difficult for historians to trace his early life. Historians, who are inclined to regard the early life of everyone to be relevant to understanding them, have generally regarded Divine as born and raised in the American South. Because of his speaking style, his biographer Robert Weisbrot believed that he was born in the rural Deep South. His more recent biographer Jill Watts, using court and census records, believed he was born as George Baker in rural Maryland. This present book not being a biography, the present author has not independently researched Divine's early life, and while admitting that there remains doubt, reports here what recent historians generally believe in regard to it.

According to some recent historians, Divine was born in 1879 as George Baker, to a poor family of ex-slaves, in a rural Afro-American neighborhood in Rockville, Maryland. Baker grew up, historians are likely to believe, humiliated by his short stature—he grew to be just over five feet tall. If he was also humiliated by his mother's extreme obesity, it was not enough to cause him to reject a common attitude of the time that for anyone to become heavy was a sign of prosperity. Baker grew up, historians believe, accustomed to poverty, alcohol abuse, and segregation. He grew up with little schooling but in the embrace of a warm, black-led Methodist religious tradition, which emphasized not so much head as heart. He also grew up with respect for the Catholic Church through his mother, whose slave masters, when she was their young slave, had required her to attend that church.[1]

By about 1899, when he settled in Baltimore, as he later himself approximately confirmed, George Baker was supporting himself as a gardener, and, turning away from established religion, he was identifying himself with loosely-organized storefront churches. Beginning to preach, he preached without pay, a practice he continued throughout his life. He fell much under the influence of a progressive religious movement of the period called New Thought, led at that time by such figures as Robert Collier (the nephew of the publisher of *Collier's* magazine) and Charles Fillmore (the founder of the Unity School of Christianity). New Thought was a liberal, individualistic, decentralized movement, and it was working its way into the American main stream. Baker adopted such New Thought beliefs as the desirability of building a better life now, on earth below, rather than waiting for it later, in heaven above; and the belief, like that of the related Christian Science, that positive thought could help bring health and prosperity.[2]

From about 1902, with considerable evidence for this period supplied by Baker himself, he became an itinerant evangelist. In the Deep South, he gathered a few black followers, and influenced by Catholic asceticism as well as by New Thought's emphasis that one's spiritual nature should control one's bodily urges, he taught them to abstain from sex. Rejecting racial segregation, he brought blacks and whites together in defiance of Southern custom. Such unconventional behavior led, historians believe, to Baker's being jailed, coming close to being lynched, and being pushed out of town.

Meantime, while both the traditional revivalistic church and New Thought concentrated on individual salvation, Baker was also embracing social salvation. He may have moved toward this view not only because of his own experience of poverty and racial injustice, but also because of the rising Social Gospel movement which sought to lead Christianity to social reform. At the same time, Baker was continuing to sort out what he was learning from a mix of such traditions as progressive New Thought, evangelical Methodism, ascetic Catholicism, speaking-in-tongues Pentecostalism, and the revivalistic storefront church.[5]

FATHER AND MOTHER DIVINE, said to have been photographed in Washington, D.C., in 1932. (Woodmont)

HIS BROOKLYN PERIOD: LEADING A BLACK COOPERATIVE COMMUNE, IN A BLACK NEIGHBORHOOD

By 1915, when his life can be more reliably traced, Baker had settled in New York City, where considerable numbers of Southern blacks were moving in search of better jobs. Having collected a handful of disciples, he organized them into a little cooperative, which was the forerunner of his many utopian communities. At first he housed his cooperative in a run-down house on West 40th Street in Manhattan, but by at least 1917, he housed it in an apartment in a black neighborhood in Brooklyn. At this time his immediate followers were all blacks, mostly women. Paring expenses, he bought them second-hand clothes, and prohibited drinking, smoking, and drugs. He ran an employment agency, which placed his followers in domestic or blue collar jobs. Although everyone in the cooperative was regarded as having equal rights, those who worked outside the community pooled their wages to support it, while those who worked inside it worked without pay. By this time, he had adopted the name Rev. Major Jealous Divine, which lent itself to the belief that he personified God.[4] He ran his community like a family, he leading it as a firm father and his wife assisting him as a compassionate mother. His wife was Peninnah, known as Mother Divine, a black of Southern origin who believed he had healed her; however, he continued to advocate a strict code of sexual abstinence, and applied this code even to married persons like himself.

HIS SAYVILLE PERIOD: MOVING HIS OMMUNE TO A WHITE NEIGHBORHOOD, WHERE IT BECAME INTERRACIAL

In 1919, Divine moved his cooperative community out of New York City, distancing himself from figures he felt to be his rivals such as Marcus Garvey, the leader of the Back to Africa movement. Divine moved his community to Sayville, a white, middle-class town, on Long Island's South Shore, about sixty miles east of Manhattan. Divine and his wife bought a house there, with his wife providing the funds. The white owner of the house, fed up in a dispute with a neighbor and seeking revenge, had advertised he wanted to sell it to "colored." This meant, as Divine well knew, that by living there he was openly defying Sayville's customary housing segregation.

Continuing to operate his employment agency, Divine secured domestic jobs for many of his followers in the nearby region, and they earned a reputation for hard, honest work. With their support, Divine enlarged the house, kept three cars, served elaborate meals free, and welcomed all kinds of people, of all ages, including the indigent, if they promised to abide by his strict rules. While residents seemed to come and go, by 1924 their number had risen to about 12, and by 1930 to about 30; these latter included a few whites, making the community interracial. Meanwhile, Divine frequented the local library, continuing to read New Thought literature, strengthening his belief that envisioning health and prosperity helped to make them happen. While he remained essentially Christian, if unconventionally so, he also studied Eastern religions, adopting from them an appreciation of intuition, reincarnation, and respect for a variety of religious traditions.

The neighbors of the community, disturbed by its increasing number of visitors, pushed the Suffolk County District Attorney to investigate it. In 1930, the District Attorney did so especially by sending to the community Susan Hadley, an attractive young Harlem woman, in disguise. Pretending to seek help as a needy prospective follower, Hadley stayed there two weeks. She was welcomed. She was not required to pay anything. She found that the followers worked hard, enjoyed generous quantities of food, and Divine encouraged them to gain weight as a sign of health. She found they lived peaceably and greeted each other with the word "peace." She learned they abstained from sex, held praise services with singing and jumping, and adored Divine as Christ come again. Divine claimed, Hadley reported, that he did not solicit donations, and since she could not discover that he did, she was at a loss to explain his apparent wealth. From her and others' reports, the District Attorney concluded he had no

DIVINE'S HOUSE IN SAYVILLE, LONG ISLAND, WHERE HE FED VISITORS FOR FREE. The house drew such crowds that neighbors complained. (*New Day*, June 15, 1974)

evidence of illegality and abandoned his investigation.[5]

Meanwhile, in response to the privations of the Great Depression, Divine, unlike many other clergy, kept protesting the injustice of the economic system toward the poor, and kept finding food and jobs for them. Moreover, he held out hope to all for salvation in this life and promised that believers would never die. He insisted on equal rights for all, fought racial segregation in any form, and with deep passion, strove to make religion a force for building a more just society.

Local merchants were pleased that Divine paid his bills at once. Neighbors, however, kept complaining that too many visitors came to his house, that their singing was too loud, and that too many of them were dark skinned, threatening property values. The complaints brought publicity, which attracted more followers, a growing number of them being whites. They were especially of middle or upper class background, many of them having previously been touched by New Thought-related groups such as Unity School or Christian Science. Such whites found that Divine's community lived according to impressively high standards—including no drinking, no sex, and no violence, but stressing honesty, hard work, respect for the dignity of each person, and expectation of health and prosperity. Such standards gave vibrancy to concepts with which they were familiar but which otherwise tended to remain abstract. By September, 1931, it was said that an average of one thousand persons, of a variety of races, were partaking of the free Sunday banquets at the house, banquets that were continuously served. Such generous quantities of free food being served during the depression kept raising the question as to how Divine could afford them, adding to the neighborhood's uneasiness with him, and Divine felt the pressure.

On a November evening in 1931, Divine seemed to orchestrate a confrontation: he allowed his usual praise service to last late into the night and be very noisy. This led to a police raid on the house, and the arrest of Divine and some of his followers as public nuisances. Taken away in buses were 63 blacks and 15 whites, including several who were later to become associated with Ulster County, such as Divine's black wife; the white John Lamb, a wealthy Massachusetts automobile dealer who was to become Divine's major secretary; and the white Rebecca Branch, an immigrant from Spain who taught Spanish to upper crust New York City families.

While the press increasingly paid attention, officials released the followers, but pressed charges against Divine himself as especially responsible for the public nuisance. Eventually a jury declared Divine guilty but recommended that the judge, in sentencing him, be lenient. On June 5, 1932, however, the judge, Lewis J. Smith, saying he considered Divine a "menace to society," gave him the maximum possible sentence of one year in jail, which Divine, evidently feeling he had little to lose, seemed to face easily. A few days later, when Divine had already begun serving his jail sentence, Judge Smith, in his fifties and apparently in good health, suddenly died of a heart attack. When Divine in his cell was asked to comment, he was widely quoted as saying, "I hated to do it." Divine never disavowed those words.

The press played up the story of the trial, the judge's death, and Divine's taking responsibility for it, catapulting him, for the first time in his life, into fame. His high ethical standards and his teaching that heaven was on earth, not in the sky, gripped attention. His apparently inexhaustible wealth combined with his refusal to solicit funds aroused immense curiosity. Before this, only some of his followers called him God. After this, more did so, and after a higher court freed him, thousands overflowed his meetings in Harlem.[6]

HIS HARLEM PERIOD: HIS COOPERATIVE COMMUNE MULTIPLIES

In the meantime, in March, 1932, Divine and his community moved from Sayville to Harlem, where most of his increasing number of followers now lived. When a black follower, Charles Calloway, who was to become a presence in Divine's movement in Ulster County, made available to him a house on 135th Street, Divine made it into his Peace Mission headquarters. Later in the same year, another follower, Lena Brinson, who was to become a buyer of property for Divine in Ulster County, offered Divine a larger house, this one at 20 West 115th Street, and he moved his headquarters there.[7] From about this time, Divine, to avoid owning any real estate in case of any law suit against him, sold his and his wife's Sayville property to his followers, and avoided buying any new property in his or his wife's name.

As the depression deepened, with Harlem's unemployment mounting to scorching rates, Divine felt increasingly pushed toward social concerns. So also did the increasing number of his white followers who were social activists. Bringing not just religion but also politics into his struggle for justice, Divine began to join political coalitions that were fighting class and racial discrimination, including coalitions that included Communists. Within his own Peace Mission movement, he took the radical step of not just encouraging racially integrated seating at banquets, but requiring it.[8]

Beginning especially in 1932, Divine's movement established in New York City and elsewhere a series of interracial, nonviolent, cooperative communities, each one independent of the others, but all based on the Sayville model. With affluent blacks and whites volunteering financial support, and poor blacks providing most of the labor, these communities took the form of both residences and businesses. Whatever their form, the movement called these communities variously kingdoms, missions, or extensions, with no clear distinction among these terms. The first business enterprises were restaurants. As they became popular, followers created other businesses, such as groceries, dress shops, shoe repair shops, and garages.

To secure Divine's approval, each cooperative community was required to operate with voluntary, unpaid labor; to shop with cash, not credit; and to sell their goods or services at less than market prices. Each, whether it was primarily a business or a residence, was expected to avoid designating people by race, to segregate the sexes, to use positive thinking and non-violent methods, and to recognize Divine's spiritual leadership.

Meanwhile Divine, being hounded by legal charges and investigations, was developing unwritten operating strategies that not only protected himself and his movement, but also enhanced his control over it, particularly the following three strategies: First, his movement kept no financial records, making it difficult for his enemies to investigate him or his movement. Second, Divine accepted for his movement gifts in kind, as of food, housing, cars, and money, including gifts from wealthy supporters, without which his movement would not have been successful, but for himself, his policy was to refuse all monetary gifts, receive no pay, own no property, and own no bank accounts. This helped him not only to avoid financial liability, but also to claim that he was above material concerns at the same time that he controlled substantial wealth for the benefit of his movement. Third, Divine's movement kept no membership lists. In fact, it rejected the whole concept of membership, adopting the looser concept of followers instead. This allowed followers to accept Divine and his teachings in varying degrees, as their consciences determined. This also helped Divine to avoid responsibility for what his followers did. When people seemed to follow him, if he liked what they were doing, he could say they were his followers, but if he did not like what they were doing, he could say they were not his followers. In the short run, these strategies seemed to work.

By 1935, when Divine was beginning to move his followers into Ulster County, observers friendly to him focused on the more positive aspects of his work, such as feeding the hungry; lifting the desperate out of poverty, addiction, and crime; forbidding his followers to be on relief; and teaching them honesty, hard work, and financial independence. But much of the public was uneasy with him, as because he promoted racial integration; controlled vast wealth and yet claimed to own nothing; seemed to have a hypnotic, magical power over his followers; and played the role of God.

By 1935, Divine had already become wondrously successful in gathering followers, and in creating intentional cooperative communities for them to live and work in. By this time, his communities were scattered across the nation, and a few were even abroad. Their greatest concentration, however, was in the New York City region, including at least twenty-three communities in Manhattan, twelve in Brooklyn and Queens, twenty-one in nearby New Jersey, and three in Westchester County.[9] But Divine, flexing his powers, was looking for new locations in which to establish still more communities.

2. ESTABLISHING THE FIRST ULSTER COUNTY MISSION: NEW PALTZ

IN 1935, when Divine was looking for sites where he could establish more of his communities, it mattered to him that much of Ulster County was within moderate driving distance of New York City, only 75 to 100 miles, north along the Hudson River. Driving by car being Divine's preferred means of travel, it was convenient for him that new highway bridges had recently been opened over the Hudson, as at Poughkeepsie (Mid-Hudson Bridge, opened 1930), and at New York (George Washington Bridge, opened 1931). Moreover, he knew that if he or his followers wished to visit by means other than driving, Ulster County was also easily accessible by ships steaming up the Hudson River and by passenger trains winding up both sides of the river.

It also mattered to Divine that Ulster County property was available inexpensively. This was so not only because the county was not close enough to New York City for easy commuting, but also because farming had long been declining in the county, causing its population to drop, and because the Great Depression of the 1930s had lowered property values. In addition, Divine was aware of Ulster County's charming landscape, including the Hudson River to the east, the Catskill Mountains to the west, and a mix of river valleys and rolling hills between. If Divine established vacation resorts in the county, as he was considering doing, visitors might easily find them appealing.

Besides, Divine believed that an important part of his mission was to desegregate America. Although Divine had been pushed away from one overwhelmingly white area, Sayville, Long Island, he deliberately planned to locate his new interracial communities in other overwhelmingly white areas. As a Divine movement periodical said at the time, the Ulster County region, highly white as it was, showed "a clear case" of having racial prejudice, and "that's just why" Divine chose to establish communities there.

In 1930, Ulster County's population was only 1.7 percent "Negro," which was less than the state percentage, even less than the percentage in such nearby counties as Dutchess, Orange, or Westchester. While more than a century earlier, in 1800, 9 percent of Ulster County's population had been black slaves, after the state had freed them in 1827, most of the former slave families had left long ago, and no significant new influx of blacks into the county had yet occurred.

When Divine first approached Ulster County's real estate dealers, he found many of them unwilling to assist him in bringing blacks into the county. When he finally discovered one dealer, John Dellay of Rosendale, willing to take the risk, this discovery was undoubtedly a significant factor in drawing Divine into Ulster County. Dellay's brother-in-law, George Sachs of Brooklyn, owned a farm in the town of New Paltz, and this farm was the first property Divine led his movement to buy in Ulster County. To purchase this farm, Divine kept to what had become his practice ever since he had left Sayville and established himself in Harlem. He did not buy the property himself. Instead, he led a follower to buy it for him.

Under the guidance of Father Divine and real estate dealer Dellay, Divine follower Clara Budds bought the New Paltz farm on July 27, 1935. Budds was a Harlem resident who apparently did domestic work—an employer praised her as having "diligence" and "lofty equanimity." Divine explained that Budds "had worked for years and years and had saved up her earnings." She volunteered, Divine said, to "give her service" by purchasing this farm. Budds paid about $5,500 for it, a price Divine considered low compared to its "actual value." Though the farm was only of modest size, about thirty-two acres, it included Wallkill

Above:
PANORAMIC VIEW OF THE PEACE MISSION'S NEW PALTZ FARM, showing the main house (left) and its garage (center). The Shawangunk Mountain ridge shows in the background. In recent years, the garage has disappeared and more trees have grown up, making the site much less open.
(*New Day*, March 9, 1939)

Right:
THE MAIN HOUSE OF THE MISSION, OFF LIBERTY ROAD, ABOUT A MILE FROM THE WALLKILL RIVER, a recent view. Women served meals here not only to Divine followers, men, women, and children, but also to the public. The building survives, recently being rented out as apartments.
(Photo by Rene F. Ramos, 2003)

DIVINE FOLLOWERS CONSTRUCTED THIS GARAGE BUILDING DOWN A SLOPE FROM THEIR MAIN HOUSE. The garage's first story, faced with brick, housed parking space for fifteen cars and, when needed, served as an auditorium.
(*New Day*, March 9, 1939)

River bottomland, which was said to be some of the "richest" farmland in the Hudson River region. It was located about a mile west of where New Paltz's Main Street crossed the Wallkill River by bridge, and slightly north off Libertyville Road.[1]

The farmhouse was conspicuous, suggesting that Divine had learned from his experiences not to hide his desegregation activities but to flaunt them. It was visible from New Paltz Village, on a rise across a stretch of river-bottom farmland, almost directly in line with Mohonk Hotel's famous Sky Top watchtower on the Shawangunk Ridge. Of four stories, the house had earlier been used, like many other farm houses in the county, for summer boarders, and it was so imposing that Divine's followers often called it a "mansion."

Once the farm was acquired for Divine, it seemed to some New Paltz observers to become "a blot on the beautiful landscape." From their point of view, the arrival of mostly African-American followers of Divine to live there, in what they feared would grow into a "lavish settlement," cast a shadow over the "quiet and slow" New Paltz region, over its State Normal School, its boarding houses, and its nearby mountain hotels.[2]

Within a month after the purchase of the farm, only three persons were living at the New Paltz Mansion, one of them being Mother Divine. However, on one Sunday in August, Divine and 125 primarily African-American followers came up from New York City to visit the farm, driving through the little village of New Paltz in a conspicuous procession. At a time when there seemed to be only one black youth growing up in the whole town, it was startling to see so many blacks driving through New Paltz, some of them in big cars. Soon afterward, on another Sunday in September, 1935, even more followers trekked to the New Paltz farm, thousands of them this time, it was said, many of them sailing up the Hudson from New York City in a chartered excursion steamer, docking at Poughkeepsie, and then driving by car, taxi, truck, or bus. Passing through New Paltz's narrow Main Street, they seemed to the townspeople like invaders. Meantime, the New Paltz *News* reported that the mothers and fathers of New Paltz "resent the very thought" of Divine's followers moving into their town. They fear that the followers will buy their necessities not from local New Paltz merchants, but from their "connections in New York." They fear, the *News* said, that the arrival of blacks would keep students away from the town's "beautiful Normal School," from the boarding houses in the Wallkill Valley lowlands, and from the nearby mountain resorts like the Mohonk Mountain House "which we have so long leaned on as a support."[3]

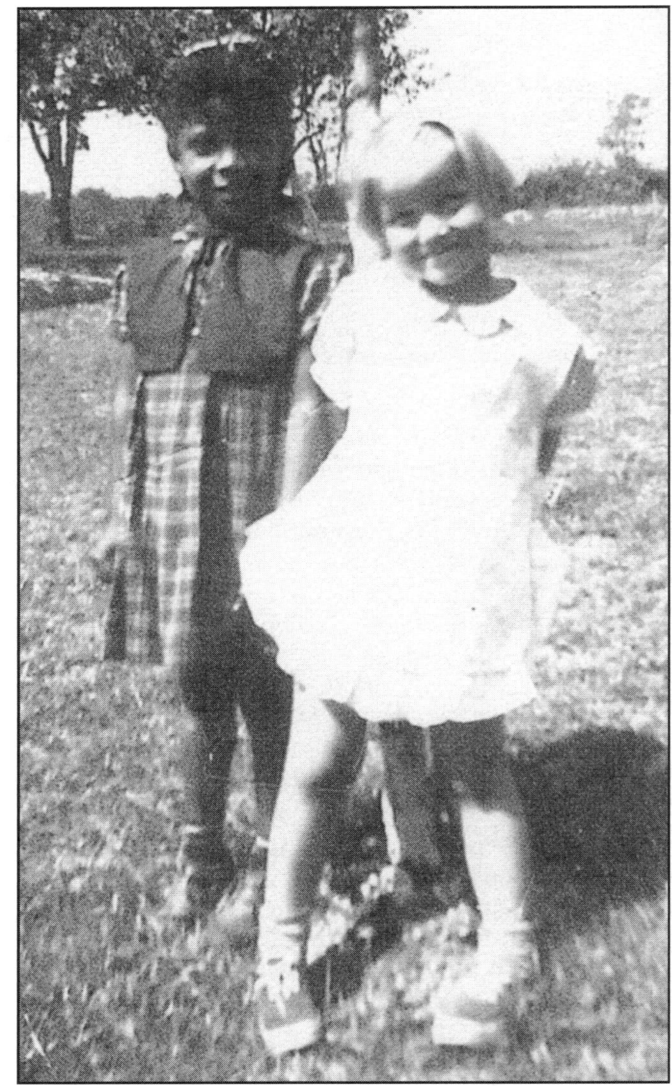

EXEMPLIFYING THE INTERRACIAL NATURE OF DIVINE'S COMMUNITIES, these two children both lived at Divine's New Paltz mansion. Sweet Love, left lived there summers only, while her mother worked in Harlem. Laura Brock lived there year round. (Laura Brock Miller)

In early November, Divine set off another disturbance by driving into New Paltz Village to look for a place to pay his new mission's electric bill, a bill from the "Hudson Gas and Electric Co." Seeing a drugstore, Divine sent in his chauffeur to ask where the "gas" office was. The chauffeur came back agitated, to say he was roughly told, in "a truthful quibble," there was no "gas" office in town. Divine himself then walked into the store, asked again, and soon came out, followed by the angry proprietor, who told Divine loudly that the people of New Paltz opposed his mission's coming to town. Then as a crowd looked on, the proprietor "did shove" Divine. In the crowd, as it happened, was the editor of the New Paltz *News*, Walter W. Kenney, who persuaded the obstreperous proprietor to return to his store, and then invited Divine to visit his newspaper office. After Divine had found where he could pay the bill and had paid it, he visited editor Kenney.

While the editor admitted that the drug store proprietor's shoving of Divine was "too ridiculous," he explained that the proprietor was "one of

FATHER AND MOTHER DIVINE LEAVING A HUDSON RIVER STEAMER AT POUGHKEEPSIE ON THEIR WAY TO VISIT THEIR MISSION AT NEW PALTZ, accompanied by followers. (*Spoken Word*, Oct. 5, 1935)

our leading merchants," and his opinion of Divine was widely shared in New Paltz. What was needed to calm the village, the editor suggested, was for the townspeople to understand how many new settlers Divine would be likely to bring in, and what effect they would have on the village. Divine then explained some of his plans, including plans for building, near the newly acquired mansion, a garage for fifteen cars. The editor asked, where are you going to buy your building supplies? Divine replied that he had already ordered some supplies in New Paltz, and, seeming to extend an olive branch, added that he preferred to buy locally. The editor was pleased, saying that purchasing in New Paltz would improve the town's attitude toward Divine.

From its opening, the New Paltz mission was run like other Divine enterprises as a cooperative, and Mother Sarah Love was in charge. She appears to have been an exemplary manager. Once when firemen came to the house to put out a chimney fire, they found Love kept the house as "clean as wax." Later a New Paltz newspaper reported that Love was "a kindly, capable woman who dispensed hospitality to venturesome townspeople, " and that "the children under her care"—at times there were perhaps as many as twenty of them—"were clean and well mannered."[4]

Among the adults who lived at the New Paltz mission at various times, besides manager Love, were three women who did kitchen work: Sister Charity, Thankful Kindness, and Dear One. When visitors were expected, these women were doubtless the ones responsible, according to a Divine periodical, for the kitchen's "aroma" of roasts and pies. Other women living there included Rosalind Real, who solicited advertisements in New Paltz for the periodical published by Divine followers; and Wonderful Victory, who went out daily to do housekeeping for a neighbor about half a mile away. Among men living there were John Joseph, a white former Christian Science practitioner, who cared for the sloping lawns; farm hands ,who raised vegetables and tended animals, including brown Jersey cows, "fluttering" chickens, and grunting pigs; and while the main house was being renovated and a new garage was being built, twenty construction men, one of them being Happy Boy, a "well-proportioned Negro." All, it should be noted, were supervised by Mother Love. In keeping with Divine's insistence on gender equality, in Divine's kingdom, women, whether black or white, were often given significant roles.[5]

In regard to the unusual names that many followers went by, it was a Peace Mission custom—

though not required—for followers to adopt new religious names as an outward sign of their having been born again. Sometimes Divine was reported to have suggested new names to followers, and sometimes guardians might choose religious names for children being raised within the movement, but usually followers chose their own religious names. Since the Peace Mission kept no registry of names, it was not surprising that sometimes several followers chose the same name, producing confusion. Women sometimes chose male names, compounding the confusion. If followers chose idealistic names, like Charity or Love, Divine said they should live up to them. If they chose endearing names like Sweet or Honey, Divine considered such names might encourage human affection, which was contrary to his teaching; to counteract any such impact, he might urge followers to do what he sometimes did, reduce such names to initials.

For the new garage building, the construction men hauled crushed stone, poured concrete flooring, laid red bricks, and installed a steam heating system. At Divine's request, they made the building fireproof. They made it fireproof, Divine explained, not because it was legally required in this rural region (it was not), but because doing so was living righteously. It was similar, he said, to driving a car with consideration for others, whether the law required it or not. The garage was "spacious." Its first floor provided parking space for fifteen cars, with a concrete floor and a high raftered ceiling; it was designed to double as a meeting hall when needed. Its second floor was claimed to provide sleeping quarters for fifty persons, if necessary. The mission's men lived in this garage residence, while its women lived in the main house, which had been renovated by dividing larger rooms into smaller ones, to provide twenty-four rooms. Both men and women ate in the main house, but the men and women sat separately.

On his frequent visits to this New Paltz site, Divine watched over its daily life. He saw to it that its bills were paid. He checked its farm crops. He presided at banquets. He often spoke, sometimes in the main house at a banquet table, sometimes in the garage's meeting hall. On one such occasion, Divine urged his listeners to be conscious of what attitudes they were developing in themselves. Were they positive or negative? Were they spiteful or loving? Whatever they were, he warned, their attitudes would be revealed not only in their minds but also in their bodies.

Within a few years, the New Paltz mission residents had somewhat reduced popular suspicion of them. One way they had done so was by often shopping locally, as editor Kenney had suggested they should. By 1939, many New Paltz businesses advertised in the Divinite weekly publication, including the Lane-Sargent Department Store; Henry's Electrical Shop; Carrol's Clothes; GLF farm supplies; and Le Fevre and Son, sellers of feed, lumber, and fuel. One of the Le Fevre family recalled that they valued Divinites as customers because they paid their bills promptly, and that on one occasion Mother Sarah Love, who did much of the shopping for the New Paltz mission, brought Divine himself to their lumberyard on a courtesy call, suggesting that Divine, bold as he could be, understood there were advantages in being conciliatory.[6]

3. STONE RIDGE FARM

IN THE FALL OF 1935, only a few months after a Divine follower acquired the New Paltz farm, another follower acquired another farm, this one also considered one of the finest farms in Ulster County. It was a farm of about 140 acres on the edge of Atwood, in the town of Marbletown. Its charming, two-and-a-half story, colonial stone house overlooked Esopus Creek. While it seemed remote, it could be reached from Route 213 (the Stone Ridge-Atwood Road) eastward, by a long, downhill right of way.

The mailing address of this farm was Atwood, a sparsely settled community nearby, but the Divine forces often called it Stone Ridge Farm or Stone Ridge Mansion, after the village of Stone Ridge, which was about three miles to the south. As was customary for Peace Missions, the mailbox

DIVINE WITH A PANORAMIC VIEW OF HIS STONE RIDGE FARM. The house (left) shows an addition, including sleeping porches, which Divine follwers had built on the front of it. Today some of the barns survivve, as the house does, also, but the addition has been removed. (*New Day*, Feb. 9, 1939; composite photo)

bore the inscription: "Rev. Divine," though he only occasionally stayed there.

Just how the Divine forces handled the down payment for this property became an issue in a trial in New York City. Arthur Hasbrouck, the seller, a descendant of one of Ulster County's old Huguenot families, asserted in an affidavit for this trial that Father Divine personally took part in the negotiations and made the first payment for it with his own hands, drawing bills out of a "little black satchel." Divine, who was being sued to pay damages from an accident involving one of his movement's buses, admitted he was present with Hasbrouck when the money was paid and that he might have handled the money, but he insisted the money was not his. He was trying to make the point that he did not possess any property of his own, whether real estate, buses, or money.

After owner Hasbrouck and the Divine forces had signed a contract for the Divine forces to buy the farm, Hasbrouck changed his mind, deciding after all that he did not want to sell it for Father Divine's use. This farm had been occupied by his Hasbrouck ancestors for over a hundred years, and neighbors were protesting his selling it for black use. But realtor Dellay, who had arranged the sale, pushed Hasbrouck to honor his contract to sell.

Hasbrouck finally sold the farm on November 22, 1935, and he did so to Divine follower Abraham Augustus, who lived at Divine's headquarters, 20 West 115th Street, in Harlem. While Augustus himself seemed to have played little role in negotiating the sale, in an affidavit Augustus attested that he paid for this property himself, and did so with his "own individual life's savings." The purchase price was $11,000. Augustus paid $8,000 directly, he said, and took out a mortgage for the remaining $3,000. (While Divine discouraged his followers from borrowing money, he seemed not yet to have applied this policy firmly to buying real estate.) Augustus asserted that he had offered money to Divine as early as 1932 to do with as he pleased, but that Divine had refused it, saying, however, that he would look for an opportunity for Augustus to invest it safely. When eventually Divine told him he had found such an opportunity in Ulster County, Augustus himself inspected the site and agreed that it would be a safe investment.[1]

FATHER DIVINE AT HIS STONE RIDGE FARM. The sign over the barn door reads: "Thank you FATHER," a common saying among Divine followers. Although the *New Day* published the photo on the right on March 9, 1939, with photos of the New Paltz farm, its issue of Sept. 12, 1940, identified the barn as at Stone Ridge Farm. (Left photo from *New Day*, Sept. 12, 1940)

In October, 1935, after the sale to Augustus had been settled, but the deed not yet signed, Divine and an entourage drove to the farm. They found it in operation. They found 2,500 chickens living in a three-story chicken house "equipped with modern improvements." They found a cow pen, corn crib, horse barn, garages, and quarters for help. They found crops ready for harvesting, including corn, apples, and vegetables. In December, after his followers had already occupied the mansion, Father Divine visited there again. At that time, a Divine periodical described the mansion's room where Divine spoke as long and low ceilinged, with "deep casement windows and two-foot-thick stone walls," like similar rooms in other Ulster County Dutch-style colonial houses. Visitors touring the farm noticed "rich cultivated soil" and "three great white horses," which followers had already named after one of Divine's slogans: "Righteousness, Justice, and Truth."

Soon this farm was producing so many chickens, eggs, watermelons, and vegetables that Peace Mission trucks were carrying them daily to New York. There was so much cabbage that a truck carrying it to New York, one thousand heads at a time, was obliged to make several trips carrying nothing but cabbage. In New York, the trucks delivered the produce to Divinite rooming houses, restaurants, groceries, and even to Divinite-run street pushcarts.

By 1936, the farmhouse had been considerably enlarged. Two sleeping porches had been added onto the front of the house, and a dining room had been added onto the kitchen at the rear. While the new dining room, Divine explained, was not as big as would be provided by Peace Missions in New York City, where large numbers of the unemployed were likely to be fed, nevertheless, he said, the room was an "expression of love and devotion" to all who cared to dine there.[2]

In 1936, Divine followers also bought another farm less than two miles south of Stone Ridge Mansion. It was also was on the edge of Atwood, on Route 213, but on the west side of the road. Being small, only about five acres, it was called Spot-on-the-Road. Before the Divinites bought it, it was owned by an Italian family, the Carmelo Calcagnos, who grew grapes there for making wine. After Divinites bought it, they continued to grow grapes, but in keeping with their beliefs, they no longer used them to make wine. They concentrated, however, on raising chickens, and they also remade a barn into a restaurant where they served dinners to the public, as did many other Peace Mission farms.[3]

DIVINE'S SPOT -IN-THE-ROAD'S FARMHOUSE, less than two miles from his Stone Ridge Farm, both near Atwood. (*New Day*, March 30, 1939)

Dr. Frederick Jones, a New York dentist, made a brief summer visit, with friends and family, to the little Spot- in-the-Road Farm, and a longer visit to the big Stone Ridge Farm. Jones recalled the big farm's kitchen as being "hot indeed," but the sisters working there, he said, seemed to have "songs in their hearts" as they prepared "sumptuous meals" for only 15 cents. A young farm hand from nearby Lomontville recalled long afterward that the farmer he worked for used to treat him to dinner there. As his fellow diners passed along to him such dishes as ham, ice cream, and pie, he became well aware that those present included both blacks and whites.

When Divine himself visited the Stone Ridge Farm, he sometimes stayed overnight, often presided at banquets, and often spoke—in 1938 he spoke there thirteen times. Speaking there once, Divine said that this community and his other Ulster County communities provide humanity with samples of "the practicality of true Christianity." Nevertheless, being well aware that even in these supposed utopias there was conflict, when he spoke there again a few months later, he warned his followers that if they continued to "squabble" and "pierce" each other, they would be "putting a crown of thorns on God's head."[4]

4. KINGSTON MANSION

ON DECEMBER 21, 1935, Divine followers completed the purchase of another site in Ulster County, this one an impressive old house in the city of Kingston. It became the administrative headquarters for the Divine movement in the county, and it turned out to be the Ulster County site which remained under the control of the Divine movement for the longest time—fifty years.

Located off Wilbur Avenue, at 67 Chapel Street, the house was built about 1870 and had once been occupied by the Sweeney family—they were dealers in a well-known local product, bluestone. The house was a huge wooden structure of three stories, with a mansard roof, bracketed eaves, and a large verandah. When it was bought, it had recently been used as a hotel which could house fifty persons. The site, limited to four acres, was not a farm like the previous Divinite purchases in the county, but it had "rolling lawns," and "lofty" old oaks. To the east of the house in a low spot, it had a large swimming "pool."

The buyers of this house for Divine's Peace

Above: **KINGSTON MANSION, facing Chapel Street in Kingston's Wilbur neighborhood. The mansion housed a suite for Father Divine on the main floor, rooms for sisters on the second floor, and rooms for brothers on the third floor. To the rear right is a new dining hall constructed by Divine followers; it was near, but not attached, to the mansion.** (*New Day*, March 23, 1939) Below: **THE FORMER KINGSTON MANSION HAS SURVIVED INTO CURRENT TIMES AS A PRIVATE RESIDENCE. It is well cared for. A cat is in the entry; pumpkins are on the steps. Karen Vassell is walking toward the steps.** (Photo below by the author, Oct., 2005)

Mission were four women, all residents of Harlem. Two of them, Esther Grace and Heavenly Rest, had been arrested in 1931 in the police raid on Divine's Sayville house. Although most of these buyers were probably black, Rest was white. She had attended Boston University. She had become curious about Divine through hearing about him at a Unity church in Boston. She had joined Divine at Sayville, when she was about twenty-six years old, and later became one of Divine's first secretaries. As was true of most of the buyers of property for Divine in Ulster County, none of these four women lived in this Kingston property after they bought it. They were buying the property not to secure a residence for themselves but to promote a cause in which they believed. They were also buying it as an investment, knowing that if the value of the property were to increase by the time they sold it, they would profit.[1]

While the public was likely to call this new site a "heaven," Divine followers themselves were more likely to call it an "extension," "mission," or "mansion." Instead of saying that the site was in Kingston, they sometimes said—playfully—that it was in "King's Town," referring to Divine as king.

During its first summer as a Divine site, a party of visitors were given a tour of it. They were guided by, among others, the "angel" in charge of the house, probably Satisfied Love. In this house, she insisted, nothing is "out of place," nothing "unpolished," nothing "rumpled." In the basement story, on a level with the garden, the visitors saw a dining hall for the resident workers, with a U-shaped table seating forty or fifty. In the adjoining kitchen, they found a slow fire burning in the range and hot biscuits, just removed from its oven, "steaming on the table." On the main floor, they passed through Father Divine's office, his bedroom, Mother Divine's bedroom, and their own dining room for special guests. On the next floor above, they saw bedrooms for "sisters," and on the top floor, bedrooms for "brothers." Passing outdoors, at the northeast corner of the house, they found a new Divinite-built two-story structure, separate from the main house, where they entered a third dining room, a grand banqueting hall, with seating for about two hundred. In this same building, above the banqueting room they visited additional quarters for men, and found their beds made and their desks in order. Also outdoors, Sister Peace Dove, otherwise known as Mary Sheldon Lyon, a wealthy white woman, showed the visitors through a separate "cottage" she was building at the western edge of the grounds. "We all sense," one of these visitors wrote, "that hers is but the first of a big series of happy dwellings that will cluster around this and other kingdom centers in the Promised Land." This was probably a reflection of Divine's plan at that time to make available small plots of land at various mission sites in the county, without cost to those willing to build houses on them, a plan that was scarcely carried out.[2]

About this same time, in August, 1936, Divine followers arranged a steamer excursion from New York City to Kingston, to celebrate the acquisition of all the sites followers had so far acquired in Ulster County, sites which followers were calling collectively the Promised Land. They chartered two river steamers for the purpose. One morning soon after 6:00 AM, the boats sailed from New York City's 132nd Street pier, with Father and Mother Divine aboard. As the boats steamed the 100 miles up the Hudson, the 1,877 passengers—most of them African-Americans, but including more than 50 whites—sang, clapped, and swayed. Approaching Kingston, the ships turned into Rondout Creek, tooted, and headed toward their docks. Crowds of onlookers, immensely curious, greeted them, some looking out windows, others standing on roof tops, while the passengers aboard sang and stomped so rhythmically that the boats shook.

When the passengers poured out of the boats, they grouped themselves for a parade. They were joined by several hundred other followers of Divine who already lived in the region, or who had come up from New York for the occasion on their own. The marchers were conventionally dressed, the men in suit coats, the women in long skirts, both usually wearing hats. They were placed in the line of march, an observer recalled, so that as much as possible the races were mixed, blacks and whites side by side. Paraders carried signs, some asserting that "Father Divine has

DIVINE EXCURSIONISTS LEAVING THEIR HUDSON RIVER STEAMER, *THE CITY OF KEANSBURG*, at a dock on Rondout Creek in Kingston, and WOMEN EXCURSIONISTS PARADING FROM THE DOCK THROUGH KINGSTON to the Kingston Mansion in Aug., 1936. Most of the women wore hats and long white dresses. (Both: Dolores A. Miller)

Healed Millions from Smoking," or "We will Work—Not Depend on Relief," or "We Have Returned All Stolen Goods." While most people in the procession marched, Father Divine and his wife rode in a blue Rolls Royce, which had picked them up at the dock, with Divine elevated, seated on the car's folded top, in a grey suit and grey felt hat, smiling and waving. Many of his closest associates also rode in cars—including Faithful Mary, who had recently bought a hotel in High Falls. As the parade moved forward, the paraders chanted. A Peace Mission Band played. Airplanes roared above, piloted by Divine followers. Sidewalks were jammed, stores were closed, and the curious gawked out of upstairs windows.

The paraders moved toward the Kingston Mansion not by the shortest way, which would have been to follow Abeel Street along Rondout Creek, but instead, to make a bigger impact, by following Broadway through the center of the city. The paraders passed City Hall, soon turned onto Greenkill Avenue, and then down hill a long way on Wilbur Avenue, finishing with a short climb up Chapel Street, a total of about three miles. When they arrived at the mansion, some of them had energy enough left to tour the house, exclaiming, "Thank you Father." Others found relief by swimming in the pool. Still others were so tired they lay down on the lawn, listening to Father Divine speak to them by loud speaker. Everyone was

PEACE

FATHER DIVINE

Boat Excursion & Outing, 2 Days to Promised Land -o- King'sTown

Better Known as Kingston, N. Y.

F R E E !

To all children 18 years & under.

ADULTS $1.00 ROUND TRIP

All Welcome, regardless of so-called race, creed or color; Religious belief or social or political affiliation.

SMALL CHILDREN MUST BE ACCOMPANIED BY GUARDIANS

Monday, August 30, 1937 A. D. F. D

Boat Leaves 132nd St. & Hudson River 6 A. M.

Returning Leaves Kingston Aug. 31, 8:30 P. M.

Staying overnight at the FAMOUS DIVINE GREENKILL PARK and other Peace Mission Extensions in The Promised Land. Sleeping Accomodations for

CHILDREN UNDER 12, 25 CENTS — ADULTS 50 CENTS

No Smoking, Drinking, Obscene Language or Immodest Conduct Permitted.

Tickets at 20 W. 115 St. and other Peace Mission Connections.

(*New Day*, Aug. 26, 1937)

KINGSTON'S JUNIOR FARMHOUSE, about 2-1/2 miles from the Kingston Mansion, off the road from New Salem to Port Ewen. The term "peace" on the building was commonly used within Divine's Peace Mission. Inset: Father Divine. (*New Day*, July 13, 1939)

THE FARMHOUSE AS IT APPEARED RECENTLY, considerably remodeled from its Divinite days. (Photo by Rene F. Ramos, Sept., 2007)

offered a chicken dinner for ten or fifteen cents, with the tickets being sold by a white follower, Glorious Illumination. An artist by occupation, she felt herself called as a Divine follower to resist the world, which she needed to do, she explained, because the world was pushing her to be a machine.

During the celebration, realtor John Dellay of Rosendale, who had been an agent for purchasing the Kingston site, told reporters that several hundred Divine followers were already living in Divine's missions in the county, that Divinites already owned almost 1,000 acres there, and that they were acquiring still more. One of Divine's lawyers, Nat Kranzler, who had also helped to arrange the Kingston purchase, said that within several months, twice as many followers would likely be living in the county, while thousands more were ready to come if work could be found for them.[3]

In late 1936, Divine followers purchased another site, a farm of 87 acres, about three miles from the Kingston Mansion. While its land was much more extensive than that of Kingston Mansion, its housing capacity was much smaller, scarcely affording accommodations to ten persons, even with the men being housed over the garage and in a barn. This new farm was in the town of Esopus, but since its mailing address and telephone exchange were in Kingston, Divinites dubbed it Kingston Junior. It could be reached from the Kingston Mansion by following southwest along Rondout Creek, crossing the creek at Eddyville, then turning east on County Route 25, but eventually turning off of it southward onto a private lane, now the public Schultz Lane, to its dead end. Because its house was small, Divine probably spoke at Kingston Junior only once during its entire existence as a Divine mission.[4]

By contrast, perhaps forty or fifty people lived regularly at the Kingston Mansion. Although the residents at both sites were mostly blacks, they were racially mixed. Among whites, who lived at Kingston Junior was Rebecca Branch, a teacher who was an immigrant from Spain, already mentioned. Among whites who lived at Kingston Mansion were not only the artist Glorious Ilumination, and Mary Lyon, the builder of a cottage on the grounds, both already mentioned, but also the wealthy Mary Bird Tree from California.

Both the person in charge of the Kingston Mansion, Miss Satisfied Love, and her major assistant, Miss Lamb, were black. They did the major shopping for the house. They were also, as a black schoolboy recalled, the mansion's chief "head-knockers." The boy, Curtis Van Demark, who often visited his young friends at the house, observed that when anyone at the house needed disciplining, it was these two women who were likely to do it, whether the transgressors were black or white.

In the next few years, Divine followers seemed to win some respect in Kingston, as suggested by the substantial number of Kingston area businesses, which advertised in the Divinites' *New Day*. Among them were Netburn plumbing, Farber's meats, Blanshan paper, Chelsea furniture, Singer coal, Spiegel school supplies, Schryver lumber, Samuel market, and Frick used cars.

As for Father Divine himself, he was intensely aware of his Kingston Mansion and often spoke there. During 1936, when it was rumored that Divine might move his headquarters from New York City to the Kingston Mansion, Divine spoke there 26 times; during 1938, he spoke twenty-nine times.

On some occasions when Divine spoke at the mansion, he made it clear that he doubted that his followers there had yet achieved utopia. He scolded some of them for ignoring guests. He scolded others for being like the children of Israel in the wilderness, "mumbling and grumbling." He scolded still others for resenting those who "think they are just a little above you in authority;" or when the table is set, for "rushing to get to the table"; or for talking to each other for hours on the "mortal minded" level, about material matters. He disdained some of them as utterly "impractical, unprofitable, and good for nothing," and seemed to want to weed them out. He advised all his followers living in the Promised Land, if you are "not happy for any cause," then "do not stay."

Yet Divine could also be proud of his Kingston Mansion. Speaking there at a banquet, Divine said, racial prejudice is not either "true Americanism" or "true Christianity." Instead, he said, "true Americanism" and "true Christianity" are the racial mixing "you observe in this dining room."[5]

5. DIVINE FARM, RESTAURANTS, AND GAS STATIONS IN SAUGERTIES

AT VARIOUS TIMES, it was rumored that Divine was arranging for his followers to buy property in the village of Saugerties. His representatives, including his real estate agent John Dellay, were sometimes there inspecting possible sites. They inspected sites on the Saugerties waterfront, including a hotel and a Hudson River steamboat dock. While they never bought any property in the village of Saugerties itself, they did buy considerable property in the town of Saugerties.

One such property was known as Quarryville. Consisting of about five acres, it included several houses, and was slightly north of the small hamlet of Quarryville, on the east side of Route 32 (the road from Quarryville to Palenville). It was bought on May 29, 1936, by two Divine followers, Ernest P. Vaughn, who lived at Kingston Mansion, and Peace Branch, who lived at Divine's headquarters, 20 West 115th Street, New York.

Although Divine followers probably operated this site as a farm, they also operated it as a set of businesses: a restaurant, gas stations, and residences for tourists. According to the *New Day*, these businesses, like other Divine businesses, took pride in selling at low, "evangelical prices," including selling gasoline for 3 to 4 cents a gallon less than nearby gas stations.[1]

A larger property that Divine followers also bought in the town of Saugerties was what they named Divine Farm. It was considered to be the northernmost of all Divine's Peace Mission sites in Ulster County, perhaps five miles northwest of the village of Saugerties. It adjoined the Quarryville Farm, but unlike the Quarryville Farm, it was on both sides of Route 32, and was regarded as in the neighborhood called Saxton.

This farm, seventy-six acres, was bought on August 31, 1936, by four Divine followers. One of these buyers, Lovely Light, already lived in the

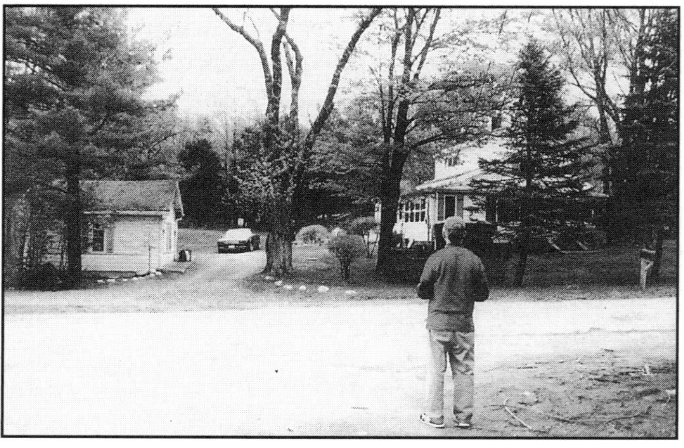

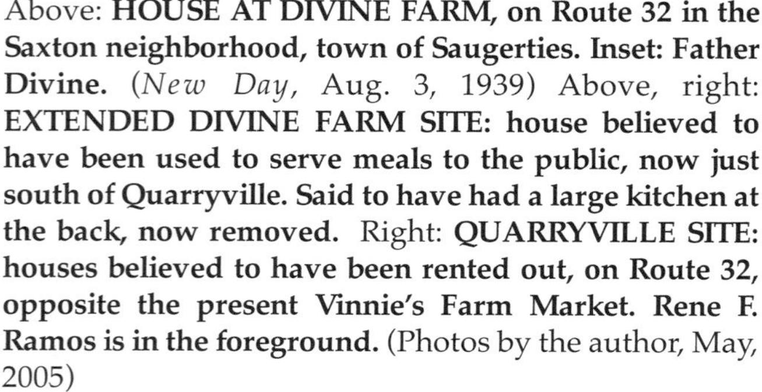

Above: **HOUSE AT DIVINE FARM, on Route 32 in the Saxton neighborhood, town of Saugerties. Inset: Father Divine.** (*New Day*, Aug. 3, 1939) Above, right: **EXTENDED DIVINE FARM SITE: house believed to have been used to serve meals to the public, now just south of Quarryville. Said to have had a large kitchen at the back, now removed.** Right: **QUARRYVILLE SITE: houses believed to have been rented out, on Route 32, opposite the present Vinnie's Farm Market. Rene F. Ramos is in the foreground.** (Photos by the author, May, 2005)

town of Saugerties, probably nearby at the Quarryville Farm. Another of these buyers was Nathan N. Kranzler of Newark, New Jersey, who served on Divine's legal staff.

According to the deeds for both the Quarryville and Divine farms, their Divine buyers bought them not as most Divinite group buyers usually bought property, as "tenants in common," so that if one of the owners died, that owner's heirs would acquire his share. Instead, these buyers, like most Divine buyers in Ulster County, bought this farm as "joint tenants," so that if one of the owners died, the remaining tenants would acquire that owner's share. Joint tenancy was a natural choice for the Divine movement because it discouraged family ties, as the Divine movement taught its followers to do.

In addition to purchasing the Quarryville and Divine Farms, in the same year, 1936, Divine followers also purchased another site on Route 32, twenty-three acres, on the west side of Route 32. It was between Divine Farm and Quarryville Farm. These three farms sites, totaling about 104 acres, were contiguous to each other, and were apparently operated together as Divine Farm.

On Divine Farm, as at other Peace Mission sites, followers worked as volunteers, in the usual "cooperative system." They raised not only cows, chickens, and ducks, but also, since some of the land was fertile, "an abundance of garden vegetables." As at many other Divine sites, they served dinners to the public, using some of their own farm produce. A resident of Palenville recalled long afterwards driving with his family to Divine Farm and stopping at a part of the farm on the east side of Route 32 to be served inexpensive chicken dinners; then as they began to drive away, crossing to the west side of the highway to another part of the same farm, to fill up their car with gas. They paid one dollar for seven gallons, and besides were given an extra quarter gallon free, to encourage them to come back.

Divine Farm became conspicuous for a large sign painted on a rock ledge, on the western side of Route 32, overlooking it. It carried a familiar Peace Mission slogan, "Righteousness, Justice, and

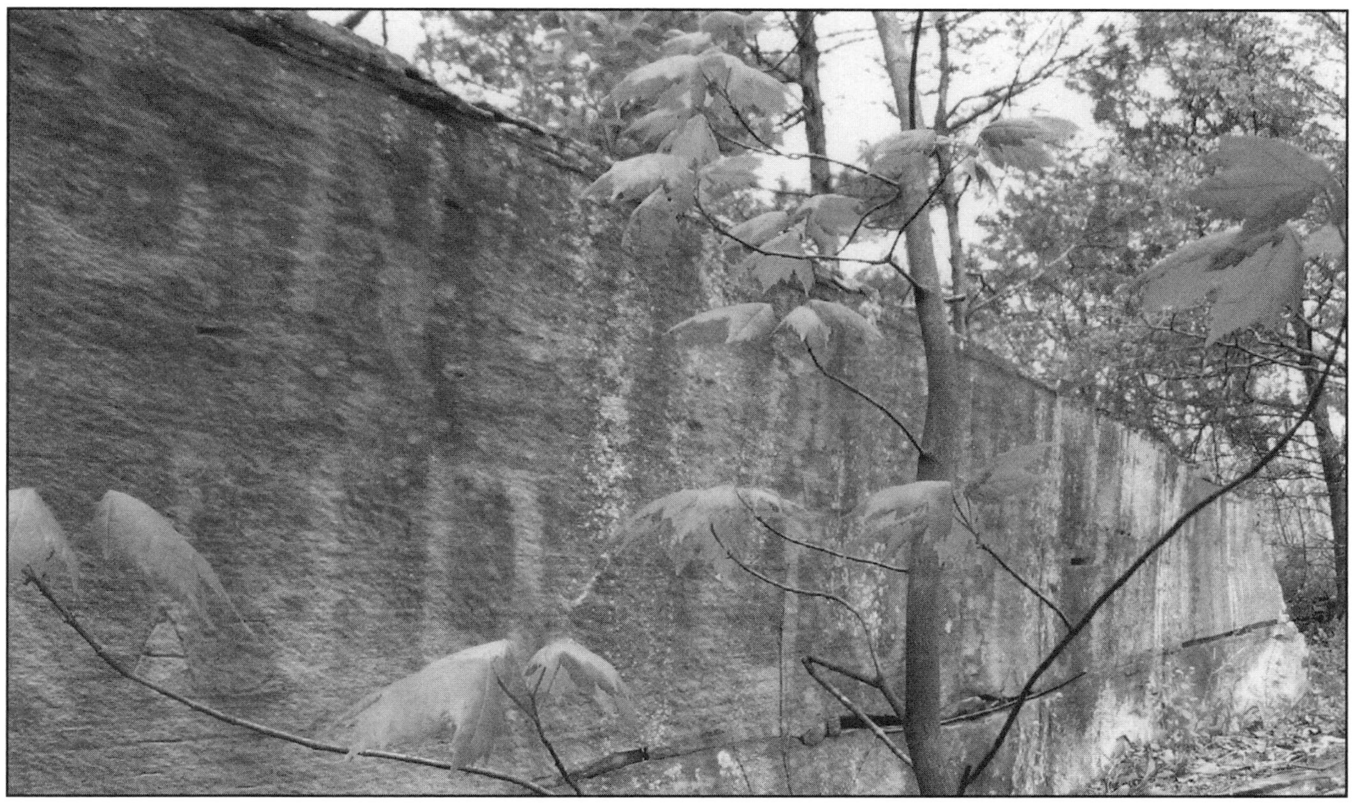

DIVINE FARM: SIGN ON ROCK LEDGE OVERLOOKING ROUTE 32, about a mile northwest of the hamlet of Quarryville and slightly northwest of some of the farm's gas stations, restaurants, and tourist homes. The sign, in fading letters, reads: "Righteousness, Justice, and Truth," which was one of the Peace Mission's familiar slogans.
(Photo by the author, May, 2005)

Truth." At this writing, the sign is still there, but, obscured by time and trees, it can scarcely be read.

Near this rock sign, according to local tradition, Divine followers kept a car in a barn ready for Divine to use whenever he needed it, as they also did at other sites in Ulster County. It was a fine car. They kept it in perfect condition.[2]

By 1937, Divine followers had also purchased still another site in the town of Saugerties about three miles south of Quarryville on Route 212, in the tiny hamlet of Veteran. This site, whose purchase was arranged by Divine's persistent realtor, John Dellay, consisted of more than one building in the center of the hamlet. It was opened by September, 1937, accompanied by the protests of neighbors. This site included a hotel, general store, restaurant, and gas station. Collectively, they were known by the conciliatory name, Peace Exchange, and they were affiliated with a Divinite cooperative in Harlem, on Madison Avenue.

Such small sites in the town of Saugerties as Quarryville and Veteran lacked adequate space for taking their turn in hosting Divine's county-wide social action events known as Righteous Government meetings. Even Divine Farm proper, having only slightly larger facilities, rarely took such a turn. But on one Saturday evening in July, 1940, it did.

This meeting was interrupted late in the evening by the arrival of a special bus in which Father Divine had taken followers from New York to Washington to lobby Congress. On its way back to New York City, the bus detoured upstate to Divine Farm to allow the travelers to report to the meeting on their lobbying.

As the travelers explained, the bus had carried

DIVINE GAS STATIONS on Route 32, town of Saugerties, where Divine followers sold gas at "evangelical prices." Probably part of Divine Farm. Inset: Father Divine.
(New Day, July 20, 1939)

"huge" boxes of petitions, bearing 250,000 signatures. The petitions, which had been collected by Divine's followers reaching out from New York City to its far suburbs, including Ulster County, asked Congress to pass an anti-lynching bill. Stubborn Southern senators had long blocked the bill in the Senate. With high hopes, the lobbyists had delivered the petitions and visited the offices of

PEACE MISSION SITE AT VETERAN on Route 212. According to the Frisbie family tradition, the building on the left housed the Frisbie family store, and the building on the right housed the Divine store. Called "Peace Exchange," the latter, in 1937-1939, was a general store, selling groceries, clothing, gas, tires, and paint as well as providing meals and rooms. (Author photo, May, 2005)

several senators. At Divine Farm, the lobbyists sang for the audience a song they had been singing on the bus as they traveled:

Pass the anti-lynching bill,
Stop prejudice and hatred,
Recognize the brotherhood of man,
And the fatherhood of God!

Senator Bilbo and Senator Ellender
Must do away with Southern pride,
And recognize the allness of God,
And the nothingness of man!

Despite Divine's leading the petition drive, Divine's followers often did not vote, a fact which was not likely to help any political cause they advocated. At times, followers did not vote because election officials would not register those who wanted to vote using their religious names. At other times, Divine protested against the refusal of election officials to register some of his followers as voters by asking all his followers not to vote, in a boycott. In any case, the Peace Mission's petitions failed to induce Congress to act on the anti-lynching bill. This failure so disturbed Divine that it soured him on struggling for social change by political methods.[3]

FATHER DIVINE WITH A FEW OF HIS STAFF LEAVING THE SENATE OFFICE BUILDIG IN WASHINGTON AFTER DELIVERING HIS ANTI-LYNCHING PETITIONS THERE. From left to right: unknown; Anne Shanewise (a former high school teacher in Chicago); Victory Dove (a former secretary of Faithful Mary); Father Divine; Sweet Love (an owner of the New Day); and Great Love (a former resident of the Stone Ridge mission). (*New Day*, Aug. 1, 1940)

6. BUY A WHOLE FACTORY VILLAGE? CHICHESTER

A FACTORY VILLAGE occupied a little valley in the Catskill Mountains. The village was in Ulster County but near the Greene County border. It was only two miles north of Phoenicia, a prime Catskill vacation center.

It was a small village named Chichester, with fewer than 400 people. Many of them worked in its one factory, a furniture factory. Some of them had worked there for almost their entire lives. The same family that owned the factory also owned the village's general store, its church, and most of its housing.

The family that owned almost the whole village were the Schwarzwaelders, a family of German origin. They had bought a small chair factory in Chichester long before, in 1884, and built it into a maker of quality wood furniture. It made office furniture for Metropolitan Life Insurance in New York. It made house furniture for Vanderbilts and Morgans. It used lumber cut in the nearby mountains, as well as special lumber brought in from a distance by railroad.[1]

The head of the family, William O. Schwarzwaelder, if somewhat like a feudal lord, was devoted, according to his standards, to both his business and his workers. He taught a Bible class at the church and served as school trustee. He created a nature preserve of 6,500 acres, which ran from the village up a trout stream into the mountains, and he opened it only to residents of the village. While the workers were scarcely warm to Schwarzwaelder, they respected him, and they took pride in their work.

After his death in 1924, however, the factory passed into the hands of his three sons who were not like their father. They sometimes used unseasoned lumber in their factory, producing furniture that eventually warped. Instead of appointing as foremen men who had worked their way up through the ranks, they brought in new foremen from the outside. Worker morale dropped. Production declined. The public's increasing use of steel furniture rather than wood furniture did not help, nor did the depression of the 1930s. For years, the Schwarzwaelder sons tried to sell off their factory, along with most of the rest of Chichester, without finding a buyer.

Then one evening, probably in 1936, after 10 o'clock when many of the villagers had already gone to bed, a Rolls Royce arrived in Chichester. It stopped in front of one of the village houses, and a uniformed black chauffeur stepped out to ask the location of Samuel B. Schwarzwaelder's house. The black's presence was startling, for no blacks were ever known to have lived in Chichester.

When the Rolls Royce reached the Schwarzwaelder ten-room house, sometimes called "the village manor house," Samuel B. Schwarzwaelder himself answered the door. The chauffeur asked if Father Divine might come in to ask about buying the village. Schwarzwaelder hesitated a moment, and then said yes. Father Divine walked into the house, accompanied by his secretary, a pretty girl of about twenty.

Inside, as the villagers learned later, Father Divine seemed well informed about the village. As the secretary recorded the conversation in shorthand, Divine inquired about the price. Schwarzwaelder said it would be necessary to consult his brothers. The brothers later agreed to negotiate.[2]

Before news of the negotiations had become generally known in the village, Divine returned to inspect it. He arrived in his Rolls Royce again, but this time in daylight, and accompanied by a parade of cars carrying a number of his adherents. They parked in the Schwarzwaelders' yard, stepped out of their cars, and walked conspicuously about the village. Divine seemed to be enjoying himself.

It is notable that in this case Divine was not negotiating through his loyal real estate agent, John Dellay. It is also notable that in this case Divine was not veiling his negotiations in secrecy, as could have given him an advantage. Instead he was making it publicly known that he was considering buying the site.

A village resident who was mowing his lawn watched as Father Divine and his retinue walked by, seeing him as "rotund, sedate, and very much

SCHWARTZWELDER HOUSE in Chichester, where Father Divine arrived late one evening to propose that his Peace Mission buy the whole village. (Photo by the author, Sept., 2007)

ONCE A COMPANY STORE BUILDING in Chichester, now the Chichester post office. (Photo by the author, Sept., 2007)

at ease." But three children playing on the lawn, never having seen blacks before, were startled. Two of them stood still and stared. The third one, a boy of eight years, waved his arms, shouting, 'Look at the niggers! Look at the niggers!'"

The mower was embarrassed. He told the boy to be quiet. But the boy was too excited. He continued to shout "Look at the niggers!" until finally the man took hold of him and shook him.

Following Divine's daylight visit to the village, everyone there knew that he was negotiating to buy it; and, having heard Divine's reputation, everyone believed that he would be able to pay the price, whatever it was. One rumor was that he might turn the village into a summer camp for Harlem children. Another rumor was that he might ask the present factory workers to stay on to train his followers to work there, but some of the workers vowed that they would never work for a black.

The three Schwarzwaelder brothers, convinced that Divine wanted to buy them out, seemed to worry about what effect such a sale would have on the villagers. But having been looking for a buyer unsuccessfully for many years, they were eager to sell. They decided to make an offer to sell to Divine, but the price they asked was $300,000, which was more than they had already asked prospective white buyers who had turned them down.

Meanwhile, as negotiations proceeded, talk in Chichester grew bitter. Some villagers believed that if Divine took over the factory, he would eventually hire only his followers and drive out the settled residents. Some villagers considered "unbridled" revenge against the Schwarzwaelders if they ever sold out to Divine. Moreover, nearby Phoenicia was "every bit as uneasy" as Chichester, one villager recalled. Its resort business, its businessmen believed, would be "immeasurably injured" if a Divine "Peace Haven" were established "at its back door."

Father Divine, on behalf of his followers, was looking for a bargain. He did not consider the asking price a bargain. Instead he offered something less, which the Schwarzwaelders, by now under strong pressure not to sell to blacks, refused.

Three years later, in 1939, the Schwarzwaelders' factory was no longer functioning. It was unable to pay its taxes or to pay what it owed a Kingston bank. It went bankrupt, and, under court order, almost the entire village was sold at public auction. The sale included the factory, with much of its machinery already having been stripped out, and many houses, a few already empty and deteriorating. Almost the entire village was sold to a variety of bidders, including some of the previous factory workers who still lived in the houses. It sold for a total of $32,000, and neither Divine or his associates were among the bidders.[3]

7. NEIGHBORING FARMS: OLIVE BRIDGE AND KRUMVILLE

WHEN NEW YORK CITY was increasing its water supply by creating the Ashokan Reservoir, farms in the Krumville neighborhood, being only five miles south of the reservoir, prospered by supplying food and housing to the swarms of workers busy on the project. But after the project wound down about 1915, Krumville farms resumed their long slide downward. By the depression of the 1930s, some of them, little used or abandoned, were for sale at bargain prices.

OLIVE BRIDGE FARM

On December 12, 1935, Divine followers bought a farm in the Krumville neighborhood, in the town of Olive. Though this farm was not in Olive Bridge, followers called it their Olive Bridge Farm because its post office was Olive Bridge. The farm as originally bought included only one house, but four months later they bought a small adjacent property including a second house. The combined farm, totaling about 175 acres, extended along both sides of Lower Sahler Mill Road, but its significant buildings, consisting of two medium-sized houses with a large barn in between, were on the road's east side. The southernmost of the two houses, on a sharp bend of the road, was the Ben Davis house, called "a delightful old Dutch stone farmhouse."

Most of this farm was sold by Benjamin O. Davis and his wife to three Divine followers, Hannah James, Hope Fullow, and Anna Reed, all of whom resided at 20 West 115th Street, New York, which was Father Divine's headquarters. The three explained afterwards that, having worked all their lives, they had "invested" their "life's savings" in this farm.

At the farm, the Divinite men lived in the house to the north of the barn, a more recent wooden structure. The women lived south of the barn in the old stone farmhouse, the Ben Davis house, and they served meals there, meals for both the men and the women co-workers, and on occasion for the public. Once when Father Divine visited this old stone house, he spoke there, according to the *New Day*, in a "cozy little banqueting room," with "every inch" occupied by "adoring" followers gazing at him.[1]

When Divine stayed overnight at the farm, he usually stayed in the old Davis house, in quarters reserved especially for him. When he did so, he was likely to keep his car, a big car such as his Duesenberg or his Rolls Royce, in a garage across the road from the house. His followers also kept a big Lincoln in the garage for him, washed and polished, ready for Divine's exclusive use, whether he needed it or not.

In the fall of 1936, visitors found "Brother Joseph" milking cows there, nine of them. They were Holsteins, black and white, with "bags filled almost to the floor." About the same time, other visitors, a group of Divinite children from New York City, found not only the cows, but also, they reported, two horses, three big pigs with eleven piglets, and sixteen ducks in a pond. Eventually the Divinites there kept more cows, twelve to fourteen of them, and also more pigs. They kept the pigs across the road from the stone house, in a low swampy area.

Divine himself, speaking at the farm in 1940, recalled that Ben Davis, when he had worked this farm, had done so with scarcely any help. Divine was proud that, now that his followers farmed it, they had considerable help, and the help was "much more hale and younger"—reason enough, Divine implied, for them to be able to accomplish more than Ben Davis had. Divine was eager, he said, for them to make a profit, suggesting that they were having difficulty in doing so.

In the summer, the farm employed extra help, which by the late 1940s included six or eight local schoolboys. According to one of these boys, Sheldon Boice, who was brought up to be familiar with horses, the work he did for the farm was especially driving a team of horses. When he drove the team to do haying, it might take him three days, he recalled: on the first day he would do mowing; on the second day, drying; on the third day, stowing the hay into a barn.

OLIVE BRIDGE FARM

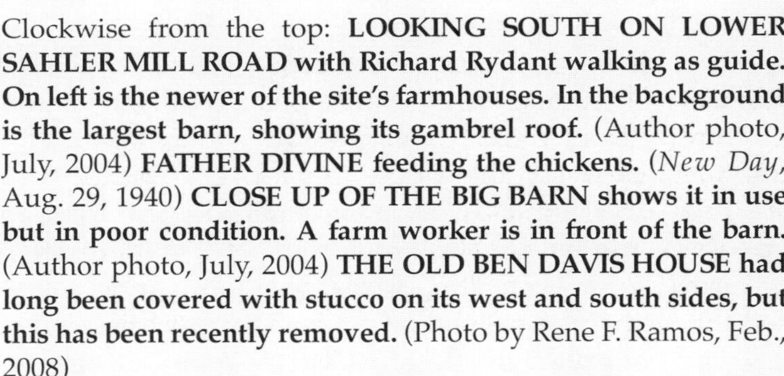

Clockwise from the top: **LOOKING SOUTH ON LOWER SAHLER MILL ROAD with Richard Rydant walking as guide. On left is the newer of the site's farmhouses. In the background is the largest barn, showing its gambrel roof.** (Author photo, July, 2004) **FATHER DIVINE feeding the chickens.** (*New Day*, Aug. 29, 1940) **CLOSE UP OF THE BIG BARN shows it in use but in poor condition. A farm worker is in front of the barn.** (Author photo, July, 2004) **THE OLD BEN DAVIS HOUSE had long been covered with stucco on its west and south sides, but this has been recently removed.** (Photo by Rene F. Ramos, Feb., 2008)

Boice recalls that he worked for the Divinites when he was about 12 to 16 years old, and they paid him 25 cents an hour, which he considered a fair wage. They paid it regularly, and, in keeping with Divine's teaching, in cash, while other local farmers, because they were hurting, might put off paying, or might try to pay in kind, as with a can of paint. The Divinites paid their extra help at the end of each day's work, according to Boice, and they were likely to pay at the barn, which was where they brought in the hay and left their equipment. Pay time was likely to be about five o'clock because that was when the regular farmers had to start milking.

At about this time, the Divinite farmers in Krumville were selling a significant portion of their produce to Divinites in High Falls. Divinites in that village, having no farm of their own, but operating a restaurant, grocery, workshops, and residences, had considerable demand for farm produce.

By the time Boice was working for the Divinites, Divine seldom visited the county any more. The two regular Divinite farmers, Jeremiah Love and Moses Lord, both blacks, invited Boice to go to Krum Elbow to hear Divine when he spoke there once, but Boice declined, and he never saw Divine. Love and Lord did the basic farm work themselves, and supervised the extra help. They were good to work for, Boice recalls. They did not swear and would not let their help swear. Nor would they permit barbed joking. Yet if one of their help wanted to take constructive initiative, as Boice wanted to do with the horses, they might let him do it.[2]

KRUMVILLE FARM

In April, 1936, a few months after Divine followers had acquired their Olive Bridge Farm, they acquired another farm in the same Krumville neighborhood. Consisting of about 76 acres, this new farm was within walking distance of the Olive Bridge Farm. Distinguishing this new farm from their Olive Bridge Farm, followers called this one their Krumville Farm. Its mailing address was Krumville.

Krumville Farm was on both sides of the road leading from Krumville to Samsonville, that is, County Route 2, slightly west of its intersection with the present Upper Sahler Mill Road. This farm had two houses, both of moderate size, both near the road and opposite each other, one being on the north side of the road, and the other being on the south side. The house on the north side of the road, the older of the two, was built on land with an eastward slope, which enabled its basement's east end to have full windows. Under Divinite ownership, this house came to be occupied by men. The house on the south side of the road, the more modern house, was closer to the road and it came to be occupied by women and children. The women often used this house to serve dinners to the public, including dinners that featured homegrown products like chicken and ham. Both of these houses were surrounded by comparatively flat, open farmland, with impressive views of Catskill Mountains to the northwest.

The Divine followers who purchased this Krumville Farm were Lettie Vaughn, who lived at 67 Chapel Street, Kingston, and Charity Davis, who lived at 20 West 115th Street, New York. They acquired this farm from Florence S. Donohue, a sister of Benjamin O. Davis.[3]

In the fall of 1936 when Divine spoke at the Krumville Farm, so many visitors were present that amplifiers were installed outside, on a lawn. In his talk, Divine stressed that his movement's having put his followers to work, as here in Ulster County, meant taking huge numbers of people off relief, saving governments enormous sums. Once in 1937, when Divine had arrived early on a surprise visit to the farm and had begun to make a fire in the kitchen before the residents were up, he soon gathered a small group of the "angels" from this and nearby extensions, to talk to them in a "front room." This time he spoke about his concern for the prices his Ulster County farmers charged, as when they trucked eggs, milk, meat, and vegetables downstate to Divinites in New York, and the prices his New York followers charged as when they trucked groceries and other supplies upstate to Ulster County Divinites. All their prices, he insisted, should be at least as low as what regular markets charged.

KRUMVILLE FARM

Clockwise from the top: **A COMPOSITE VIEW WITH THE CATSKILLS IN THE BACKGROUND. The house to the north (right) was the men's residence; the one closer to the road (left) was the women's residence. This open land is now wooded.** (*New Day*, Mar. 2, 1939) **FATHER DIVINE AND RIDING HORSES.** (*New Day*, Sept. 5, 1940) **VIDA VICTORIA (center), WHO OPERATED THE FARM'S CANDY STORE AND GAS STATION, with two other Ulster County followers: New Hope (left), who operated the tea room in High Falls, and Sweet Inspiration, who was a chef at Hope Farm.** (*Spoken Word*, Sept. 8, 1936) **THE CANDY STORE was directly on County Route 2 in front of the men's residence; now it's in George Kruger's yard.** (Photo by Robert Tucker, July, 2004) **THE MEN'S RESIDENCE** (*New Day*, Mar. 2, 1939)

When several of Divine's secretaries visited Olive Bridge Farm, they observed that some of the followers there were quick to give "eloquent testimonies" of their loyalty to Divine's cause, but in "their daily occupations were entirely different persons, showing slothfulness, resentment, and dissatisfaction," and were failing to do their "practical" part "to establish the Kingdom of God on earth." On the other hand, one of the children who was brought up at the Krumville Farm, Peter Love, when he later looked back at his growing up there, was grateful for the values he learned.[4]

A group of Divinite children, visiting from New York City in the fall of 1936, found at the Krumville Farm "nine hundred chickens, four pigs, two horses, nine cows, eight cats, and four calves." In time the Krumville Farm came to specialize more in vegetables and chickens, while the Olive Bridge Farm specialized more in pigs and cows.

In 1938, when some 18 or 20 people lived at the Krumville Farm, a manager of the farm was True Heart Love. When Love was driving near Stone Ridge, and was arrested for passing two trucks on a curve, a local newspaper identified her as "colored," from the Krumville extension. But a passenger in her car, also from the Krumville extension, was Vida Victoria, a white woman of English origin, who, according to the newspaper, had previously lived in Victoria, British Columbia, Canada, and was a woman "of apparent refinement." While both blacks and whites lived at both the Krumville and Olive Bridge Farms, a life-long resident of the neighborhood recalled their residents as predominantly blacks.[5]

GASOLINE AND MELONS

Local boy Sheldon Boice recalled long afterward that most of the Divine farm workers at both farms had previous farm experience in the South. They had little education, it seemed to him, but they were polite, decent people. Inside their houses, he was struck by the big photos of Divine on the walls. He was also struck by the women and men staying apart. The women did the cooking, washing, and cleaning, he recalled, but they were careful to clean the men's quarters only when the men were out.

The Krumville Farm had a tiny store building, on the north side of the Krumville-Samsonville Road, close to the road, where Divinites sold candy and ice cream inside and gasoline otside. A Divinite woman who often operated this store and sold the gas was Vida Victoria who often wrote for Divine publications, including arguments for economic and political reform.

Sheldon Boice recalled this store sold gas for 11 cents a gallon, while his grandfather, who also had a gas station in the neighborhood, sold gas at the more usual price of 18 cents a gallon. Many drivers in the area, Boice recalled, would buy gas from the Divinite station during the day, when it was open; but if they needed gas at night, when the Divinite station was closed, they would buy it at his grandfather's.[6]

The land that Divinite farmers worked included not only the two farms they owned but also additional land they rented nearby. They rented such land as a portion of the old Owen farm, which stretched from Route 2 north to near the Krumville Cemetery. At the time the owners of this old farm were Ed and George Ekersen, who used it especially as a hunting site. They welcomed having the land farmed because they did not want it to grow up to brush.

George Kruger recalled that Divinite farmers in the Krumville region worked the fields on both sides of what is now the one-lane entrance road that leads from County Route 2A into the cemetery. He remembered that Divinite farmers, particularly Moses Lord, grew hay on the north side of that road and melons on the south side. During the season when the melons were ripening, if some of the melons seemed to disappear, and farmer Lord found shoe tracks in the melon field, he would say, tolerantly, that racoons must have feet remarkably like shoes. Lord and other Divinites, Kruger recalled, had good relations with neighborhood youngsters. They not only employed several of them in the summer, but also sometimes gave them melons, and invited them into the Divine farmhouses.

Moses Lord sometimes drove a rickety "doodle bug," really a truck stripped down to be like a tractor. Lord used it to haul a wagon to various local boarding houses and summer camps to pick up their scrap food to feed to pigs. If the "bug" stalled on a hill, Lord might be heard to say "darn," but he would not swear. Neighborhood youngsters, doubting the completeness of any such discipline, would listen sharply to Lord and other Divinites, ready to pounce on any lapse into swearing. They rarely found a chance to pounce.[7]

8. ELTING CORNERS: THE INN THAT BURNED

THE ELTING FAMILY, of Huguenot ancestry, had long conducted a tourist boarding house at Elting Corners. It was in the town of Lloyd, about three miles east of the village of New Paltz. It was on a little hill on New Paltz Road, which was the main road leading from New Paltz toward Highland, at the corner of North Elting Corners Road.

When Divine followers bought this property in October, 1936, it consisted of about six acres, including a large house with about twenty-two bedrooms, and two barns. Following the Elting family tradition, Divine followers sometimes called it "Orchard Terrace," or more often, adapting this old name, they called it "Divine Terrace."

The four Divinites who bought Divine Terrace were all women: Charlotte Becker, Grace Faith, Mary Davis, and Wonderful Peace. They all gave addresses in Manhattan, three of them on West 123rd Street, in Harlem, and the fourth, the white Charlotte Becker, on West 106th Street. Becker, also a buyer of several other properties related to Divine in Ulster County, soon afterwards said she lived at Divine Terrace.

Why were the buyers of properties for the Divine movement—whether in Ulster County or elsewhere—more often women rather than men? One reason was that there were more Divine followers who were women than men. But beyond that, Divine said he saw a another reason. Many of the women who became his followers had grown up with different values from many of the men who became his followers. The women grew up obedient to their elders, he said, while the men grew up obedient to nobody. Moreover, as the women grew up, they "saved their money," but the men, as they grew up, did not. That was why his women followers became more successful in business than his men followers, he said, and that was why the women had more money available to buy property for his movement.

Soon after Divine followers purchased Divine Terrace, they operated it as a resort. Situated on elevated land among "spreading trees," its main building had "wide verandahs" with a view of distant mountains. They put a large sign on it saying, "Peace to the world at large. God is in the land, walking like a mighty man."[1]

Then one night in April, 1937, only six months after Divinites had purchased it, the main building caught fire. To escape the fire, according to the New York *Times*, several residents "scrambled down rain pipes or jumped from windows," but no one was seriously hurt. The New Paltz and Clintondale firemen arrived at the scene too late to control the fire, however, and the building was destroyed.

At the time of the fire, Divine himself was in New York City. When he heard of it by radio, he rushed by car to the site, accompanied by his leading secretary, John Lamb. They helped arrange for most of the followers who had been living in the building, about fifteen of them, to be housed for the time being at the New Paltz mission.

Since it was known that Divine Terrace's neighbors were not happy with Divine followers living there, rumors quickly circulated that the fire had been deliberately set. Secretary John Lamb believed the rumors, explaining that numerous threatening telephone messages had recently been received at various Divine sites in Ulster County. The night before, two crosses had been burned at Atwood, near the Stone Ridge Mansion, about seventeen miles from Divine Terrace. Besides, before the fire, County Sheriff Abram Molyneaux, aware of the hostility to the Peace Mission in the county, had recommended that Divinites keep their lights burning all night, as a protection. However, Sher-

ORCHARD TERRACE INN, AFTER DIVINE FOLLOWERS BOUGHT IT, WAS OFTEN CALLED DIVINE TERRACE. It was on a slight rise at Elting Corners on the southeast corner of the junction of New Paltz Road with North Elting Corners Road. After the inn burned to the ground in 1937, it was never rebuilt. (Postcard, no date, Elting Memorial Library) **SECRETARY JOHN LAMB BELIEVED THAT THE DIVINE TERRACE FIRE HAD BEEN SET DELIBERATELY.** (*New Day*, Jan. 23, 1941)

iff Molyneaux and other officials doubted that the fire was the result of arson. The New Paltz fire chief pointed out that the fire could have started near a second floor chimney, and that a stove connected to that chimney had recently been in use. The cause of the fire was never officially determined.

The loss was estimated to be probably more than $15,000. In line with Divine's teaching that relying on insurance indicated lack of trust in God, the property was not insured. Followers who had lived in the building, however, seemed unconcerned about the loss, confident that Father Divine would take care of it. Secretary Lamb predicted that Divine would see to it that a new building would be built, and that it would be larger than the one destroyed.

A year later, in 1938, Divine was saying he would arrange to rebuild the building if the county adopted a policy that would exempt all property improvements from taxation for five years. But the county did not adopt such a policy, and anyway, Divine was more inclined to encourage repairing old structures than building new ones. He never arranged to rebuild the building.[2]

Meanwhile, several Divine followers, black men, continued to live at the site, in barns left untouched by the fire. They slept in a large barn, and used a small adjoining barn as their kitchen and dining room. To help support themselves, they sometimes did a little farming. One of them sometimes worked outside as a handyman for Bill Van Vliet, a New Paltz real estate dealer. By the 1950s, another one of them was Frederic N. Crabb, who worked as a New York City public school teacher.[3] As we will see later, Crabb long continued to live at Divine Terrace.

9. CREATE A CHILDREN'S HOME IN SAUGERTIES OR NEW PALTZ?

IF PARENTS became dedicated followers of Divine, it was expected that they would not raise their children, once they had grown out of infancy. Instead, the children were expected to be scattered among various Divine communities, the children apart from their parents. By 1936, when the number of such children had grown significantly, the Peace Mission decided it would be appropriate to house them in a children's home.

The Peace Mission planned to establish a children's home in Ulster County, and to name it the "Peninnah's Children's Home," in honor of Mother Peninnah Divine. The Peace Mission's application to New York State for permission to operate the home listed among its incorporators John Dellay, the Rosendale real estate dealer who was making himself conspicuous on behalf of Divine. The State Board of Social Welfare arranged a hearing on the application, to be held in New York City.

The application provided that the home could be located anywhere in Ulster County. Verbally the applicants explained that it might be located in West Saugerties, but opponents suspected this might be a ruse to cover up plans to locate it in some other location, near other already established Divine communities.

The New Paltz Chamber of Commerce, fearing the home might be located in New Paltz, called a meeting for November, 1936, to prepare for the state's hearing, and the meeting was crowded. A judge told the gathering that if the home was established without adequate means of support, the children might become public charges. The County Welfare Commissioner declared that wherever such a home was established, the local school district would be compelled to accept the home's children in its schools. The meeting arranged for Attorney Peter H. Harp, a conservative attorney who was a descendant of the early Huguenot settlers of New Paltz, to write a letter explaining the New Paltz Chamber's opposition to the proposed home.

Harp's letter, as presented at the hearing in New York City, was fierce. It read in part:

> Since 1678 this [Wallkill River] valley has been inhabited and developed by our ancestors. By inheritance, possession, industry and thrift, we have a prior right upon the social, educational and welfare units of this community.
>
> Most of the social and religious doctrines of that element known as the followers of Father Divine are diametrically opposite, obnoxious and repugnant to our principles on religious, social and economic standards. We cannot mix but one must eventually exclude the other.
>
> The migration and transportation of a disproportionately large number of people into our midst without visible means of support, enchanted and hypnotized by a mortal who is financed in an unknown and mysterious manner, sustained by the most part with ignorant people of low intelligence, is shocking and obnoxious to our social order.
>
> He and his kind were not invited and are not wanted in our community. In the name of Peace we request them to depart.
>
> The desirability of New Paltz as an educational center and as a vacation and recreation community has been tremendously damaged by this new and untried cult.
>
> We respectfully petition that the application herein be absolutely denied.

At the hearing, Divine's Peace Mission was represented by the black attorney, Arthur Madison, who, as he admitted under questioning, considered himself a follower of Divine. Madison explained that at first the proposed children's home was expected to take only girls, from about six to twelve years of age. The home could charge parents for the care of their children, he said. As discussion brought out, however, this would not be likely if the parents became fully devoted followers of Divine, since then they were no longer encouraged to take individual responsibility for their children.

Ulster County Welfare Commissioner Bob Park told the hearing bluntly that when parents become followers of Divine, they "abandon" their children, and therefore might refuse to pay for their care in this children's home; and he warned that if the home did not have adequate financing, the county might then become responsible for the children.

Dr. Lawrence Van Den Berg, the New Paltz State Normal School's principal, attended the hearing personally and presented a letter of his

ATTORNEY ARTHUR A. MADISON (left) represented the Peace Mission when it applied to the state for permission to establish a children's home in Ulster County. Brought up in Alabama, he earned a masters degree from Columbia, a law degree from Wisconsin. He volunteered his legal service to Divine, but somewhat uneasy as a follower, he maintained his own marriage, his own home, and his own law office in New York City. (*Our World*, Aug., 1949) **PETER HARP, a New Paltz attorney of Huguenot ancestry, passionately opposed Divinites in their attempt to create a children's home in Ulster County.** (Elting Memorial Library)

own. It was a more temperate letter than attorney Harp's. He said that if the proposed children's home were situated near New Paltz, it might well be intended that the children of the home were to attend the New Paltz Normal School's Practice School, which at the time served as New Paltz's public elementary school. If so, this would require "considerable expense" in enlarging the plant and hiring more teachers. Moreover, he wrote, "Appreciating the fact that an argument based upon purely racial objections would necessarily have little weight, we nevertheless wish it to be understood that we at New Paltz view this encroachment upon the village by the organization backing this proposed incorporation with considerable trepidation." He explained, "Two pieces of property have recently been purchased" by the Divine group near the village of New Paltz: "one a farm site [the New Paltz Farm] directly across the Wallkill River to the west of the village," and the other [Divine Terrace]," a large home formerly used as a summer boarding house" about three miles to the east. "Those of us who are interested in the welfare of the State Normal School located at New Paltz can see but one result to the establishment of [another] colony by this group in or near the village. Attendance at the Normal School College would drop materially."

On Dec. 16, 1936, the State Board of Social Welfare denied the Peace Mission's application. One reason it gave was that financial resources to operate the home had not been assured.[4]

At about the same time, the Divine forces also considered establishing a children's home across the Hudson River in Dutchess County, in Pine Plains. They succeeded in acquiring an option there on the eight-acre estate of the Eno family, a prominent family of lawyers. The option included, according to a Poughkeepsie newspaper, what had once been a grand mansion, in the town's finest residential district, on North Main Street.[5]

But if the state would not allow Divine followers to establish a children's home in one county, it was not likely to allow it in another. After the state turned down their application for Ulster County, followers seemed to abandon their plans to establish a children's home anywhere in the mid-Hudson region.

10. HOPE FARM, WEST SAUGERTIES

HOPE FARM consisted of about forty-five acres in the West Saugerties neighborhood of the town of Saugerties. It was located on a road leading from West Saugerties south to Pine Grove, a road now known as Band Camp Road, slightly south of its junction with the highway from West

Saugerties to Woodstock. As a visitor described it, Hope Farm's "peace," its easy racial mixing, and its "brisk mountain air" provided many Divine followers relief from the "degradation" they had known in New York City.

On October 31, 1936, four Divine followers bought Hope Farm for $6,500. Two of them already lived at Divine missions in Ulster County, one, an elderly white, Charlotte Becker, at Divine Terrace in the town of Lloyd, and another, Aquilla Matthews, a black domestic, at the mission in New Paltz. The remaining two lived in New York City, in Harlem. The four bought the farm from the Hermann Benninks.

Herman A. Bennink, an immigrant from Holland, had studied agriculture, and then for ten years had operated Hope Farm. Speaking at a meeting at the Kingston Mansion two weeks after the sale, he expressed his confidence that in time Divine followers, because of their "consecration," would become "outstanding" farmers. He also gave them farming advice, such as urging them, when they removed their wood ashes from their stoves every morning, to save them, and then in the spring when they planted their potatoes, to apply the ashes as fertilizer.[1]

The new owners seemed pleased that the Benninks had called the farm Hope Farm, and decided to retain the name. Father Divine liked it, he said, because it suggested to him hope for overcoming the world.

The new owners arranged to remodel Hope Farm's "antiquated" house, and to do it extensively. Within a year, according to the *New Day*, with more than twenty Divinite volunteers doing the major work, they had enlarged the house, constructing a two-story addition at the front and a three-story addition at the rear, giving the house altogether at least thirty bedrooms, though small ones. They also installed a dining hall in the basement able to seat 200 guests, which, thanks to a convenient slope in the lay of the land, had ground-level entrances. Divine, who himself participated in designing the renovations, was particularly proud of placing the laundry facilities—including space for hanging out clothes to dry—upstairs rather than in the cellar. This meant, Divine said, that the laundress would not have to "lug" the clothes "up the cellar way," to hang them "out in the cold." Meanwhile, as was typical of Divine, he specified no source for the funds that paid for such "glorious" renovations, only insisting, when he spoke there at a banquet, that such renovations are possible if the participants concentrate on the "positive" and "visualize harmoniously."[2]

As Hope Farm opened, its manager was Simon Peter, a white who earlier, as a physician, had deliberately burned down his own office for the insurance, but once reformed under Divine's lead, had become a persuasive leader. Later a "dignified Negro woman," Sister Lovely Sweetness, a former teacher, was in charge. One visitor found Sweetness' greeting of "peace" to be "so natural" that nearly anyone would be apt to respond with the same greeting. She kept the banquet tables always set, ready to serve guests. The chef, Sweet Inspiration, delighted in the foods the farm was able to provide, including milk, eggs, apples, ducks, and turkeys. A farmer there was Unison Heart who, following Divine's teaching against the use of violence, became a conscientious objector in World War II. At various times, two young people who lived at Hope Farm, both children of Divine followers, were Jean Becker, who tried to hide there from her parents, and Son Peter who, under the inspiration of Faithful Mary, was a rebel against Divine. Another resident was the college-educated Deborah Newmind, by origin an Orthodox Jew, who often read aloud at meetings. She claimed that Divine, at Hope Farm as well as elsewhere, was creating "the Kingdom of Heaven on earth."[3]

In the Kingdom, while Divine taught that family members should be separated from each other, he sometimes seemed ambivalent about the degree to which they should be separated, as the following account of his relation to the child Free Will suggests. Free Will was born in Florida, but her mother, not yet a Divine follower, brought her to New York, with her other children, early during the depression of the 1930s, hoping to improve their lives. In New York, where the mother and her children often stood in bread lines, her mother met a Divine follower, and through her became a fol-

HOPE FARM

Clockwise from the top: **DIVINE FOLLOWERS RENOVATED HOPE FARM'S MAIN HOUSE, as shown here, markedly increasing its capacity. In the background are Catskill Mountains.** (*New Day*, Oct. 1, 1942) **FATHER DIVINE IN HIS HOPE FARM OFFICE.** (*New Day*, Feb. 27, 1941) **FEEDING HOPE FARM'S CHICKENS** (*New Day*, Oct. 3, 1940)

lower herself. Thereafter their lot began to improve.

Once when Free Will was about six years old, she was standing near Divine, when he called her over and asked her if she wanted to go to the Promised Land. Free Will did not know where it was, but wanting to please Divine, said yes. When Free Will was seven, in about 1937, Divine took her, along with her mother, brother, and sister, upstate to Hope Farm, all of them to stay there, although it is not clear whether Divine considered it ideal for all of them to live at the same mission. On arrival, Free Will was startled, she recalled afterwards, by seeing chickens and apple trees for the first time. She had been accustomed to eating on paper plates, and now for the first time she began eating on chinaware. At first she was thin from lack of adequate food, she recalled, but provided with abundant food, she soon filled out.

Altogether there were eight children staying at Hope Farm at the time. Free Will's mother and other mothers, some of whom were followers and some not, did cleaning, washing, and cooking there, indirectly helping care for their own children. It was not the mothers who were designated as having primary responsibility for their children, however. Rather it was the farm's manager.

Several of the children, including Free Will, attended the nearby one-room public school, the Blue Mountain School. In good weather the children would walk there, but in bad weather it was not any of the mothers who drove them to school. The person who often chauffeured them was one of the mission's white followers, Deborah Newmind.

Speaking at Hope Farm, as Divine often did, he sometimes felt the need to urge his followers to live up to their ideals. Once Divine scolded many of his followers for claiming that to follow his teaching they "gave up" their families, but "when you are weighed in the balances," you are found still "loving" them.

Illustrating the difficulty of followers breaking their family ties, at another time a follower visiting Hope Farm from California said she was troubled by criticism that she still lived at home with her husband. They were living together only as brother and sister, she explained defensively, adding that her husband, being like a child, needed her care. In reply, Father Divine said that for the right relationship with God, you must not be devoted to your families. It is necessary "to lose your identity." It is necessary to make "a complete surrender." "Your minds and attention, your love and devotion, your ideas and your opinions," he said, "all must be concentrated on the Fundamental."[4]

FATHER DIVINE VISITING HOPE FARM with Mother Divine in the background.
(*New Day*, Oct. 10, 1940)

11. "IN THE CUP OF THE MOUNTAINS": RESORT AT SAMSONVILLE

OF ALL THE DIVINE SITES in Ulster County, the Samsonville resort was the farthest into the Catskill Mountains. It was in the town of Rochester, near the border of the town of Olive. Although officially called Divine Lodge, informally it was called Samsonville, after the nearby hamlet of that name. It was reached from Samsonville by driving on Palentown Road, then by climbing northwesterly up Rocky Mountain Road, which merged into what is now Etheline Road. It was at the far end of Etheline Road.

Although Townley had furnished the resort fashionably, it was not successful enough to survive. In October, 1936, Townley's family sold it to Divine followers. As a teenager who helped the actors move out recalled long afterward, when followers moved in, they found a stash of liquor inside. In accordance with their beliefs, they carried the liquor bottles outside and smashed them, spilling the liquor on the ground.[2]

When Divine followers found their way to the Samsonville resort, they found that while the main house lacked electricity, its living room had the charm of "Rochester oil lamps," as well as a stone fireplace. A New York lawyer, visiting there with his family, found the hostess, Miss Rebecca Well, to be "gracious," and her assistant, Miss Blessed Faith, "indeed blessed in her manner." Another visitor, a young woman from a family which had owned the resort before the Townleys, said her family had been distressed when the resort was taken over for "drinking and carousing," but were glad now that Divine followers owned it, that it would be used instead for "spiritual" uses."

PANORAMIC VIEW OF DIVINE LODGE, OFTEN CALLED SAMSONVILLE RESORT, high in the Catskill Mountains. At left, a big farm barn. In the center, the main house, which served as a women's residence. At riight, the largest building was a barn, which served as a men's residence. (*New Day*, March 16, 1939)

Visitors liked to say the Samsonville resort was "in the cup of the mountains." It offered striking views of the mountains hovering over it, including Little Rocky, which, at 3,015 feet, was high for the Catskills. Inside the resort's buildings, according to the *New Day*, the "fragrant air," as it "sifted in" through the screened windows, was "rejuvenating" for the guests. Outside, hiking trails were available, giving access to mountain brooks and wild game such as deer and bear.[1]

Before Divine followers had acquired this site, it had been a resort for actors. It had been operated by Barry Townley, himself an actor—in 1932-1933, he appeared in two Broadway plays, the longer lasting of which was *It Happened Tomorrow*.

Divine followers cared for the resort year-round, keeping perhaps six followers in residence there even during the winter. They kept only one riding horse, but several workhorses, and they raised hay, barley, and pigs. While they served dinners to guests for the usual low charge which Divine requested, fifteen cents, they scarcely seem to have opened their dining room to the public. According to a long-time resident of the area,

SAMSONVILLE RESORT

Clockwise from above: **THE MAIN HOUSE, WHERE THE WOMEN SLEPT, has a striking view of the valley below.** (Photo by Robert Tucker, July, 2004) **DIVINE WITH A RIDING HORSE FOR USE AT THIS RESORT. He was more often pictured with workhorses. THE BIG BARN IN AN OPEN FIELD. The barn is now almost empty, suggesting the farm is scarcely active anymore.** (Photo by the author, July, 2004) **DIVINE IN A FARM FIELD.** ***New Day*** **described the resort's farm as "formerly unprofitable" but now yielding and "abundance."** (*New Day*, Sept. 26, 1940) **A RESORT BARN, WHICH DIVINE FOLLOWERS HAD RENOVATED AS SLEEPING QUARTERS FOR MEN, with eight bedrooms. Shown with Rick Rydant acting as guide (right) and Robert Tucker (left).** (Author photo, July, 2006)

those who lived nearby who were looking for Divine-related public dinners customarily went not to the difficult-to-reach Samsonville resort, but to the more accessible Krumville Farm.[3]

When Divine visited Samsonville, he was likely to come in one of his impressive big cars, such as his Duesenberg. When he first arrived, if his followers in neighboring missions did not know he was there, they soon got the word by telephone, and many were likely to drive over to see him. As when he visited other missions, Divine was likely to inspect the mission's facilities, preside at its banquets, speak, and stay overnight in special quarters always kept ready for him. According to a Divinite periodical, his Samsonville quarters were graced with "beautiful mahogany furniture," a "private bath," and a "reception room."

If followers drove up from New York at the same time Divine did, they sometimes closely followed Divine's car, partly because they were not familiar enough with what one of them called the "twists and turns of these famous mountain roads." Occasionally Divine felt required to reprimand some of these drivers for being "reckless." They cut in and out of the line of cars too often, trying to get their cars closer to his.

One evening in September, 1938, Divine arrived at the Samsonville resort so late that he found the main house, where the women slept, in darkness, everyone already having gone to bed. His arrival awakened some of the sleepers, however, and they soon produced a banquet in his honor. By 2:05 AM, as they sat at the banquet table, Divine, who needed little sleep, was speaking to them. Among the concerns he spoke about was which sites in the county were the most suitable for holding county-wide Righteous Government meetings in the early fall. The most suitable, it seemed to Divine, did not include Samsonville, its facilities being too small. The most suitable were the sites that could house large indoor meetings, but not necessarily in heated spaces, sites such as New Paltz, High Falls, Milton, and Greenkill Park.

On another occasion, Divine was at Samsonville presiding at a banquet at a more conventional time of day, the early afternoon. It was November, and in the dining room of the main house, "logs blazed in the fireplace." Divine spoke. Although he seemed concerned to provide both himself and his followers quality resort accommodations, he advised his listeners, "Still yourselves." "Observe the nothingness of matter."[4]

12. "THE CHOICEST SPOTS": HIGH FALLS

BEFORE 1900, High Falls had been a canal center. From High Falls, canal barges had shipped out logs cut in nearby forests, and had also shipped out barrels of cement produced from stone mined in nearby quarries. By the depression of the 1930s, however, the forests were depleted, the cement plants were gone, the canal was no longer functioning, and population had dropped. Property in High Falls was for sale inexpensively, and that attracted Divine followers.

The first property they acquired in the High Falls area was about three miles southwest of the hamlet. Purchased in October, 1935, it was a farm of about 62 acres, on Cherry Hill Road, in the town of Marbletown, near the Rochester town line. Its house was a neat story-and-a-half structure, with a generous porch, shaded by maple trees, and surrounded by open fields. The Divine follower who bought it was St. Mary Bloom of Harlem. Though lacking any significant level of education, she inspired trust, and was later to become a Divine's movement administrator. On a visit to this Cherry Hill Farm soon after it was acquired, Father Divine and a group of followers found it provided with a "modern equipped house," and stocked with cows, pigs, and horses.

The most significant properties that Divine followers acquired in the High Falls area, however, were in the hamlet of High Falls itself. They began acquiring them beginning in August, 1936, when follower Faithful Mary acquired a hotel, the old Belmont Hotel, at the northeast corner of Main Street and Third Street (now Bruceville Road), in the heart of the village. After enlarging this build-

Above: **HIGH FALLS: PEACE MISSION DEPARTMENT STORE BUILDING (showing its cupola on top), with an attached barbershop on its left and an attached two-story house on its right. Other Peace Mission structures showing are farther left (on Main Street), a separate two-story dress shop with its attached one-story shoe repair shop; and farther right (on Church Street), a sparate dwelling.** (*New Day*, Feb. 16. 1939)

Below: **FAITHFUL MARY'S HOTEL, one of the Peace Mission's facilities in High Falls, was on Main Street at the corner of Bruceville Road, opposite the department store. Beside serving as a hotel, the building provided a restaurant and grocery inside, as well as gas pumps outside (foreground). Faithful Mary , in the course of rebelling against Divine, lost control of this hotel. The site is now empty.** (1930's[?], Richard Rydant)

Top: **PEACE MISSION'S CANDY FACTORY, LATER A TEA ROOM, on the north side of Main Street at the corner of Second Street, High Falls. The building does not survive.** (*New Day*, Feb. 16, 1939)

Above: **PEACE MISSION'S ECONOMY STORE, housed in a flatiron-shaped building on Second Street, south of Main Street in High Falls. This shop advertised that it sold used clothing, including hats for ten cents, dresses for fifteen cents, coats for a dollar. The building, remodled, survives.** (*New Day*, Feb. 16, 1939)

Top: **PEACE MISSION'S BAKERY, TAILOR SHOP, AND RESIDENCE on the south side of Main Street at the corner of Sixth Street in High Falls. At present the building houses the High Falls post office.** (*New Day*, Feb. 16, 1939)

Above: **PEACE MISSION'S AUTO REPAIR GARAGE (left) AND NEARBY RESIDENCE (right) on the east side of Lucas Avenue at the corner of Main Street on the edge of High Falls. The garage included a heated hall for meetings where Divine spoke. Both buildings survive.** (*New Day*, Feb. 16, 1939)

ing, Faithful Mary arranged to place a sign on its front, saying "Father Divine's Peace Mission Hotel." Faithful Mary operated it not only as a hotel but also as a grocery, a dwelling for Mission workers, a restaurant that served the public chicken and duck meals at the usual low Mission prices, and outside the building, a gas station with several gas pumps.[1]

That same month, four other Divine followers, Eva Barbee, Victory Luke, Jean Bright, and John Truth, all of New York City, acquired what had been a shoe store across Main Street from the hotel, on the corner of Main and Church (now Mohonk Avenue). By the next January, they had turned it into the Peace Mission Department Store. This store was diagonally across the street from the Reformed Church's parsonage, and was acquired while the pastor was away on vacation. On the Sunday after he returned, when he began preaching his sermon, he was reported to have had tears in his eyes as he announced his theme, "We're All God's Children."

In October, 1936, two other followers, Faith Love and Charlotte Becker, the latter of whom was also a purchaser of Hope Farm, acquired a building only a block west of the hotel and department store. This was a three-story building on the north side of Main Street, between Second and Third Streets, and had formerly housed a bakery. Followers remade it into a candy factory, but soon they themselves raised questions about the quality of the candy it produced, and with Father Divine insisting it produce the best possible quality of candy or stop production, by July, 1937, they had converted the factory into a "tea-room restaurant." According to the *New Day*, it became busy because, after the hotel's restaurant had ceased to operate, it was the only restaurant in High Falls.[2]

Top: **THE LUCAS AVENUE RESIDENCE FOR DIVINE FOLLOWERS ON THE EDGE OF HIGH FALLS, now a private residence. (Photo by Rene F. Ramos, Jan., 2004)**

Above: **THE PEACE MISSION'S CHERRY HILL FARMHOUSE outside of High Falls on Cherry Hill Road, just south of an old cemetery, near the Rochester town line. The house survives.** (*New Day*, Feb. 23, 1939)

By February, 1937, Divine followers had bought so many key properties in High Falls, that a Divinite periodical, the *Spoken Word*, claimed they already possessed its "choicest spots," but Divine followers continued to buy still more High Falls property. In March, followers acquired a building on the south side of Main Street, at the corner of First. This building, the present High Falls post office building, they turned into a tailor shop, and after Faithful Mary's hotel grocery had ceased to operate, also into a grocery, with a residence on the top floor. The next month, April, 1937, they bought still another property in High Falls, this one considerably west of the heart the village, across Rondout Creek, on the southeast corner of Lucas Avenue and the highway to Stone Ridge (Route 213), in what they called the "Rondout" neighborhood. This property consisted of a large blacksmith shop directly on the corner, and adjacent to it, southward on Lucas Avenue, a dwelling, with its back toward Rondout Creek. The buyers included two Divine followers who already lived in Ulster County: Mary Bird Tree, who lived at the Kingston Mansion, and John Fountaine, who lived in Saugerties. The buyers kept the dwelling as a residence for Divine followers; and the demand for blacksmiths having faded, they turned the blacksmith shop into a garage servicing automobiles. By that same month, April, 1937, Divine followers were operating still another new establishment on High Falls's Main Street, east of the Divine department store. This was a dress making shop, which was "kept supplied continually with orders." For several years, Mother Divine herself managed this dress shop, and lived much of the time apart from Father Divine, across the street in a "cottage" behind Faithful Mary's hotel.[3]

As usual whenever Divine's movement acquired property in predominantly white neighborhoods, there were signs of opposition. Someone threw a brick through the window of the department store, and someone burned a cross at a door of Faithful Mary's hotel. In the case of the property on Lucas Avenue, neighbors tried to prevent Divine followers from buying it by pooling their assets to buy the property themselves, but did not succeed. On a Sunday evening in the fall of 1936, when Divine was speaking in the hotel building, it became so crowded that his followers set up loud speakers to carry his voice outside, to a crowd gathered there, as they often did in similar situations. The noise, however, disturbed neighbors. They called County Sheriff Molyneaux. On his arrival, the sheriff directed Divine's supporters to remove the loudspeakers, and when they refused, he disconnected them. In March, 1937, the New Paltz *Independent* pointed to High Falls as a warning that Divine threatened the whole of Ulster County. "One has only to drive through High Falls," the newspaper said, "to realize the pitiful wreck the whole county may become unless drastic measures are taken."[4]

Meanwhile, the grocery—which was managed by the white Simon Peter, who had earlier managed Hope Farm—was doing well because of its low prices. What it sold included produce from Divine's nearby farms, such as fruit, meat, and eggs. In April, 1937, when the grocery was still located in Faithful Mary's hotel, the *Ulster County Press* reported that it was "the main source of food supply" for "most" Divine "missions" in the county, and was open to the public as well. By December, according to Divine's secretary John Lamb, when the grocery had moved slightly west on Main Street, its low prices were attracting customers from twenty-five miles around. At least a few area residents came to believe that the Divine movement's arrival was a blessing to High Falls, explaining that it was helping the poor and rescuing the village from depression-induced economic collapse.[5]

By 1939, followers had also acquired a building on Second Street, just south of Main Street, a two-story building that was shaped like a flatiron. They put there an Economy Shop, which was affiliated with another such store in Harlem. This shop often advertised in the *New Day* that it sold used clothing, including dresses for fifteen cents.

The buildings that Divine followers bought in High Falls came to be easily recognizable as Divine-related, because followers eventually painted all of them similarly, the same as they did their buildings in the rest of Ulster County. They painted them in a variety of light colors, such as white, ivory, grey, or yellow, but always with red trim. All their enterprises in High Falls, like Divine enterprises generally, were run as "cooperatives," that is, not consumer cooperatives, but producer cooperatives. They were owned and operated by Divine followers, who sometimes lived on the premises and always worked without wages, but were provided with the necessities of life, including food and clothing. All these enterprises were interracial. Followers were deliberately placed in them so that persons of different races worked and lived together. According to the recollection of two white children, who not only grew up in High Falls but also attended school with Divinite children and shopped in Divinite stores, the proportion of Divine children who were white was higher in High Falls than in other such Divine communities, perhaps more than half being white.

Divine himself often came to High Falls. He checked there both on his wife and on his followers. When one of them publically charged that followers "fight up here just like wild dogs," Divine responded that if they really were his followers, they would not fight, but in any case the fighters were only "a limited few." He spoke at Righteous Government meetings, as at the garage on Lucas

Avenue, and at the dress shop on Main Street. He spoke at a banquet in the "cheerful little dining room" at the Peace Mission residence on Lucas Avenue, beside the garage. He also spoke at a "sumptuous banquet," on Main Street, at the "lovely residence" above the tailor shop and grocery. In 1938, it was rumored that Divine followers were buying so many buildings in High Falls, that "it is only a matter of time" until they "own that whole village." But, Divine explained, "I am not interested in their owning the whole village." What I want, he said, is "to work cooperatively, unselfishly," not just for our own movement. "I want our work," our businesses, to reduce prices for the "general public." Some wholesalers have stopped selling to our High Falls grocery, he admitted, because they say we sell for less than their cost of production, but, he insisted, our low prices help bring down the prices of the "high priced merchants," aiding everyone.[6]

When Divine visited High Falls, he was likely to arrive in one of his big cars, such as his Duesenberg or his Rolls Royce, along with a caravan of other cars. Followers hurried to gather around. They shouted. Divine, wearing a hat at a sporty angle, waved. He smiled. He was vigorous. He was handsome. To some onlookers, "he looked like a million dollars."

Charles R. Barnett, a white boy who spent his summers at his grandfather's in nearby Rosendale, remembered long afterwards being in a crowd when Divine arrived in High Falls. "I was looking straight at God," Charles remembered."Well, not exactly straight. I had to look up a little because I was pretty small." Charles was only seven years old at the time. "I couldn't get a really clear view of him, either. There were too many people in the way. They seemed enormous and kept shifting back and forth and shouting. It was hot and humid but we were in heaven so who cared? The people were happy and they wanted God to know it. So they swayed back and forth and they shouted and waved. Some of them sang songs. That seemed to make God happy because he had a big smile on his face. He was wearing a rumpled suit that looked heavy with perspiration but he didn't seem to mind. On his head was a creamy white fedora as cool as a summer cloud."

His mother often took Charles to High Falls to the Peace Mission barbershop on Main Street, in an addition built onto the eastern end of the Mission's department store. When Charles "came bouncing" into the shop, he would say "Peace, brother," in accordance with the expected ritual. The barber, Brother Nicodemus, "a tall, spare, black man," would always smile and answer "Peace," and wave him to a "huge enamel and leather chair that sat on an hydraulic pedestal."

With a "series of snippety snips," Charles recalled, "Brother Nicodemus would swing me around, back and forth," clipping my head. "Finally, I'd feel him smear a dollop of shaving cream on the back of my neck and one behind each ear." Then "Brother Nicodemus would take out a straight razor and slap it back and forth against a leather strap that hung the rest of the time from one arm of the great chair. That sweeping motion of steel against leather" gave the razor a "keen" edge. Soon "a splash of witch hazel, a careful parting of my hair with the help of some perfumed water and I was done."

"'Next,' called Brother Nicodemus as he held out his hand to me for payment. In his palm, I would place the nickel my mom had given me. It was warm and moist from my excited grip."

"'Thank you, little man,' he would say and smile gently."[7]

13. BUY KINGSTON AIRPORT?

IN 1935, only a few months after Divine forces had acquired their first property in Ulster County at New Paltz, its neighborhood was "aroused" by the roar of Father Divine's airplane passing overhead. Over the next few weeks, it roared over several times.

During the previous decade, dramatic advances had occurred in the development of aviation. In 1926, Floyd Bennett and Richard Byrd had flown to the North Pole. In 1927, Charles Lindbergh had flown across the Atlantic solo. In 1932, Amelia Earhart had also flown across the Atlantic solo, the first woman to do so. In the early 1930s, however, carrying passengers on regularly scheduled commercial flights was still not common. Commercial flights paid for themselves not so much by carrying passengers as by carrying mail.

By 1935, however, Father Divine had become a flying enthusiast. While he usually traveled to Ulster County by car, he sometimes flew, and was considering flying more often. When he flew, he flew not on scheduled commercial flights, but on private planes.

In 1936, *Newsweek* reported that Divine had "bought" an airplane. It is probable that he did not actually buy it himself, as it was his settled policy not to own property; perhaps followers bought it in their names for his use. However, any reports that Divine was flying private airplanes created immense public curiosity as to where Divine found the funds for such extravagance.

FATHER DIVINE STEPPING OUT OF A RENTED AIRPLANE, A TEN-SEAT BELLANCA, during the early 1930s. He often flew his own plane. (*New Day*, Oct. 4, 1975)

For Divine to fly was costly, but according to the *New Yorker* magazine, not as costly as it might seem because the planes he used were old. Sometimes, the magazine reported in 1936, Divine rented "an ancient Bellanca ten-seater." He rented it at Floyd Bennett Field in Brooklyn. Divine also sometimes flew to Ulster County, the magazine added, in a plane said to be his own, "an old Ryan monoplane of the type Lindbergh used on his first transatlantic flight."[1]

Among those who piloted planes for Divine were two prominent black followers. One was Colonel Hubert Julian, a former Garveyite, who was famous for having regularly piloted a plane for Emperor Haile Selassie of Ethiopia. Julian was flamboyant. He made himself conspicuous by doing aerial stunts over Harlem. While unwilling to follow all of Divine's teachings, Julian nonetheless identified with Divine and gave flying lessons to Divine followers. The other such pilot for Divine was a young woman, Flying Angel (also called Flying Determination). She flew a little red plane that had painted on it a sign saying, "Father Divine, Peace Mission." She believed that her faith in Divine had saved her from several flying disasters, such as once when her plane was in the air and ran out of gas.

Although Flying Angel was inspired by Amelia Earhart, still it was rare for a woman, and especially a black woman, to be a pilot. Divine's choice of Flying Angel to be one of his pilots was an example of his defiance of the prevailing conception of the proper role of both women and blacks. Divine often defied custom by encouraging women, including black women, to chauffeur Peace Mission cars, manage Peace Mission stores, hotels, or restaurants, and be officers of Peace Mission churches.

In spring, 1936, Divine proposed to buy an airport in Ulster County. According to the New York *Times*, Divine proposed to buy it "for the use of his own planes." He wanted to fly himself and a few of his associates from New York to the county, and to do it easily and quickly, not to mention dramatically.

In April, 1936, Divine traveled by plane at least twice from New York to Ulster County. One time he and some of his staff left his home in Manhattan early, avoiding the crowd which usually assembled for his departures, and drove to Queens to Holmes Airport (later part of LaGuardia Airport). When a little plane arrived there to pick him up, he squeezed in with him as many of his staff as possible, leaving the rest to follow by car. They flew north up the Hudson River, passing over Tarrytown with its "great automobile plants," and over Ossining with its "Sing-Sing Prison." When they reached the Bear Mountain region, "the air became slightly bumpy," but as one of his followers on the plane explained afterwards, "Father was there to guarantee complete comfort and safety." Reaching southern Kingston, "the red roof of Father's Kingston headquarters was plainly visible," but the plane continued on north across the city, to its only known airport, "where one of the Promised Land's new station wagons" was waiting to pick them up.[2]

On another occasion that same month, Divine again flew up to Ulster County, this time, according to the *Spoken Word*, looking for a possible site for an airfield on Peace Mission land. Still another time the same month, he drove up by car, as he usually did, and inspected the Kingston Airport. He went there with his favorite Ulster County real estate dealer, John Dellay of Rosendale.

At the time, Kingston's airport, a private one, was little known and little developed. It was located just beyond the northern city limits, only five minutes from Kingston's main business district, just off the main road from Kingston into the Catskills. Consisting of thirty acres, it was a moderate size for this early period in the development of flying, and it had a large hangar, but it did not have the lighting necessary for night landing, and was not approved by government regulators for commercial flying. It was, however, conveniently located for Divine's purposes, being within about twenty-five miles of all the Peace Mission properties in the county.

While visiting the airport, Divine talked to its owner, Milton Walker, about the possibility of buying it. He told Walker that he would pay for it with cash, which he hoped would induce Walker to sell. However, finding themselves unable to agree on a price, Divine said he would come back again in a few days to discuss the matter further.

In August, 1936, when a crowd of Divine's followers sailed up the Hudson by steamer and then formed a parade through Kingston to the Peace Mission mansion on Chapel Street, two planes flew over the paraders, both piloted by Divine followers. At that time, real estate dealer Dellay reported that Divine had abandoned his plan to buy the Kingston Airport. After that, while Divine continued to fly occasionally, his enthusiasm for flying seemed to diminish.[3]

14. RISK TAKER: JOHN DELLAY, ROSENDALE REALTOR

BY OCTOBER, 1935, it had become well known that Rosendale real estate agent John Dellay had arranged the sale of a New Paltz farm to Divine followers. At that time, a descendant of one of the old Huguenot families of New Paltz, Lanetta Elting DuBois, declared that if any one in New Paltz had done what Dellay had done, he would be "run out of town."

Despite such antagonism, by the next month Dellay was arranging the sale of two more properties to Divine followers: the Cherry Hill Farm outside of High Falls, and the Hasbrouck farm, called the Stone Ridge Farm, outside of Stone Ridge. While arranging these sales, Dellay wrote Divine, telling him about the hostility aroused by the Hasbrouck farm sale. According to Dellay, a few days after Divine forces had paid a deposit and signed a contract for buying the farm, its owner, Arthur Hasbrouck, had told Dellay that neighbors were complaining, and had asked to cancel the contract. Hasbrouck "offered me double the fees due me and your deposit back," Dellay wrote Divine, "if I could convince you to cancel the contract. I refused to do so." I told Hasbrouck that you would not "consider taking any money back, and that they should quiet down and let a few days pass by, and I will go to all the neighbors and talk to them personally, telling them who Father Divine is."

By this time, Dellay's association with Divine, beset by popular hostility to Divine though it was, had become important to Dellay. "Since I have met you and have done business with you," Dellay wrote Divine, the people I have been doing business with "have more confidence and respect for me than before. Even the former owners of the Cherry Hill Farm at High Falls are always talking about you, and the wonderful work you are doing, and the good luck you have brought to them in which they were very much in need. You were really God to them as well as to myself. I want to thank you, Father, and I hope that hereafter, any business we may do will go a little more smoothly than previously. The people now are better convinced, and they will be, more and more later on. Through faith in Father we will all have better luck throughout our lives. I assure you that I will be faithful to you and do my utmost to help along with you to make this Ulster County the Divine City."[1]

John Dellay was born in Venice, Italy. He spoke not only his native Italian, but also, according to his son, four other languages, French, German, Spanish, and English. He came to the United States around 1900, at the age of 14. For a time he lived in New Jersey, where he married a young German woman. By 1905, while still very young, he had begun a real estate business in Ulster County in Rosendale, and in a few years he had become popular enough to be elected to the Rosendale town board, serving from 1925 to 1929 without pay.

According to Dellay family tradition, when Divine was first looking for real estate in Ulster County, Divine tried to work through real estate brokers in Kingston, but found they were hostile. When Divine tried Dellay, however, Divine found him cooperative. Discovering Dellay was undoubtedly a factor in Divine's concentration on Ulster County as a key location for his model communities.

As Divine's association with Dellay lengthened, it seemed to grow closer. Early in 1937, the Kingston *Freeman* claimed that Dellay "has been the exclusive agent for Father Divine in his real estate transactions in Ulster County." Soon afterwards, the Stone Ridge *Ulster County Press* published a photo of Dellay, identifying him as a real estate broker for Father Divine. The photo showed Dellay with his wife; their son John Joseph, about eleven; their daughter, a little older; and a black woman—incorrectly identified—in their midst. Afterward Dellay, explained to a *Press* reporter, as he could have avoided doing, that the black woman pictured was in fact Mother Divine.

According to Dellay's son John Joseph, Dellay was driven to helping Divine locate property to buy because during the Great Depression, the Dellays were desperately poor. John Joseph recalls he grew up eating potato sandwiches. His family were sometimes unable to pay their electric bills, and their electricity being cut off, he was forced to do his school homework by candle light. To help warm their house, he used to pick up coal dropped along the railroad tracks near their house—the Dellays lived on Rosendale's Depot Hill, near the Wallkill Valley Railroad depot, at the southern end of the high railroad bridge over Rondout Creek.

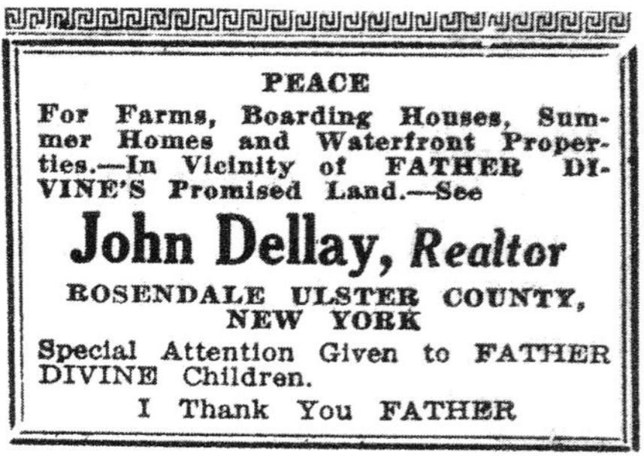

A SAMPLE OF JOHN DELLAY'S MANY ADVERTISEMENTS in Peace Mission periodicals.
(*Spoken Word*, Aug. 18, 1936)

Even though John Dellay was profiting by acting as Divine's real estate broker, it could not have been easy for him to serve Divine in such a public role. Even if Dellay had been hardened by his early immigration experience, and by his poverty, and by his service as a town official—he recalled that as an official he "received a great deal of abuse"—still, considering the region's pervasive distrust of blacks, it must have been stressful, year after year, to be known for assisting more blacks to settle in the region.[2] Nor could it have been easy to be John Joseph, the son of such a stigmatized real estate dealer. John Joseph recalled that when he climbed onto the bus which drove him to high school in New Paltz, other children would call out, "Here comes the nigger lover." He also recalled that he avoided reading newspapers because he was afraid he would come across unfriendly news about his father.

According to John Joseph's recollection, his father John Dellay was a hard taskmaster. He expected his son to weed the garden and trim the hedges. He expected him to pick up the family's mail at the Rosendale post office. When John Joseph was old enough to want a bicycle, his father expected him to earn it by cutting asparagus for a grower in nearby Tillson. His father also expected him to work for the Knaust Brothers, helping them grow mushrooms in abandoned cement mines, and to deliver newspapers in Kingston on Sunday mornings, where he would ride on a delivery car's running board, occasionally jumping off to throw a paper at someone's doorway.

John Dellay, as his son presented him, was an aggressive businessman, eccentric, and tough. He was like Divine in believing in hard work and disdaining government relief. He did not like to pay taxes. According to his son, to throw income tax agents off his case, he might try to hide the names of persons he did business with. To reduce government regulation of what he did, he avoided securing a real estate broker's license; his son doubts he ever secured one.

John Dellay publicly defended his role as a real estate agent for Divine, and he did so when many residents of the county seemed unusually aroused against Divine. At the time, in early 1937, Divine followers had just purchased the well-known Greenkill Park, and had done so secretly, by ruse, disturbing many Ulsterites. Also at the time, a white follower of Divine, the wealthy Californian John W. Hunt, was being charged with seducing a seventeen-year-old girl, and Hunt and the girl were said to be hiding among Divinites in Ulster County. At the same time, County Sheriff Abram F. Molyneaux claimed that his office was receiving complaints that Divine's acquisition of property "is based on a policy of making an initial investment of a large sum in an area for the purpose of deflating the value of surrounding properties." The county was heading toward launching a grand jury investigation of what local newspapers called the Divine "cult." Moreover, it was rumored that a secret movement was rising to force Divine out of the county, even if to accomplish it, participants would have to go "night riding," in the style of the Ku Klux Klan.

Just when Divine was under these accumulating pressures, in April, 1937, Dellay wrote a letter to the press defending Divine. Dellay, while not claiming in his letter nor at any other time that he was a Divine follower, denied that Divine wanted, as reported, to control the politics of the county, claiming instead that Divine merely wanted to obtain "the respect of officials." Admitting that Divine intended to continue to expand his missions in Ulster County, Dellay said that "thousands" of landowners, including landowners "in every town and village in Ulster County," had written him, offering to sell their property through him to the Divine movement. In a county where many farms had been abandoned, sales to Divine forces, Dellay said, were good for taxpayers. Divine "pays cash" for properties," Dellay said, and also "remodels" the buildings he buys, sprucing up the county. Moreover, Dellay described Divine's movement as attempting to "eliminate unnecessary relief" and instead "give everyone a chance to work." This also, Dellay said, is good for taxpayers. While most of his statement emphasized economic benefits, Dellay also added a more idealistic view. In regard to Divine's followers, Dellay said, "No one is to blame if some happen to be colored. They are all our brothers and sisters, so we should have respect for all. . . . As long as I know that I am doing right," he said, "I have no fear of what people say."[3]

Soon after Dellay had publicly defended Divine, Dellay was indicted, whether justifiably or not, for having a still operating on his property. This was the second time he had been faced with such a charge, the first time being for property he was said to own in Cottekill, and this time for a farm of his between Rosendale and Creek Locks. But he denied the charge. Meanwhile, Dellay was buying up dilapidated houses, to prepare them to rent out or resell, and he was renovating them by using Divine movement labor. He would call a Divinite agent in High Falls, ask for a carpenter, electrician, or the like, and consistently find the workers the agent sent to be inexpensive, competent, and honest. In the summer of 1937, Dellay's habit of employing black Divine followers to renovate his houses led, the Dellay family believed, to the burning of a Rosendale house Dellay was renovating. This house was in a neighborhood of hotels and boarding houses, west of the Rosendale railroad bridge, at the junction of Rosendale's Main Street (Route 213) with a road to Binnewater. After the fire, signs threatening Dellay appeared on the house's charred remains. The neighbors, the Dellays believed, mistakenly thought that because black Divinites were working to repair the house, they were slated to live in it, and they feared this would keep summer visitors away. Later another house Dellay was having repaired by Divine followers was also burned, this one west of Kingston off Route 28A. It was probably burned, the Dellays believed, for similar reasons.

HOUSE IN ROSENDALE, OWNED BY DELLAY, DESTROYED BY FIRE. It was suspected the fire had been set by someone who believed Dellay was renovating the house for it to become a Divine mansion. (*Ulster County Press*, Aug. 6, 1937)

Despite such harassment, Dellay publicized his cooperation with Divine by advertising in Divine's weekly publications. In such advertisements, he used the Divine-approved greeting, "Peace," and offered for sale farms, boarding houses, and summer homes, often in the vicinity of existing Divinite property. In the fall of 1937, after the main hotel building at Divinite-owned Greenkill Park burned to the ground, and rumors were that this blow, combined with all the other blows raining down on Divine, meant Divine was "going on the rocks," Dellay wrote to the *Ulster County Press* denying the rumors, and asserting that Divine had enough support "to face anything that comes along." He scolded local officials for raising the assessments of Divinite-held Ulster County property by up to 600 percent, and claimed they were doing it to punish the owners for being followers of Divine. He also claimed the federal income tax charges being brought against these same followers who owned Ulster County property were "engineered" by "crooked politicians." He wondered how federal tax officials could claim these followers have taxable incomes when "every cent they earned during their life went into real estate, and now all they get out of it is room and board and they have to work besides to keep up the properties."[4]

In 1938, continuing to advertise in the Divine-related periodical, the *New Day*, Dellay offered houses for sale near the Divinites' Greenkill Park. In 1939 and 1940, he offered Saugerties farms for sale, in advertisements embellished with the familiar Peace Mission slogan, "Thank you, Father." By this time, Dellay was doing well enough to have two offices, not only his usual office in his residence in Rosendale, but also an additional office in Kingston. Despite popular distrust, Dellay, stubborn as he was, continued to serve Divine-related real estate interests even as late as 1942. Dellay went on to become, a local resident recalled long afterwards, "a big wheeler-dealer," and in fact continued in the real estate business in Ulster County for the rest of his life, into the 1960s.[5]

15. RESORT ON RONDOUT CREEK: GREENKILL PARK

IN EARLY 1937, Divine's Peace Mission was considering acquiring a resort south of Kingston, between the hamlets of Eddyville and Bloomington. Called Greenkill Park, it comprised about 177 acres and fronted on Rondout Creek. It was mostly in the town of Ulster Park, but extended slightly into the town of Rosendale.

The Consolidated Rosendale Cement Company had created the resort in 1910, when the natural cement industry was declining, on property the company had originally bought for cement production. Within a few years the resort had grown to include not only an inn which could accommodate about fifty guests, but also seventeen bungalows, each with a fireplace in its living room. The resort featured a swimming pond, golf course, casino for music and dancing, and docks on Rondout Creek for fishing and boating.

By early in the depression of the 1930s, however, when the resort's patronage had declined, it stopped functioning. In 1932, the German boxer Max Schmeling temporarily used it as a training camp to prepare for his fight with Jack Sharkey. After that, the resort, unused, fell into the hands of the Kingston Trust Company.

On March 13, 1937, the Trust Company sold the resort for $75,000, to the white Charlotte Becker, who gave her address as East 106th Street, New York. As the company explained defensively afterward, they sold it to Becker without knowing that she was a follower of Father Divine. In the atmosphere of public hostility that surrounded the Divine movement, the movement sometimes acquired property through intermediaries who did not identify themselves as Divine followers. Three days after Becker, who was the intermediary in this case, had bought the Greenkill Park property, she resold it, evidently by pre-arrangement, to Anna Reed of Olive Bridge, another Divine follower. Reed, in turn, quickly resold it, evidently also by pre-arrangement, to twenty-seven Divine followers who retained it.

Most of these twenty-seven followers were women, and most of them, in giving their address-

PANORAMIC VIEW OF GREENKILL PARK, overlooking Rondout Creek. At this time, before it had become a Divine Mission site, it already could accommodate more than 300 guests. (Postcard, ca. 1913, Century House Historical Society)

THREE GUEST HOUSES AT GREENKILL PARK, named by Divinites "Rose of Sharon," "Bright and Morning Star," and "Way Shower." Inset: Father Divine. (*New Day*, May 18, 1939)

es for their deed of purchase, gave them as in New York City. But eight of them indicated they lived in Ulster County. One of these eight was Charlotte Becker, the original intermediary, who this time gave her address as Divine Terrace, at Elting Corners in the town of Lloyd. Four others lived at Divine sites near Greenkill Park: Rebecca Branch, who lived at the Kingston Junior farm in the town of Esopus; and three, Light Child, Gertrude Kommer, and Mary Bird Tree, who lived at the

Above: **IN 1945, DIVINE TRIED TO PERSUADE A RESTLESS SWIMMING TEACHER, DAVID RIGHT, FROM CALIFORNIA, TO CLEAN UP THIS GREENKILL PARK POND and give free swimming lessons there, but Right, short of funds, returned to California. A diving platform shows at the right.** (*New Day*, June 1, 1939)

Right: **A GREENKILL PARK HOUSE IN THE WOODS** (*New Day*, Aug. 21, 1941)

Kingston Mansion. The remaining three were Agnes Hammond of New Paltz, Elizabeth Shelton of Saugerties, and Sarah Alberman of Olive Bridge. The Peace Mission explained that in acquiring this park, its intention was to move its headquarters from Harlem to the park, with the hope of drawing more Divine followers to live there or elsewhere in Ulster County.[1]

When a few Divine followers first moved into their new Greenkill Park site, a music teacher who lived nearby was so alarmed, one of his pupils recalled, that he considered installing floodlights to protect his house. Someone in Rosendale wrote an anonymous letter to the Kingston Trust Company, charging that the company was "guilty" for selling the property to Negroes, and saying, "Hitler should be here."

Brushing aside such alarms, Divine and his associates concentrated on improving the property. For this purpose, one day Divine drove in his Rolls Royce to a plumbing supply company on the Kingston waterfront, where he arranged to purchase a large quantity of supplies. The proprietor, being uneasy as to how Divine would pay for them, was astonished when Divine, having settled on an order of about $2,500, walked out to his car, and after some time returned with a paper bag filled with small bills. Divine handed the bag to the proprietor, saying that if the amount of money in it turned out to be wrong, they should let him know, and he would make it right. Then he walked out. When an assistant counted the money, it took him a long time, but he found the amount correct.

After a few months of improving the new resort property, Divine followers planned a grand opening celebration for July 8-9, 1937. One of Divine's lawyers, the black Arthur Madison, said this opening "should mean more" to Divine's followers "than any event thus far recorded" in the Divine movement's history. Madison explained afterwards that even though he himself was relatively privileged, he had never visited any such "rural estate," but he rejoiced that Divine had made it possible even for poor Afro-Americans, who "for years" had to "put up with" appalling conditions in New York, to "enjoy" such an estate as if they were wealthy.[2]

For the opening, Divine followers chartered a steamer, the three-decked *State of Delaware*, to leave New York, from a pier at 132nd Street, at 7:00 AM on a Thursday, to take celebrants up the Hudson to Kingston, and to return the next day in the evening. The only persons to be allowed on board, Divine announced, were those who were "evangelical" and had paid all their debts, with the individuals themselves to judge whether they were qualified. The charge was to be only a token $1 for adults, round trip, raising the inevitable question as to the how the cost for the rest of the excursion would be paid. Divine's secretary, John Lamb, answered the question, telling the press that the wealthy New York City follower, the black Charles Calloway, was financing the excursion.

Father Divine, dressed in white, arrived at the pier in New York late, about 7:30 AM, and the boat left just before 8:00AM, with 1,750 passengers. On board, no smoking was allowed. Soda and watermelon slices were sold, both at three cents each. Father strode about the decks, chatting with passengers, and posing for photographers. Two bands played almost continuously. Many passengers sang, clapped, and tapped their feet, praising God.

When the ship docked in Rondout Creek at Kingston at 1:40 PM, the plan to have busses transport the excursionists the four miles to Greenkill Park fell apart. It did so, according to the excursion leaders, because the bus managers were charging more than excursionists understood they were to pay. Amid confusion, the organizers scrambled to arrange for taxis, private cars, and trucks to drive the visitors to Greenkill Park, but many excursionists were obliged to walk all the way.

At the park, the visitors found that Divine followers, in accord with their beliefs, had given all the buildings new names such as Love, Joy, Good Will, Harmony, Morning Star, and Rock of Ages. They found that new electrical wiring had been installed; floors had been re-laid; large bedrooms had been partitioned into smaller ones to accommodate more guests; and many bungalows had been newly painted in popular Peace Mission colors, red and ivory, all these renovations once again raising the question as to the source of the funds to pay for them. While no answer to the question seemed to be forthcoming, the park was "spic and span" for the celebration, according to the park's long-term caretaker, C. E. Keyser who, as Divinites had arranged, continued to live at the site. The number of visitors present, Keyser said, was the largest the site had ever had. Because all the accommodations in both the hotel and the scattered cottages were quickly taken, some of the weary visitors had to sleep that night in the auditorium, or outdoors on the grass, or drive to other extensions, as in Kingston, High Falls, or New Paltz.

During the day, visitors, if they had the energy, could play baseball, tennis, or cricket—the cricket being intended especially for followers from the West Indies. Visitors could swim near the hotel in a brook-fed pond, which was especially welcome because the temperature topped 100 degrees. They could participate in a parade, marching from the hotel past the auditorium and various cottages on the park grounds, with the marchers carrying such signs as "Peace," or "Father Divine is God." They could dine at banquets, offered with repeated servings, at which, according to the *New Day*, Father Divine spoke and Mother Divine danced "in sweet humility."[3]

The celebrants reflected different points of view. A student of Eastern religions declared that for celebrants to sleep outdoors reminded him of the holy men of India who consider houses to be for "weaklings." A follower having socialist leanings interpreted the opening of this park as emancipation from "wage slavery." A health-oriented visitor felt that the "verdure" in this "Garden of Eden," filled with Divine's spirit, was "healing." Perhaps it was an introvert who hung up a streamer bearing the inscription, "Watch carefully the seed you sow in your little garden, down in the depths of your soul." A speaker in the auditorium, Melchizedeck Matthew of the Krumville extension, declared that Divine's "renovation" of old Ulster County properties was like his "renovation" of his followers' "minds, souls and bodies." A newcomer said he had prepared himself to settle in the Promised Land by cutting himself off from "all old acquaintances"; he was "just waiting," he explained, for Father Divine to tell him where he could settle. Divine himself predicted that 200 to 300 of the excursionists would settle in the Promised Land.

Although Divine had personally written many officials inviting them to participate in the celebration, among them President F. D. Roosevelt, New York Governor Herbert H. Lehman, Kingston Mayor John Schwenck, and Ulster County District Attorney Cleon B. Murray, no such officials are known to have come. After the excursion, Divine, seemingly hurt, threatened that "final woes" would result from their failure to come.

Only four months after the optimistic excursion to Greenkill Park, in November, 1937, one of its major buildings, its hotel, burned to the ground. One possible cause was sparks from a fireplace. Another possible cause was arson.

At the fire, the proprietor of a Kingston jewelry store, a volunteer fireman, was playing a hose on the fire at the same time that he continued his usual habit of smoking his corncob pipe. One of Divine's followers, apparently more disturbed by the smoking of the pipe than by the burning of the building, told the smoker several times that Father Divine did not allow smoking. When the fireman nevertheless continued to smoke his pipe, eventually the follower, frustrated, grabbed the pipe out of his mouth, and ran off with it.[4]

Although in accordance with Divine's teaching his followers carried no insurance on the resort buildings, Divine assured them that, if they had the Spirit within them, it was an "impossibility" for them to be "losers." They believed, as Divine told them, that they had Jesus' "blessed assurance," as promised in the familiar hymn of those words which they sometimes sang. At first Divine intended to see the hotel rebuilt, but when he became convinced that the town assessors had over-assessed the park property, he moved away from his plan. In any case, as the aftermath of the Elting Corners fire suggested, Divine followers generally preferred to renovate old buildings rather than build new ones. Although Divinites never rebuilt the hotel, later when they acquired

POLICE SEARCHING FOR DIVINE AT GREENKILL PARK'S HOTEL, when he was charged with assault in New York City. The charges were later dropped.
(*Ulster County Press*, April 23, 1937)

AIR VIEW OF THE RUINS OF GREENKILL PARK'S HOTEL, taken soon after it burned.
(*Ulster County Press*, Nov. 9, 1937)

two other resorts, both on the Hudson River, at Milton and Krum Elbow, Divine claimed that they were replacements for Greenkill Park's hotel, only "better."

Without its hotel, Greenkill Park lost its intended role as Divine headquarters, but it remained a vacation resort. It also remained a site where some followers lived and fanned out from there into the surrounding communities to work as handymen, farm help, housekeepers, or the like. It also remained a site where dinners were served to the public.

The family of Raymond Le Fever, who farmed nearby, were among the many residents of the region who visited Greenkill Park to enjoy its inexpensive, home-cooked dinners. On one occasion, when three of his family went there for dinner, they found three empty seats together. The youthful Raymond, being big, chose the biggest chair for himself, but as he sat down, he was suddenly surrounded by several followers, insisting, "Get up, get up!" He was startled. The followers explained that the big chair was reserved for Father Divine. They always reserved the big chair for Divine, they said, whether he was expected or not.[5]

16. ART COLONY ON THE HUDSON: MILTON

BY THE FALL OF 1937, Divine followers were negotiating to purchase yet another property in Ulster County, this one in the county's south, at Milton, in the town of Marlborough. This property had been an art colony and was located directly on the Hudson River. The people of the vicinity regarded it, Father Divine said, as its "most valuable" property.

Several nearby residents tried to prevent Divine from securing control of the colony. According to a local newspaper, they "did everything in their power" to stop the take-over, including starting a fund to buy the property themselves, but they did not raise enough money.

This property, about twenty-eight acres, was about a mile south of the center of Milton, off Indian Road. It had a deep-draft pier on the Hudson River, which would permit steamers to dock. The owners asked $35,000 for the site, but Divine followers purchased it, Divine said, for "much less than that."

ANDERS H. ANDERSEN, THE ARTIST WHO SOLD THE MILTON ART COLONY TO DIVINITES and then continued to live there. (Elverhoj Lectures, Milton, NY, 1920s?)

The art colony, primarily a summer colony, was founded about 1912, one of its major figures being the Danish-born silversmith, Anders H. Andersen. He gave it a Danish name, Elverhoj, meaning home of the elves. The colony centered on a bluff overlooking the Hudson, in an old house with four tall pillars. The colony's artists removed the pillars, and enlarged the house into a Moorish-style building. They decorated its outside

Facing page:
MILTON SITE

Top: **MAIN BUILDING, showing its striking arches, as well as a glimpse of the Hudson River behind it to the right.** (*New Day*, July 31, 1941)

Bottom: **MAIN BUILDING AS SEEN FROM THE HUDSON RIVER. The West Shore Railroad's right of way shows close to the shore.** (Photo by William B. Rhodes, 1976)

doorways with ironwork, and its outside walls with "porcelain plaques" depicting classical scenes. Nearby they laid out gardens, and enhanced them with statuary. Up the slope behind the house, they built cabins for themselves to live in, perhaps ten rustic cabins, all without electricity or running water. On a low, flat space close to the river, they built a theater.[1]

The colony was part of a major art movement of the time which protested against industrialism by cherishing individual craft work. The colony's artists were themselves likely to be craftsmen such as jewelers, weavers, metalworkers, and potters. Andersen invited them to hold shares in the colony, as a cooperative enterprise. Some settled permanently at the colony, while others came and went. With the Hudson River and its dramatic bluffs providing inspiration, the artists both practiced their arts individually and taught them to others. They swam in the Hudson. They presented plays in their theater which came to be called one of the first summer theaters in the mid-Hudson region.

Under Andersen's tactful management, for a time the colony seemed to scrape by, but by the early 1930s, with the Great Depression hitting hard, Andersen could not make the payments on his mortgage, and was forced to sell the colony. He sold it to Alfred Heckman and others, who also could not make the payments on their mortgage. When their mortgage was being foreclosed, Divine followers bought the colony, on April 25, 1938, for an amount variously reported as $10,000 or $15,000. Thereafter, Andersen himself continued to live at the site in a cottage which he had reserved for himself, and he became what the *New Day* called an "enthusiastic adherent" of Divine's movement. About nine months after Divine followers took possession, Andersen said that he had enjoyed their presence "every moment."

The deed for the Divinite purchase of the colony named fifteen followers of Divine as buyers, including several residents of Ulster County: Marjorie I. Burns of High Falls; Peace Harmony of Olive Bridge; two from New Paltz, Agnes Hammans and Thankful Daylight; as well as two from Krumville, Bliss Love and Vida Victoria. A buyer from New York City, Henri Stephen, unlike many such buyers, himself moved to the site to live.[2]

Divine followers continued to call the site an art colony and tried to retain the allure that artists had given it. In consultation with Andersen, they enlarged the main house for use as a hotel, so that it became a four-story, 27-room, white stucco building, trimmed in marine blue, but still Moorish-style. They provided it with space to serve 500 diners at once. Just north of the main building, down the river bank, beside the water, the followers themselves built a huge new pier building to house males, both co-workers and guests.

In August, 1938, even though renovations were still in progress, followers celebrated the acquisition of the art colony, along with the opening of another site farther north, Krum Elbow, purchased almost at the same time. They ran two steamboats from the 132nd Street pier in Manhattan, up the Hudson River, crowded with 2,500 passengers. The steamers docked at the art colony's own newly renovated pier, which was decorated with white pennants for the occasion. Passengers swarmed out of the steamers into what the New York *Times* called a "paradise," with "shady groves of oak and elm, winding woodland paths and trellised arbors of honeysuckle, clipped green hedges, bowers of rambler roses, tennis courts bordered by leafy magnolias, and a tumbling mountain stream crossed by rustic bridges." After the followers had looked around, they feasted at a banquet served for them in shifts in the main house, on tables that seemed to stretch endlessly. Among the speakers was the former art colony

Facing page:
MILTON SITE

Top: **MAIN BUILDING AS IT FACES THE HUDSON RIVER. A round classic relief showing close to the corner is a sample of the art colony' work, which was already in place before Divine followers bought the site.** (Author photo, Aug., 2007)

Bottom: **TWO DIVINE FOLLOWERS VISITING FROM PENNSYLVANIA, Roger Klaus (left) and Aaron Enaharo (right) in front of the main building viewing a string of passing barges on the Hudson River.** (Author photo, Aug., 2007)

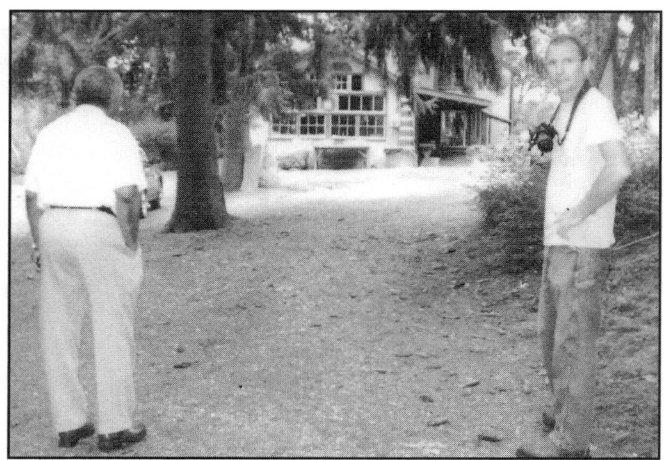

MILTON SITE

Left: **RESIDENCE BUILT BY DIVINE FOLLOWERS ON A PIER, north of the main building, between the West Shore Railroad tracks (foreground, left) and the Hudson River (rear). This residence no longer survives.** (*New Day*, Feb. 2, 1939) Right: **THIS COTTAGE WAS OCCUPIED BY ANDERS H. ANDERSEN after he sold the site to Divinites. It is now occupied by an artist. Visiting it recently were Divine follower Aaron Enaharo (left) and one of the present owners, Bruce Weiss (right).** (Author photo, Aug. 2007)

leader Andersen, who said he hoped the Divine followers would enjoy the site as much as artists had before them. Divine also spoke. Accompanied by cries of "Thank you, Father," he declared that the site was another outward sign of God's blessing.[3]

In 1937, before the purchase of the Milton site, the New York *Evening Journal*, although admitting that Divine did not own property in his own name, claimed that Divine "owns more of Ulster County than any other living man." By 1938, after the purchase of the Milton site, according to the New York *Times*, "nearly 2,000 people are living the communal life" in Divine enterprises in the county. These enterprises stretched as far north as the farm in the Saxton section of the town of Saugerties, near the Greene County border; as far west as a resort near Samsonville, well into the Catskill Mountains; and as far south as the art colony at Milton, near the Orange County border.

When a teacher from Atlantic City spent a vacation at the Milton colony, she marveled that, as a black, she could stay at such a place. "I never did think," she said, "that I would ever rest on the banks of the Hudson." When a correspondent from the New York *Herald Tribune* visited Milton, he decided that the "expensive automobiles" he saw there testified "to the means of some of Father Divine's adherents." He found a "broad glassed veranda" overlooking the Hudson, and in it, banquet tables always kept laid for 160 guests, with fresh linen, and "matched china aligned so precisely as to suggest the use of a surveyor's line." The woman in charge, Sister Martha, explained that the only manager the site had was "the father," and everything "turns out beautifully by doing as he would have one do."

Followers at Milton did not, however, always do as Divine would have them do. Once a few of them, attracted by grapes on a neighbor's vines, picked some for themselves, and the neighbor complained to police. Responding, police came to the Milton site. They found followers at dinner, with Divine at the head of the table. When they reported to Divine that his followers had picked some of the neighbor's grapes, Divine scolded them, and assured the troopers that it would not happen again.[4]

17. BECOMING A NEIGHBOR OF PRESIDENT F. D. ROOSEVELT: KRUM ELBOW

IN ULSTER COUNTY, Divine avoided acquiring property in what few African-American enclaves there were, as in Kingston. Rather his policy was to scatter his residences and businesses about the county in white neighborhoods, to help integrate them, neighborhood by neighborhood. When the opportunity came to buy property along the Hudson River, which would enable Divine to help integrate even what he considered to be the neighborhood of the President of the United States, this opportunity was naturally attractive to him.

In 1938, a Hudson River estate known as Krum Elbow became available for sale. On the west bank of the river, in Ulster County's town of Lloyd, its main entrance was on Red Top Road, and its principal buildings were on a height of land at a bend in the Hudson, affording, directly across it, a stunning view of President Franklin D. Roosevelt's house at Hyde Park.

Krum Elbow belonged to the family of Howland Spencer, an eccentric socialite. A distant relative of President Roosevelt, he had been married to a sister of Mrs. William K. Vanderbilt. Although he owned other estates, as in Newport, Rhode Island, and Palm Beach, Florida, his financing for this Krum Elbow estate had recently become so shaky that it was threatened by foreclosure.

KRUM ELBOW'S LANDING ON THE HUDSON RIVER included a boat house (left), a dock (center) suitable even for such large vessels as steamers, and a barn bearing Divine's familiar slogan, "Peace."
(*New Day*, Aug. 14, 1941)

KRUM ELBOW ESTATE

Above, left: **THE MAIN HOUSE AS SEEN FROM A SLOPE, which dropped down toward the Hudson River. The house no longer exists. (New Day, Aug. 7, 1941)** Right: **THE GATE HOUSE on Red Top Road, Highland, NY. (Photo by the author, Sept., 2004)** Below: **THE OBSERVATION TOWER ON A BLUFF OVERLOOKING THE HUDSON RIVER. Divine followers cherished this tower because from its upper floor they could easily see across the river to President Roosevelt's house at Hyde Park. On the tower's lower floor, Divine followers operated a tea room. (Photo by the author, Sept., 2004)**

Spencer's estate, about five hundred acres, stretched from the Hudson River westward across Route 9W, which was a major New York-to-Albany highway. The estate featured about a mile-and-a-half frontage on the Hudson River, as well as orchards, vineyards, and at least twenty-eight buildings, including a main house, tenant houses, barns, a tower observation building, and a three-story boathouse.[5]

Spencer, who knew President Roosevelt a little socially, and had voted for him in 1932, had come to despise him as becoming a dictator like Stalin. By 1936, Spencer had purchased a local newspaper, the Highland *Post*, and used it to campaign fiercely against President Roosevelt's re-election. Meantime, Spencer was also conducting a feud with Roosevelt about the use of the name "Krum Elbow." The name had historically been used for both sides of the river, and it had traditionally been used for Spencer's estate on the west side of the Hudson, but it was also a name Roosevelt wanted to use for his estate on the east side of the river. In 1938, the federal Board of Geographical Names, acting in response to an inquiry by the President, declared that the name properly applied only to the President's side of the river, not to Spencer's side. The press delighted in claiming that Spencer was considering selling his estate to Father Divine in order to spite Roosevelt over such issues as its name, and Spencer played slyly with this idea, while at the same time insisting that he needed to sell the estate because he could not afford to keep it.

A follower of Father Divine, the white Mary Bird Tree (Florence Hunt), a resident of Divine's Kingston Mansion, visited Spencer's estate to inspect it. In doing so, unlike some other followers negotiating to buy other property in the county for the Divine movement, she made clear that she was doing so as a representative of the Divine movement, which was considering buying it. In negotiating with Spencer, she suggested he investigate the Divine movement for himself, and Spencer did so. He visited several existing Divine establishments in the area, accompanied by his chauffeur, both of them dressed to prevent anyone from knowing why they came.

Spencer found the establishments clean, and the people living there working hard. He was impressed that the men and women lived separately, having taken vows of chastity, he said, almost like Franciscans or Sisters of Charity. He rejoiced to discover that they were making the land produce well, rather than following President Roosevelt's policy of limiting production to raise prices. He also rejoiced to discover that Father Divine forbade his followers to be on relief. Spencer claimed that he could not find suitable laborers to work his farm because they preferred to be on relief, for which he blamed the President.

Although some people living nearby were disturbed by the proposed sale, in July, 1938, in a deal completed by a Poughkeepsie attorney, the African-American Gaius C. Bolin, Jr., twenty-one followers of Divine jointly purchased Spencer's estate, except for a "cottage" and a few acres that Spencer's family temporarily retained. According to Divine, Spencer sold his estate to Divinites at much less than its actual value "because he wanted us to have it."

Spencer understood that Mr. Peace Harmony of Olive Bridge, and Miss Tree of Kingston, both wealthy whites, supplied much of the money for the purchase. Although Tree's name was not listed on the Krum Elbow deed, it may be that Harmony and Tree donated generous amounts of money for the purchase which Divine, to prevent the property from being owned by only a few, combined with small amounts donated by others, to make the property widely owned. Among the twenty-one names listed on the deed, almost all women, most lived in New York City, but a few lived in Ulster County, including Marjorie I. Burns in High Falls, Cassandra Rylander in Krumville, and two, Redeemed Love and Peace Harmony in Olive Bridge.[6]

According to Spencer at the time, "thousands of colored" would be coming to Divine's new resort to picnic or swim in the Hudson. "Whether we meant it or not," quipped Spencer, "this really will annoy Franklin a great deal, won't it?" By contrast, Divine himself said that, regardless of what may be true for Spencer, his followers were not engaged in any argument with President Roo-

sevelt. When reporters pressed Divine on his attitude to the President, Divine said, "I couldn't have a finer neighbor, could I?" As for Roosevelt himself, at a gathering of his Hyde Park neighbors, when several of them teased him about the "heaven" across the river, Roosevelt responded diplomatically, "I'm confident that the people in that 'heaven' in Ulster County will be good neighbors to us here in Dutchess County." Eleanor Roosevelt, in her newspaper column, was also conciliatory, writing that it is "pleasant to feel that in the future this place will be 'heaven' to some people, even if it cannot be to its former owner."

Predictably, some area leaders were not enthusiastic that the Divine's movement was acquiring Krum Elbow. Jesse D. Rose, president of the Highland Board of Education, whose jurisdiction included Krum Elbow, said "I regret exceedingly that Father Divine has purchased another estate in Ulster County." William B. Carr, a justice of the peace in the neighboring town of Plattekill, declared, "I am very glad to say that we have none of the heavens within our township."

At about the same time, however, the New York *Times* reported that "nearly every community" in Ulster County "contains some sort of a Father Divine 'Peace'

Top: **THE KRUM ELBOW ESTATE STRETCHED SO FAR THAT THESE TWO OF ITS FARMHOUSES WERE ON HIGHWAY 9W, about a mile from Krum Elbow's main buildings on the Hudson River. Inset: Father Divine.** (*New Day*, Ap. 27, 1939)

Left: THREE KRUM ELBOW HOUSES AS SHOWN ON A *NEW DAY* COVER. Top, the "Cottage," which Howland Spencer kept for himself when he sold the Krum Elbow Estate to Divinites. Lower left, a building sometimes called the "Hotel," which included accommodations for Divine, his wife, and his staff, and on its lower floor, a large banquet hall. Lower right, the Gate House. Inset: Father Divine. (*New Day*, Ap. 13, 1939)

Spring

enterprise." While most of those participating in these enterprises were blacks, the newspaper said, "hundreds of them are white people, and scores of them are persons of substantial means." The acquisition of Krum Elbow, "one of the choicest of the old manorial estates in the county," declared the *Times*, was "the crowning event" of Divine's move into Ulster County.[7]

A year later, in 1939, when Krum Elbow was fully open as a Peace Mission resort, about sixty Divine followers were reported to be living there regularly. At about that time, workers living there were remodeling various buildings, tending such stock as horses, cows, pigs, sheep, and goats, and growing such fruits as apples, grapes, pears, and cherries. In the mid-1940s, when the number of followers living there had dropped to about thirty to thirty-five, including a few whites, Mr. Love, a big, determined black, was in charge of the men. A person who did business with him recalled, "I would not want to cross Mr. Love." Meantime, Sister Noah Endurance, the "efficient and charming" household manager, was in charge of the women. Loyal to Divine as she was, once when someone asked her what remodeling was going on, she replied that nobody but Father Divine knows.

Among outsiders who sometimes visited Krum Elbow for meals were the Coy family from Clintondale, who brought their

Top: **A STEAMER APPROACHES THE KRUM ELBOW DOCK. At right, a signalman in a dark suit guides the steamer in. A sign painted on the steps, center foreground, reads, "Father Divine Shall Cover The Earth."**

Right: **DIVINE FOLLOWERS ON THE BOATHOUSE PORCH, WATCHING FOR THE ARRIVAL OF A STEAMER. The arches below invite small boats to pass through to tie up.** (Both: *Poughkeepsie Evening Star*, Aug. 10, 1938)

WHEN DIVINE FOLLOWERS CELEBRATED THEIR OPENING OF KRUM ELBOW, VISITORS OVERFLOWED the porches and lawn of this main house. *(Poughkeepsie Evening Star,* Aug. 10, 1938)

child William with them. Years afterwards, what William Coy especially recalled was that if Divine was expected, everybody had to wait for his arrival, guests included, and the followers who waited were so excited they were "in stitches." Another outsider who occasionally came for meals was a young Highland man, Kenneth Erichsen, who sometimes drove Krum Elbow workers to a local farm to pick apples. Erichsen remembered the tables as being set with fresh linen, and his being served homemade pie. While he assumed that for Divinites to offer such fine meals so inexpensively might be a goodwill gesture on their part, even so, like many visitors, he wondered how they could possibly afford to serve such fine meals.

Visitors often came to Krum Elbow not only to dine but also to vacation. For two summers, a girl of eleven or twelve years, from Harlem, spent several weeks there. She enjoyed the food, including "rich milk straight from the cow." A Massachusetts shoe manufacturer, vacationing there with his family, found the facilities clean, the meal prices a welcome "surprise," the people "neat," and their faces "shining."[8]

In 1939, former owner Spencer regarded the Divine followers' handling of Krum Elbow as "so wonderful" that he had become, he said, "almost a follower myself." In 1947, when Spencer was living on an island he owned in the Bahamas, he visited his former estate at Krum Elbow, and said that he never regretted selling it to Divine followers because they had turned it into a "veritable heaven." In 1951, he visited Krum Elbow again, staying in Father Divine's quarters, and felt a "wonderful relaxation" come over him that he seemed able to attribute only to Divine's mystical powers.

Of course, Divine knew that most people were impressed with Krum Elbow, impressed with its meals, its cleanliness, its views, its peace. But what Divine especially emphasized about Krum Elbow was that, while previously people had not been able to come there if they were poor, or of "darker complexion," or not in the social register, now all those who are willing to "lay down the world" could come.

Still, Divine was well aware that beneath the surface, all his followers at Krum Elbow had not fully laid down the world. Presiding there once at a banquet, he warned his followers that, despite their struggling to live in the spirit, they could easily fall into selfish, "detestable tendencies." He warned them not to speak if they were doing so for "self-aggrandizement." He warned them not to try to please God if they did so to benefit themselves. He warned them not to limit themselves to thanking God for themselves having a "special home" to live in, whether here in the Promised Land or anywhere else. To do so, he told them, would still be "living in mortal consciousness." Rather, he urged them, thank God for all his blessings to all mankind, and on more than a material level. "Get away from materialism and go on into infinitude."[9]

Top: **DIVINE FOLLOWERS OPERATED GAS STATIONS ON BOTH SIDES OF ROUTE 9W, as part of the Krum Elbow Estate.** (*New Day*, Aug. 14, 1941)

Right: **AMONG THE CROPS THAT DIVINE FOLLOWERS CONTINUED TO GROW AT KRUM ELBOW, after they took control of it, were grapes.** (*Poughkeepsie Evening Star*, July 30, 1938)

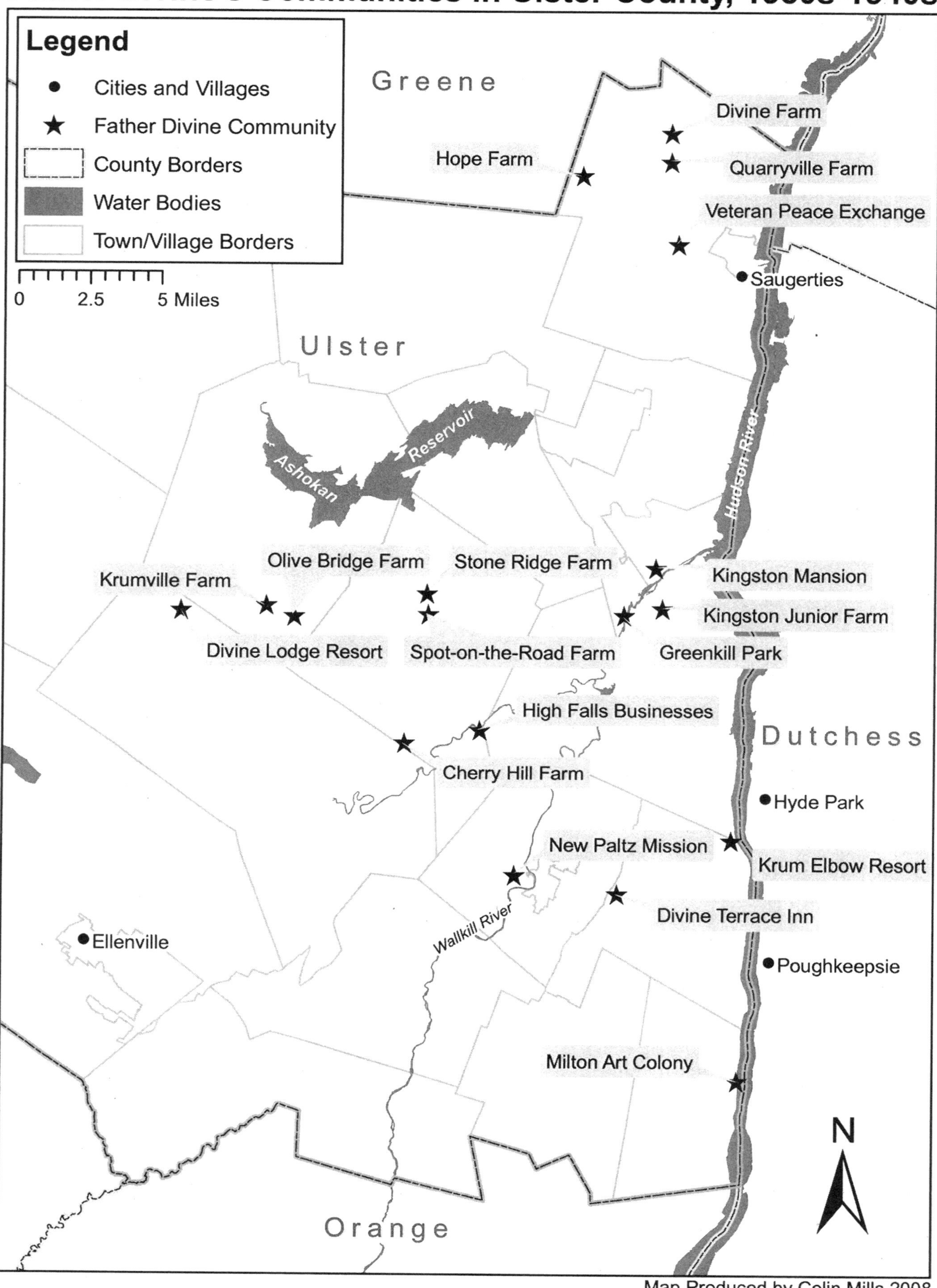
Father Divine's Communities in Ulster County, 1930s-1940s
Legend
Cities and Villages
Father Divine Community
County Borders
Water Bodies
Town/Village Borders
0
2.5
5 Miles
Greene
Ulster
Dutchess
Orange
Divine Farm
Hope Farm
Quarryville Farm
Veteran Peace Exchange
Saugerties
Ashokan
Reservoir
Hudson River
Olive Bridge Farm
Stone Ridge Farm
Krumville Farm
Kingston Mansion
Kingston Junior Farm
Divine Lodge Resort
Spot-on-the-Road Farm
Greenkill Park
High Falls Businesses
Cherry Hill Farm
Hyde Park
New Paltz Mission
Krum Elbow Resort
Divine Terrace Inn
Wallkill River
Ellenville
Poughkeepsie
Milton Art Colony
N
Map Produced by Colin Mills 2008

MAJOR PEACE MISSIONS IN ULSTER COUNTY: DATES BOUGHT AND FEATURES

NAME	DATE	FEATURES
New Paltz Farm	1935	First property acquired in the county; quality river-bottom farm land; auditorium; served dinners to public
Stone Ridge Farm	1935	A productive farm, with old stone house overlooking Esopus Creek; served dinners to public
Kingston Mansion	1935	Divine headquarters for county; offered swimming pond; many children living there attended Kingston High School
Olive Bridge and Krumville Farms	1935-1936	Substantial farms; included old stone house; mountain views; children attended one-room Krumville School
Divine Lodge, near Samsonville	1936	Resort high in the Catskills; westernmost Divine property in county; offered fishing, hiking, horse back riding
Hope Farm, in West Saugerties	1936	Farm; much expanded main house; fishing; children attended nearby Blue Mountain School
Divine Farm, in Saxton	1936	Farm, rooms for tourists, restaurants, gas stations; northernmost Divine property in county
Elting Corners, in Town of Lloyd	1936	Boarding house; fire destroyed its main building in 1937, but thereafter followers lived in its barns
High Falls Businesses	1936-1939	Included a hotel, grocery, department store, shoe shop, dress shop, barber shop, garage, bakery, and restaurant. These businesses dominated the High Falls economy
Greenkill Park, near Kingston	1937	Resort on Rondout Creek; hotel burned in 1937, but many bungalows remained; open-air auditorium; offered swimming pond, fishing, boating; served public dinners
Art Colony, Milton	1938	Moorish-style main building on Hudson River, with dock for river steamers; offered swimming and boating in the Hudson; southernmost Divine property in county
Krum Elbow, near Highland	1938	Estate on Hudson River, with dock for river steamers, farm, and views across the river of Pres. F. D. Roosevelt's house in Hyde Park

18. BUY THE VANDERBILT ESTATE, ACROSS THE HUDSON, IN HYDE PARK?

In the summer of 1939, the Vanderbilt estate in Hyde Park, Dutchess County, was for sale. According to the Poughkeepsie *Star*, it was "one of the most magnificent baronial residences in America." It was a huge estate of about 700 acres, with stunning views of the Hudson River. While it had a long history reaching back before the American Revolution, its main house, built only in 1899, was an opulent Greek-pillared palace designed by Stanford White. The former owner of the estate, Frederick W. Vanderbilt, of the well-known shipping and railroad family, had recently died in his old age, and having no children, had passed ownership to his deceased wife's niece, Margaret L. Van Alen, who wanted to sell it.

Several of Father Divine's wealthy followers proposed to buy the Vanderbilt estate, which would make it the Divine movement's first property in Dutchess County. They proposed to buy it for several purposes, it was said, including providing another residence for Divine. But did he need another residence? By this time, he had suites in many of his extensions in Ulster County, not to mention a fifty-room mansion at 1887 Madison Avenue in Manhattan, and mansions in the fashionable parts of Yonkers and New Rochelle. Moreover, they hardly needed to buy the Vanderbilt estate to provide Divine's followers more living space in the mid-Hudson region. At the time, according to the New York *Times*, Divine followers already had housing in Ulster and Westchester Counties combined which could lodge "perhaps 10,000," but, as Divine said, they were far from fully utilizing it. Then what were their purposes?

Divine's followers entered into negotiations to buy the estate secretly, Divine said, both without telling Divine that they were doing so, and without informing the estate's owner that their intent was to buy it for Divine. They suspected that if the owner, Mrs. Van Alen, knew they would be purchasing it for Divine, she would refuse to sell it to them.

Once Divine learned of his followers' plans, he was slow to approve them. He decided to delay the negotiations, he said, until he "could get in communication with the President and Mrs. Roosevelt," because he "did not wish" to "embarrass" them. Such a plan raised questions. If Divine secured replies from the President and his wife, would he not be likely to make them public? If he did make them public, would that not make the Divinites' intention to purchase the Vanderbilt estate also public, and would that not in turn likely lead Mrs. Van Alen to refuse to sell it to Divinites? Were Divine and his movement serious about purchasing the estate?[1]

The Roosevelts could have had reason to be concerned. President Franklin D. Roosevelt's family home was only about a mile-and-a-half from the Vanderbilt estate, the latter being just north of the village of Hyde Park, and the Roosevelt estate being just south of it. Moreover, the President's church, St. James Episcopal, of which he was a senior warden, was almost opposite a main entrance of the Vanderbilt estate.

Carrying out his intention to communicate with the Roosevelts, Divine wrote Eleanor Roosevelt first. Although he was writing to none other than the wife of the President, he included in his letter three idiosyncratic features which were typical of his letters, but which we have usually omitted in condensing his letters for this book: First, following his custom, in dating his letter he noted that his year of writing was "A. D. F. D," meaning Anno Domini Father Divine. Second, following his custom, he capitalized certain words which are not usually capitalized, including words referring to himself, such as "Me" and "My." Third, following his custom, in closing his letter, he used a standard formula which boasted of his own health and prosperity. Divine's letter, including these three idiosyncratic features, follows:

Buy the Vanderbilt Estate, Across the Hudson, in Hyde Park?

VANDERBILT MANSION, Hyde Park, showing its south facade. Divine followers proposed to buy it.
(Photo by Rene F. Ramos, Feb., 2008)

1887 Madison Avenue
New York City
Aug. 7, 1939
A.D.F.D.

Mrs. Franklin D. Roosevelt
The White House
Washington, D.C.

My dear Mrs. Roosevelt:

Out of My appreciation for your graciousness, and your democratic stand on so many phases of life, I am writing to you as a matter of courtesy, to ascertain your views on a matter which intimately concerns your Hyde Park home.

A group of My Followers have become interested in purchasing the Vanderbilt Estate near your home on the Hudson. They would like to maintain this property as a private residence for ME and My Staff, and as a place where I can receive distinguished guests.

However, the present Administration at Washington has been so democratic and so liberal, I would not for a moment wish to embarrass you or your friends in any way.

I have therefore withheld My approval of the plans of My Followers until I had an opportunity to consult your wishes in the matter.

If you would be so kind as to let me know whether or not it would be entirely agreeable to you for this property to be occupied for such purposes, I should appreciate a frank statement on your part, and I shall withhold My approval of the plans of My Followers until I hear from you.

With sincere wishes to you, desiring that you and all who are concerned might be as I AM, this leaves Me Well, Healthy, Joyful, Peaceful, Lively, Loving, Successful, Prosperous and Happy, in Spirit, Body and Mind, and in every organ, muscle, sinew, joint, limb, vein and bone, and in every atom, fibre and cell of My Bodily Form.

Respectfully and Sincere, I Am
Rev. M. J. DIVINE
(Better known as FATHER DIVINE)

The next day, Divine telegraphed a similar enquiry to President Roosevelt, but Mrs. Roosevelt was the first to reply:

August 12, 1939
Hyde Park, New York

My dear Father Divine:

I have talked with the President in regard to your letter and your telegram to him, and he is writing you, telling you that there can be no reason against any citizen of our country buying such property as he wishes to acquire. He is also writing you in regard to the history of the Vanderbilt estate, especially in regard to the fact that it is probably the only place in the United States which contains such a remarkable collection of mature and rare trees of many kinds. For some time he has been trying to interest some public or quasi-public body in the acquisition and preservation of the place because of its public value as an arboretum.

With thanks for your good wishes and with appreciation of the work which you are doing for the good of your own people as well as others, I am

Very sincerely yours,
Eleanor Roosevelt

FATHER DIVINE WROTE ELEANOR ROOSEVELT, asking if it would be "entirely agreeable" to her if his followers bought the Vanderbilt estate, near her residence in Hyde Park. She replied. (Photo 1940, F. D. Roosevelt Library)

Two days later, President Roosevelt also replied to Divine in the form of a letter written by his secretary Stephen Early. The letter explained the President's special interest in the Vanderbilt estate:

The White House
Washington
August 14, 1939

My dear Father Divine:

The President before leaving on his cruise asked me to thank you for your telegram of August eighth and to tell you that you have, of course, the right which all citizens have to purchase any property which you may desire to acquire.

In regard to the Vanderbilt estate at Hyde Park, the President asks me to tell you something of its history which you may not know.

This old place was originally developed about 1750 by Dr. John Bard, a famous physician of New York, who was George Washington's doctor during the Revolution. Dr. John Bard was also a naturalist and began the planting of specimen trees. The place was then for many years occupied by his equally famous son, Dr. Samuel Bard. The latter was one of the founders of the College of Physicians and Surgeons in New York. He planted trees from many countries in Europe, and the place therefore took on the character of an arboretum.

He, in turn, was succeeded by his partner Dr. David Hosack who was also a naturalist and added to the collection of trees, going as far as Russia and Scandinavia to get specimens.

Later the place was owned by Mr. Walter Langdon Sr., Mr. Walter Langdon Jr, and Mr. Frederick W. Vanderbilt. All of these gentlemen, like their predecessors, took special pains to preserve the many interesting examples of trees and shrubs, replacing them with new ones when necessary.

Thus, the place for nearly two hundred years has acquired a character of an arboretum containing many mature species of trees from all over the world that can be found no where else in America.

For all these reasons, the President has felt for many years that the Vanderbilt place should be acquired by some public or government body in order that it might serve the public in perpetuity as a point of interest to visitors from all parts of the nation. The house itself which is comparatively modern is somewhat expensive to keep up because the rooms are very large, the main floor of the house would probably serve well as a public museum for the display of forestry, landscaping and similar exhibits.

There is, of course, no public appropriation for such a purpose at the present moment, but ever since the death of Mr. Vanderbilt the President has been trying to interest public and quasi-public organizations toward this end.

Very sincerely yours,
Stephen Early
Secretary to the President

In what may or may not be regarded as an appropriate response, Divine replied to the President's message on August 15, not mentioning the estate's trees, but saying that he would instruct his followers to proceed with the negotiations to buy the Vanderbilt estate, with the intention of using the big house as the President had suggested, including placing a "public museum" on its main floor, but with Divine, his staff, and his guests having accommodations elsewhere in the same building.[2]

Of course, Divine could see advantages if his followers bought this estate for him. He would be pleased with such a dramatic step toward the racial integration of President Roosevelt's neighborhood, a step in addition to his followers' already having already purchased Krum Elbow. Probably also Divine relished the possibility of entertaining guests in such a grand place. Moreover, perhaps it seemed significant to Divine to write President Roosevelt, whether the purchase actually took place or not, to nudge him into declaring that anyone, of whatever race, had a right to buy such an estate. Probably also at some level, in pushing for the purchase, even if he guessed that it might not actually take place, Divine, as a skilled publicity man, welcomed the attendant publicity—it was publicity which could benefit not only Divine's movement but also his sacred cause of racial integration. Probably also Divine, in releasing to the press his correspondence with the Roosevelts, as he could have avoided doing, knew that estate owner Mrs. Allen, when she learned that Divine forces wanted to buy her estate, was likely to refuse to sell it to them, and probably Divine, regarding the purchase of the estate as not being a pressing matter for him, was prepared for her refusal.

Once the Divine-Roosevelt correspondence was released to the press, thus making public the intention of the Divine movement to purchase the property, public reactions varied. The secretary of the Dutchess County Real Estate Board, Don C. Thew, while admitting that Divine followers had been "models" of good behavior, urged that the estate should be acquired not for Divine, but instead for the site of the proposed Franklin D. Roosevelt Library, as part of a public park. The Hyde Park supervisor, Elmer Van Wagner, disagreed, however, saying that his town was already "parked to death," and that for Divine to buy the estate would have the advantage of keeping it on the tax rolls. At a time when opposition to the Peace Mission had been considerably reduced, the Poughkeepsie *Evening Star* felt able to support the Divinites' buying the property, saying editorially that the Divinites are "good neighbors." Mrs. Van Alen's real estate agent, however, declared that Divine's attempt at purchase "has all the earmarks of a cheap and mischievous bid for publicity."

Once the release of the Roosevelt-Divine correspondence warned Mrs. Van Alen that Divine followers were contemplating the purchase of her estate, she announced, as Divine surely must have suspected she might, that she would not sell it to Divine followers.

It is likely that the interest of Divine's followers in buying the Vanderbilt estate pushed Mrs. Van Alen not only to refuse to sell it to them, but also to give it away instead. It is also likely that their interest in buying the estate provided a convenient opportunity to the President to encourage Mrs. Van Alen to give her estate to the government. Six months after Divine had written the Roosevelts, in February, 1940, when the Presidential library was already being constructed not on the Vanderbilt estate, but on the Roosevelt estate, the President announced that Mrs. Van Alen had deeded the Vanderbilt estate to the federal government for one dollar, so that it could become a national park.[3]

PROPERTIES CONSIDERED BY DIVINE FOLLOWERS FOR PURCHASE IN ULSTER COUNTY OR NEARBY,

but either not purchased, or (as in the case of the Goelet Estate) if purchased, not developed

Date	Property	County	Comment
1936	Virtually the whole of Chichester village	Ulster	A factory-owned village
1936	Kingston Airport, off Rt. 28	Ulster	Kingston's only airport, a private one
1936	Goldrick Brickyard, at Goldricks Landing, north of Kingston	Ulster	On the Hudson River, the brickyard employed 200 men.
1936	Hudson River steamer dock, in Saugerties village	Ulster	Former Saugerties & NY Steamboat Co. dock
1936	South Side Hotel , in Saugerties village	Ulster	The hotel was near the dock (listed above), which was also being considered
1936	Eno Family house, a family of lawyers, in Pine Plains	Dutchess	For a proposed children's home
1939	Robert Goelet Estate, on Glenmere Lake, near Chester	Orange	Over 2,000 acres
1939	Vanderbilt Estate, in Hyde Park	Dutchess	Grand estate overlooking the Hudson River

Proposed Property Acquisitions for Father Divine's Movement in the Mid-Hudson Region, 1930s, Not Completed

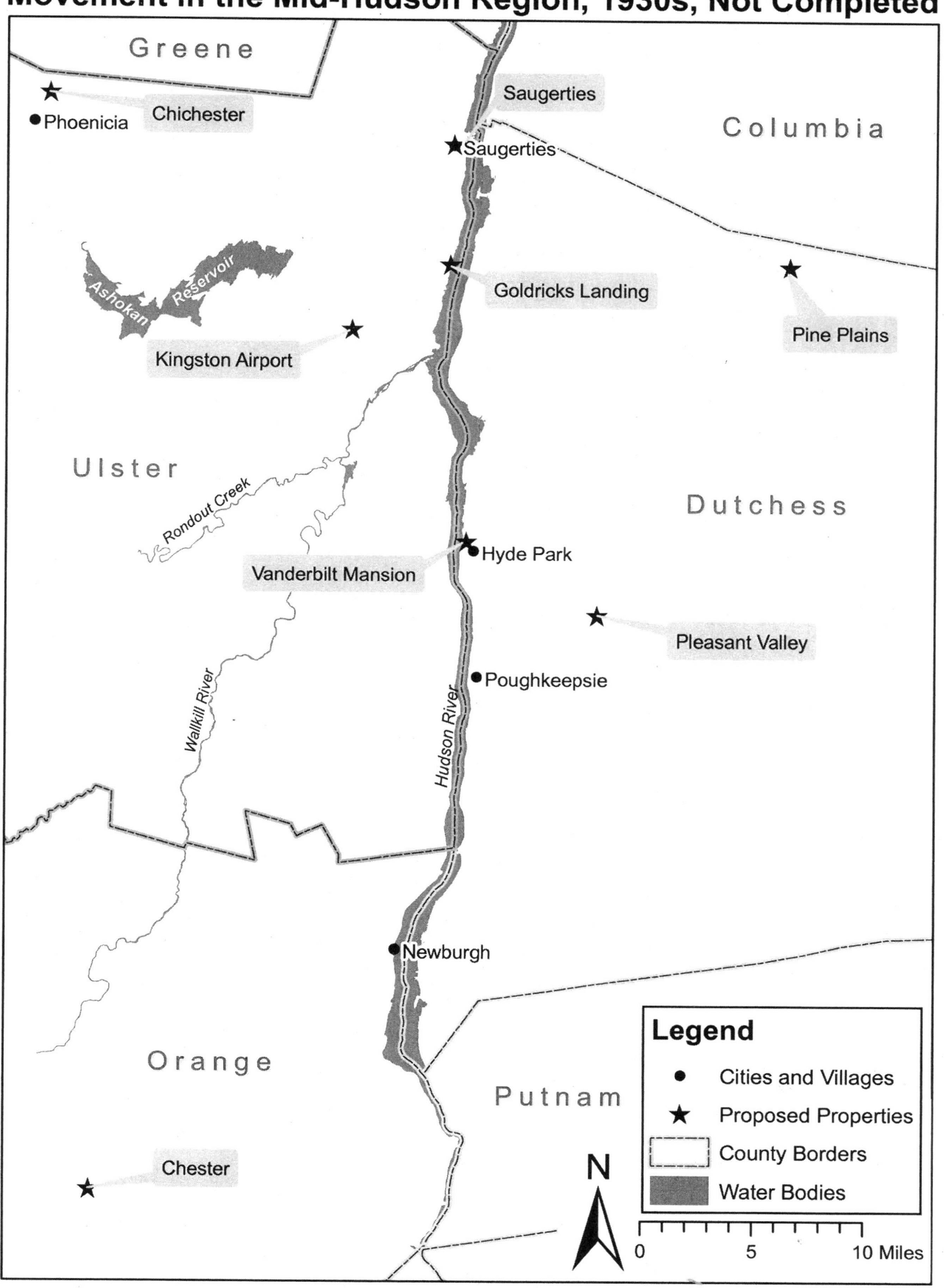

Map Produced by Colin Mills 2008

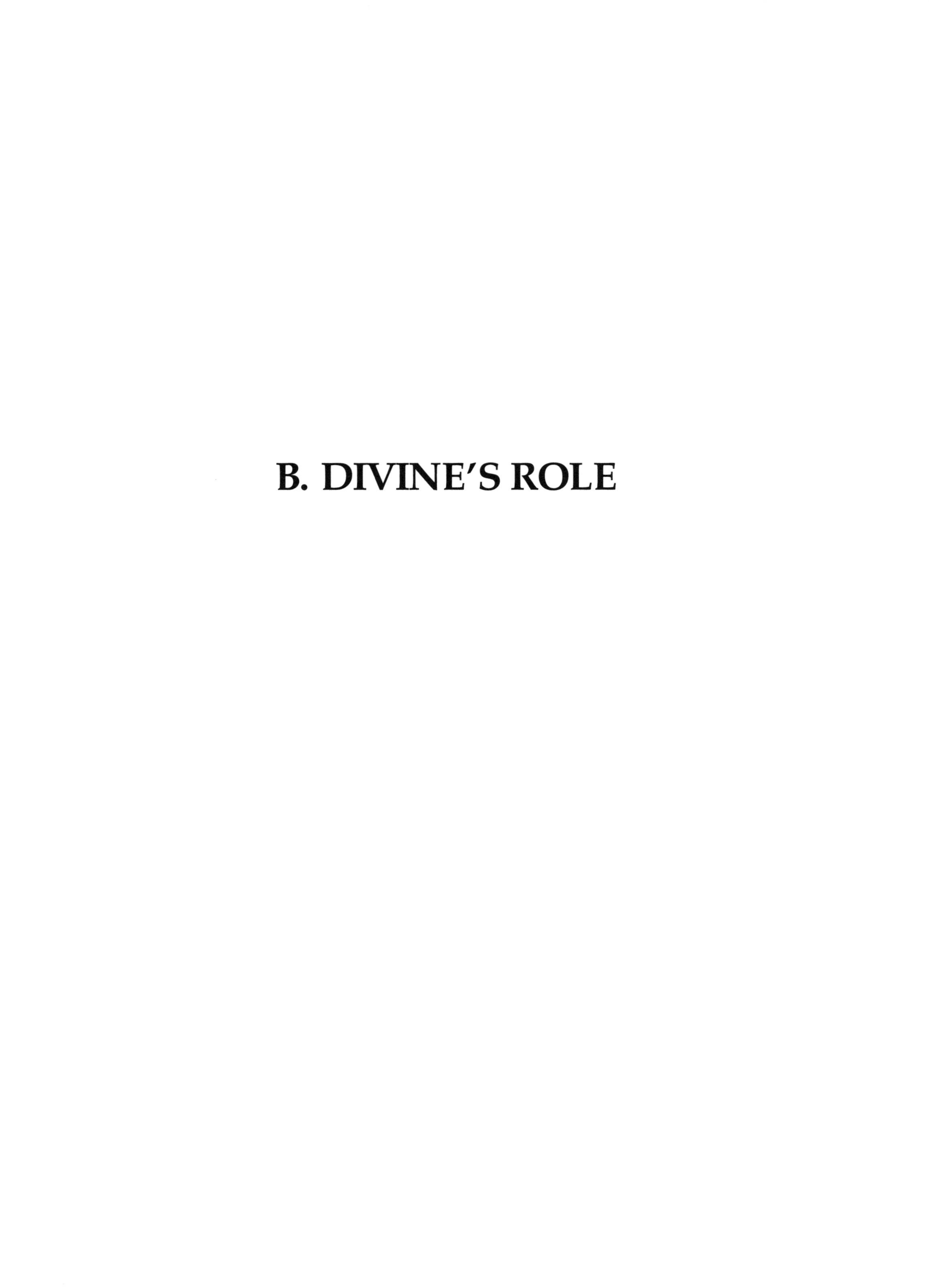

B. DIVINE'S ROLE

19. DIVINE'S PERSONAL TRAITS

FATHER DIVINE worked intensely, for long hours. He seemed to work both day and night. He wore out his secretaries, so they worked for him in shifts. He scarcely seemed to need sleep. It was claimed that he meditated as a means of rest.

At times he spoke softly. At other times he shouted, filling a hall without a loud-speaker. Though he was unusually short, only five feet two or three inches, his voice, energy, and bearing enabled him to take easy command.

By early experience a handyman and unpaid preacher, Divine nevertheless learned to adjust his rhetoric to a variety of circumstances. He learned to avoid legal liability. He learned to counsel followers, whether aspiring or backsliding, whether asking for healing or business advice. He learned to parry journalists, politicians, judges. He was called one of the most skilled publicists in the world.

His followers usually found him not distant, not satiric, but reassuring. Whether they were black or white, rich or poor, they felt him to be a visionary who was promoting innovative alternatives for them and the world. They might not be certain what he would do next, but they were likely to feel he cared. They might feel he was wrenching them from their complacency, trying to move them up to a higher plane, and they were likely to believe him to be infinitely capable.

Divine moved about often, being capable of speaking in New York in the afternoon, in Kingston after midnight, and then the next morning touring several Ulster County missions before lunch. He seldom traveled far. Although he had missions scattered about the globe, as in Canada, the West Indies, Europe, and Australia, he rarely left the American Northeast. He was present everywhere in spirit anyway, he explained, and could work more effectively if he was personally "out of the way."

He avoided making appointments, explaining that he did not want to run his life by clocks. He might suddenly leave a location without announcing where he was going. "It is not my custom to tell anyone, not even those of my immediate Cabinet, where I am going," he said. I "rely entirely upon my spirit, which moves me volitionally." His sudden arrivals and departures were likely to throw his followers off balance, making them more likely to cling to his presence. If he arrived somewhere unexpectedly, a crowd would usually soon gather around him. As he said, people "stick to me like flies stick to fly paper."[1]

FATHER DIVINE ON A VISIT TO ULSTER COUNTY, showing his electric energy. (*New Day*, Oct. 13, 1938)

When Divine spoke, he was normally accompanied by a bevy of his stenographers who took down his words verbatim. Afterwards, he would proofread their typescripts, and then make them available to his movement's weekly publication, the *New Day*, which routinely published them.

From the 1930s up to 1942, Divine gave most of his speeches in New York City because it was his base. But he also spoke often in Ulster County, the missions there where he spoke the most being Kingston, Stone Ridge, and New Paltz.

SEEMING CONTRADICTIONS

While Divine claimed he had no money, he often traveled in a Cadillac, Rolls Royce, or Duesenberg. He avoided wearing clerical garb, instead usually wearing tailor-made business suits. Sometimes he also wore expensive jewelry, and according to the *New Day*, his "reputation for smart dressing is unexcelled."

He recommended being generous in welcoming guests, but in daily life he urged being frugal, and on certain matters he could be frugal himself.

Speaking at Hope Farm, he said that to avoid unnecessary work, he made it his custom when he was dining not to use a knife unless it was necessary, and when in a bathroom to use a towel sparingly, to make it last a week. In many ways, he lived an ascetic life. He was not known to gamble, smoke, or drink intoxicating beverages—what he jokingly called his customary "mixed drink" was a combination of Postum and cocoa. He did not use profanity. According to a prominent New Thought lecturer who stayed with him for a month, he "manifested to an extreme degree" a "transparent purity of life."

He seemed committed to major principles, but under pressure to adapt to new circumstances, he was capable of revising them. Although he taught nonviolence, during World War II when he was pushed to oppose Hitler's Germany, he endorsed buying war bonds; and after the war, when he was pushed to oppose Stalin's Russia, he supported building atomic bombs. While for years he encouraged his followers who had received benefits either from governments or from private institutions to repay the amounts received, nevertheless, when he wanted to punish governments and private institutions for failing to recognize his followers' religious names, he abruptly asked his followers to stop repaying them. Moreover, although he taught his followers to cooperate with the law, when he himself was ordered by the courts to make a payment to a former follower, he refused, and to avoid paying it, moved out of New York State.

He taught denial of self, but when he was photographed, he said he wanted to be shown "better than I am," He wanted to be shown as having "lighter" skin than the way he was usually shown, he said, and shown to be closer in height to Mother Divine—his second wife—so that she was not "towering" over him, as photographs often made her seem to be.

He taught mercy, but he threatened retribution to those who crossed him. When an Ulster County phone company balked at giving him a clergy discount unless he showed them his ordination papers, Divine threatened that cosmic forces would punish the company. When Divine was annoyed by persistent Ulster County reporters, he said he would "get" those "devils." When Kingston suffered a destructive hailstorm, Divine said it happened because Ulster County had persecuted him.

While Divine sometimes seemed to bend to public opinion, at others time he seemed to defy it, regardless of the consequences. In a nation which valued guns, he advocated they be thrown away. In a nation devoted to racial separation, he brought different races together as equals. In a nation, which encouraged competition, he discouraged competitive games because, instead of bringing people together in harmony, he said, they turned people against each other. In a nation which valued patriotism, however, he claimed he was patriotic. He came to regard America as God's chosen vehicle for reforming the world. He repeatedly indicated his respect for the Declaration of Independence and the Constitution. But he emphasized that Americans, corrupt and greedy as he saw many of them to be, often did not put the ideals of the Declaration and Constitution into practice.[2]

HIS LANGUAGE

At times, Divine seemed to order his followers precisely what to do. Some of these orders were broadly related to the settled principles of his movement. For example, he told his followers not to go on relief, or drink, or smoke. He told them to pay their debts and not to borrow money. He insisted his missions charge low prices. Other of his orders, however, seemed to arise in response to particular events, and could be interpreted as egocentric. When his caravan of cars was arrested for speeding on the New Jersey Turnpike, and he considered the troopers treated him discourteously, he ordered all his followers to stop driving on the Turnpike. When Sara Harris published a book about Divine which the Harvard historian Oscar Handlin praised as providing the best available understanding about him, Divine found the book distorted, and declared that anyone who sold it or even read it would be cursed. Moreover, he was capable of what his critics considered to be grand-scale bluster, as when, at the end of World War II, he claimed that he was the one who had given the allies their victory.

Much of the time, however, Divine expressed himself cautiously. He would often say—especially when dealing with controversial, complex matters—that if his followers did what he taught, they should do so not because he taught it but because they felt it was right from within, according to their own "highest intuition." Similarly, when he gave interviews, he would tend to make only conditional promises to those he was interviewing, promises which would be true only if what they had told him about themselves was true, and only if they had faith and lived the evangelical life.

Divine did not write out his speeches ahead of time. He did not even prepare notes. He spoke "inspirationally," he explained, from "within," that is, from God, the "source" of "all wisdom." He sometimes seemed to punctuate his speeches with often-repeated expressions, as if filling in until he decided what to say next. He would assert, "How glorious it is to live in such a recognition." Or he would ask rhetorical questions like "Aren't you glad?" to which his listeners often shouted their agreement. Or he would say, "Peace, it's wonderful," an expression that became so well known that Dwight Eisenhower, when he was running for President in 1952, used it at a press conference, and the New York *Times*, reporting what Eisenhower said, identified the expression as Divine's.[3]

Divine often used expressions borrowed from New Thought. Long before the New Thought term "vibration" became popular, Divine was using it, as at Milton in 1939, in an interview with a woman who was seeking healing, when he promised her, "Stay in the vibrations of thanksgiving and praise, and you will find yourself restored." He also often used another New Thought term, the "allness of God," as when speaking at Kingston in 1936, he said he kept himself in the "consciousness of the allness of God."

DIVINE, REGARDING HIMSELF AS PATRIOTIC, ADVOCATED THAT THE U. S. LEAD IN REFORMING THE WORLD. The "A. D. F. D." letters in the upper left corner meant Anno Domini Father Divine. (Cartoon, often republished in the *New Day*, as on April 28, 1956)

A term which the press commonly used for Divine-related establishments was "heaven." As we have seen, both President F. D. Roosevelt and his wife used it to refer to the Divine colony at Krum Elbow. Divine, however, called such a use of the term a "misunderstanding," and discouraged using it. For him, "heaven is not a place geographically," he said. For him, heaven is "a state of consciousness" within a person, a mental condition in which Christ "reigns" within, and "tribulations" drop away. Divine and his movement preferred to call his establishments by such terms as missions, kingdoms, extensions, or connections.

Since Divine, according to the *New Day*, was "humanly uneducated," it was hardly surprising that he sometimes used not only unconventional words but also unconventional grammar. He was conscious of doing both, and interpreted them as desirable. Speaking at the Stone Ridge mansion, he said that Christ identified especially with the "under-privileged" and "illiterate," and that he did too. This freed him, he explained, to "chop up all of the 'King's English' when it gets in the way." As he explained to a reporter, he reached common people "on the plane where they are functioning that I might be one with them."

RETROACTIVE COMPENSATION

PEACE **July 28, 1951 A.D.F.D.**

ALL NATIONS AND PEOPLES WHO HAVE SUPPRESSED AND OPPRESSED THE UNDER-PRIVILEGED, THEY WILL BE OBLIGED TO PAY THE AFRICAN SLAVES AND THEIR DESCENDANTS FOR ALL UNCOMPENSATED SERVITUDE AND FOR ALL UNJUST COMPENSATION, WHEREBY THEY HAVE BEEN UNJUSTLY DEPRIVED OF COMPENSATION ON THE ACCOUNT OF PREVIOUS CONDITION OF SERVITUDE AND THE PRESENT CONDITION OF SERVITUDE.

THIS IS TO BE ACCOMPLISHED IN THE DEFENSE OF ALL OTHER UNDER-PRIVILEGED SUBJECTS AND MUST BE PAID RETROACTIVE UP-TO-DATE.

REV. M. J. DIVINE, Ms.D., D.D.
(Better known as FATHER DIVINE)

IN THIS 1951 PEACE STICKER, DIVINE EXEMPLIFIED BOTH HIS WILLINGNESS TO ENDORSE RADICAL PRINCIPLES and his difficulty in expressing himself concisely. (*New Day*, Sept. 15, 1956)

A noticeable expression which Divine often used, despite its seeming redundancy, was "sample and example." Speaking in the Peace Mission's new "garage auditorium" in High Falls, Divine said that the creation of this auditorium was "a sample and example" of what God's spirit could do. Also among his noticeable expressions was "tangibleate," a term said to be original with him. He seemed to use it as a verb to mean make tangible, as, in speaking at Greenkill Park, he explained that in his movement, we are "tangibilating" our "fondest imaginations" by bringing "them to the earth plane." Another such expression was "extremiate," seeming to mean to push down to the extreme. Speaking at Milton, he said that when people are at their "extremiation," down at their lowest state, God has a better opportunity to reach them.

His unconventional language provided doubters an opportunity to ridicule him. Divine was like Gertrude Stein, the critic Katherine Woods claimed; they both conveyed not so much sense as emotion. Much of his talk "seemed virtually unintelligible," said the New York *Times*, but this may have been true especially for people who seldom listened to him. When he spoke, he seemed to enthrall his listeners, and his unconventional language helped to enthrall them.[4]

HIS USE OF HISTORY

Among historical precedents for the Peace Mission, Divine followers often referred to the predominantly white Quakers because they advocated both nonviolence and rights for the underprivileged. Divine himself often welcomed Quaker visitors, and praised Quaker work, such as their work against racial discrimination in employment. But Divine followers seemed to identify more directly with the also predominantly white Shakers. As Divine publications pointed out, both Divine and Ann Lee, the Shaker founder, believed they were reincarnations of Christ. Both encouraged honesty, frugality, and industry. Both practiced faith healing and taught non-resistance. Once Divine became aware that Lee had created a Shaker community up the Hudson near Albany, he said that his communities in Ulster County were following her not only "spiritually, but geographically." Speaking in Stone Ridge, he recalled that Ann Lee, like himself, taught that "marriage in the sexual way" was not "holy in the sight of God," and in fact Shakers "stressed" almost "everything we are stressing."

In referring to American heroes, Divine usually spoke of white ones rather than black ones. He often referred to such founding fathers as Washington and Jefferson. When he referred to entrepreneurs, he often mentioned Ford and Woolworth, praising them for selling at low prices. Among inventors, he cited Edison as only needing three hours of sleep at night. Among leaders who worked against slavery, he often named John Brown. He seemed to avoid identifying with any such black freedom fighters as Harriet Tubman, Frederick Douglass, or Sojourner Truth, perhaps avoiding them because his education hardly included such black freedom fighters, or because he wanted his movement to be known as non-racial rather than black.

In fact, Sojourner Truth had long lived as a slave in Ulster County. After being freed from slavery, she became a Christian evangelist, like Divine. She chose to change her original name to a religious name, as Divine and many of his followers did, and the name she chose—Sojourner Truth—was like the names many Divine followers chose. She chose to live in three different intentional communities, like Divine's intentional communities. She became, like Divine, not only an opponent of tobacco, alcohol, and violence, but also an advocate of both blacks' and women's rights.

Despite his similarity to Sojourner Truth, when Divine visited his mission in Kingston, he is not known to have spoken of Truth as having lived in Kingston. When Divine was called to testify in the Ulster County Court House, he is not known to have indicated that he was aware that Truth had gone to that same building to recover her son from slavery in Alabama. When Divine followers bought the Krum Elbow estate, Divine did not seem aware that Truth had long lived as a slave within three miles of it, in West Park. When he advocated racial integration and women's rights, he seemed to ignore that Truth had done much the same. Divine seemed little attuned to parallels between his experience and the experience of historic black figures before him.[5]

HIS CONTROL: THE EXAMPLE OF JOY LOVE

Divine's charisma gave him power, and he seemed to exercise it easily, almost unconsciously. He seemed to exercise it in speeches, singing, presiding at banquets, or just waving to a throng. At times he seemed to exercise it flamboyantly, as when he arrived at a site in a luxurious car, or exercise it on a large scale, as when he gave blanket orders that he expected all his followers to obey. At other times, however, he seemed to exercise it quietly, on an individual level, but effectively nonetheless, as the following examples suggest.

Joy Love was one of the buyers of Greenkill Park in 1937. By the 1940s, she had become treasurer of one of the Divine churches, the Peace Center Church, and had been several years in charge of the mission on West 128th Street in Manhattan. At this mission, Love was one of those who especially cared for the child Laura Miller, who earlier had lived in the New Paltz mission. But also at this same 128th Street mission, Love took major responsibility for putting on banquets.

In 1944, while planning a banquet, Love found herself with limited funds, and that is when she made a mistake. The merchant she was buying supplies from, the meat merchant Samuel Miller, who had an outlet on Twelfth Avenue, was not clearly a Divine follower. He pushed her into buying more than she had cash to pay for at the time, and extended credit to her—probably credit of less than fifty dollars. He told her not to worry about the credit, and she accepted it.

When Divine heard about this, he called it a "disgrace." Both Love and merchant Miller should have known, he said, that it was contrary to his teaching to buy on credit. Not buying on credit seemed to have become a precise rule, which he required all followers to obey; it was not a matter he left to each individual follower's conscience. To punish Love, he asked her to "go off" to Ulster County, to "the Promised Land," to "take a vacation for a long time." Soon afterwards, when an annual meeting of Divine's Peace Center Church was being held, although Divine was not reported as having spoken against her in the meeting, many members already seemed to know of Love's transgression, and with Divine's consent, instead of reelecting Love as treasurer, they unanimously elected someone else.

At about the same time, Merchant Miller went to see Father Divine, to try to appease him. Miller assured Divine that he doubted there was another follower who "loves the Kingdom as much as Joy Love." Anyway, Miller insisted that he himself felt responsible for her buying on credit. Because of that, he said, he was willing to have what she owed him "stricken out." But Divine did not make it easy for Miller. He pointed out that Miller was not allowed to make a donation to Love's church because he was not "an immediate member" of that church.

Miller pleaded for Joy Love. He asked Father Divine to let her go back to her usual banquet work. Divine, however, was uneasy. He said, "Maybe she might buy things on credit again." But Miller insisted he would not allow it. "You can trust my word; she would not buy on credit again." Divine finally relented in part, saying,"If you want to cancel the would-be charges, you may."

It seemed to be easier for Divine to be forgiving to someone who was not a regular follower than to one who was. Several years later, Love was again elected to office by the Peace Center Church—not as treasurer this time, however, only as a second assistant treasurer. In still later years, she was repeatedly re-elected, but only to the same lesser office.

As far as available information indicates, it was not the New York mission which Joy Love served which decided that Miller should be forgiven. It was not the mission she served, which decided that she should be punished. It was not any mission in the Promised Land which decided she should be sent there. It was not her Peace Center Church which took the initiative in demoting her. It was Divine.

HIS CONTROL: THE EXAMPLE OF GRACE QUIETNESS

In regard to paying for the children of followers who lived in Divine missions, it seemed to be understood among many Divine followers that if you were a true follower, you would not have to pay for your children to live there, but if you were only a plain follower, you would be regarded as an outsider and expected to pay for them. However, there was no precise demarcation between a true follower and a plain follower. There were no initiation rites for entry into any such groups, and no lists of membership in such groups. Moreover, if your behavior or circumstances changed, you could pass back and forth from one group to the other. Who would decide in what group you belonged?

In 1944, Divine interviewed Grace Quietness about who should pay for the care of her child in Ulster County. The interview was held in a Divine office in Philadelphia, and it was, as usual, recorded by a secretary.

Quietness had previously lived in Oakland, California, where for several years she had operated a Divine movement restaurant. It seems possible that at that time she could have been regarded as a "true follower." In recent months, however, she had moved to Philadelphia where she was not working in any Divinite enterprise, but temporarily just "helping" a Divine follower. Was she a "true follower" or not at this time? Should she be required to pay for the care of her daughter?

Grace Quietness's child, named Precious Love, was living in Ulster County, at the Peace Mission's cooperative farm at Krumville. At the interview, the mother said this child had already been cared for there for eight years, and was now eighteen years old. Divine explained that he knew that Precious Love was not yet working to support herself. Divine said that for some time he had been expecting Quietness to come to him to arrange to pay for her daughter's care, if "not entirely," at least "in some way."

Divine explained that for years, Peace Mission followers in New York City had been sending weekly truck loads of food and clothing to the Krumville Farm, to help support all those who stayed there, including the children. Such assistance had to be paid for somehow, Divine said, and particularly at present, during World War II, the Krumville Farm, short of help as it was, was not earning much, and by itself could scarcely pay for such assistance.

Some followers who lived at missions, Divine told Quietness, were "fully consecrated," as by "investing their money" in them, and working for them unselfishly, "absolutely gratis." Such persons or any who were otherwise "true followers" were not expected to pay for their own care, he said, or for the care of any of their children who stayed at any Divine missions. But "outsiders," even if they lived at missions, he said, were expected to pay something for their own care or the care of any of their children who lived at missions. He seemed to be considering Quietness to be an outsider.

The state, Divine said, when it had charge of a child and placed it in an institution, paid about seven dollars a week for that child, but in our homes we charge less, only five dollars a week. Paying this, he said, would be a "small thing to do."

Quietness said that she "could have sent money from Oakland" to pay for her child, but those around her advised that "so long as Father did not say anything, don't bother."

Divine responded, "I did not have to say anything" because our usual child-care payment is "generally known" among us. Those who are not true followers "pay five dollars a week for the care of children."

Quietness replied, "If I would have known it, I would have been only too glad to send it." Defending herself, Quietness reminded Divine that his teaching, as she understood it, was that followers should distance themselves from family ties, removing children or other any other family from their minds. She said, "I must have got the wrong conception. I did not even want to mention it to you. I did not even want to have her in my consciousness."

That would have been appropriate, Divine replied, "if you had been consecrated to the service," or "if you had bought property in the Promised Land and would have invested all you had in that way for the common good." Then "you would not have had an obligation."

As far as available information indicates, it was Divine himself who was in control of this situation. It was he who was deciding how to classify Quietness. It was he, not the Krumville Farm, who was insisting that she should pay for its care of her child.[6]

NUMBER OF PUBLISHED MESSAGES (SPEECHES OR INTERVIEWS) GIVEN BY FATHER DIVINE,
in Ulster County Peace Missions, by Locations Where Given, 1935-1952

PEACE MISSION	NUMBER OF MESSAGES
Kingston Mansion, Kingston	126
Stone Ridge Farm, near Atwood	101
New Paltz Farm, New Paltz	75
Hope Farm, West Saugerties	66
Art Colony, Milton	56
Krum Elbow Estate, near Highland	51
Divine Lodge, near Samsonville	43
Greenkill Park, near Eddyville	26
Garage, Lucas Ave., High Falls	25
High Falls Extensions, High Falls	20
Divine Farm, Saxton	14
Olive Bridge Farm, Krumville	12
Krumville Farm, Krumville	11
Divine Terrace, Elting Corners, Town of Lloyd	2
Kingston Jr. Farm, May Park, Town of Esopus	1
Spot-in-the-Road, near Atwood	1
Total	630

20. DIVINE'S DUESENBERG

ONCE when Father Divine rode in his Duesenberg from New York up to Ulster County, he took along a Philadelphia reporter who was overwhelmed to be riding in such a "great" car. With a chauffeur at the wheel, they drove to Hope Farm, where on arrival, according to the reporter, the car's "powerful air-horns" were blasting, and followers "were running to the car from every direction." Of course the reporter wondered where the money came from for Divine to ride in such a luxurious car. "The whole world has been worrying," he wrote, how Father Divine "can ride around in Duesenbergs, Rolls-Royces and Cadillac sixteens."

Divine's luxury cars were a sign of his power. His Duesenberg was especially awesome. While he received some of his cars second-hand, he received his Duesenberg new, and it was built especially for him. It was 22 feet long, could seat ten passengers, and was called the largest Duesenberg ever built. It was expensive. It was reported to have cost $28,000 at a time when a new Ford might cost $400 to $600, and even a new Cadillac might cost only $1,645.

Duesenbergs were considered the best American-made cars in existence. They were named after the race car designer, Fred Duesenberg, who first built them, and they became status symbols. Such prominent families as the DuPonts, Vanderbilts, and Wanamakers owned them. Such individual celebrities as New York's Mayor Jimmy Walker, aviation entrepreneur Howard Hughes, and Hollywood actor Clark Gable also owned them. Duesenbergs were famous for their speed. At a time when many cars could not reach 70 miles per hour in any gear, Duesenbergs could reach over 90 miles per hour in second gear. Sometimes the Duesenberg penetrated American awareness enough to switch the spelling of the familiar slang expression, "it's a doozie," into "it's a duesie," after the car.[1]

Divine's Duesenberg was, like all his possessions, not literally owned by him, but rather by a follower who made it available to him. Divine sometimes seemed reluctant to reveal who this owner was.

The chassis of Divine's car, a model J, was built in Indianapolis, at the Duesenberg factory, but this factory did not build Duesenberg bodies. Bodies were built to order by customers, in whatever body shop they chose. For Divine, the body of his Duesenberg was ordered to be built in Pasadena, California, by Bohman and Schwartz who had built other Duesenberg bodies. It was a Divine follower, Howard B. Smith, who, acting as a secret agent, ordered the body in 1936, and production was under way by April, 1937. The design, as Smith originally ordered it, called for the back of the car to have a "raised single throne-chair." As the car neared completion in October, 1937, however, Smith toned down the design. Instead of a calling for a single special seat, the new design provided for two, more modest seats, though observers still called them throne-chairs. The two seats were intended for Father and Mother Divine. The roof over them was retractable, which would be handy during parades.

Eventually it became known that Smith had ordered the Duesenberg body to be made for Divine on behalf of the Hunt family. Smith had often assisted John Hunt with technical services at the Hunt family base in Los Angeles. An engineer by education, Smith could explain to the car builders what the Hunt family wanted in language they could understand. According to the *Saturday Evening Post* soon afterward, John Hunt "wanted to install a revolving throne in the rear of the big sedan, with a retractable gold halo which could be extended out over the spot where Divine's head would be." While the *Post* said, "Divine forbade this as contravening good taste," Divine himself claimed afterward—as we shall soon see—that the car was built without his knowledge.

When the Duesenberg was completed in the fall of 1937, it was not John Hunt who delivered it from California to Divine in New York. At the time John Hunt was serving a sentence in a California prison. It was also not John Hunt's brother Warner Hunt who delivered it. He was busy editing a

THIS LUXURIOUS DUESENBERG CAR WAS SPECIALLY ORDERED FOR FATHER DIVINE by Mary Bird Tree, who lived at the Kingston Mansion. The photo shows the car in Philadelphia, where Divine was officiating in October, 1940, at the opening of a facility on South Broad Street which later became his headquarters.
(Auburn Cord Duesenberg Museum)

Divinite periodical in the East. It was a third brother, Joseph Hunt, who delivered it to Divine.

It was also Joseph Hunt who in November, 1937, drove Father and Mother Divine and several secretaries in the new Duesenberg from New York to Ulster County, on the car's first visit there. On their way to attend a banquet at Hope Farm in West Saugerties, Divine stopped the car at the office of the *Ulster County Press* in Kingston to show the car, as he did not need to do. Showing the car, according to the *Press*, he was "beaming with pride."

As the *Press* reported it, the new Duesenberg was "a rolling palace." A "glass panel" separated "the driver's seat from the rear compartment." The car had "retractable" running boards. It had "built-in" spare wheels and tires on each side and "two large white lights on the rear of the car" which "flash on as soon as the car is thrown in reverse so that the driver has the same amount of light to back up as he has when driving ahead."[2]

It was the mother of the family, Florence Hunt, a wealthy but quiet follower of Divine, who, through engineer Smith, had ordered the car's body to be built. She paid for it from money she had acquired from her family's various enterprises in Cleveland, including the manufacture of candy, and it was she who made the completed car available to Divine. Known in the Divine movement as Mary Bird Tree, she was the mother of the deliverer of the car, Joseph Hunt. She was also the mother both of the flamboyant John Hunt who was imprisoned in Los Angeles for seducing an under-age girl, and of the steadier Warner Hunt (known in the Divine movement as John DeVoute), who was the editor of the Divine movement's weekly periodical, the *New Day*. By early 1937, Florence Hunt had moved from Los Angeles to Ulster County and was living at the Divine mission in Kingston, known as the Kingston Mansion.

In September, 1938, when the Duesenberg could still be considered new, Divine seemed indirectly to apologize for having such a luxurious car. This car, Divine said, was built to be his "office-car." It was built, he explained, so that he could take with him not only Mother Divine and a guest, but also several secretaries who could work with him as they drove. The usual work they did, as Divine described it, was "proofreading." They could proofread letters, which he had written before they were sent, or they could proofread the copies of his speeches, which his secretaries had recorded before they were released to the press. Speaking at the Samsonville resort, Divine claimed that they could proofread in this car even when driving the crude, twisting Catskill Mountain roads which led to this resort. "We can ride along almost any sort of a rough road," he insisted, "and read right along as though we were in the office."

Ten years later, in 1948, when Divine scarcely used the car anymore, he seemed to be apologizing for it more directly. At this time, a car buff, who was gathering information for a history of Duesenberg cars, had asked Divine for his recollections about his "Throne Car." Answering him, Divine rejected the label "Throne Car" as a "misconception." My Duesenberg, Divine wrote, "was built without my request, knowledge or desire, and had I been previously informed, I would have made an effort to prevent such an extravagant and unnecessary waste." It was because of "my respect for the one who owns the Duesenberg that I permitted her to place her car at my disposal." He added that she still owned it.

Ironically, by about this time, the car's owner, Mary Bird Tree, was elderly and frail, living in Philadelphia, and dependent on the Divine movement for her care. Her son John Hunt claimed she no longer managed any money of her own.

After the Peace Mission secured a new estate at Woodmount, outside of Philadelphia, as a residence for Divine, and he was no longer using the Duesenberg, he stored it there.

After Mary Bird Tree died, the car made its way to an auto museum in Las Vegas. Recently, however, it has been on display in an auto museum in Auburn, Indiana, in the state where its chassis was originally made. At the museum, despite Divine's distaste for the term, the car is still known as the "Throne Car."[3]

21. SCARCELY ORGANIZED

DIVINE'S PEACE MISSION organized excursions, parades, and political campaigns. It operated residences, hotels, farms, businesses. It was called the biggest landlord in both Harlem and Ulster County. It was not only strong in the United States on both the East and West Coasts, it was also international, having missions on several continents. Even so, it had no board of directors. It had almost no paid staff. It seemed to have no obvious means of support. Divine liked to say that the Peace Mission was not an organization, but a movement, and that he, as its head, was only a "volunteer servant."

The movement never had a membership system. Participants in the movement could live in a Divine mission or not, as they chose. When the *New Day* published lists of Peace Mission branches, as it often did, it often called them missions, or extensions, or connections, but there was no clear distinction among these terms; they were not administrative categories. Even the individual missions themselves were only loosely organized. Speaking at the Milton mission in 1939, Divine explained that none of his Peace Missions was "organized as an organization." Nevertheless, he said, all his missions were "governed by my mind and my spirit," which is to say, "by the Christ."

John Lamb, Divine's leading secretary, declared in 1939 that the movement has "no organization of any kind," and "therefore there are no officers, trustees, or even members." The movement was kept in line, Lamb explained, by Divine himself, his "slightest word" to his followers being their "rule of conduct." In the mid-1940s, even after the Divine movment had organized churches, the anthropologist Arthur H. Fauset took a similar view. Having studied Divine communities in Ulster County and elsewhere, Fauset wrote, "Father Divine is the organization." More harshly, a critic in the New York *Times* voiced a common view among Divine's detractors: Divine's movement did not need an organization because Divine was a "despot." His many followers who came to him for relief from their "hunger and humiliation" found it, she said, only by "dulling" their "reason" and losing themselves in "primitive emotion."[1]

On the level of individual missions, each was independent of the others, and each was expected to be self-supporting. It is not clear that missions were expected to report to any larger entity, except they all were expected to regard Divine as their spiritual adviser. Many individual missions were organized, however, to the extent of designating specialized workers. For example, Walking Jerusalem was designated a farmer at Samsonville resort, Mina Brock was designated a chauffeur at New Paltz, Little David was designated a boys' guardian at Kingston Mansion. In High Falls, Divine-related businesses often had individuals in charge: Wrestling Jacob ran a residence, New Hope ran a restaurant, Simon Peter ran a grocery, Sincere Heart ran a garage, Mother Divine ran a sewing workshop, and Brother Nicodemus ran a barber shop.

CREATION OF CHURCHES

Beginning in 1940, Divine's movement organized itself more by forming churches. The movement may have moved in this direction to provide tax advantages, to fend off law suits, or to make the movement more understandable to the public; or also, although Divine seemed little concerned about his movement's survival, to give it more institutional framework to help it survive.

The first Divinite church, the Palace Mission Church, was founded in 1940. Taking the initiative in founding it were a small group of followers, including Attorney Arthur Madison, Editor John DeVoute, and two wealthy Ulster County-related followers, Charles Calloway and Mary S. Lyon.

The other four Divinite churches were created in 1941: the Circle Mission Church, Peace Center Church, Unity Mission Church, and Nazareth Mission Church. Each of the five churches was separate from the others. Each had branches. But all five churches operated under the same by-laws and discipline. All five churches held annual meetings, at which they elected officers, but only if Divine approved of them. Most officers were women, a substantial portion of them related to Ulster County. Divine was the pastor of all of the churches, but they elected assistant pastors, at least one being a woman.

Continuing the Peace Mission's tradition, the staff and members of these churches served without pay. All these churches offered food and accommodations at low rates, and free to many in need. All these churches continued the movement's practice of keeping no membership lists, and hence, as Divine cheerfully admitted, many even of his "true followers" did not know whether they belonged to any one of the churches or not. But to be elected an officer of a church, they were required to declare that they were members of that church. To be recognized as a Divine follower, however, it was not necessary to be a member of any church at all.[2]

METHODS OF CONTROL

The paucity of formal organization allowed Divine more freedom to control his movement as he wished. The movement's lack of a membership system meant that Divine could declare an individual to be a follower or not, as he chose. Even if he had once recognized an individual to be a follower, he could later punish him by stripping him of that designation, washing his hands of him. When he did so, Divine might say he had "excommunicated" him, which could happen without any procedure for due process.

Similarly, Divine could exercise control by giving or refusing to give his approval to mission enterprises, whether churches, residences, farms, or businesses. The workers at each such mission seemed eager to secure and keep his approval. When Faithful Mary led a rebellion against Divine, his response was to withdraw his recognition of her and the extensions she led, including her hotel in High Falls. With Divine's approval withdrawn, nearly all Divine followers deserted her, and her rebellion crumbled.

Divine made explicit which mission enterprises he approved by publishing lists of them. He did so in the *New Day*. He also did so on his letterheads. In doing so, he often implied that he himself lived or worked there. Thus for Ulster County, he listed the Hope Farm address as Rev. M. J. Divine, Hope Farm, West Saugerties, N. Y.; the estate at Krum Elbow as Rev. M. J. Divine, Krum Elbow, Highland, N. Y.; and a tailor shop as Rev. M. J. Divine, Tailor Shop, High Falls, NY.

Though Divine claimed that he had nothing to do with admitting residents into his missions, he sometimes seemed to direct people to them. He took the initiative in sending an erring youth, Son Peter, to Hope Farm. He took the initiative in sending the baby Laura Brock to New Paltz, and later in persuading her mother to work there. When follower Sing Happy, of New York City, wanted to take a temporary job in Kingston, he understood he had to ask Divine's permission because, he said, any follower had to have Divine's permission to change his "routine." When Joy Love broke his rule against buying on credit in Manhattan, he punished her by ordered her to Ulster County.

Divine sometimes exerted control by making verbal threats of retribution. While Divine clearly did not consider these threats to be coercion, others might consider them so, especially given Divine's enormous power over his followers. However, he made it clear that retribution should not take place by human intervention, but by the spirit, by God. Nevertheless, transgressors would be punished inevitably, automatically, he often said, as by an accident, or illness, or natural disaster. Given that he increasingly referred to himself as God, he was in effect claiming for himself the power to inflict retribution, thus setting up a powerful psychological tool, based on fear, for him to exercise control.

In the climate of adulation that surrounded Divine, his giving or withholding approval of any action, whether it was minor or major, could seem highly significant to followers. Attorney Arthur Madison, speaking in Father Divine's presence, described Divine's control over his followers matter-of-factly, without any implied criticism, saying, Divine's influence on his followers was so great, that "it does not matter how well a thing is being done;" until Divine personally puts "an approval on it, we don't feel free to go on."

Divine's control was limited, however, by his followers' inability to live up to his severe standards. It was also limited by his own awareness that his teachings were fundamentally aimed not as much at outward conduct as at inward, voluntary growth. While Divine sometimes directed his followers exactly what to do, he often avoided, as he frequently said, coercing his followers to do anything, especially in complex matters."In any sacred work," he was fond of saying, "when coercion begins, the work of God that moment ends."[3]

THE GREETING "PEACE"

Using the word "peace" was a ritual, which helped to hold Divine's movement together. The word was used in the name of the movement, the Peace Mission. With Divine's encouragement, followers came to say "peace" as a personal greeting both among themselves and to outsiders. They used it to answer the telephone. They placed it on placards in parades, as a sign on buildings, as a salutation in letters, and as a slogan in advertisements.

Father Divine often used the word "peace" in opening his speeches, as by saying, "Peace, everyone." If his followers met his exacting standards in their business enterprises, Divine encouraged them to use "peace" in the names of their enter-

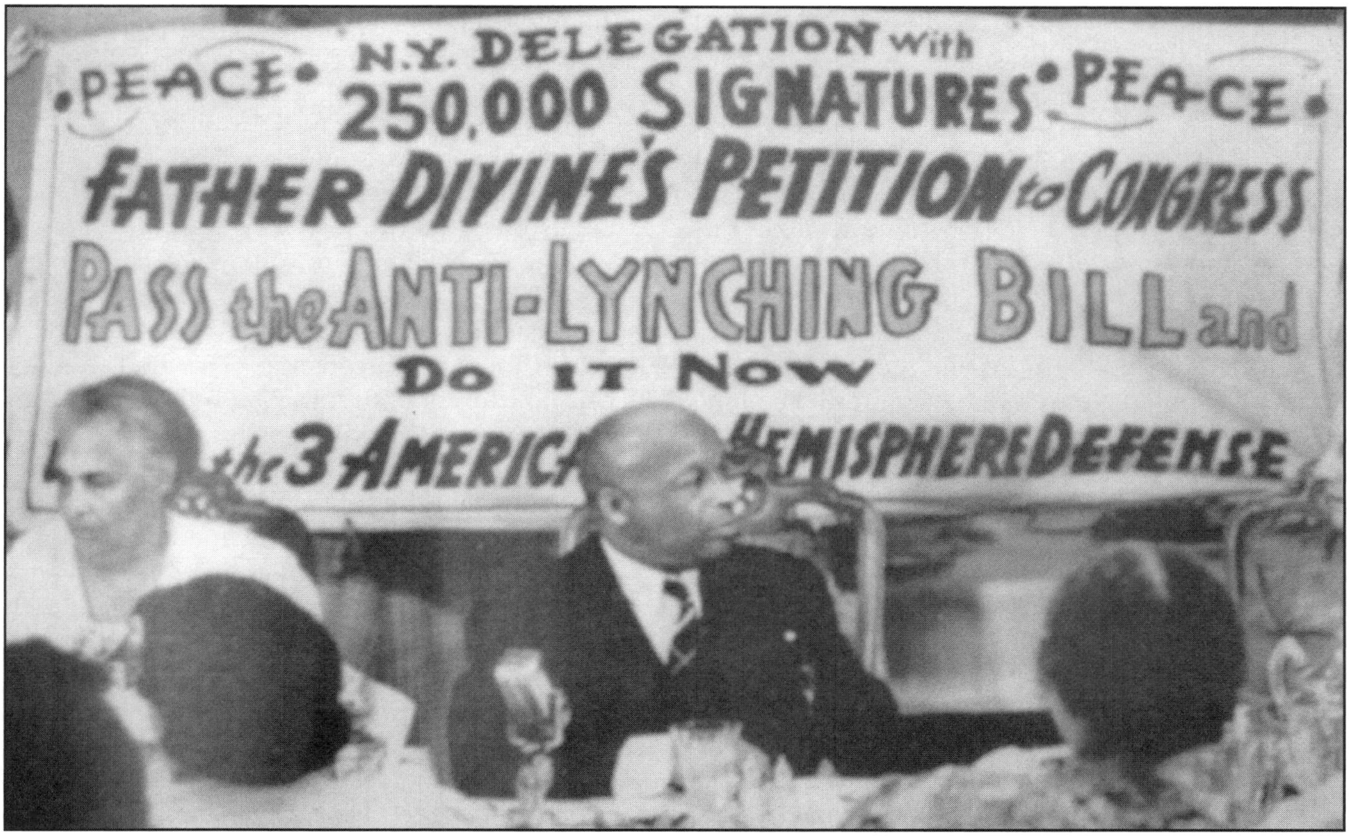

FATHER DIVINE AND THE FIRST MOTHER DIVINE at a banquet at Rockland Palace in Harlem. The banner behind them proclaims the Peace Mission's opposition to lynching and support of uniting the Americas. (*New Day*, July 25, 1940)

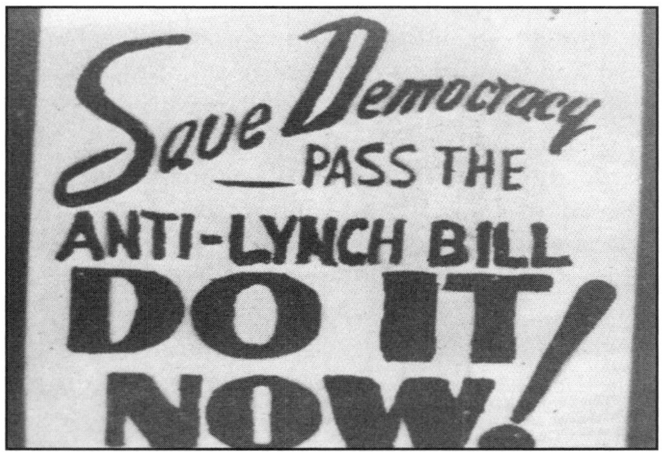

POSTER AGAINST LYNCHING, displayed at such Divine communities as Rockland Palace and Greenkill Park. Divine campaigned to persuade Congress to pass an anti-lynching bill, saying Americans are hypocrites to condemn Germany for its cruelty to Jews while it tolerates the lynching of blacks. (*New Day*, Sept. 11, Nov. 13, 1941)

DIVINE SECRETARIES SIGNING AN ANTI-LYNCHING PETITION TO CONGRESS. The three secretaries at the table in the act of signing are, from left: Mary Justice (enthusiastic for the UN), Great Love (originally from the Midwest, lived at Stone Ridge), and Quiet Devotion (originally from South Africa, a secretary to John Hunt, later lived at Stone Ridge). Standing in center right background is Heavenly Rest (a buyer of Kingston Mansion). (*New Day*, Aug. 8, 1940)

prises, as in the name of the Peace Department Store in High Falls. While of course Divine was likely to use the term "peace" when exhorting his followers to commit themselves to nonviolence, Divine gave the term "peace" many other meanings, spiritual and mundane, personal and political. Whether at meetings or banquets, or on bus and steamer excursions, both followers and visitors seemed warmed by greeting each other with the term, and singing about it, and hearing testimonies about finding it. Frequent use of the term "peace" provided part of the magic that, along with the singing, clapping, and swaying, helped to provide a welcoming, joyous sense of community at Divine gatherings, for thousands of participants, of all ages, of varying degrees of education and wealth, of varying religious, racial, and national backgrounds.

RITUAL DINNERS

Dinners were another significant ritual within the Divine movement. Divine followers, whether in their missions or churches, often treated dinners as the sacrament of communion, which was the only traditional Christian sacrament that Divine's movement practiced. They radically reshaped their communion, however, from that of the conventional church. Instead of the communion meal consisting only of slight portions of bread and wine, they remade it into a sumptuous meal. Instead of offering it only at limited intervals, they offered it frequently, sometimes several times a day. Instead of restricting participation in it, they welcomed everyone. Instead of accompanying it by formal singing, as from hymnbooks, the singing was likely to be spontaneous, and during periods of enthusiasm, accompanied by swaying and clapping. At communion dinner tables, men were expected to wear coats and ties, women to be modestly dressed. Men and women sat separately, as at separate tables, or across from each other at the same table, but those of different races were likely to be deliberately mixed. Partaking of such a communion feast meant having an interracial experience, and satisfying the bodily hunger of those in need—the poor were often invited to participate free, and for everyone the cost was small, for many years only 15 cents for a regular meal, a bit more to include dessert. For those spiritually ready, it also meant participating in a sacred rite, which promised forgiveness, healing, prosperity, and victory over all obstacles.

In practice, followers served such communion banquets elaborately. They served them with the best china and silverware, on white tablecloths. The food was likely to be prepared by expert cooks, tastefully displayed, and more abundant than the diners could consume. The food was not served to diners individually, by waiters, but served family style, with serving dishes passed down the tables by the diners, from hand to hand, symbolizing sharing. If Divine was present, as the dinner began he would bless the food by placing a spoon or fork in each dish before it was passed, and later he would speak. Divine maintained, however, that it was not necessary for him to be bodily present, whether at communion dinners or similar occasions, as his presence could be just as real in the spirit as in the body. Whether Divine was present or not, seats and place settings were customarily reserved for him. Seats might also be reserved for Mother Divine, and for Divine's immediate staff, including, as he explained, stenographers and chauffeurs who might be asked to leave quickly with him if necessary. No other seats were to be reserved, he said, and if any mission did try to reserve other seats, he threatened to stop going there.[4]

SPONTANEOUS MEETINGS

As for meetings, although practice could vary, Divine tended to prefer them to be spontaneous. Drawing on his early experience, he often held meetings without the use of Bibles, hymn books, or any set program. Meetings did not include prayer as such, as Divine did not encourage formal prayer, teaching rather that all of life should be prayer. Meetings often consisted largely of singing and testimony, both unplanned.

Especially at first, however, the meetings of the Righteous Government Department, the social and political action arm of the Peace Mission movement, were organized enough to be led by

DIVINE AND ASSOCIATES IN HIS OFFICE AT ROCKLAND PALACE, in Harlem. From left, James C. Thomas (also called Chester Thomas), a lawyer for Divine who had recently been appointed a New York State Assistant Attorney General; Dr. Joseph Broadman, a physician with an office in mid-town New York; Father Divine; John Lamb, a major secretary to Divine; and "Mr. Weiss," the proprietor of Rockland Palace. (*New Day*, Aug. 8, 1940)

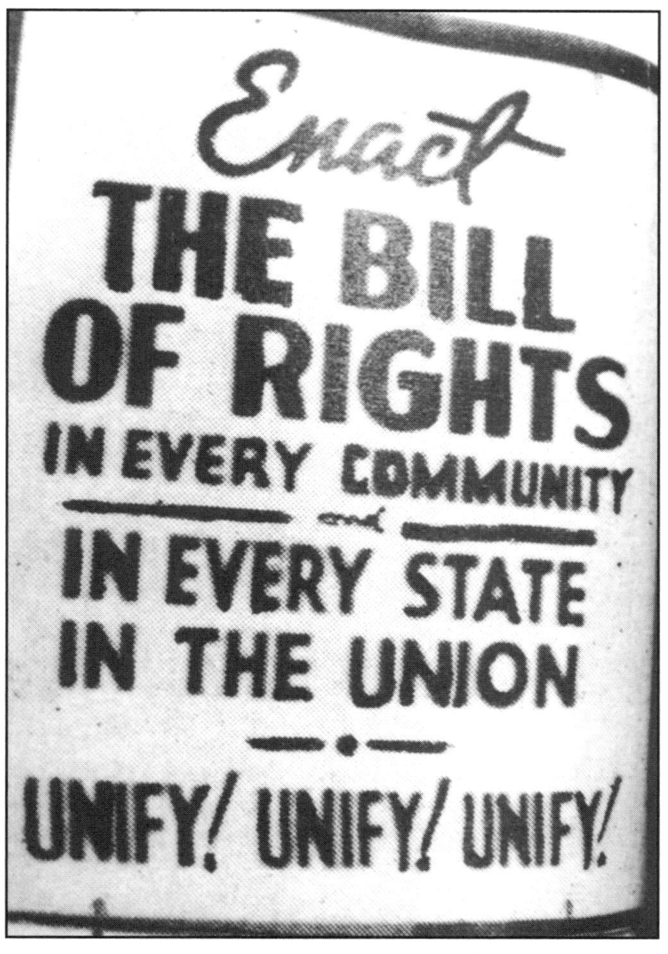

POSTER DISPLAYED IN DIVINE COMMUNITIES ASKING THAT THE BILL OF RIGHTS BE CARRIED OUT EVERYWHERE. For Divine followers, the Bill of Rights meant rights for all, regardless of race, rights such as free speech, freedom of religion, and equality before the law. (*New Day*, Sept. 11, Nov. 13, 1941)

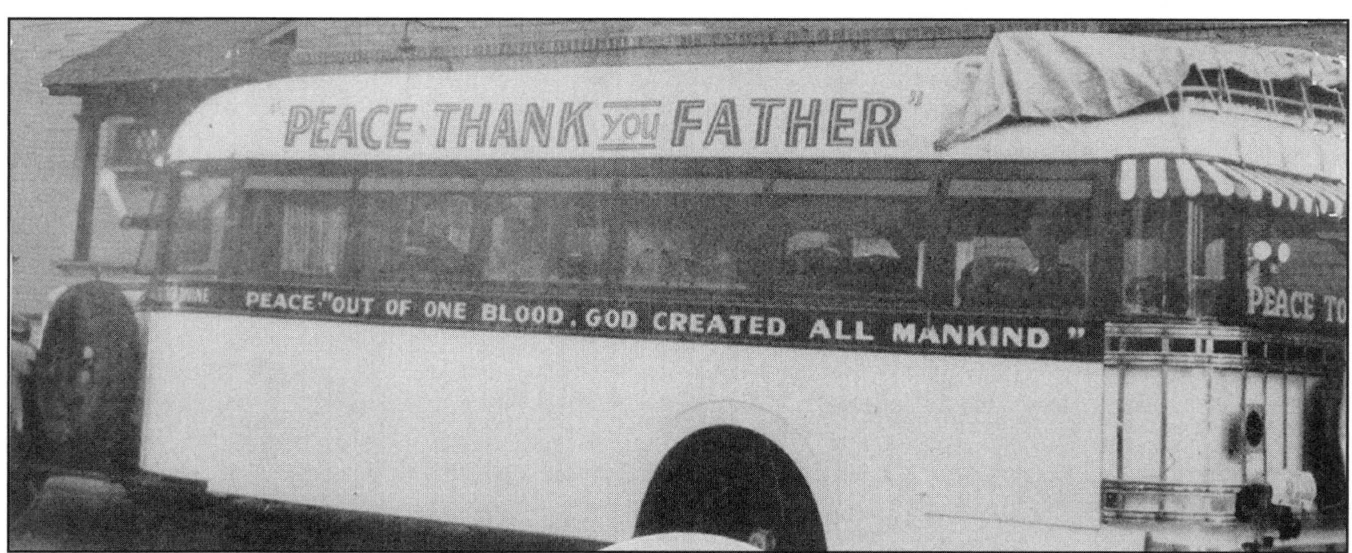

BUS OWNED BY DIVINE FOLLOWERS
used for transporing followers, as between missions in California and New York.
(*New Day*, Ap. 11, 1940)

PEACE MISSION "EXCURSIONS" TO ULSTER COUNTY, 1935-1952

DATE AND PURPOSE	MEANS OF TRANSPORT	IF BY SHIP, DESTINATION WHERE IT DOCKED, and dock's distance from NY City	FINAL DESTINATION and if transport was by ship, miles from dock to destination	FEATURES
1935, Sept. 29. To celebrate the opening of New Paltz Farm	Ship's name unknown. Excursionists were expected to be "evangelical" in behavior	Poughkeepsie, 75 miles up the Hudson River	New Paltz Farm, off Libertyville Rd., 12 miles from the dock	Fare round trip: 75c. Divine said God was transforming "lacks" into "abundance"
1936, Aug. 20. To open both the Kingston Mansion and the whole Promised Land	Two ships: Calvert and City of Keansburg, with 2,000 passengers. Welcomed were only those who had paid their debts	Kingston (Rondout Creek), 100 miles up the Hudson River	Kingston Mansion, in the Wilbur neighborhood of Kingston, at 67 Chapel St., 2 miles from the dock by the shortest route	Fare round trip: $1. From the dock to the Mansion, most excursionists paraded on foot, part of the way on Broadway, about 3 miles
1937, July 8-9. To open Greenkill Park	Ship upriver: State of Delaware (left dock at 132 St., with 1,750 singing passengers on board). Ship on return: City of Keansburg	Kingston (Rondout Creek), 100 miles up the Hudson River	Greenkill Park, near Eddyville; 3 miles from the dock, much of it on Abeel St. Because buses over-charged, many excursionists walked	Fare round trip: $1. Temperature over 100 degrees. At the Park, a swimming pond was available

1937 Aug. 30-31. Especially for children, but not as many came as hoped.	**Ship: City of Keansburg, with more than 2,000 passengers**	**Kingston, 100 miles up the Hudson**	**Greenkill Park. Transportation from the dock, 3 miles, provided by buses and cars**	**Fare round trip: $1, children under 19 free. Overnight accommodation 50c, children 25c**
1938, Aug. 8-9; to open both the Milton Art Colony and the Krum Elbow Estate	**Two ships: City of New York and Manhattan, with 2,500 singing passengers**	**Milton (own dock), 70 miles up Hudson; Krum Elbow (own dock), 80 miles; Kingston, 100 miles**	**Three final destinations: Milton Art Colony, Krum Elbow Estate, and Kingston Mansion**	**Fare round trip: $1. Overnight accommodations were available at several sites**
1939, June 19, to check on remodeling, and to find "peace," not "hate"	**Ship: State of Delaware (departed from NYC's 132 St. pier)**	**Milton (own dock), 70 miles up the Hudson; Krum Elbow (own dock), 80 miles**	**Two destinations: Milton Art Colony and Krum Elbow Estate**	**Fare round trip $1; children under 18 and co-workers free**
1940 -- --------	**------------------**	**[No excursion because**	**participation in excursions had**	**dropped]**
1941, Oct. 12 (Columbus Day) (two months before the attack on Pearl Harbor). Especially to enlist support for Civil Defense	**Steamboat service on the Hudson having declined, 18 buses departed from Harlem's Rockland Palace, and other buses from New Jersey**		**Greenkill Park. Thousands packed the auditorium and overflowed outside. Speakers urged volunteering for Civil Defense**	**Fare round trip: $1.33. Divine explained, "We do not believe in taking up arms," but we can "rescue the perishing and care for the dying"**
1942-50 -- ------	**-----------------**	**[No excursions because of such**	**factors as the war and**	**Divine's move to Philadelphia]**

1951, Sunday, June 17, to celebrate the 5th anniversary of Divine's remarriage	**With regular passenger steamboats on the Hudson having stopped, transportation was by buses**		**Kingston Mansion**	**Swimming in the pool, baseball, banqueting, concessions for hot dogs and ice cream**
1951, Sept. 2-3 (Labor Day), to celebrate again the 5th anniversary of Divine's remarriage	**Chartered buses from Philadelphia; Newark, NJ; and NY City**		**Krum Elbow**	**Fishing and swimming in the Hudson, picnicking on the grounds, and banqueting inside**
1952, Aug. 31-Sept 1, (Labor Day). To celebrate the 6th anniversary of Divine's remarriage	**"Hundreds" came in a "caravan" of cars from Philadelphia**		**Krum Elbow and Kingston Mansion**	**Krum Elbow being crowded, Divine stayed at Kingston Mansion. This was Divine's last known visit to Ulster County**

designated officers. The Department had an international chairman, the black lawyer Arthur Madison, and an international board, two members of which lived in Divine missions in Ulster County. In Ulster County itself, for a time the Righteous Government Department was also organized enough to have its own chairman—that is, to use her own woman-conscious terminology, a "chairlady." She was Miss Melchizedec Matthew, who had been a long-term teacher in the New York City public schools. Although she was one of the purchasers of the Spot-in-the-Road mission, she was reported to live at either Olive Bridge or Krumville Farm. Matthew sometimes chaired countywide meetings, although at least once, Happy Heaven, the operator of a Peace Mission candy factory in High Falls, presided instead. If at any time Divine arrived, however, whoever was presiding would defer to him.

From 1936 to 1942, Righteous Government meetings for the whole of Ulster County were held frequently, with Divine himself often being present. They were usually held on Saturday night, and most of them in Kingston, the rest in scattered locations. Since no set schedule was made out ahead of time, sometimes it was not decided where the next meeting would be held until the Saturday before, with the decision being made by Divine or by vote. In the early years, discussion topics were sometimes planned ahead, as, for example, one meeting being devoted to agriculture, another devoted to politics. At a county-wide meeting in the fall of 1936, a Presidential election year, followers explained that literacy tests were necessary to register and vote, and announced the locations in various towns where such tests might be taken.

By 1937, however, after some experience with set programs, Divine made it clear that he preferred meetings to be freer. While meetings might still be devoted to specific topics, he wanted all present, visitors included, to feel able to speak "volitionally," in the same manner in which he spoke himself, or, as he once said, in the manner of the early Quakers. But, he warned, if participants wander from the subject, we may be obliged to "bring programs back," choose a "master of ceremonies," and "call on individuals" to speak "systematically." He long continued to encourage "volitional" meetings. As late as 1958, the *New Day* noted that a major distinction between Divine's meetings and conventional church's meetings was that Divine's tended to be "spontaneous," while the conventional church's tended to be planned.

In the 1940s, Divine's movement created not only churches but also orders. A substantial portion of the most committed followers became members of one of the movement's three orders: Rosebuds for the younger women, Lily-buds for older women, and Crusaders for men of all ages. Each order met, sang, and performed demonstrations separately. Each wore its own distinctive uniform, especially on ceremonial occasions. Each had its own creeds—including for the Rosebuds, who were sometimes called the nuns of the Divine movement, a promise to do only what Divine "would admire"; for the Lily-buds, a promise to "never argue, fuss, or fight"; for the Crusaders, a promise to live "daily lives of virtue."[5]

VOLUNTEER STAFF

Wherever Divine was, he was likely to have staff around him. Except for certain lawyers, they were volunteers, receiving no pay. Among them were such leading secretaries as the college-educated, competent white, John Lamb. Among them also were many other secretaries, all ardent followers, most of them white, nearly all females, said to vary over the years from as few as twelve to as many as twenty-five. Certain secretaries were assigned particular responsibilities, such as screening Divine's visitors, typing his enormous correspondence, recording his speeches and interviews verbatim, or caring for transportation or property records. Several secretaries normally accompanied Divine when he visited the Promised Land, some riding in separate cars, others riding with him in his car and working with him on the way; and then on arrival at a mission, if he stayed there any length of time, working with him in the office space provided at each site. All his secretaries were likely to be considerably educated. Speaking at a banquet at Krum Elbow, Divine explained that some of his staff had found their way to him after being dissatisfied with taking "all sorts of high occult courses in psychology and in metaphysics."

Among his secretaries with ties to Ulster County were the white Heavenly Rest, a buyer of Kingston Mansion, and the white Quiet Devotion who came from Los Angeles with John Hunt, lived at Stone Ridge, and for a time was a secretary to Faithful Mary until the latter broke with Divine. Another secretary was the dark-complexioned June S. Peace who had grown up at Krumville and New Paltz. Still another was the light-complexioned Dorothy Darling, who in the 1970s and 1980s, was an officer of Unity Mission Church when it became the owner of two Ulster County missions, Kingston Mansion and Greenkill Park.

Many professionals who were close to Divine—including not only lawyers and secretaries, but also photographers, architects, and editors—were white rather than black. Though some followers complained that Divine favored "a certain complexion," he denied any such bias, and most followers seemed to understand that it was especially the whites in the movement who were likely to have the educational qualifications necessary for professional positions. It was also understood that blacks did have the opportunity to rise in the movement, as exemplified by Divine himself, as well as by Arthur Madison, Priscilla Paul, Sara Washington, Faithful Mary, Charles Calloway, St. Mary Bloom, and leaders in many individual missions, like manager True Heart Love at Krumville, manager Lovely Sweet at Hope Farm, and farmer Moses Lord at Olive Bridge.

Of Divine's panel of lawyers, most were white civil libertarians, not fully committed as followers of Divine, and likely to be paid. Among them was Nathan N. Kranzler, of Newark, New Jersey, who was enough of a follower to be allowed to be one of the buyers of Divine Farm, in Saugerties. Kranzler admired Divine, he said, for his ability to remake "the scum of the earth" into "respectable men and women." Also among the lawyers was Kevie Frankel, who had his office in mid-town New York. He called Divine's teaching the "grandest since the world began," and during the long drawn-out Verinda Brown case, said he "always followed Father's advice." Also among the lawyers was the black Arthur A. Madison who had roots in Alabama, but had studied law at the University of Wisconsin. He maintained his own home and office in New York. But he donated his services to Divine and served as one of his most trusted advisers, at the same time that he sometimes struggled over the question of Divine's deity.[6]

22. CALLING DIVINE *GOD*

IN 1938, Divine explained that in order to bring out the divine nature within himself, he had tried to put away his human concerns. By "consecration," and "self-denial," he tried to put aside "all things that pertain to this life," such as money, knowledge, and flesh. He was trying to reach his "nothingness" as a man, he said, because "when man disappears," then "God will appear." Having been through this process, he believed he had become a "new creature," with Christ reigning within him, and he was leading others to do the same.

Already in the early 1930s, however, Divine allowed followers to call him God if they wished, even though he knew that allowing them to do so subjected him to ridicule. He "could very easily have refuted" such talk, he once explained, by claiming that "the same God" was in "all men," but seeming to be aware of his charismatic powers, he said he did not do it because people needed a model. They need to "have something to gaze upon," he explained. Without it, their spirits would be "dampened."

In the 1930s if his followers called him God, Divine often avoided calling himself so, especially not for any public record. In 1933 when a committee appointed by a judge was investigating him, Divine said at a committee hearing, "I teach that God has the right to manifest himself through any person or thing he may choose. If my followers, however, believe that I am God and in so doing they are led to reform their lives and experience joy and happiness, why should I prevent them from doing so?" In a hearing in 1935, when a presiding justice questioned him as to whether he taught that he was God, he answered, "I preach the gospel of Jesus, and that God dwells in every man." When the justice kept pressing him further, Divine said, "I don't have to say I am God, and I don't have to say I am not God." In 1937, while he was in Kingston, when a British reporter asked him by telephone, whether he was God, Divine answered, "to millions I am, and to many I am not." I am "as a person thinks in his heart."[1]

At the same time, Divine developed the theme that he was encouraging others to let God grow within them. In the early 1930s, he seemed to feel that he had almost brought both his light secretary John Lamb and his dark disciple Joseph Gabriel—a fiery, rhythmical preacher—to the point where they were ready to surpass him in developing the "God-head" nature within them. Divine explained that when they had become "greater" in "expression" and in "love than me," they won't "need me" any more. Then, he said, he would be ready to "detach myself" from them, and they could be independent. Speaking at Kingston in 1939, Divine said he wanted the Christ within everyone to "be brought to fruition" so that everyone attains "the characteristics of the Christ." Similarly, speaking at Olive Bridge in 1940, he said, if you develop the same love that God has, you "will take on the characteristics and the nature of your God." As late as 1952, he was still saying that not only does God live in all people, but all people could produce in themselves "the likeness of God."

Already in the 1930s, however, most of his followers were calling him God. Later, looking back, Divine emphasized that he had been slow to say he was God, explaining that "millions" regarded him as God before he was willing to admit that it was true. But in the 1930s, he sometimes claimed to be God, if indirectly, and gradually he seemed to become more open about it. In 1938, speaking in Stone Ridge, Divine called himself "Jesus." In 1942, speaking to his followers in Samsonville, he said "if the whole world would love me just as you say you do, I would bring peace on earth." In 1947 when a State University of Iowa professor advocated tolerating Divine's calling himself God, Divine responded fiercely,"The universe shall know I am God unadulterated." Speaking in Kingston in 1951, he said that his followers "find the abundance of the fulness" by "believing sincerely in my deity." In 1952, writing to a follower, he declared, "Just the fact that I have lifted thousands and thousands off the doles, and caused them to go to work and be self-supporting, independent and prosperous, is sufficient proof that I am God."[2]

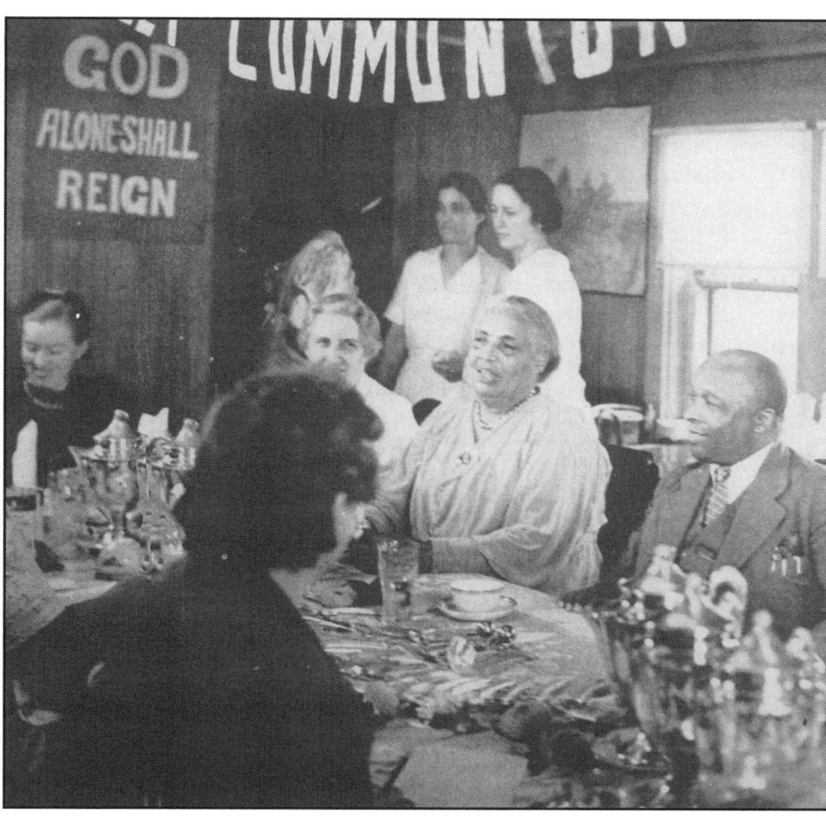

DIVINE AS GOD: According to the original caption for this photo, Divine, as pictured at a communion banquet at Hope Farm, was "fulfilling" the "prediction" that "God" will "set up a kingdom" in a "new dispensation." The first Mother Divine sits at Divine's right, in one of her last public appearances. (*New Day*, Ap. 17, 1941)

Even for some of those who wanted to follow Divine, however, doubts regarding his deity persisted. When he was speaking once at Kingston, a follower present asked, why, if he were God, would he have to ask someone such a question as, did you have a good trip? His answer was, for the same reason that he had earlier asked Adam, Where art thou? and had asked Cain, Where is thy brother Abel? Similarly, Son Peter, when he was running away from Hope Farm, asked himself, if Divine really were God, would he not know that I was running away, and stop me? Divine's loyal lawyer, the black Arthur A. Madison, said it took him ten years "to recognize Father Divine is God," and even then he seemed to see him differently from other followers. He was able eventually to call him God, Madison explained, because he saw that the good he taught was really "reflected in him."

When the young Baptist minister Leon Sullivan, a future civil rights activist, visited a Divine meeting, he said he found there, with light and dark people associating freely together, the "heaven" which he had "been talking about for years." Having seen the leader of this heaven "whom people say is God," he felt able to say, though he conceded "many people may be surprised" for him to say it, that "God is any spirit" or "being in the flesh" who "provides us with those things that give us life."

Ross Humble, a psychologist who traveled across the continent from Alaska to Key West lecturing on behalf of Divine, once told a Peace Mission audience that it was not necessary to call Divine God. "If anyone does not want to call him God, then call him what they like." But whatever they choose to call him, he is " beyond the concepts of the human mind."

For years, a Methodist minister, Clarence V. Howell, who had taught at New York's Union Theological Seminary, led students, teachers, and ministers to visit Divine functions. In answer to a reporter who asked him if he believed that Divine was the Creator of the Universe and the God that Christians are expecting to come to judge the world, Howell said no, he did not see Divine that way. But to the question, is Divine the personification of God, he replied. "God has no hands but your hands, no feet but your feet, no voice but your voice. When God speaks, he speaks with your voice and my voice. In-so-far as anyone of us reacts perfectly to the will of God, we become very God of very Gods. In that sense, I can call Father Divine God."

Many observers, however, ridiculed Divine for claiming he was God. McKelway and Liebling wrote in the *New Yorker* as early as 1936 that neither in his "early years" nor in his "later years" "has Father Divine ever hinted that he considers himself to be anything more than God." Later the theologian Georgia Harkness, writing in the *Christian Century,* declared that Divine, in claiming he was God, was either "self-deceived" or "an extraordinarily clever showman," and she was inclined to believe he was the latter. In fact, many outsiders, regarding it as outrageous to call Divine God, saw the belief that he was God so deeply enmeshed in the daily life of his communities, that, even though they might regard some features of those communities as intensely appealing, they found it impossible to regard those communities as models that should be copied.[3]

WHAT IF?
What if Divine, instead of calling himself God, had continued to say that he was working to develop his divine nature, and everyone else could do the same?
Then would he have had fewer followers? or more?

23. A JEW REFLECTS

FATHER DIVINE often identified Christianity as an offspring of Judaism, and coupled the two religions together almost as if they were one. He sometimes said he preached Judaism as much as Christianity.

Among his many followers who were raised as Jews was Deborah Newmind. She said that while she was growing up as an Orthodox Jew, from a "line of rabbis," it was "pounded" into her that to "hold up" her "tradition," she should only associate with "certain kinds of people." But she searched for a satisfying religious experience of her own. She tried Unity, Yoga, and Bahai. It was only some years after she had graduated from college and was living in Seattle in 1929 that she first heard of Father Divine. She did so, she recalled, when she heard "metaphysical" lecturers tell about a visit they had made to Divine in Sayville, Long Island. Later when she visited Divine meetings in Oakland, California, she was impressed to hear people testify that Divine had healed them even though he was not present with them in person. She wanted to visit Divine at once, but for several years "obligations" prevented her from doing so. By 1935, however, when she had already become a follower of Divine, she traveled to New York, and for the first time saw Divine.

By 1938, Newmind had settled in the Divine community of Hope Farm, in West Saugerties, Ulster County. While she was living there, Divine publicly protested the treatment of Jews in Germany, and invited them to move to his American communities, as in Ulster County. Newmind grieved that they did not come. They did not come, she later explained, because New York's "yellow" newspapers, by telling "lies" about Divine, scared them off. If they had come, she maintained, "thousands" of them could have settled on Divine's ample Ulster County estates, making them a "haven of refuge," safe from being "slaughtered" by Hitler.[1]

It was while Newmind was living at Hope Farm that she wrote the following open letter to Father Divine, explaining her view on calling him God:

Hope Farm, The Promised Land
June 12, 1938

Peace!
Dear Father:

Strangers, visitors, coming in our midst, ask, "Why do they call him God?" and they call us fanatics for so doing.

Show me another on the face of the earth who has thrown open the doors of his home, saying, "Come all ye that labor and are heavy laden, and I will give you rest," and has let them come—of every nationality, race, creed and color; and fed them and clothed them and healed them and blessed them—free—asking nothing, giving all—and I will call him "God" too.

Show me another one on the face of the earth who can change underworld characters, committers of all sorts of vices and crimes, into law-abiding citizens over night; taking out of them all desire for evil; turning their hearts and minds unto righteousness—and I will call him "God" too.

Show me another one on the face of the earth who could cause his followers to willingly pay back all debts of many years standing, and return stolen goods, and openly confess their sins—and I will call him "God" too.

Show me another one on the face of the earth who can stand before the multitudes, and without any preparation whatever—without book, Bible or reference of any kind, unfold to a hungry world, the mysteries of the life more abundant; mete out justice; and teach victory over sin and sickness, death and the grave—and I will call him "God" too.

Show me another one on the face of the earth who, in a world filled with wars and rumors of wars, is causing his followers to open Peace Missions, set up banquet tables, break down the walls of segregation among the children of men, and in an atmosphere of Godliness and cleanliness, with songs and praises and joy, feed the multitudes good meals for 10 and 15 cents (and no price at all if they cannot pay), and make the Kingdom of Heaven on earth an actual, practical reality—and I will call him "God" too.

Show me another one on the face of the earth who is actually doing what all the socialists and communists and idealists and utopians have talked and dreamed of doing, but have never had the wisdom nor the understanding of how it actually could be done.

You, Father Divine, are the Christ, the Messiah, "the Lamb of God that taketh away the sins of the world." Now is the time of the end, the end of mortality, and the dawn of the millennium! I thank you Father. It is wonderful!

Deborah Newmind[2]

By 1944, after Divine had moved to Philadelphia, Newmind had followed him there. She lived in Divine mission housing, and worked for the federal government as a clerk.

DEBORAH NEWMIND (second from left), singing in a Peace Mission procession.
(From an old video, Woodmont)

As that year's Presidential election approached, voter registration officials notified her that they were canceling her registration because she had given her name as Deborah Newmind rather than giving her birth name. Her response was vigorous. She told officials that in fact Deborah Newmind was her correct name. She said it was the name on her driver's license. It was the name by which she paid her taxes and bought Liberty bonds. It was the name by which she had taken a federal civil service test, and passed it, and was now employed in civil service. While she admitted it was not the name she had been given at her birth, she insisted that as a follower of

Father Divine, she had been "born again," so that a new name was appropriate for her.

The next year, when she was still in her civil service position and her supervisor presented her holiday gifts, she returned them, explaining that it was against her religious beliefs to accepts gifts. When Divine publicly praised her for returning the gifts, he admitted that this practice invited many outsiders to regard Divine followers as "peculiar people." But that did not seem to bother Newmind. In that same year, speaking in one of the Divine churches in Philadelphia, she said that it was "wonderful"to be aware of "the nothingness of matter," "the nothingness of myself," and the "allness of God."

Newmind continued to work as a federal government clerk. She worked steadily, year after year, without ever taking sick leave. In the 1950s, she was still working at the same position, still living in the Philadelphia area, still speaking and writing for Divine. She was still saying, as she had many times before, that for Jews, Divine was the Messiah, and for Christians, he was Christ come again.[3]

24. HEALING

MANY PEOPLE became followers of Divine through believing that he had healed them. They believed Divine had healed them from injury or illness. Or they believed he had healed them from drinking, smoking, abusing drugs, or other obsessions. Or they believed he had healed them from being criminals.

Divine said that faith healing can work anywhere, in any context. It can work at home, at a Peace Mission, or at a shrine. It works, Divine said, not because it is administered by any particular person, or in any particular ritual, or at any particular location, but because of a person's faith.

Speaking in Ulster County, Divine often emphasized healing. At Greenkill Park, Divine told his followers, God has "given you victory over sickness." At New Paltz, Divine declared that none of his followers who lives right and stays "in the vibrations" should even "have an ache." At Milton, he promised everyone, "if you love God" and "keep his commandments," "you will be delivered" from any "undesirable" condition "forever."

A well-known Ulster County resident who claimed Divine had healed him was Howland Spencer, from whom Divine followers had bought their Krum Elbow estate. Some time after Spencer had sold the estate but was still living there, and had been laid up with his toes crippled by gout, Divine telephoned him at five o'clock in the morning. Spencer jumped out of bed, ran downstairs to answer the telephone, and when Divine asked him how his toes were, Spencer suddenly realized that they seemed normal.

A visitor whom Divine counseled in faith healing was Minnie Shey who came from Roxbury, Massachusetts, to see him in his office at Milton. Her knees had troubled her for about four years, she told Divine. Her doctors called it neuritis, Shey explained. She told Divine that if he was not God, at least she believed that God was "working through him," so she hoped he might be able help. Divine did not scold her for seeming to doubt that he was God, nor did he scold her for having sought medical help. But he told her that sickness was caused by "the condition of the mind," and that can be changed, he said, "according to your faith." When the woman explained that she felt Christ had left her, Divine advised her to "get back" in "fellowship with your God." Saying it another way, he used one of his favorite words, "vibration": if "your vibration drops low," he said, you may "give in" to poor health. But "stay in the vibrations of thanksgiving and praise, and you will find yourself restored."[1]

When should followers of Divine seek medical care and when should they seek faith healing? This was a sensitive question for Divine's followers. Was it clear what Divine advocated on this question? Were his followers consistent in their practice in regard to it?

While there was a long-term pattern of followers being reluctant to seek medical care, Divine's policy in regard to it could seem fuzzy. The Peace Mission's platform, as adopted in 1936, noted that, according to New York State law, if a child was seriously ill, the child's parents were required to call a physician. Divine seemed to accept this law, and applied it also to adults, saying, in a statement which was included in the platform, that if his spirit could not heal a sick person, a physician should be called. But he added an additional requirement, also included in the platform, which raised uncertainty: if physicians were called in, they "must guarantee a cure." This requirement seemed so impossible that it could be interpreted as prohibiting followers from seeking medical help

When Divine followers were admitted to Kingston hospitals, according to a 1937 newspaper report, they were sometimes admitted under assumed names, suggesting that Divine followers were reluctant to acknowledge that any of them received medical care. At Hope Farm, one of the workers who helped care for its children declared in 1940 that the children did not receive medical care because "medical attention is not necessary for them." At about this same time, the *New Day* was following the practice of accepting medical service advertisements, but explaining to its readers that the services were intended only for those who were "not yet true followers of Father Divine." In the 1940s, when a group of followers living at Krum Elbow were working outside of the mission at a nearby farm, standing on ladders as they picked apples, one of the group fell, hitting his head. His employer arranged to send him to Vassar Hospital in Poughkeepsie. When his Divine associates heard where he was, according to one of his farm associates, they explained they did not believe in hospitals, and arranged to remove him. In regard to eye care, in 1949 Divine himself even went so far as to discourage wearing glasses. When a follower wore glasses to read aloud at meetings, and according to Divine, did so "emotionally," attracting attention, Divine asked him to stop wearing glasses because, he said, reading with glasses was "stressing imperfection."[2]

Despite followers often avoiding medical care, and often being led by Divine to do so, confusion about when it might be appropriate to seek it surfaced in 1937 when a long-time white follower named Crystal Star, who had been living in New York near Divine's headquarters, visited the Stone Ridge mission. He arrived while a meal was in progress, and was invited to speak, as visitors regularly were. He told the gathering, which included Divine, that he had recently come to Ulster County, with his wife Golden Star, their several children, and others, looking for a farm to buy. They wanted to establish a new cooperative farm, he said, which they would like to place under Divine's jurisdiction.

As Star spoke, another follower told Father Divine that Star and his wife were wanted by New York City authorities. They were wanted because when a child of theirs, thirteen years old, was ill with tuberculosis, they had not provided her with medical care until too late.

Divine, apparently ignoring Star's invitation to take supervision over his proposed new farm, responded to Star that if authorities had a warrant for his arrest, he should surrender. In response, Star explained that he and his family had left the city several days before, early one morning, when the death of his child under questionable circumstances had already become known, but he had left the city to flee reporters, he said, not to flee the authorities. He heard only later that the authorities were looking for him. "All I can say is, in great humility, if I had had any idea that anything like that was going to occur, I don't believe we would have left."

While their child was still living, the Star parents had been investigated by a child protective society for not providing her adequate medical care. Only then did they send her to Harlem Hospital. She died at the hospital.

Divine scolded Star now, at the banquet, for not having given his child adequate medical care. "I have always said," he told Star, that "if for any cause my spirit cannot or does not reach the condition of the patient immediately, they should have a physician, and you all know that!"

Star replied that he had " never read" any such message."For some reason I never saw it." But he had "no idea of going against your wishes."

Divine seemed angry with Star. Divine knew that Star was an educated man—he was a graduate of Purdue University's School of Agriculture, and had been a teacher. Divine also knew that Star had previously been a believer in metaphysical theories which were more absolute in opposing medical care than Divine was. Divine publically scolded Star at the banquet: "You have been following me all this time, and you, an intelligent man, and especially a teacher and a reader! ...You should be one to know definitely, in preference to others, what I have said in all of my messages." Divine charged Star with holding onto his former metaphysical belief against securing medical help, and attributing that belief unjustly to Divine.

Divine asked Star to find out definitely whether there was any warrant against him, and if so, to surrender, and not be a "fugitive from justice." Divine also asked him to declare that it was not on Divine's account that he and his wife had failed to provide appropriate medical care, but that they had "violated my teaching" and also had "violated the law."

Star and his wife did surrender to authorities. They were taken to court on the charge of not providing appropriate medical care for their child. They pleaded not guilty. They testified they had given the child medical care, as by taking her to Harlem Hospital, even though it was too late. The charges were dismissed.

While no record is available that Father Divine ever took jurisdiction over any cooperative farm in Ulster County such as Crystal Star said he was helping to organize, five years after the Stars were taken to court for neglecting their daughter's care, in 1942, the wife, Golden Star, was still living in Harlem, and still identifying herself as a follower of Father Divine. At that time, under the influence of Divine's teachings, she paid $12 to Harlem Hospital for the four days in the spring of 1937, when her daughter Morning Star was treated there, until she died.

Five years still later in 1947, Golden Star was still living in a Divine facility, this time in the Bronx. By this time, ironically, she was a nurse, and Divine was encouraging her to work as a nurse. The Divine movement clearly approved of followers becoming nurses even if they were the kind of nurses who provided medical care. But in approving his followers becoming nurses, what Divine was approving was not medical care in general: rather he was approving of his followers providing medical care to those who were not themselves true followers.[3]

25. DIVINE'S TWO MARRIAGES

THE FIRST MOTHER DIVINE, called Peninnah, came to know Divine in the South, when Divine healed her, she believed, of debilitating rheumatism. She was an Afro-American like Divine, but taller and older. Being compassionate and having a stately presence, she became an effective supporter for him. She testified to his healing powers, assisted him in serving banquets, sang songs in his praise, and supervised work projects for him.

According to Divine, his marriage to her was always "without physical cohabitation." This was in keeping with his long-term teaching that not even husbands and wives should have sexual relations with each other. Faithful Mary, as critical of Divine's claims as she became, declared that Father and Mother Divine followed this teaching.

After Divine had established missions in Ulster County, Mother Divine lived there much of the time. Once when she was there, she told a reporter, "I'd rather live here than in New York." Divine usually came up to Ulster County once a week, she said, so she could hope to see him often.

In 1935, soon after Divine had created a mission in New Paltz, Mother Divine stayed there, helping to put it in order. A little later she seemed to be living at the Stone Ridge Farm, as if running it. By the fall of 1936 she was living in High Falls, in a residence behind Faithful Mary's hotel building, and soon she was operating a dressmaking shop nearby, across Main Street from the hotel.

On several occasions in 1936 and 1937, however, Mother Divine was taken to Benedictine Hospital, in Kingston. On at least one such occasion, it was Faithful Mary, according to her claim, who arranged to send Mother Divine there. Father Divine, who seemed to be trying to keep her illness secret, seemed reluctant to let her go there unless she registered under an assumed name.[1]

According to Divine, anyone who truly followed his teachings, including Mother Divine, would never die. While sometimes he seemed to mean only that his followers would never die spiritually, often he seemed to mean literally that they would never die in their bodily form. Speaking to his followers at Milton, Divine said, you can "overcome death." You can "transcend" it "mentally and spiritually." Speaking at Kingston, Divine said that all who died did so because they lived "selfishly." At a banquet at Greenkill Park, someone sang a song which Divine commended:

> We have heaven right here in Greenkill.
> Take your eyes out of the sky.
> We have heaven right here in Greenkill,
> Live the life and you won't have to die!

A group of High Falls followers once put a notice in the *New Day* thanking Divine for being here on earth "to save our bodies alive," as if they believed doing so was a major purpose of his. In the light of such teachings, when Mother Divine became hospitalized and seemed about to die, Divine seemed afraid that his followers, if they knew, might lose faith in him.

In 1937, when Mother Divine was hospitalized for months, according to Faithful Mary, Divine rarely visited her. According to the *Ulster County Press*, Divine "deserted" her. Faithful Mary, however, felt close to Mother Divine, and for some time, according to the New York *Post*, visited her "almost daily." Though Mother Divine was in a charity ward, Faithful Mary was said to have paid her hospital bills.

Despite attempts to hide Mother Divine's identity while she was in the hospital, the hospital nurses soon learned that their patient was related to Father Divine, and reporters, persistently poking into Divine's affairs as they often did, eventually discovered who she was. After this discovery, a reporter, visiting her in her hospital room, described her as white haired, having "enormous, gentle eyes and a soft voice," but being in pain. While the hospital nurses said she was dying of heart and kidney failure, Mother Divine, loyal to her husband as she was, would not acknowledge that she was in danger of death. In keeping with Divine's teaching, she struggled to believe that with God, she would overcome her illness.

She told the reporter that she was fond of living in Ulster County. "This is the Promised Land of the Bible, here in Ulster County," she said. While she hoped to go back to her "farm in the hills," it was Divine, she explained, who would decide where she would live. [2]

By early 1938, Mother Divine had recovered. In April, 1938, she took part in a youth meeting in High Falls, urging youth to be unselfish. In September, 1938, she attended a banquet at the Kingston Mansion, on Chapel Street, at which she thanked Father "for the lovely little home he had given her," evidently meaning the "cottage" she was then occupying in High Falls.

In 1940, when she was one of the followers who bought an estate in Tarrytown, she was listed as having the same Harlem residence as Divine, 1887 Madison Avenue, New York. In the summer of 1941, however, she was again staying in High Falls in her "cottage" near her dress shop, and was showing both of them to visitors. In the summer of 1942, she attended a banquet in New York with Divine, and sang a song.

By 1943 she had disappeared. Apparently in the latter half of 1942 or in 1943 she died, on a date and at a location which Divine and his staff did not disclose. They seemed reluctant to talk about her death. It was their custom to explain the death of followers as having occurred because they did not sufficiently follow Divine, but they would scarcely wish to say that about Mother Divine.[3]

In 1946, about three years after Mother Peninnah Divine's death, Divine married his second wife, a young white Canadian, Edna Rose Ritchings, who was only 21 years old. She had grown up in Vancouver, the daughter of a florist. Becoming part of Divine's movement while still living there, she adopted the name Sweet Angel, moved to Philadelphia, and became a Divine secretary. When they decided to marry, she and Divine tried

THE SECOND MOTHER DIVINE: Divine's marriage to this gracious young Canadian raised questions of interpretation. (Laura Brock Miller)

to secure a marriage license in Pennsylvania or Maryland, but found that interracial marriages were forbidden there, as they were in most states. When they tried in Washington, D. C., however, they succeeded in securing a license. They were legally married there by a Baptist minister, on April 29, 1946. Apparently uneasy about their marriage, however, they did not make it known for several months.

Once Divine was willing to talk about his remarriage, he claimed that the second Mother Divine, Mother Sweet Angel Divine, always occupied a bedroom separate from his. Assigned to her was a "secretary, Peaceful Love, who stayed constantly with her, to assure that her marriage was without physical co-habitation. According to one of Divine's secretaries, the second Mother Divine lived a complete "life of denial," with her life kept constantly public, as if she were a fish in a fish bowl.

Even though this remarriage was understood not to be a physical union, some Divine followers were upset by it. As Attorney Arthur Madison, Divine's long-term ally, explained later, this marriage "almost knocked a lot of us 'coo-coo.'" Madison refused to talk against Divine because of it, he recalled, but "we just did not understand." Some followers were uneasy that the new wife was so young compared to Divine. Others were uneasy that she was white. Still others were upset that Divine would remarry when he discouraged his followers from marrying at all. While Divine himself declared that for anyone who condemned his marriage "retribution is assured," others predicted that Divine's remarriage was so disturbing that it would destroy his movement.

Divine and his second wife, defending their marriage, interpreted it in various ways. Interpreting it in one way, only six months after the marriage, Divine, employed the concept of reincarnation. He wrote that the former Mother Divine "had repeatedly asked me" for a new youthful body, "a Rosebud's body" and he added, paraphrasing First Corinthians 15: 38, "I have given her a body as it pleased me," the body of the Second Mother Divine.

Before his remarriage, had Divine taught that

even if his followers died, they could be reincarnated in other persons? While writers have differed on this question, anthropologist Arthur H. Fauset, writing in 1944, declared that Divine already taught reincarnation. Divine taught that "a true follower" of his "will never die," Fauset wrote, but if a follower does die—presumably he would be a follower of less than complete devotion—his "spirit enters another body and continues thus to live."[4]

MEEKNESS LOVE, WHO WAS ONCE IN CHARGE OF A DIVINE RESIDENCE IN HIGH FALLS, came to regard the Divine's conception of reincarnation as not rigid doctrine, but generous compassion. (Taylor Street Studio)

In his formative years, Divine had been influenced by New Thought-related movements such as Theosophy and the Unity School of Christianity which were aware of reincarnation. Divine himself frequently used the term reincarnation. He sometimes seemed to use it loosely, as when speaking in Kingston in 1937, he said that the spirit of Jesus "has been reincarnated" in the "hearts and lives of millions." He later seemed to use it somewhat more literally, as when speaking to followers at Hope Farm in 1941, he said, what God has declared must be fulfilled, "if not in you, it will in others in whom you will be reincarnated." In a 1942 interview, he explained that if persons have not been "completely purged of all mortality," then their spirits will be "incarnated" in other bodies, giving them an opportunity to move on to a "more perfect state of being." If Divine seldom seemed to detail what he meant by reincarnation, certainly the concept floated around him, available for him to pluck as needed, as eventually it seemed to be needed in the case of Mother Divine.

After Divine claimed that the first mother Divine was reincarnated in the second one, many followers seemed to accept this interpretation, and reincarnation seemed to become a fixed principle for Divine. For him reincarnation became a principle applicable not only to the Mothers Divine, but to his followers in general. When in 1952 a visiting pastor asked if someone now in this room with us died, would he "be reincarnated in another body?" Divine said, yes, "God would give it a body as it pleases him." However, Divine recognized limits to the concept of reincarnation: when a follower claimed to be the reincarnation of a Biblical figure, Divine rejected this idea, finding it disturbing that anyone could recognize himself or herself as a reincarnation of someone else—except of course for the second Mother Divine.[5]

Attorney Arthur Madison did not warm to the idea that the second Mother Divine was the reincarnation of the first one. However, after a struggle, Madison came to accept the remarriage as appropriate anyway because it was both interracial and international, and thus was in line with Divine's teaching. Divine himself, besides interpreting his remarriage as exemplifying reincarnation, also interpeted it as interracial and international, citing the example of Moses marrying an Ethiopian. Henri Stephen and Frederic N. Crabb, in an advertisement for their Harlem and Ulster County-based trucking service, congratulated Mother and Father Divine for showing in their marriage, "the practicality of real true inter-raciality and brotherhood." However, Divine seemed to fear that any such interpretation could lead to his followers feeling free to marry if they did so interracially or internationally, when marrying in any manner was contrary to his teaching—except, of course, for Father and Mother Divine themselves. When a close associate of Divine, Millard J. Bloomer, wrote Divine that his remarriage provided an example of interracial and international "unity" for "other open-minded children to follow," Divine reprimanded Bloomer. His marriage, Divine countered, was not an example for mortals to follow, so no mortals "had better try it."

It was not the interpretation of the marriage as interracial and international that Father and Mother Divine encouraged the most. It was also not the interpretation of it as having been enabled by reincarnation that they encouraged the most. Rather it was the marriage's virginity. As Mother Divine said within a few months of the marriage, the marriage was a "sample and example of the virginity of Mary" for everyone. Over the years it came to be the custom to celebrate the marriage as an example of virginity, and to combine it with the idea that the marriage, in accord with Ephesians 5: 32, was the marriage of Christ to his church.

In 1951, when Father and Mother Divine celebrated their fifth wedding anniversary in a big occasion at Krum Elbow, with "countless thousands" present, Divine, speaking there, did not mention that his remarriage was made possible by reincarnation. He mentioned but did not emphasize that his remarriage was international and interracial. What he emphasized then, and what he and his followers continued to emphasize long afterwards, was that his bride was and continued to be a "spotless virgin," and that his marriage represented the "marriage of Christ to his church."[6]

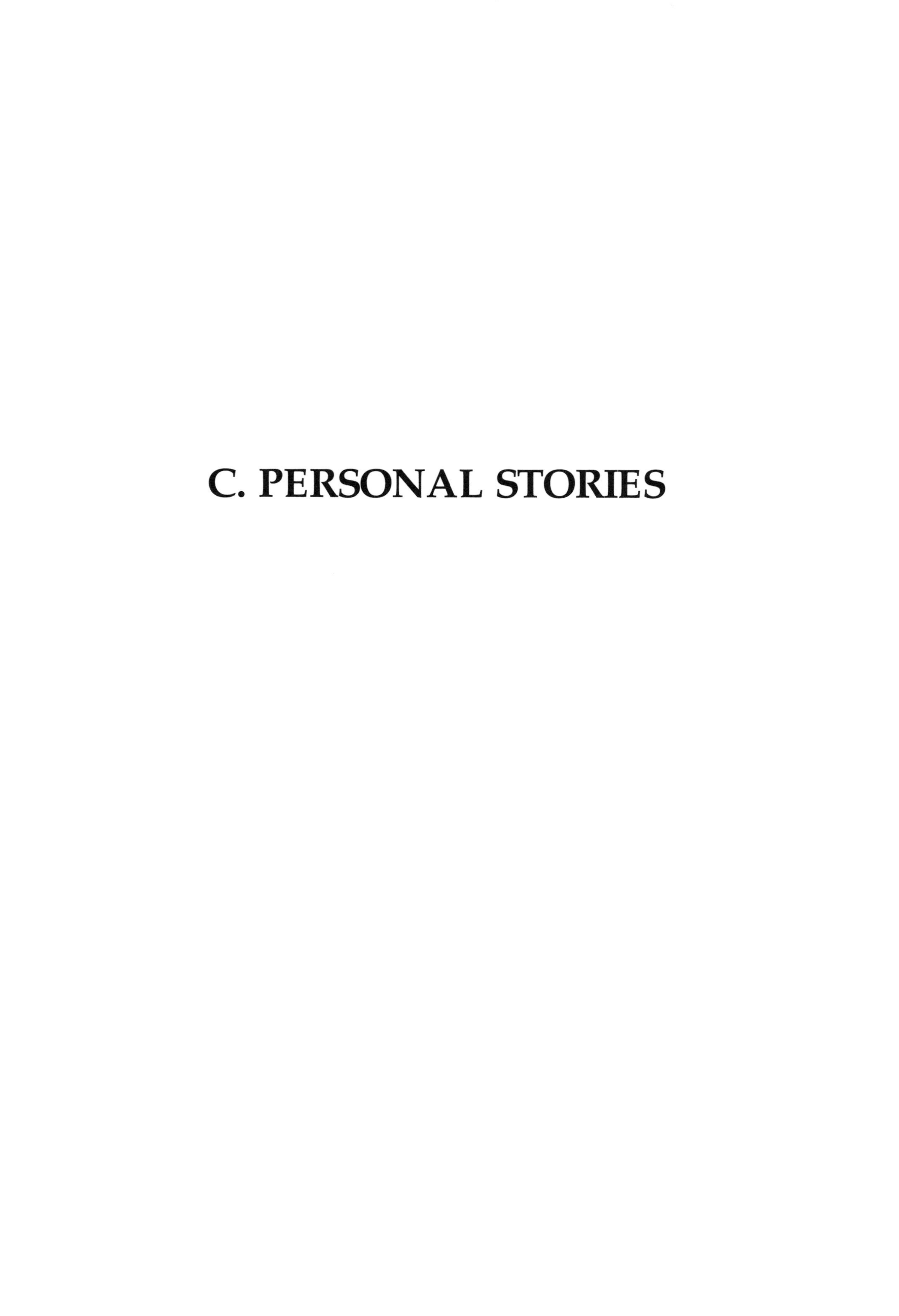

C. PERSONAL STORIES

26. FAITHFUL MARY: FROM GUTTER TO THRONE AND BACK

AT ONE TIME, she was a notorious drunk and prostitute. Reformed, she learned to be active in Divine's Peace Mission movement. In time, she took on heavy responsibility. She did it joyously, and rose to become a star.

By her own account, Faithful Mary was born in rural Georgia, one of sixteen children of a black father who was a Baptist minister on Sunday and a drunk the rest of the week. She ran away from home at the age of fourteen, and sometimes worked in cotton fields. After World War I, she joined the surge of Southern blacks migrating north, herself settling in Newark, New Jersey. There for some time she worked as a domestic or as a Pennsylvania Railroad matron, but circulated in a "fast crowd." Then, after having shed three husbands, she became a confirmed drunkard and prostitute, well known to the Newark police.

One morning in 1932, according to her recollection, she presented herself at a Divine mission in Newark, sick, "ragged, dirty and with no stockings on." Welcoming her, Divine followers escorted her to a banquet where "long tables" were "covered with food." Later, when Father Divine, "a little bald-head Negro," arrived, there was "a great commotion" to greet him, she recalled. But Divine noticed her. He drew her into his movement. When she first listened to his "beautiful words," she considered them the "manifestation" of "power within." It seemed to her, as she afterward recalled, that if God could reveal himself in one son, Jesus, he could do so also in other sons, as in Divine. "With God all things are possible," she explained. Soon she felt he was healing her. He was healing her from tuberculosis, from drink, from degradation. In accord with the movement's custom, she abandoned the name her family had given her, and adopted the new religious name of Faithful Mary.[1]

With the support of the Peace Mission movement, Faithful Mary developed her talents, and soon felt able to lead in founding a new Peace Mission extension. "I thought at first that Divine would finance me to do so," she recalled, "but I was wrong, as each person must find a way of financing his or her own extension. I succeeded in getting the money and I started an extension. Once you had an extension the followers came to room with you and eat with you. From the profits of my first venture I was able to acquire several more extensions over in Newark, and I made such rapid progress that Divine was very pleased."

By 1935, with Divine's encouragement, Faithful Mary had taken over an old Turkish Bath in Harlem on West 126th Street, and turned it into yet another extension. Continuing to enlist the contributions necessary to make her establishments prosperous, in 1936 she leased an imposing building on West 123rd Street, which had been a branch of the Poughkeepsie-based Eastman Business College, and made it into her Harlem "headquarters." By about this time, she was said to be directing over a dozen businesses for the Divine movement, including two dress factories—one in Newark, another in Harlem.

Many of her enterprises operated in space she leased or encouraged other Divine followers to lease for her. On August 3, 1936, however, she bought a hotel building in Ulster County, in the center of the village of High Falls. It was on the north side of Main Street, between Third and Fourth Streets. Intending to make it into both a hotel and grocery, she bought it in her name alone, as three other Peace Mision buyers had already done in Ulster County: Budds at the New Paltz Farm, Bloom at the Cherry Hill Farm, and Augustus at the Stone Ridge Mansion. But none of these other three was known to be in sole control of any additional Divine movement property, while Faithful Mary was.

Whether in Newark, or New York, or High Falls, Faithful Mary seemed to be not only a practical manager but also a warm friend to everyone, including the unfortunate, with whom, as a result of her own past, she easily identified. When she participated in the usual praise services, though grown heavy in her middle age, she radiated joy and danced gracefully. Comfortable with herself as she was, success seemed to come to her easily. All her extensions, she recalled, "were packed with followers" and were "remunerative." At banquets she was often seated beside Divine. She was provided with secretaries. She was provided with a chauffeur and a car, sometimes a new Ford V-8, sometimes a Rolls Royce, enabling her to travel easily among the various Divine enterprises she managed. For many of Divine's followers, she became an outstanding example of Divine's ability to lift a wreck, particularly a black wreck, from degradation to honor.[2]

While Faithful Mary was riding high in the Peace Mission, however, she began to question it, suspecting it of not being all that it pretended to be. Divine, seeing her becoming uneasy with him, seemed to feel threatened by her. He came to feel she controlled too much property in her own name. As she recalled later, they began to quarrel.

At about this time, a follower from Ohio, William Gottlieb, offered to donate $10,000 directly to Divine. When Divine, following his custom, declined the offer, Gottlieb, who had lived in a New York City extension managed by Faithful Mary, offered the money instead to her, for her use in Ulster County. Early in April, 1937, she accepted it, and was about to go with Gottlieb to High Falls to purchase a large garage and accompanying residence, and do so in her own name, when Divine heard of her intention. He insisted she drop her plan, and surrender the money, so that, according to Divine, the property would be bought not in her name alone, but in the names of a number of followers. While she insisted she was acting only for the cause, she did drop her plan, but only under protest, and Divine was furious with her. He threatened to demote her by sending her to the Promised Land to work in a kitchen.

Later that same month, on April 19, in New York, an official process server, trying to hand Father Divine a summons, was violently attacked by several persons including, according to one witness, Divine himself. Divine was charged with assault, and then, to avoid being summoned, according to the press, he went into hiding, seeming to flout his own teaching that everyone should cooperate with the law. The charges were eventu-

Above: **WHEN ULSTER COUNTY'S DISTRICT ATTORNEY CLEON B. MURRAY CALLED FOR A GRAND JURY INVESTIGATION OF DIVINE, he did so especially in response to Faithful Mary's charges against him.** (*Ulster County Press*, May 7, 1937)

Facing page:

Top left: **FAITHFUL MARY, AT HER HOTEL IN HIGH FALLS, ENUMERATING CHARGES AGAINST DIVINE TO A STATE TROOPER. A few hours later she vacated her hotel.** (*Ulster County Press*, Ap. 30, 1937)

Right: **FATHER DIVINE (CENTER) AS HE ARRIVED IN KINGSTON FOR THE GRAND JURY INVESTIGATION INTO HIS AFFAIRS. Towering in the center background was his chauffeur who, according to the Press, had been threatening news cameramen, until Divine stopped his doing so.** (*Ulster County Press*, May 7, 1937)

Bottom: **A CROWD GATHERED AT THE ULSTER COUNTY COURT HOUSE, Kingston, as a Grand Jury investigation of Divine began inside.** (*Ulster County Press*, May 7, 1937)

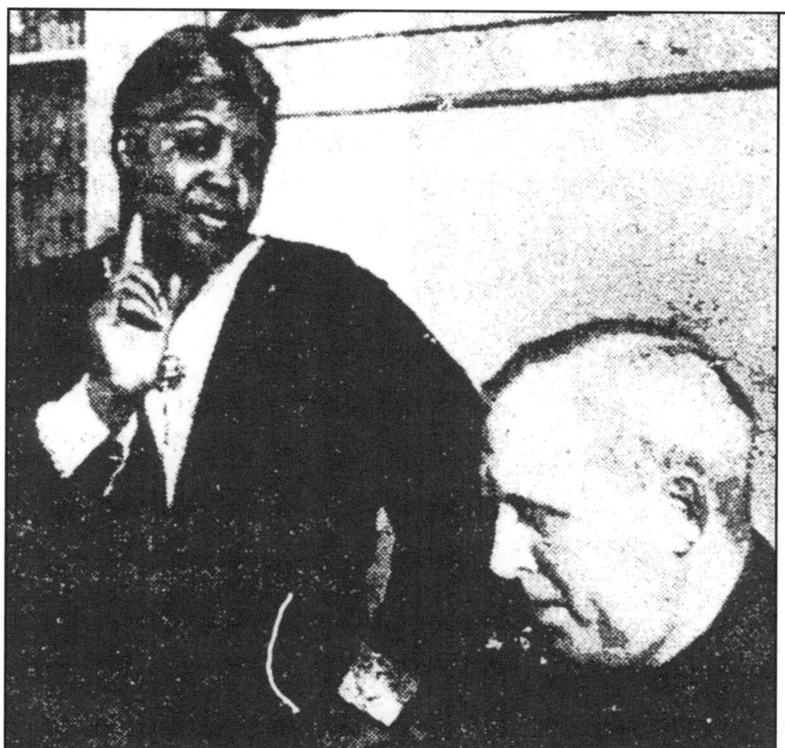

ally dropped, but while they were still pending, the police conducted a widespread search for Divine—at one point, twenty-five officers were searching for him in Ulster County alone. Meantime, the police were also looking for Divine's conspicuous wealthy follower, John Hunt, for having seduced an under-age girl.

Just when the conjunction of these two blows seemed to suggest that Divine's kingdom might topple, Faithful Mary seized the opportunity to denounce Divine and start a new Christian mission of her own. She intended that her new movement, which she called Universal Light, instead of recognizing Father Divine as God, would recognize God as present in everyone. On April 22, she went up to High Falls, and tried to take control of various Divine movement extensions there, hoping to make them, along with the hotel she operated there, into a center for her new movement. Unfortunately for the now-unfaithful Mary, most Divine followers in High Falls, continuing to be loyal to Divine, resisted her. Some became contentious, and state troopers were called in to preserve order.[3]

When the Hearst newspapers, intent on discrediting Divine, heard that Faithful Mary was breaking with him, they sent reporters to follow her to High Falls. According to Faithful Mary afterwards, they kept telling her that they wanted derogatory stories about Divine. When they tried to photograph her and related High Falls scenes, some of Divine's followers became angry, and tried "to smash the cameras," but, as Divine explained afterwards, "we suppressed" the anger. At about this time, Divine, feeling betrayed, found it difficult to prevent himself from sliding into "violence" against Faithful Mary, but he managed to bring himself, he said, "into subjection to righteousness." While he made it clear that he would not personally harm Faithful Mary, he admitted that his "spirit" might do so. In fact, he put a "curse" on Faithful Mary, he said, and also on anybody who "even sympathizes with her."

At about the same time, Hearst reporters were assuring Faithful Mary that while she would lose her usual livelihood from Divine, they would lodge her in first class hotels, and supply her with money besides. According to Faithful Mary's account later, the reporters, to get her to talk more freely, plied her with drink, which she had been avoiding. They got her drunk, she said, and she "went plumb crazy."

The reporters put her up in hotels—first in Kingston, then in Poughkeepsie, later in New York. They kept her four or five weeks, she said, all the time trying to get information out of her that would discredit Divine. They asked her to sign statements charging Divine with scandalous acts, including sexual escapades, and she did sign some of them, though whether she was sober enough to know what she was doing was a question.

On April 28, the Ulster County district attorney, Cleon B. Murray, who had been looking for an opportunity to investigate Father Divine's activities in Ulster County, decided, with a flourish of publicity, that the time had come. The first persons he summoned to testify before a grand jury were Faithful Mary and her young chauffeur, John Victory. According to Faithful Mary afterwards, reporters supplied her with alcohol before she testified to make sure she would talk freely. They especially wanted her to make statements about Divine having sex with girls of around 14 or 15. She did not know anything about that, she recalled later, but they said she had already signed statements that she did.

During the investigation it became known that Faithful Mary did not any longer own the High Falls hotel which she claimed was hers—this was a revelation that helped to undermine her credibility. In fact, she had sold her hotel several months previously, in January, 1937. She had sold it to a Newark, N. J., corporation, headed by Nathan Kranzler, an apparent follower of Divine who often served as Divine's lawyer, who let her continue to manage the property as if it were still hers. Undermining her credibility still more, however, was the dearth of other witnesses willing to appear before the grand jury to substantiate her charges. After several months, when the press was scarcely any longer paying attention, the grand jury felt unable to produce an indictment of Divine, and quietly abandoned its investigation.

Meanwhile, although Divine had no legal control over Faithful Mary's hotel in High Falls, he ordered Faithful Mary out of the building. For a few days she wavered as to what to do, but finally, convinced that she was not getting enough support in High Falls, she decided to move out. On May 24, 1937, the hotel's owner, lawyer Kranzler's corporation, sold the building to Sonia Zwick, whose family continued to operate it as a hotel, without any connection to Divine.[4]

Faithful Mary persisted in her revolt, however, still attempting to set up her own movement. In July, she returned to High Falls, where she visited the new owner of what had been her own hotel, and said that she liked High Falls, and would like to buy other property there.

By about this time, Faithful Mary was writing a book, with the aid of a ghost writer, detailing her charges against Divine, charges which the grand jury's failure to indict Divine was rendering questionable. Published by August, 1937, with the help of the *Amsterdam News*, a Harlem newspaper critical of Divine, the book was entitled *God: He's Just a Natural Man*. In this book, Faithful Mary claimed that her work with Divine's followers in the Peace Mission movement "was a real pleasure, and it was with regret that I withdrew my affiliation." But she charged that Divine, having "reached heights beyond his expectations," had become "drunk with his success." He had become, she said, a blasphemer, a demagogue, a false prophet. While most of his followers still believe he is God, and "become hysterical in his presence," his staff, she claimed, knows that he is "a fake." By discouraging his followers from seeking medical care, she charged, he caused some of his followers who were seriously ill to die, in effect murdering them. While she admitted that most of his followers obeyed Divine's teaching that they should refrain from sex, nevertheless, she claimed, among some followers sex was "rampant," in both homosexual and heterosexual forms. Moreover, she claimed, Divine himself did not practice the sexual abstinence, which he preached. Recalling one evening when she sat next to Divine at a banquet at High Falls, while a woman was testifying that Divine was helping her to overcome her sexual desires, Faithful Mary claimed that Divine had his legs entwined with hers. Faithful Mary believed, she claimed, that "it would be very difficult to find any person more sex-crazed" than Divine.[5]

Towards the end of the summer of 1937, Faithful Mary still was in control of an extension in Harlem, a four-story house on Fifth Avenue near 127th Street, and she was still leading her separatist movement. Generously, she was undertaking to provide free or inexpensive meals to all in need, to offer educational courses to adults and children, and to reconstruct old houses to make them available at low rents to her followers, as havens from the world. Underlining her distinction from Divine, who opposed beauty shops, she planned to open one herself.

As more months passed, however, Faithful Mary came to see that her effort to start an alternate movement was foundering. Feeling defeated, she herself slipped back into frequent drinking. By the end of 1938, she felt so low that she abjectly confessed to Divine that her charges against him were lies, and begged him to take her "back home to the fold."

In response, Divine gave her the opportunity to make a public confession. He arranged for it to take place on January 1 and 2, 1939, in the Rockland Palace in upper Manhattan, where Divine often held big meetings. There, as thousands of followers listened, she confessed she had allowed forces opposed to Divine to push her into lying. They had got her drunk, she said, so that she had lost control of herself. They had offered her bribes, though they never actually gave her a penny. Under their pressure, she said, she had brought false charges against Divine. While it may have been difficult to believe a person who admitted she had lied earlier—how would one know she was not lying again?—her dramatic confession was a tremendous triumph for Divine, greatly enhancing his authority.

Responding to Faithful Mary's confession, Divine accepted her back, saying that anyone who confesses her sins deserves mercy. At the time, Divine directed his fury, he said, not as much against her as against his newspaper enemies for pushing her, against her will, to lie. He threatened that if they did not repent, he would "bring them lower than I did Faithful Mary."

As for Faithful Mary herself, he explained that he had brought her up "from the garbage can to the throne." But then when she had fallen off the throne and become "malicious," he had turned his back on her, he said, and brought her low. As a result, she had lost all her joy in life. That had induced her, he said, to beg to return to the fold.

The mercy Divine offered Faithful Mary was limited. He did not restore her to her former positions of responsibility. After all, she was hardly to be trusted any more. Divine demoted her to an insignificant role in one of his missions in Newark. Later she moved to Los Angeles, where, unhappy, she often became drunk, dirty, and sick. After suffering years of torment, in 1949 she took an overdose of pills and died. Hearing of it, Divine said, "retribution is assured."[6]

27. SON PETER: A DOUBTER AT HOPE FARM

WHEN HIS PARENTS joined the Divine movement at Sayville, Long Island, they took their son along with them. Because the movement did not encourage keeping families together, it eventually separated him from his parents, sending him to live at one of Divine's Harlem communities. There the community's leaders gave him the name Son Peter, and put him to work. He worked downtown for a dress factory, as a delivery boy, for ten dollars a week.

For a time Son Peter lived in a community on 116th Street which Faithful Mary managed. In April, 1937, however, when Faithful Mary defected from Divine, and left the community, at first Son Peter left with her. But later, evidently considering him too young, she sent him back to the community. The followers there, according to the *Amsterdam News*, chastised him for deserting Divine, threatening him with "bodily punishment of the worst kind." Later, he was taken to see Divine, who scolded him, and sent him upstate to Ulster County, to Hope Farm, in West Saugerties.

By this time, Son Peter was about twenty-two years old, dark-comlexioned, slim, and mild-mannered. At Hope farm, he was put to work assisting in the kitchen and laundry for the twenty-five "brothers" and "sisters" who lived there. He was given his food, housing, and clothes, but like the other workers there, he received no pay. Because it was known that he "leaned" toward the defector, Faithful Mary, the Hope Farm leaders worked him "unmercifully," he later claimed. He felt that he "was constantly being shoved around."

SON PETER WITH HIS MENTOR, FAITHFUL MARY, as pictured in her book. (Faithful Mary, *God*, 1937)

Within a few months, Son Peter began to consider walking out, and Faithful Mary was sympathetic to his doing so. Faithful Mary was coming to believe, she said, that because all the mission workers in the Promised Land, including Son Peter, worked without pay, they were slave laborers. According to Faithful Mary, since mission workers worked without pay, they could serve meals more cheaply than regular restaurants, competing unfairly with them. In keeping with such beliefs, Faithful Mary sent Son Peter the bus fare to help him walk out.

Meanwhile, despite the Peace Mission's reputation for serving generous meals to visitors, Faithful Mary was also coming to believe, she said, that Divine's followers in Ulster County did not have enough to eat except when Divine came to visit. Although this was a difficult claim to believe, Faithful Mary insisted that the followers were so hungry that many of them sneaked into Kingston stores to buy crackers.

In line with Faithful Mary's claim, Peter decided, according to an *Amsterdam News* report, that he and the other Hope Farm residents did not have enough meat to eat. During one of Divine's visits, Peter asked him, so Peter later claimed, for more meat to serve to the followers. According to the *Amsterdam News*, Father Divine replied, "They've got money of their own, some of them. I know that, and so there's no reason they shouldn't buy their own meat."

But Peter persisted. Once he asked Divine, whether as a cook, he could take chickens from the farm, and cook them. But Divine would not give him any such permission. With that, according to the *Amsterdam News*, Peter decided the time had come for him to leave the farm.

By this time, Peter had begun to doubt that Divine really was God. It seemed to Peter, as he said later, that if Divine were God, he would have known that Peter was planning to leave, and tried to prevent it. But Divine did not seem to know. Peter prepared to leave quietly, according to the *Amsterdam News*, "afraid to let the farm angels know that he was leaving," He simply walked out, "carrying his few meagre possessions with him in a battered suitcase."

He caught a bus, and made his way to the Bronx. At the time Faithful Mary was staying there while trying to start her own religious movement, in defiance of Divine. Faithful Mary took Peter in.[7]

When Faithful Mary made a visit to Ulster County in July, 1937, she drove up in her "large black sedan," with Son Peter and also her loyal chauffeur John Victory. They visited High Falls and Kingston, but not Hope Farm. At about this same time, Son Peter was making public charges against Divine, in support of Faithful Mary. He publicly repeated his charge that the Hope Farm community lacked adequate food.

After it had become apparent that Faithful Mary was not being successful in creating her own alternative movement, both she and Son Peter abandoned their revolt against the Divine movement, and both begged to be taken back into it. At great public meetings in Rockland Palace in early 1939, while it was Faithful Mary who received almost all the attention, Son Peter as well as Faithful Mary confessed that his charges against Divine were lies.

After his confession, Son Peter separated himself from Faithful Mary, and returned to being a Divine follower. During World War II, when he was in the armed forces, Divine kept in touch with him.[8] Divine seemed to find it easy to forgive Son Peter. Away from Faithful Mary, Son Peter was hardly a threat.

28. JOHN W. HUNT, HABITUAL SEDUCER

JOHN W. HUNT, a flamboyant white follower of Divine, took Delight Jewett, a white schoolgirl, on a trip. He was 33; she was 17. They traveled by car from her parents' home in Denver, Colorado, to his home in Beverly Hills, California, in 1936, accompanied by several other persons, including a chauffeur and Howard B. Smith, Hunt's assistant. According to the charges that he would face later, Hunt brought Delight for sexual purposes.

In Denver, Delight's parents had already been drawn to Divine, attending banquets at Divine's mission there regularly. Both in Denver and then also in California, Hunt dazzled their daughter with gifts of clothing and jewelry, and under Hunt's guidance, Delight became a devoted Divine follower. In fact, Hunt persuaded her that she was another Virgin Mary, who would become the mother of another messiah, who in turn would succeed Father Divine.

Hunt, a smart, rotund young man, was from a

wealthy family of Cleveland, Ohio. According to Hunt himself, he had long led a dissolute life. He was an alcoholic. He hardly seemed to have any ethical standards. In the various private schools to which his parents sent him in the 1920s, he had scarcely made an effort to study. He regularly cheated on tests. He regularly seduced girls. He was admitted to Michigan's Hillsdale College using false credentials. Various institutions dismissed him, and some of them readmitted him.

Once he had settled in California, Hunt ran an advertising agency, and, with his engaging bravado, seemed to succeed. He lived in Beverly Hills in a palatial house, in the neighborhood of such movie stars as Lionel Barrymore. Soon he had married three times, and while married, according to his own account, he sometimes swapped wives and was often over the Mexican border "with loose women." Serving as an officer of his college fraternity's alumni association in the Los Angeles area, and its president for 1935, Hunt drew alumni to association meetings by showing them what he afterwards called sexually "obscene" movies. In time, he said, he could "keep going only by remaining under the influence of liquor," and his business was failing. His body was becoming "bloated." He could hardly eat. He felt "corrupt in body and mind and soul," he afterwards recalled. He considered suicide.

Desperate, he sought a way out. While testing various groups which might help, he attended a meeting of Father Divine's followers, and was struck by their joy. He listened to them. He turned to the spirit of Father Divine for help, he recalled, and felt he was beginning to heal.

Soon Hunt became prominent in the Divine movement in California, where it was strong, especially among whites. He became known by his new religious name, St. John the Revelator. In his luxurious home, he hosted parties for the movement, with as many as two hundred guests. He spoke for the movement and became a major figure in helping to finance it. As a photographer, he made movies of its activities, and showed them in tours across the continent. In addition, his wealthy mother, Florence Hunt, a widow, came to believe that Divine had cured her of cancer. Becoming a Divine follower herself, she adopted the name of Mary Bird Tree.

JOHN HUNT HIDING BEHIND TWO FLAGS, the left one saying Father Divine is God, and the right one saying Peace. With two other followers. At the time Hunt was on Divine's personal staff. (*Spoken Word*, Sept. 8, 1936)

GOING TO EXTREMES

In February, 1936, while John Hunt was visiting in a Divine Mission in New York, he wrote a long, open letter confessing his previous life of debauchery, and claiming to having been cleansed from it by Father Divine, so that he was now "living the exact life that Jesus taught." A Divine-related periodical, the *Spoken Word*, called the letter "one of the most astounding confessions and exposes ever made public," and published the letter in full, taking five pages to do so. Brashly, Hunt mailed copies of the letter to hundreds of prominent people, including all members of Congress, governors of all states, presidents of major colleges, as well as to President F. D. Roosevelt, King Edward, Lady Astor, Henry Ford, J. P. Morgan, and the Pope. As a result, Hunt became, according to the *Spoken Word*, "internationally famous," and federal officers in New York arrested him for sending obscenity through the mail. A court then sent him for psychiatric observation to Bellevue Hospital where his doctors, believing that Hunt did not intend his confession to be obscene, decided that he was fanatic, but not psychotic. Officials then released him.[1]

Free again, Hunt became part of Divine's personal staff, serving as Divine's official photographer, and was often in Ulster County. He joined an excursion, which went there by Hudson River steamer. He spoke there, as at New Paltz, where he held his audience spellbound telling of his healing from debauchery. Still, Hunt continued to be rash. In later 1936, at a time when he regarded New York City to be his legal residence, he applied there for a driver's license, but following Divine's teaching against his followers identifying themselves by race, Hunt refused to state his race, and ran into trouble over it.

At about the same time, other Divine followers applying for driver's licenses in New York State also ran into trouble, but they were scarcely as confrontational about it as Hunt was. When Quiet Devotion, a white who lived at the Stone Ridge mansion, applied for a driver's license, where her application form requested her to indicate her "color," she at first refused to write in anything, but after officials discussed it with her, she wrote in "olive," a compromise, and received her license. When another white Divine follower, Deborah Newmind, who, as we have already seen, later lived at Hope Farm, applied for a driver's license at the Motor Vehicle Bureau in Jamaica, Long Island, where the application form asked for "color," she also left a blank. When a clerk asked why, Newmind explained her religious scruples, and later the clerk, after discussing it with her, filled in the space with a question mark, and accepted her application.

When Hunt refused to state his color, he was denied a license, and then, instead of trying to

THE DENVER PEACE MISSION WITH WHICH THE JEWETT FAMILY WAS ASSOCIATED. On Larimer Street. (Vivian Wadlin)

negotiate with officials to find some way to avoid the problem, he demanded that the fee of one dollar he had paid for his application be returned to him, which they refused. By this time angry, he announced to them that until they refunded him his dollar, he would drive without a license.

Soon afterwards, Hunt was driving out of Ulster County, following Divine's rapidly moving car and trying to keep it in sight, when he was overtaken by a motorcycle policeman and charged with speeding. When the policeman asked Hunt for his driver's license, he replied bluntly, "I don't carry one." In court, Hunt explained that it was contrary to Divine's teaching for a person to designate his race, and since designating it was required for a license, he did not have one. The judge, sympathetic to Hunt's explanation, fined him only two dollars, but Hunt, again declining to be conciliatory, refused to pay it, saying that paying it would be against his religious belief. The judge then gave him the choice of paying the fine or spending a day in jail. Hunt chose jail.

Still later that same year, 1936, Hunt returned to California. Buoyed by his success in the Divine movement there, he continued to call his young companion, Delight Jewett, a second Virgin Mary, and began calling himself a reborn Jesus, the son of Father Divine. For his part, Divine, at a banquet in the Kingston mansion, boasted that he was receiving several telegrams a day from Hunt in California, about what Divine seemed pleased to say was Hunt's "unfoldment" into becoming "my real son Jesus the Christ." But at the banquet, others around Divine were uneasy, including one who was familiar with the Divine movement on the West Coast. They warned Divine that Hunt might be more focused on himself than on Divine.

A few days later, Divine seemed to have heeded the warning. He wrote John Hunt and his companion Delight Jewett, calling her "Virgin Mary," but saying he was not willing to call Hunt "Jesus." Divine reminded them that, in signing his letters, he did not even call himself Father Divine, but merely "Rev. M. J. Divine, better known as Father Divine." He warned them against any self-indulgence, including having any sexual relations with each other. He warned them to abstain from even any appearance of human affection for each other, including walking or riding together, but instead to concentrate on living the "evangelical life." Otherwise, he said, they could no longer be his "real followers."

In the meantime, while Hunt was attracting attention in Divine's movement in California, Hunt's mother, Mary Bird Tree, who had been living in California, by early 1937 had moved to New York State, and was living at the Kingston Mansion. While doing so, she became prominent as a buyer of major Ulster County properties for the Peace Mission Movement, one being a garage and residence in High Falls, and another being Greenkill Park.

Besides having a mother prominent in the Peace Mission, John Hunt also had a brother prominent in it, Warner Hunt. Quieter than John and steadier, Warner Hunt, known in the movement as John DeVoute, was the wealthy proprietor and editor of the *New Day*, the weekly Divine-related periodical. He founded it in 1936, and at first published it in Newark, New Jersey. By 1937 he had moved it to New York City, where it became the major periodical associated with the Divine movement—Divine was eventually to call it "the perfection of all publications."[2]

SENTENCED TO PRISON

In Colorado by early 1937, Delight's parents, Elizabeth and Lee Jewett, despite their own participation in the Divine movement, had become upset by John Hunt's treatment of their daughter. They publicly charged that Hunt had seduced her while she was still a minor. They wanted to punish Hunt in some way. They hoped to prevent such a "tragedy" from happening to other girls, they said, and demanded an investigation. The Hearst newspapers, including the New York *Evening Journal*, encouraged them, with relish.

In March, 1937, when the charges were beginning to be known, Hunt and the girl fled by car from California to New York State, accompanied by Hunt's assistant Howard B. Smith. They tried to hide in Divine establishments, as in both New York City and Ulster County.

Soon federal agents were hunting for Hunt, the

girl, and Smith. When the agents questioned Divine as to their whereabouts, Divine denied having any responsibility for Hunt, since Hunt, he said, was no longer his follower. Divine explained that if any follower of his becomes bad, "his badness expels him from me." Since it had been publicly reported that Hunt had been seen in Kingston, the agents looked there and at other Divine communities in Ulster County, but did not find either Hunt, Delight, or Smith.

Meanwhile, Delight's parents, the Jewetts, came from Colorado to New York State to find their daughter. Visiting Father Divine in New York City, they were received politely by him, housed, banqueted, and assured that their daughter was safe. Before helping them find their daughter, however, Divine began to draw Lee Jewett out on his experiences as a county agricultural agent in Colorado, and how he might improve the quality of the Peace Mission's farming in Ulster County. On March 29, Divine drove with them to Kingston, for a visit of four days. In accordance with the usual Peace Mission separation of the sexes, Elizabeth Jewett was quartered with women in the main Kingston Mansion building, Lee Jewett in a separate building nearby, in a men's dormitory.

In the dormitory, Lee Jewett met Hunt. At first Jewett was so angry with Hunt that he refused to speak to him; but gradually, after meeting him several times, he came to sense that Hunt had fervent faith in Divine, and became calmer. Meanwhile, Divine arranged for the Jewetts to be shown around the various Divine-related farms in a chauffeured car. Lee Jewett was impressed. Everywhere he found that the fences were in shape, the buildings painted, and livestock cared for. He became engrossed in writing reports for Father Divine, recommending better care for the fruit trees, better-bred cattle, better quality seed to improve the pastures. He was considering Divine's offer of becoming the manager for several Divine farms. He seemed to be on the verge of forgiving Hunt.

But Elizabeth Jewett, less impressed than her husband, continued to search anxiously for her daughter Delight. Eventually, while visiting a female dormitory at one of the Ulster County Peace missions, she found Delight. Their reunion was strained. Delight insisted she was the Virgin Mary, and at first repelled her mother's embrace. The mother, unlike her husband and daughter, resisted all blandishments from either Divine or John Hunt. She insisted on withdrawing her daughter, who, after all, was still a minor, from the Divine movement, and through her persistence, succeeded in doing so. She and her husband then returned to their idea of punishing Hunt, and secured Delight's help in arranging to do so.

Early in April, 1937, while Hunt was still at large, it was reported that Hunt's assistant Howard B. Smith, known in the Divine movement as John the Baptist, was in Kingston. When Hunt had originally transported Delight Jewett from Colorado to California, Smith was with them, and then when the Jewett girl lived in Hunt's Beverly Hills house, Smith was living with them there. Smith, a white-haired, mild-mannered man, who believed that Divine had brought him back to life when he was considered dead, was reported to have been living in Kingston for some time, at the mansion on Chapel Street, where Hunt and Delight also stayed more briefly. Smith was often seen at the Ulster County Clerk's office, checking over Divine-related property deeds.

Late in April, John Hunt surrendered himself in Los Angeles, and was charged with violating the Mann Act. Smith also surrendered, and was indicted with Hunt, as part of a conspiracy.

At the trial that followed, Delight Jewett testified against Hunt. With Father Divine insisting that Hunt tell the truth, Hunt confessed to seducing Delight. The jury acquitted Smith but convicted Hunt, and he was sentenced to three years in prison. Father Divine approved of the sentence.[1]

After Hunt was sent to prison, Divine wrote him a letter which, despite the bad name Hunt had given Divine's movement, is notable for showing him mercy. Perhaps it was easier for Divine to show mercy to Hunt because he and others of his family had contributed generously to the movement:

July 10, 1937, A. D. F. D.

Mr. John Wuest Hunt
L. A. County Jail
Temple and Broadway
Los Angeles, Calif.

My dear Mr. Hunt:

I am writing to say it is a consolation to know the Court's Sentence was not as severe as it might have been, and that it was lenient by My Spirit with Mercy and Compassion.

As I have often instructed, an open confession is good for the soul. Hence, "He who confesses and forsakes his sins shall have Mercy, but whomsoever it be who will cover his sins, shall not prosper."

It is understood, by others as well as yourself, that even the act of any person participating with the opposite sex, is a violation of My Teaching, as the Life of Christ must be enacted in all of your dealings. Sanctification means separation—to separate you from human affection and self-indulgence. When you fully abide by My teaching, you also abide by the Federal law of our great Country.

However, as you have made open confession to both God and man, if you have forsaken all of those tendencies, fancies and pleasures, your sins are forgiven. All you must needs do is to continue to live it and express it in prison, as well as when you receive your freedom, and continue to live Evangelically, without accusation, resentment or condemnation, and you will be Blessed continually. For the open confession and the forsaking of your sins in every way will give you your real emancipation, and no doubt will give you your freedom before the time expires.

This leaves me Well, Healthy, Joyful, Peaceful, Lively, Loving, Successful, Prosperous and Happy in Spirit, Body and Mind and in every organ, muscle, sinew, joint, limb, vein and bone and even in every atom, fibre and cell of My Bodily Form.

Respectfully and sincere, I am
Rev. M. J. Divine
(Better known as Father Divine)[2]

After Hunt left prison, he resumed his participation in Divine's Peace Mission. Divine did not seem to limit Hunt in his restoration to the movement as much as he was to limit Faithful Mary in her restoration. With Hunt's energy and wealth, he was able to help the movement significantly. Meanwhile, Hunt's brother DeVoute continued as the competent editor of the movement's *New Day* periodical, and Hunt's mother, Mary Bird Tree, continued to figure in Divine's movement, as by leading the negotiations to buy Krum Elbow, and when Divine acquired a new mansion in Yonkers, New York, appearing as the hostess of its opening ceremonies.

During World War II, both John Hunt and his editor brother, in accord with Divine's teaching, opposed killing under any circumstances, and served as conscientious objectors. As we will observe later, it is hardly surprising, however, that John Hunt, as he served, did so confrontationally.

29. JEAN BECKER, HIDING AT HOPE FARM

JEAN BECKER was a white girl who grew up in Hollywood, the daughter of Divine followers. Her mother was in charge of a Divine mission in Los Angeles. Her father was a chemist.

In 1934, when Jean was about seventeen, Ross Humble, a psychologist who frequently lectured on behalf of Divine on the West Coast, was making a trip to New York. He was taking along Divine followers who wanted to see Divine in person, and, with the approval of her parents, Jean accompanied him. According to her father, Jean's interest in Divine was only a minor factor in her going, a major factor being she wanted to see New York City.

Once in the city, Jean wanted to stay. With the consent of her parents, she lived in a residence run by Divine disciples, but took a job outside of the Divine community, in a laundry. Working there meant that she was obliged to contribute to the Social Security System (begun in 1935). Deepening her association with the Divine movement as she was, however, she eventually came to accept Divine's teaching that participating in the Social

Security system meant she did not trust in God, so she quit that job. In its place, she took a position in a Divine restaurant, where, being like the other workers there only a volunteer, she had no obligation to participate in Social Security.

After some time, however, having heard of Hope Farm in Ulster County, she decided she wanted to move there. To arrange it, she went to see Divine, having her first conversation with him. Divine believed from what Jean told him, he explained afterwards, that she was twenty-one, which was the age of majority in New York State at the time, so that she was able to make her own decisions. He consented to her moving to Hope Farm if she could find a job there. She did find a job at Hope Farm, and in the summer of 1937, moved there.

During the several years that Jean had been away from home, her parents had sent her messages, and at first she had responded to them. But as Jean came to take Divine's teachings more literally, she came to believe, as Divine taught, that unless you turn away from your family, in accord with such scriptural passages as Luke 14:26, you cannot be a true disciple of Jesus, and she stopped responding to her parents. As a result, her parents worried. They especially worried because at the time they were hearing the story of Delight Jewett, another white girl from the West whose parents were Divine followers, and who eventually hid herself from them among Divine followers in New York State. While they did not claim that Jean had been seduced, as Delight Jewett had been, the Becker parents, in their uncertainty about where Jean was, grew suspicious of the Divine movement, as they had not been before.

Finally the Becker parents decided to make the trip to the East to try to locate their daughter. They drove across the continent towing a trailer. In New York City, finding Divine followers reluctant to help them locate their daughter, they appealed to the police for help.

Understanding that Jean might attend a big rally which Divine was holding in New York, Mr. Becker went there, accompanied by an assistant district attorney. Becker spotted Jean in the crowd and approached her. He tried to take her by her arm, intending to lead her out. but she resisted. Though using violence was against Divine's teaching, a female disciple of Divine, perceiving Becker as trying to take the girl away against her will, "struck" Becker. Other nearby followers, in support of the woman, "arose in protest." A riot seemed to threaten. Becker gave up. He and the assistant district attorney withdrew.

The parents explained their daughter's reluctance to leave the Divine "cult" by saying it had rendered her "virtually will-less" by its "proselytizing." Divine followers countered that their movement did not proselytize and that Jean was following her own will.

Later when the Beckers heard that Jean was staying somewhere in Ulster County, they drove up to Kingston to look for her, staying there two weeks, sleeping in their trailer. Not locating Jean by their own efforts, they eventually went to the county courthouse for help. There they swore out a warrant for her arrest as a wayward minor, saying she was only twenty years old, that is, by the New York State law of the time, still a minor. By taking this action, the parents explained, they believed "they would be doing a service to other girls who might be lured into the cult."[3]

County sheriff's officers made several attempts to locate Jean Becker. They looked for her at various Divine locations in the county, including Hope Farm. But with followers withholding their cooperation, they could not find her.

Meanwhile, Mrs. Becker had written Divine saying that she and her husband were looking for their daughter Jean, that she was under age, and that she was being sought by the Ulster County Sheriff. Divine was out of town when the letter arrived at his address, but once he returned home on November 4, he read the letter. Because he now understood that the sheriff was looking for the girl, Divine went to Hope Farm the next day, showed Jean the letter, and asked her if it really was in her mother's handwriting. When Jean said it was, Divine, in accord with his usual policy of cooperating with the law, asked Jean to turn herself in to Sheriff Molyneaux. Divine arranged for Lovely Sweet, who was in charge of Hope Farm, to take Jean to Kingston to the sheriff's office.

Once Jean arrived at the office, the sheriff arrested Jean as a wayward minor. When the office called her mother in, Jean told her that she continued to have faith in Divine. With the help of Divine followers, Jean secured an attorney to defend herself; he was the Afro-American Gaius C. Bolin, Jr., of Poughkeepsie, who was friendly to Divine.

When Jean was arraigned in Kingston at the county court house, both lawyer Bolin and Hope Farm manager Lovely Sweet were present inside in support of Jean, while outside in front of the courthouse, a crowd of Divine followers, blacks and whites, paraded on her behalf. When the judge set bail at $1,000, however, it seemed high, and since neither Jean nor her Divine movement friends furnished the money, she was jailed.

Attorney Bolin, believing that Jean's parents had the law on their side, advised Jean to avoid a court battle. Under the impact of Bolin's advice, as well as her jailing and her mother's pleas, Jean relented. She agreed after all to return home with her parents to California. By November 8, she was released from jail, into a crowd of officials and Divine followers, who were there to support her. When someone in the crowd—perhaps a reporter—asked Jean if she really thought Divine was God, she answered: "I don't think it. I know it." In the confusion, while her father was almost silent, her mother found an opportunity to thank Sheriff Molyneaux warmly for returning Jean to her family.

As Jean was about to join her parents in their car to drive back to the West, she insisted that when she became twenty-one, and was free to go wherever she wished, she expected to return, to live with Divine followers again. It is not known, however, that she ever did.[4]

30. THE BROCKS: A FAMILY WITH QUESTIONING DAUGHTER

THE BROCKS were a white family, who at first lived in Seattle, Washington, where Arthur Brock, the father of the family, was a marine pilot. After he developed cancer, he became unable to get out of bed and seemed about to die. It was only then that his wife Mina first heard of Father Divine. Soon afterward, she appealed to Divine for help, and though he was at a great distance from Divine, Brock seemed to begin to heal.

Brock was in a Seattle hospital, with his doctors expecting him to die any time from cancer of the stomach, when his healing began. From the hospital, Brock wrote Divine to thank him for the signs of healing:

> I, knowing Doctors could not save me, said 'I leave it to God.' Sister [meaning his wife Mina] got your address, Dear Father, sending you a telegram saying, "Husband dying, please save."
>
> In a short time, I awoke, feeling much better. I had only been able to drink water through a glass tube very slowly. The next morning I could drink water by the glass.
>
> I thank you, dear Father, for the healing. I thank you for taking the desire of smoking away from me. I thank you, Father dear, for the wonderful appetite you gave me. Drs not understanding healing, wanted to give me medicine and a sleeping remedy, which I refused to take, telling them Father Divine was taking care of me.[1]

Against the advice of Brock's doctors, his wife, hoping that his being in the presence of Divine would heal him further, decided to take him from Seattle to New York City. Leaving behind in Seattle their baby Laura, born earlier that year, 1936, to be cared for by a nurse, Mina Brock brought her husband across the continent by train, with the help of a stretcher. Arrived in New York, they were met by an ambulance, which drove them to Harlem to Divine's headquarters.

There Mina Brock tried to arrange for her husband to see Father Divine, but Divine sent word through a secretary that he was too busy. Divine's policy was that it was not necessary for him to see the sick to heal them. Healing occurred, he taught, not by the laying on of hands or any other ritual, but by each patient's own faith. Later, however, as one of the family understood it, Priscilla Paul, a long-time follower of Divine who bounced with energy and purpose, intervened. Despite continuing word from Divine that he was too busy to see Brock, Priscilla Paul "threw open" a door, ushering Brock into Divine's presence. Thereafter Brock continued to heal, it seemed to him. He found himself able to get out of bed and into a chair. He found he could eat more. From a skeleton weighing about 80 pounds, over some weeks he gradually recovered his normal weight.

Meanwhile, the Brocks stayed in Divine-related housing, on West 115th Street, near Divine headquarters. While day after day Arthur Brock attended Divine meetings, telling and retelling the story of his continued healing, Mina Brock worked as a nurse, outside of the Divine community—neither Divine nor Arthur Brock, despite their belief in faith healing, had any problem with her being a nurse. Later Divine followers even opened their own school of nursing, in Newark, New Jersey. They seemed to regard nursing care and all medical care as questionable for followers, but appropriate for non-followers.[2]

Within a few months the Brocks arranged to have their baby Laura sent from Seattle to them in New York. At first the parents kept the baby with them. But as the baby grew a little older, Divine, in keeping with his teaching against families staying together, urged them to send their daughter to the Divine extension in New Paltz, in Ulster County. They sent her there in 1937, when Laura was only fourteen months old. Later they also sent there Laura's older brother, an adopted boy, Robert Mace, with Mina Brock paying for the care of both of them.

In New Paltz, the baby Laura was given a new

ARTHUR BROCK WHEN HE WAS A MARINE PILOT, LIVING IN SEATTLE (Laura Brock Miller)

religious name, Happy Heart, and her older brother Robert, the name Happy Determination. Their father, Arthur Brock, who did not adopt a religious name, occasionally visited New Paltz. It is not clear that Arthur Brock came especially to see Laura and Robert, which was not encouraged. He evidently came largely because Divine, when he traveled, liked to bring him along as an example of successful faith healing. When Brock came to New Paltz, he did not necessarily have a chance to spend any private time with his baby Laura. If they were in a crowd together, someone might hold her up so that she could at least see her father at a distance.

Laura's mother, Mina Brock, visited her children in New Paltz more openly than her husband did. Since at first she continued her regular work as a nurse in New York, she was not able to come frequently. When she came, she brought presents

ROBERT MACE (HAPPY DETERMINATION), a relative of the Brock family who had been adopted by them. He grew up at the Divine community in New Paltz. (Laura Brock Miller)

with her, but in accord with the Divine teachings, she brought them not just for her own children but for all the children staying in the mission. When Mina Brock was there, even though everyone knew she was Laura's mother, Laura was not supposed to call her mother, but to call her by her new religious name, which was Mighty Love.

Some time later, Mina Brock became eager to live nearer her children, particularly nearer the infant Laura. Although Divine did not encourage family relationships, he seemed at least able to tolerate Mina Brock's seeking to be near Laura because she was still so young. Needing to earn money to pay for the care of her children, Mina Brock looked for a job somewhere near Laura in New Paltz. Depression time, as it was, she was unable to find a job such as she would have preferred, as a nurse. She finally found a job working in a hotel in a neighboring village, Highland, and was thankful for it. However, when Divine, visiting New Paltz, heard that Mina Brock was working in a hotel nearby, he drove over to the hotel, and seeming to stretch his policy against families staying together, offered her a job as chauffeur for the New Paltz extension, saying that doing that work would support her children there. Gratefully Mina Brock accepted.

At New Paltz, the person who especially had been caring for Laura, and continued to do so even after her mother came to stay there, was "Mom Sarah."[3] She favored Laura. She allowed Laura to ring the dinner bell to call in the farm workers from the fields. She tended to excuse Laura's faults. Laura, looking back later, came to feel that Mom Sarah spoiled her. If she misbehaved, as she had a tendency to do, Mom Sarah and others looking after her would ask her, what would Father Divine say? At first this led Laura to fear Father Divine. But gradually as she came to know him better, she came to feel that she was a favorite of his too. Divine, she felt, seemed to forgive her for anything she did wrong.

While Laura was living at the New Paltz community, older children living there, including her brother Robert, attended the New Paltz public schools. Robert, who had red hair, freckles, and was near-sighted, was cruelly teased by the other children, but he withstood the teasing. When Laura was old enough, she tried to attend the same school, intending to attend it regularly. It happened, however, that there was one black boy in her room. The other children, who were hostile to blacks, told Laura, who was white, that the black boy was poison. Even though she was accustomed to associating with blacks, Laura believed the other children, and not understanding that the children claimed that the boy was poison only because he was black, she was terrified she would be poisoned by associating with him. She refused to go back to the school. Her Divinite care-givers did not insist that she go back. From then on, she was taught regularly at home, being, as she looked at it afterward, increasingly spoiled.

When Laura was about seven years old in

THE PEACE CENTER, 12-17 W. 128 St., in Harlem, a Divine facility, to which Mina Brock moved from New Paltz in 1943, with her two children. ("Come Ye...to Woodmont," pamphlet, 1950s?)

1943, Laura's father, Arthur Brock, died, and because Divine's New Paltz Farm community was showing signs of breaking up, Laura herself, her brother Robert, and her mother Mina Brock moved to a Divine community in New York, at 13-17 West 128th Street. There mother Brock lived in a Divine facility for women, in a room on one floor, while Laura stayed in a children's dormitory on another floor. Across a court from their building was a men's building where Robert lived, in a room of his own. Mina Brock, to pay for her own and her children's room and board, looked for outside work again, as a nurse. She found work for a doctor whose patients needed her often to be away over night, and when she was away, the Divine community looked after Laura and Robert, as they usually did anyway.

Robert continued in a New York high school until he graduated, and then went back to Seattle where others of his family still lived. Meantime Laura was now well into the age when she was expected to attend school. While other Divinite children accepted the vaccinations that were required for anyone to attend the city's schools, Laura, having heard that a girl she knew in the Divine community had died after being vaccinated, refused. Her mentors, uneasy with forced vaccination anyway because Divine avoided medical care, accepted her refusal. They arranged for her to be taught at home by an experienced teacher, a follower from England named Ferne Slaughter. She was a red-haired woman who taught in Divine's evening schools, sang enthusiastically, and learned to tolerate Laura's follies. Thus, as Laura looked at it afterward, she continued to be spoiled. It was only when Laura became ten years old that she consented to being vaccinated, and so was able to attend school. Meantime, she often played outside in the streets, including playing with boys, which according to Divine's teaching was inappropriate for girls. She believed, she said afterwards that it was discriminatory not to allow her to associate with boys. She recalled that she was so absorbed in the world of children, that she did not pay much attention to Divine, but she felt he continued to watch over her. He kept telling her that he knew he had not yet won her heart.

Her mother tried to instruct Laura in Divine's teachings, but Laura did not necessarily learn what her mother intended. When her mother tried to teach her to be generous, promising her, as Divine taught, that if she gave generously, even more would be returned to her, Laura, to her mother's disturbance, gave away some new clothes her mother had given her, expecting more new clothes to arrive any time. Moreover, although Divine encouraged cooperation more than competition, Laura was competitive. She seemed to enjoy playing games only if in the end she could brag that she had won. She enjoyed twirling a baton because doing so made her a leader in Divine parades. She was assertive even with Father Divine. After he moved out of New York to Philadelphia to escape being served a legal summons in New York State, she knew that he could visit New York State only on Sundays and holidays when summonses could not be served. Once on a Sunday evening when Divine seemed not to be paying attention to the approach of midnight, Laura reminded him of it. Some of her associates scolded her for being so bold with Divine, who, after all, in his role as God, was supposed to be aware of everything, including time. Meantime, Divine would see Laura, as she became a teenager, continuing to play outdoors in the streets with everybody about her age, including hoodlums, learning to know their deception and brutality, and he was disturbed.

In 1950 when Laura was fourteen, Father Divine encouraged both Laura and her mother, Mina Brock, to move to Philadelphia, to be near him. In their new location, while mother and daughter both lived in the same Peace Mission building, but in separate rooms, Mina Brock continued to work outside as a nurse. Laura, seeing little of her mother, continued to attend school, and continued to distance herself from Divine's beliefs. She found herself asking questions about a variety of other beliefs, including Christian Science, Catholicism, and Eastern religions, and Father Divine, playing a tolerant role, did not discourage her from doing so, but continued to look out for her. While she was in high school, when she attended school events in the evening, she was brought home afterwards by school buses, which sometimes delivered her home late. A Divinite sister who helped care for Laura complained about her being late, but Divine defended her, saying she was under his "personal jurisdiction."

When Laura was nineteen, and her mother was sending her to nearby Temple University, Laura went to see Father Divine. She told him frankly that her thinking was not like his. In response, he told her he knew, and laughed, suggesting to her that he was tolerant, and she was grateful.

Soon afterwards, Laura Brock left the Divine community, and in 1955 married in New Jersey, with a minister officiating, becoming Laura Brock Miller. Later, however, she was to come back into the Divine community, not as a full follower, but in loose connection to it, and as we shall see later, she did so in Ulster County.

31. MARY SHELDON LYON, FRUSTRATED PHILANTHROPIST

MARY SHELDON LYON was one of the Sheldons, an old New York State family who had lived in Auburn, in the Finger Lakes region. The family had connections to Cornell University. Not only Lyon's father but also her two brothers had attended there. Moreover, the family owned a substantial residence in Ithaca, called Sheldon Court, which had been rented out to Cornell students for more than twenty-five years.

By the 1930s, Mary Lyon, a childless widow, was residing in a penthouse apartment in upper Manhattan, in the Washington's Heights neighborhood on Cabrini Boulevard, apart from any of her family. Her closest living relative, her brother William H. Sheldon, a retired physician from whom she was estranged, had long been living in Italy.

About 1930, when Mary Lyon was in her sixties, she visited Divine's house in Sayville, Long Island, with several other wealthy women. Impressed with Divine's assistance to the needy, they offered him a substantial donation, but Divine, in accordance with his usual policy of refusing donations, refused their offer. He told them that while their millions were "exhaustible," he drew from an "inexhaustible supply." He added, using his usual explanation in such situations, that "the spirit of the consciousness of the presence of God is the source of all supply." Divine's mysterious response, instead of discouraging Mary Lyon, enhanced her interest.[1]

By 1936, when Lyon was in her early seventies, she had become a Divine follower, and had adopted a religious name, Peace Dove. While retaining her apartment in New York, she lived much of the time at the Kingston Mansion, and was building a one-story house in a western corner of the mansion's grounds. When a group visited the mansion, according to one of them, Lyon showed them "happily" through her new house. It was a house for which she apparently did not secure any legal ownership for herself. She seemed to be building it for the Divine community, but for the time being she furnished it and occupied it as she wished.[2]

Lyon became attached enough to this Kingston site to take there at least a few of her collection of paintings. She may have hung them at the mansion or in her own house nearby, or both. They were paintings that she eventually bequeathed to the Metropolitan Museum of Art.[3]

While staying in her Kingston house, Lyon attended meetings at the Kingston Mansion. At one such meeting, according to a Divine movement weekly, she participated in a dialog with Divine. When Divine said that a " positive suggestion" was "as operative" as a "negative" one, she said, "More so, isn't it?" and he responded, "Sure, the positive is eternal. The negative only has a short time to live." Later when someone said, "Father, I love you," she interjected, "Father, I try to love you by serving you."

By 1940, Mary Lyon was attending Divinite meetings near her New York apartment at the Rockland Palace, a huge auditorium on 155th Street. At that time, she became one of a small group, including Arthur Madison, Charles Calloway, and John DeVoute, who took the initiative to create a church, the first of several Divinite churches. Based at Rockland Palace, it was named the Palace Mission Church. Mary Lyon became one of the trustees of this new church, and for the benefit of the church, she regularly paid the rent for the Rockland Palace building. In addition, in 1942, Lyon was one of the many Divine followers, who bought the substantial Brigantine Hotel, on the ocean near Atlantic City, New Jersey, which became a branch of the Palace Mission Church.[4]

Meantime, Mary Lyon was cared for over a long period by Patience Budd, an Afro-American follower of Divine who lived near Lyon on West 155th Street. Budd served Lyon not only as her maid but also as her nurse and chauffeur, and became her close friend. Budd often drove Lyon to look for fine chinaware to buy for Divine banquet tables. She also often drove Lyon to Divine sites, including her house near the Kingston Mansion, and also another Ulster County site, the Cherry Hill Farm, near High Falls. Lyon became well acquainted with the competent St. Mary Bloom, the dark-complexioned owner of Cherry Hall Farm, who lived primarily in Harlem. About 1930, Bloom had been ill, given up by doctors, and was almost ready to die, when she visited Divine at Sayville, and without even telling him what her illness was, felt cured. Although Bloom lacked even a high school education, by 1943, when Lyon wrote her will, she had become so trusting of Bloom, that she made Bloom one of executors of her will, the other being a Brooklyn attorney who had also long been associated with Divine.

In 1946, Mary Lyon, suffering from cancer, died. When her will was probated, the New York *Times* featured the story on its front page, the headline reading: "Woman, 81, Bequeaths $500,000 to 2 Father Divine Organizations." By this time, when much of the Divine movement had been organized into five churches, executor Bloom was president of one of the churches, the Circle Mission Church. But Lyon willed most of her money to two branches of the Palace Mission Church, one of whose headquarters was at Rockland Palace near where Lyon, Budd, and Bloom lived. Lyon left money to this Palace Mission Church, Divine explained, because, according to his movement's usual rule, Lyon being a member of that church, it was the only Divinite church to which she was allowed to make donations.

In addition, Lyon left to her maid, Patience Budd, $2,500, along with her 1941 Packard car, jewelry, clothing, and the furnishings of both her apartment in New York and her house on the Divine mission property in Kingston. Lyon left to her brother, Dr. William Sheldon, only a token $500, explaining that she knew he was "financially well able to take care of himself." She also left only $100 each to several upstate cousins.

When the brother, Dr. Sheldon, heard the terms of the will, he contested it. While he himself

MARY SHELDON LYON CONSTRUCTED THIS "COTTAGE" ON THE KINGSTON MANSION GROUNDS in 1936. Thereafter she divided her time between the cottage and her apartment in Manhattan. (*New Day*, March 23, 1939)

ST. MARY BLOOM tried New Thought, Unity, Christian Science, and Spiritualism before becoming a follower of Divine. By 1935 she had become the owner of a Divinite facility, Cherry Hill Farm, near High Falls. By 1946, when Mary Lyon had named her as an executor of her will, she was president of Divine's Circle Mission Church. (Laura Brock Miller)

LYON'S "COTTAGE" SURVIVES IN OUR TIME. As does also the Kingston Mansion which shows in the background. (Photo by the author, Oct., 2005)

remained in Italy, he charged through a New York lawyer that when Lyon made her will, she lacked the capacity to make it, and that Divine and his associates had fraudulently convinced her that Divine was God, and had brought "undue influence" on her to prevent her from favoring her family.[5]

In turn, the lawyers who were defending Divine's interests charged that Dr. Sheldon's claims were made in malice, and that Sheldon himself had been "scandalous" in his treatment of his wife, his children, and his sister, Mary Lyon, bringing her "heartache," and making her "ashamed." However, as the dispute passed through the courts, both parties recognized the advantages of settling out of court. By May, 1947, lawyers representing both sides had agreed on a settlement. In a statement signed in the presence of executor St. Mary Bloom, Dr. Sheldon's lawyers retracted the charges they had made against Divine and his movement. They said that "no statements previously made should be construed in derogation of Father Divine himself, the Father Divine Peace Mission Movement, or any of his followers, and that there was no fraud or impropriety on the part of Father Divine himself, the Father Divine Peace Movement, his church extensions, or by anyone else concerned in the making of the will." They also agreed to share the proceeds of the will, as a court later explained, arranging that the Divine forces would still receive a large portion of the estate. A surrogate judge accepted the settlement.[6]

However, certain of Mary Lyon's cousins, Lucy Latham and others who lived in upstate New York, as in Auburn, Oneida, and Syracuse, were dissatisfied that they were left out of the settlement. They went to court, asking that most of the proceeds of the will be turned over to them. In doing so, they made more extreme charges against the Divine forces than had already been made. They charged that shortly before her death, Lyon had asked certain lawyers to draft a new will for her, which would have given the complainants most of the proceeds of the will, and that the Divine forces, to prevent her from signing this new will, used "physical force." In fact, they charged the Divine forces "conspired to kill, and did kill the deceased." They killed her, the contestants claimed, "by means of a surgical operation performed by a doctor engaged by the defendants without the consent or knowledge of any of the relatives of the deceased."

Divine replied to these charges by saying there was no basis for them "in the least." He said he had not seen Mary Lyon at all from "long before" she made her will, and that the doctors who treated her had no connection with the Peace Mission. By July, 1948, the Supreme Court's Appellate Division held unanimously that the cousins' claims were "shadowy," and dismissed the case. The lawyers representing both Dr. Sheldon and the Divine forces then reached a another out-of-court settlement, similar to their earlier one, and in September, 1948, a surrogate judge ordered that the new administrators of the will, who were lawyers representing both sides, make payments in accordance with the new settlement.[7]

The cousins, however, appealed this decision, and in 1949, the state's highest court, the Court of Appeals, voted four to two that the cousins' claims were reasonable enough to be tried. In turn, the Divine lawyers appealed this decision, but in 1950, the Court of Appeals dismissed their appeal. No further appeal was possible.

Thereafter, as far as available information indicates, the Divine forces abandoned their defense of Lyon's will, evidently regarding further defense as too costly. It is doubtful that the Peace Mission ever received any money from the will. It is also doubtful that the allegation that Mary Lyon was murdered ever led to criminal charges against anyone.[8]

D. OPERATIONS

32. PAYING WHAT YOU OWE

FATHER DIVINE led his followers to develop a standard of character which was remarkably high. A black newspaper, the Pittsburgh *Courier*, declared that "the morals of the Divine followers are probably the highest of any group in this nation."

For many years, a significant aspect of the standard achieved by followers was their obligation to pay off their debts. When Divine taught this obligation, he so thoroughly committed his New York followers to it that, according to one of his leading followers, Priscilla Paul, "not one" of them would "take a subway ride to Brooklyn," even to attend a Divine meeting, until his debt was paid.

When Divine urged followers to pay their debts, how did he arouse such passion in them to do it? Divine did so especially by asking his followers, when they paid back what they owed, to notify him. Divine's followers, buoyed by his charisma as they were, craved his attention, and when he asked them to notify him, they considered it a sign that he cared about what they were doing. Moreover, notifying Divine made it possible for him to publicize their repayments. According to Divine, while the media focused on publicizing crime and debauchery, it was better to publicize acts of righteousness, so that "righteousness might cover the earth as the waters" cover "the mighty deep." In fact, Divine arranged to flood Divine-related periodicals, issue after issue, over many years, with records of his followers paying what they owed, along with letters from Divine commending them for doing so.

For example, Jeremiah Love, an African-American of Southern rural origin, was living in central New Jersey in 1929 when he failed to pay a telephone bill. It was only $1.25, but fourteen years afterwards, in 1943, when he had become a follower of Divine, and was living at a Divine site in High Falls, in Ulster County, he remembered the bill and finally paid it, to the New Jersey Bell Telephone Company.

When Love notified Divine that he had paid the bill, Divine saw to it, in accord with his custom, that correspondence to this effect was published in the *New Day*. Included in this correspondence was a letter Divine had written to the Telephone Company, stating an argument he used to persuade his followers to pay off their debts: my followers are "ashamed" to owe money, he wrote. They want to be economically "independent."[1]

While urging his followers to pay off their debts, Divine also taught that if any person, whether one of his followers or not, truly needed public assistance, that person had a right to it. When Hannah Faithful, who lived in a Divine residence in High Falls, became ill, and went to Kingston Hospital, she was without the means to pay her bill. The hospital, through the Ulster County Welfare office, asked Divine about her, and in reply Divine did not say whether she was a follower, whether she had donated any assets to the Peace Mission, or whether the Peace Mission had previously helped her when she was in need. Divine simply said that any citizens who find they are "unable to meet their obligations," are free "to apply for assistance from the public funds." If they apply, he said, all such citizens "should receive the necessary assistance from the public welfare," regardless of "their religious affiliations."

Despite Divine's insistence on everyone's having a right to public assistance, Divine urged his true followers not to seek such assistance. But if they did, and received it, he taught them to pay it back as soon as they could—and he persuaded thousands of his followers to pay it back.

Paying back public assistance was startling. It was taking an action that most Americans who received public assistance would never even consider taking. How then did Divine persuade his followers to swim against such an overwhelming tide? Divine did so primarily by publicizing their repayment of public assistance as if it were the payment of an old debt.

While the Afro-American Grace Love had been living in Richmond, Virginia, she had once become a patient at Richmond's City Home. She was in and out of the home for three or four months. The service was free. But more than twenty years later,

THE GAS STATION WHERE ITS OPERATOR, FOLLOWER JOHN MILL, FOUND A RATION BOOK AND RETURNED IT TO ITS OWNER WAS ON ROUTE 9W, near its junction with Red Top Rd., just north of Highland. The station's shed and gas pumps show to the left. A tourist home shows behind them among trees. A restaurant shows to the right, with the sign "Peace" on its end. All these facilities were part of the Divinites' Krum Elbow Estate. (*New Day*, July 24, 1941)

in 1943, after she became a follower of Divine and was living at the Divine Farm, in Saugerties, New York, she felt she should pay for the service. She saved up what was a sizable sum for the time, $300, and sent it in stages to Richmond. She explained that she was sending the funds through Father Divine's "influence, no goodness of mine."

The superintendent of the home replied that Father Divine "should be proud of you." When Divine read this statement, he arranged to quote it in the *New Day*, along with his own letter to Love, saying that by "living righteously, soberly, and godly," she was becoming, as others could also, "independent and free."[2]

PAYING BACK PRIVATE CHARITY

Just as Divine taught that his true followers should not accept governmental assistance, he also taught that they should not accept private charity. This teaching reached Max Wollenberg, who during the depression of the 1930s, when he had lived in San Francisco, had received private charity from the Salvation Army. A decade later, after he had become a Divine follower and moved to Greenkill Park in Ulster County, he felt an obligation to reimburse the Salvation Army for its help. Sending his payment, he wrote them, in a letter, which the *New Day* made public:

> Greenkill Park
> Kingston, N. Y.
> Sept. 18, 1942
>
> Salvation Army, Headquarters
> San Francisco, California
>
> Gentlemen:
>
> Around the year 1932 or 1933 during the depression, I enjoyed for some time the hospitality of the shelter managed under the auspices of your organization.
>
> Following the teachings of Father Divine, who according to the scriptures is "the tabernacle of God amongst men," it became my religious conviction to reimburse you for services rendered.
>
> I enclose herewith US money order for the amount of $10.00 which you may use as you see fit, provided you notify Father Divine of this act. I must confess that without his spiritual influence I never would have been inspired with the understanding to undo my past transgressions.
>
> Yours truly,
> Max Wollenberg

The Salvation Army replied to Wollenberg, saying : "Because of the funds that you have given to us we are able to help someone else who is in less fortunate circumstances than you are." When Divine learned of Wollenberg's action, he publicized it, along with his own letter to the Salvation Army, explaining that the repayment was a result of Wollenberg's attaining self-control, and quoting Proverbs, "He that conquers his own will is greater than he that taketh a city."[3]

RETURNING THE LOST

Moreover, when Divine followers found something that someone else had lost—whether money, or an umbrella, or a coat—Divine taught them to regard it not as many Americans were likely to do, as a bonanza to be seized for themselves. Instead, Divine taught them to regard it as another kind of debt. If the owner could be located—lost articles were regularly listed in the *New Day* to facilitate locating owners—Divine taught followers to return the articles and to refuse to accept any reward. If Divine did not motivate them to return lost articles by the hope of a reward, how then did he motivate them? One means was by publicizing such returns, the same as he publicized paying back debts.

In an incident during World War II, at a Peace Mission gas station on Route 9W, operated as part of the Krum Elbow estate, in Ulster County, a customer, W. L. Schweikert, accidentally dropped his ration book—the kind that everyone was required to carry during the war to buy gasoline. The Divine follower who ran the gas station, John Mill, found the book, located Schweikert's Brooklyn address in it, and mailed the book to him. In response, Schweikert wrote Divine, saying that having the book returned to him was one of "the benefits of your teaching." Divine, replying to Schweikert, in a letter which he published as usual in the *New Day*, declared that returning the book might seem "insignificant," but in fact "such acts are momentous in their spiritual import."[4]

RETURNING THE STOLEN

Besides trying to persuade his followers to pay off old debts and return lost articles, Divine tried to reform thieves. He did so not so much by increasing their fear of being caught as by erasing their desire to be thieves. This meant he tried to change them within, in accordance with the traditional Christian conception of conversion. He tried to change them into new creatures, he said, changing them from "nature to grace," so that they would want to repay what they had stolen.

When Andrew Hasting was employed by a pipe manufacturer in Ampere, East Orange, New Jersey, he stole tools from his employer. Once Hasting had become a follower of Father Divine, and was living at a Divine community, Hope Farm, in Ulster County, he came to believe, in accord with Divine's teaching, that he should pay the pipe manufacturer for the tools he had stolen. After Hasting had sent the payment, the manufacturer replied to Hasting as follows:

Lock Joint Pipe Co.
Ampere, N. J.
March 25, 1937

Mr. Andrew Hasting
Hope Farm
West Saugerties, N. Y.

Dear Dan:

We received your letter, in which you sent us $5.00 because of the claw hammer, pair of rubber hose and the spigot ax which you say you took from us when you were working for us.

We are very pleased to know that you felt like you should pay for these things, but so long as you have confessed and have shown your willingness to send us the money, we will cross it off and I am sending you back the $5.00 and suggest that with it you do a good deed for some of your brothers who are more nearly broke than you are. You worked for us a long time and we thought a lot of you, and maybe you were entitled to the claw hammer, the pair of rubber hose and the spigot ax.

We are glad to hear that you are happy in your new surroundings, and Fr. Divine must have done a good job with you. As requested by you, I am sending a copy of this letter to Fr. Divine so he will know just how honest you are.

With best wishes,
Very truly yours, Lock Joint Pipe Company
A. M. Hirsch. President

In response, Divine wrote Hirsch stating a long-familiar staple of his teaching, that while material blessings were not the purpose of righteous living, "the blessings of abundance" were a natural by-product of it. As Divine explained it to Hirsch: "As men allow righteousness, justice and truth to enter into their lives, they will receive a satisfying portion of all good things." This was an aspect of Divine's teaching that troubled some observers. It could seem inconsistent with Divine's emphasizing, as he often did, the "nothingness of matter." But of the various arguments Divine used to persuade his followers to pay what they owed, the promise of material reward was probably among the more effective.

Yet it remains a question whether his followers would have been inspired to pay what they owed by such an argument unless they first had been enthralled by Divine's presence, that is, by his charisma. His charisma seemed basic in his work.

Divine aroused passion to pay off old debts, return lost items, and return stolen goods especially in his more idealistic, more radical period, that is, from the early 1930s into the mid-1940s. As he became older and more conservative, he ordered his followers to continue to pay back any debts that they were legally required to pay back, but to stop making donations that were merely voluntary, that is, to stop paying back any governmental relief they had received, to stop paying back any private charity they had received, and to stop paying back anything they were not legally required to pay back. He issued this stop order abruptly in 1946. He did so, he explained, in an "economic boycott." It was a boycott to bring pressure on public officials who refused to allow his followers to vote, or to be issued driver's permits, or be granted tax exemptions for their churches on account of their using their adopted religious names rather than their original family names. Divine's curtailment of his pay-back policy led to a long-term decline in his followers paying back.[5]

A FUGITIVE PAYS HIS DUES

Although Divine curtailed his promotion of paying back debts, he continued his long-term teaching against stealing. The following example illustrates how he applied his charisma to such a situation.

In the 1930s, Joseph Bullock was only about seven or eight years old when his mother, a Divine follower, took him to a banquet at Greenkill Park where he met Divine, and Divine told him to have faith. "I didn't have faith then," Bullock recalled in an interview with Divine in 1955 when he was twenty-seven years old, "and I don't seem to have it now. If I would have had faith, I believe, I would have been able to come to you," he told Divine, "and talk to you, and I wouldn't have been confused like I am now." At this time Bullock was a fugitive from justice.

In the 1940s, when Bullock was about sixteen, he had been arrested in Brooklyn for possessing stolen goods, and because he was a minor, he was put on probation. In 1953, he had been arrested again in Brooklyn, this time for forgery, and was sentenced to eighteen months. Soon after his release, he visited Kingston, especially to see his mother who lived in Divine facilities there, but he did not stay long.

In 1955, he was living with a brother in Brooklyn, on Myrtle Avenue, when he took part in an armed robbery. When he knew that the police were hunting for him, he fled to Philadelphia, where he stayed at a Divine facility, the Lorraine Hotel, and supported himself by working temporarily as a house painter. Meanwhile, as his mother had urged him to do, he asked to see Divine. After waiting for some time, Divine finally called him into his office, at the Circle Mission Church on Broad Street, with secretaries present as usual, to record the interview. Divine, after saying he had no recollection of having met Bullock before, asked him why he wanted to see him. Bullock said, "I have gotten myself in some trouble in New York. I was involved in a stick-up and shooting."

When Divine asked if someone got killed, Bullock replied, not killed, but a policeman was shot. "There were three of us."

Divine asked whether all three were "dark complexioned."

Bullock said yes, and explained, "The other fellows got caught and I got away. At the time it happened, they picked me up and I lied myself out of it. I told them I wasn't involved and they did not seem to have any proof, so they took me down and questioned me and they let me go the following morning."

When Divine asked why he had not written to him, the young man replied, "I guess I felt I wasn't worthy," and continued: "When I would get in trouble I would think of you. Then when things were running smooth I would never think to seek you out." But now, he explained, the authorities were looking for him.

When Divine asked if he had carried a gun during the robbery, Bullock answered, "one of the fellows had a gun." When Divine asked if they had robbed a store, Bullock replied, no, we robbed a taxicab, on Halsey Street, and we took in about twenty-seven dollars.

"Crime does not pay," Divine said, "in any way whatsoever." Divine advised him to give himself up, and "then never compromise with any such act of dishonesty again." Since they are looking for you, "they would no doubt eventually get you. So it would be better for you to give yourself up. . . . If you do, of course I will be with you, and you will come out all right."

Bullock said he was willing to turn himself in. One of the secretaries then suggested that it might be to his advantage if they called the Philadelphia police at once, from Divine's office. Divine agreed, saying, "If they knew you came here to me and you made up your mind to go straight from now on, it might make it better for you," and offered to call from his office. "Then they will know you are under my influence," explained Divine. "So, if you accept of that," and "if you confess" and forsake such behavior, "I am sure you will not be sorry." Bullock consented, and they arranged for him to go downstairs to the dining room, have coffee, and wait. Then one of the secretaries called a nearby police office, and asked that they send someone to pick up the fugitive.

Within a few minutes, three officers arrived, and were shown into Divine's office. Divine explained to them that Bullock had confessed, was turning himself in, had promised to go straight, and that God had forgiven him. The officers thanked Divine for doing "a wonderful job." After Divine had arranged to serve them coffee, the officers chatted, explaining that they were familiar with the Divine movement, being accustomed to going to Divine facilities for lunch. After Divine sent one of his secretaries to bring Bullock up, Bullock entered the office humbly, saying "Peace." The officers questioned him for a few minutes, said they would notify the New York police, thanked Divine, and took the fugitive away.

Once the officers had gone, Divine assured his secretaries that since Bullock had turned himself in, the police in both Philadelphia and New York would give him "clemency." About a month later, Bullock wrote Divine that indeed, the authorities had treated him "wonderful," that he would be sentenced soon, and after he was freed he would like to come back to Philadelphia, to Mother and Father Divine.[6]

33. THE MYSTERY OF FINANCING

THE QUESTION of how Divine and his Peace Mission movement financed their activities aroused immense curiosity. It was natural to ask how Divine could drive in expensive cars and fly in private planes, yet claim he possessed no money. It was also natural to ask how his movement could feed the public at extraordinarily low prices, but claim it did not take up collections. It was also natural to ask how the movement could purchase extensive real estate, at the same time that it taught against purchasing anything on credit.

When anyone asked Divine about the source of his funds, he might say that they came "automatically," or that they came from "the spirit of the consciousness of the presence of God."[1] By giving such obscure answers, Divine was inviting his followers to suppose that in some mysterious way, he himself produced the financing, but he was also inviting his critics to wonder whether Divine and his staff, behind their appearance of benevolence, were charlatans. Such common suspicions sometimes led to legal charges, including a suit brought by Verinda Brown against Divine, which we begin to examine here. Divine's response to this suit eventually hurt Divine's communities in Ulster County, and did so profoundly.

VERINDA BROWN'S SUIT

According to Verinda Brown, Father Divine convinced her that "banks were not secure, but that money deposited in his heavenly treasury was always safe," and she had given him funds. She understood that she had the right to reclaim the funds on demand. But when she demanded their return, Divine would not return them. Eventually Brown brought suit to regain the money.

Verinda Brown and her husband Thomas Brown, as the *New Yorker* magazine presented them at the time, were of West Indian origin, little educated, but "decent, honest people." They had lived in the United States for thirty years. They had worked together in Forest Hills, Queens, Verinda as a housekeeper and Thomas as a butler. They worked for the family of Ordway Tead, who was chairman of New York City's Board of Higher Education. In 1929, a follower of Divine, Priscilla Paul, who worked as a cook in a neighboring house, invited the Browns to visit Divine's house in Sayville, Long Island.

At first the Browns were amazed that Divine did not charge for the splendid meals he served. According to the *New Yorker* account, they only gradually understood that he would accept donations. Hearing him teach against laying up treasures on earth where thieves break in and steal, eventually the Browns, considered by this time to be true followers, began paying over to Divine much of their regular wages, as, according to the *New Yorker*, other followers also did. That is, Verinda Brown did this continually, according to her claim, from 1930 to 1933, while Thomas Brown did it only briefly, since for much of this time he was no longer working for the Teads, but instead working directly for Divine cooperatives, without pay.

Eventually, however, both of the Browns became suspicious of Divine and withdrew from his movement. In 1934, Verinda Brown asked Divine to return what she had given him, to no avail. By 1937, she had begun a suit against Divine for the recovery of her donations to him, which she claimed by this time totaled about $4,500. Brown charged that Divine put a large share of the money she had given him into purchasing property in Ulster County, but he recorded it as coming from other followers, although, she charged, they had no money of their own with which to purchase property. Later other plaintiffs joined Brown in her suit, and they broadened it to sue not only Divine but also seventy-eight owners of Peace Mission-related property, most of it in Ulster County.

Brown's "chief witness," according to the court, was Faithful Mary. Later, after Faithful Mary declared that her charges against Divine were lies, Divine claimed that the enormous publicity given to Faithful Mary's false charges had so poisoned public opinion against him that, as the Brown case moved through the courts, its handling became twisted.

Moreover, Divine contended, in keeping with his usual claim that he never accepted donations of money for himself, that neither Brown nor any one else had turned money over to him directly, for any purpose, whether for a "heavenly treasury," or for investment in Ulster County properties. Many followers who were believed to be reliable, including Charles Calloway, John Lamb, and Priscilla Paul, testified that to their knowledge Divine, while he handled money for others, never accepted money donations for himself.[2]

However, a state court decided in June, 1937, that the evidence indicated that Brown had turned money over to Divine, and ordered Divine to repay it. On appeal, in early 1940, a court dismissed the charges against the defendants other than Divine, including the owners of property in Ulster County, holding that none of the money alleged to have been given Divine had been traced to these co-defendants. But the court held that Brown's charges against Divine himself should stand.

Although this was not a victory for Divine per-

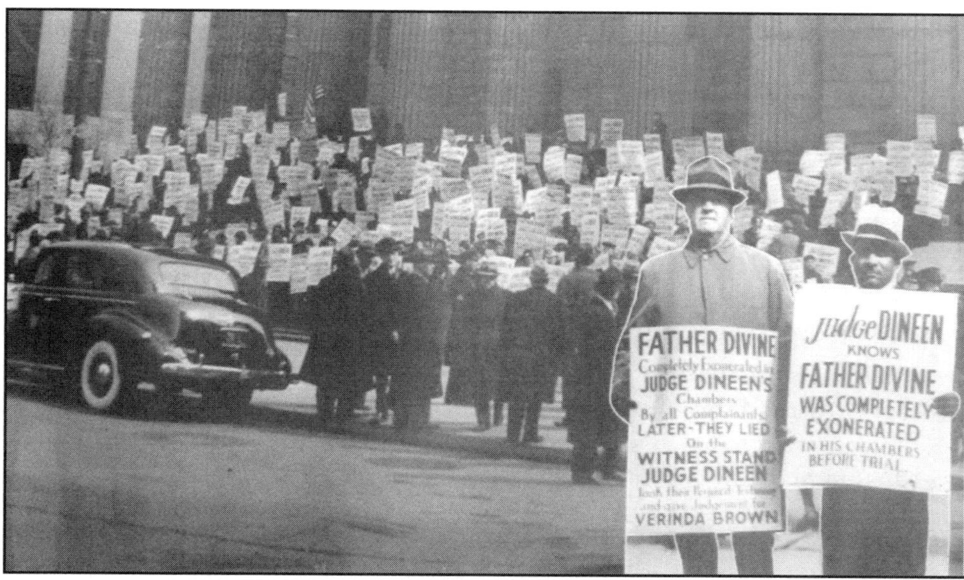

DIVINE FOLLOWERS PICKETING ON THE STEPS OF A NY CITY COURTHOUSE AGAINST JUSTICE DINEEN'S DECISON IN THE VERINDA BROWN CASE. Insert: Two picketers hold signs. The one on the right says, "Justice Dineen Knows Father Divine Was Completely Exonerated in his Chambers Before Trial," referring to a proposed out-of-court settlement. The one on the left says, "Father Divine Completely Exonerated in Judge Dineen's Chambers by All Complainants. Later They Lied." (*New Day*, March 28, 1940)

sonally, it was a victory for the Peace Mission property owners in Ulster County. Divine, speaking in Milton, pointed out that if the Brown case against the Ulster County property owners had succeeded, other "legal bandits" would also have come after the property owners in the county, as well as elsewhere, threatening them all. But now at least the property owners were safe. However, not only did the court retain the charges against Divine, but when Divine appealed to higher courts, these other courts upheld the charges against him.

In this case, perhaps neither the Browns nor the courts understood or wanted to understand that according to Divine's financial system, if it was already in place at the time, the Browns might not have been donating to Divine personally but to a cooperative, each of which managed its own finances. Or perhaps the Browns misinterpreted Divine's religious talk about putting funds into a "heavenly treasury," taking it more literally than Divine intended. In any event, perhaps both the Browns and the courts did not understand, or did not want to understand that, given Divine's financial system, Divine personally did not need monetary donations from anyone. Aside for any such uncertainties, perhaps the courts were inclined to believe that anyone who called himself God was, by this fact alone, a fraud.

Although Divine taught his followers to cooperate with the law, he refused to pay the monetary judgment against him, which by this time, with costs and interest, had grown to about $6,000. With hundreds of his followers picketing the courthouse to protest the judgment given against him, he nevertheless would not allow anyone else to pay the judgment for him. He explained his apparent violation of his own teaching by saying that in this case the courts had interpreted the law unjustly. He seemed to feel this deeply. He may have felt so especially because the Brown charges could seem to threaten his whole financial system.

His refusal to pay the judgment led to a state Supreme Court justice holding Divine in contempt of court, which Divine believed, if he continued to refuse to pay the judgment, would lead to his being sent to prison. This led in turn to Divine's moving out of the state, as we will follow later in detail.[3]

DID DIVINE ACCUMULATE WEALTH FOR HIS MOVEMENT OR FOR HIMSELF?

While the powerful are often tempted to use their power to steal, Divine is not known to have done so. As various legal suits and investigations make clear, there is no plausible evidence that Divine took advantage of his situation to enrich himself personally, as by storing up a private stash of funds in cash, stocks, or bank accounts, in the United States or in any off-shore location. He was known to have refused the offer of a gift of an island in the Bahamas, to which he could have retreated from his troubles with a stash of funds, if he had any—he was offered such an island by Howland Spencer from whom followers had bought the Krum Elbow estate.

In the 1930s, Divine's movement sold its dinners to the public for only ten or fifteen cents. Even in 1949, despite inflation, the movement was still keeping its prices down, a complete meal, including dessert, costing only twenty five cents. Why would any movement keep its prices so low if it was devoted to enriching itself?

When the Peace Mission provided classes to learn English or stenography or bookkeeping, as it often did in New York City, Newark, and Philadelphia, the classes were free. Similarly, when Peace Mission extensions anywhere, including those in Ulster County, provided employment services, they too were free. If the Mission was greedy, why would it provide such services free?

Divine taught his followers not to accept any such public assistance as relief, free hospital care, Social Security benefits, or veterans' pensions. Moreover, when Divine's followers purchased property in Ulster County, they did not ask for tax exemption for these properties, even though these properties could be said to be non-profit properties and used for religious purposes. Such refusals of public aid do not suggest fraud. They more nearly suggest a desire to be independent, and free of bureaucratic control.

Agents who lectured on Divine's behalf not only were not paid but they also were not allowed to take up collections or otherwise solicit contributions. When Ross Humble had been a lecturer for other causes, he had raised enough money in the course of doing so to pay his own way, but when he became a lecturer for the Divine movement, he was not allowed to raise money in doing it because Divine taught that the gospel should be preached free. "Now I am obliged to earn my money elsewhere," Humble explained, "and devote only my spare time to the work which is really dearest to my heart." Such limitations seemed to reinforce the Divine's movement's financial restraint.

Also when Divine encouraged his followers to make restitution for any past stealing or unpaid debts, he encouraged them to pay such restitution to the persons to which it was due, and if they could not find these persons, he encouraged them not to give it to Divine himself, nor even to Divine's movement, but to give it elsewhere, as to a charity. This hardly suggests Divine was looking for underhanded ways to acquire wealth.

On other levels, however, Divine publicly encouraged donations to his movement's cooperatives, but only from the members of those cooperatives. He also publicly accepted donations to himself—not in money, he insisted, but, as he freely acknowledged, in kind. He accepted luxurious cars, luxurious housing, luxurious clothing. He could have driven only inexpensive cars. He could have accepted only the simplest accommodations, like those his followers usually used. He could have worn only ordinary clothing. But he did not.

Moreover, since he believed that prosperity was a sign of goodness, he seemed to believe that he, as all-good, should exemplify prosperity. It seemed to be part of his conception of himself that as the leader of his movement, he should live in luxury and do so conspicuously. At the conclusion of his letters, he routinely boasted that he was not only "healthy"and "joyful" but also "prosperous."[4]

WHEN FATHER DIVINE WAS ASKED THE SOURCE OF HIS FUNDS, he often answered with this saying. Observers often found it mystifying. (*New Day*, Jan. 25, 1940)

THE COOPERATIVE SYSTEM

Since Divine and his movement in fact did have significant wealth under their control, even if not in Divine's personal bank accounts, how then did they acquire it? Although Divine often seemed hesitant to clarify it, the method which more than any other seems to explain how Divine and his movement acquired wealth was already being developed as early as Divine's Brooklyn and Sayville periods. It came to fruition early in Divine's New York City period. Divine brought this method to Ulster County already developed. It was the cooperative method. This method lent itself to keeping Divine himself out of direct entanglement in financial affairs. It also lent itself to bringing out the idealism among Divine's followers. It provided a relatively stable economic base for Divine's communities, allowing them to emphasize service and justice rather than making money. It sustained an alternative life style.

As developed, this method meant establishing a series of producer-run cooperatives. Each cooperative was independently owned and operated, but each was loyal to Divine and his Peace Mission movement. Each cooperative ran on such principles as volunteering, with members expected to work without pay; buying and selling only for cash, not credit; and equality, with each owner sharing equally in the ownership of the cooperative's property no matter what size contribution each one had made—this allowed large donations by a few, without much attention being paid to them.

Critics frequently claimed that when followers first joined the Divine movement, they were required to give all they had to the movement, or at least to whichever of the movement's co-operatives they were joining. In reply, Divine denied that there was any such requirement. But he admitted that even though it was not required, there was a "tendency" for the most "consecrated" followers to "bring all they have "to their cooperative, for the use of the movement. "It works out for the good of the people," he said, and was in accord with such sayings of Jesus as "Except you forsake all you have, you cannot be my disciple."

Since only followers who were financially independent were allowed to become members of cooperatives, they might well have assets to donate. Such members were likely to include many who were of only moderate means, but also a few who were of ample means. Although Divine was not inclined to publicize contributions from the wealthy, there are hints that donations from the wealthy became significant in his movement. For example, Mary Bird Tree (Florence Hunt) and Mr. Peace Harmony, both wealthy, contributed substantially to the purchase of Krum Elbow. Charles Calloway made New York City real estate available to Divine's use, and paid for the expenses of a mass excursion up the Hudson to Kingston. William Gottlieb tried to give Faithful Mary $10,000 to purchase Ulster County real estate, but Divine forbadeher to receive it, himself providing the money to other followers to assist them to buy Ulster County property. The wealthy follower Mary Lyon built a separate cottage on the grounds of the Kingston mansion, and regularly paid the rent for a major Divine meeting place in Harlem. She willed to the Divine movement $500,000, an enormous sum for the time, and after her death, Divine's movement fought in the courts to secure it.

Divine did not wish to emphasize the role of wealthy contributors in his movement. When poor followers became able to live in a resort in the Catskills or on an estate on the Hudson River, the explanation Divine preferred to give of this was not that wealthy donors made it possible, but that with faith in God, poor followers—many of them blacks—having pulled themselves away from drink and relief and crime, had learned to work hard, be honest, and live frugally, and so, as God's had promised, deserved abundant living.

In any event, some of the wealthy contributors evidently did not give all they had to their cooperatives when they first joined them. It seems likely that Frederic Crabb did not put all his assets into his trucking cooperative when he created it, as a few years later he had saved enough money to build a house near New Paltz. Also it seems likely that John DeVoute did not pour all his assets into the cooperative which published his *New Day* weekly when he led in forming it about 1936, for

AFTER JOHN DEVOUTE GAVE THE WOODMONT ESTATE to the Divine movement, Father Divine led a tour of the site in 1953, accompanied by Mother Divine (the tall woman to Divine's right, on the sidedwalk) and DeVoute (the tall man to Divine's left, on the grass). (*Life*, Sept. 28, 1953)

in 1952 he was the principal donor of funds for the purchase of the magnificent Woodmont estate, on Philadelphia's Main Line, as a residence for Father and Mother Divine.

Within each cooperative, when followers pooled their funds in it, the pool could be used for many different purposes, including paying for real estate, improvements, or supplies, and it was the cooperative rather than the donor who was likely to decide what a particular contribution would be used for. As Divine explained, some donors to a cooperative pool might find it "quite surprising" to find themselves listed as owners of their cooperative's real estate.[5]

Divine learned to prefer that a number of followers be listed on a deed as purchasing a particular property on behalf of the movement, rather than to have only one person listed as buying it, because one person controlling property alone, like Faithful Mary, might become a threat to his leadership. When more than one person shared in owning a property, the custom was to make the owners legally joint tenants, not tenants in common. That is, if any owner died, his share was not inherited by anyone else, but rather it was divided equally among the remaining owners. If large numbers of followers pooled their funds, as when in the 1930s in Ulster County, fifteen followers bought the Milton art colony, twenty-one bought the Krum Elbow estate, and twenty-seven bought Greenkill Park, they could muster considerable sums of money, and they could do so especially if some of them were wealthy. Although Divine preferred not to emphasize it, substantial contributions to the cooperatives from a few wealthy donors was a means to help the cooperatives prosper, help distribute wealth to the poor, and still give the wealthy contributor no more than an equal share in the ownership of the cooperative, the same share in ownership as the owner who had contributed the least.

Beginning in 1940, after the Brown suit had spotlighted the loosely organized character of the financial organization within the Divine movement, the movement organized itself more by incorporating churches. They incorporated five churches, each having branches. While for many years thereafter, most Peace Mission real estate remained in non-church, cooperative ownership, gradually these new churches came to control significant property. While these churches were not cooperatives, they were nevertheless similar to them. While each of the five churches was financially independent of the other churches, each was composed of followers who received no pay for their service to the church, but pooled their resources to help it. Each church was likely to include a few members who were wealthy and many who were not. Both the cooperatives and the churches, in accord with Divine's teaching, did not solicit, did not take up collections, and did not accept donations from the public, but they did accept donations from their own members. Moreover, these cooperatives and churches not only accepted payments for meals, room rent, child care, or other services they provided, but by at least 1949, allowed outsiders who were served meals to pay more than the small amount required, if they wished, in whatever amounts their conscience indicated. This loophole, in effect, permitted outsiders to give to the cooperatives and churches after all.[6]

Giving free labor to Divine's movement, whether in churches or cooperatives, was a central aspect of the movement's nature. As Divine explained in a 1938 interview, co-workers in the cooperatives, instead of receiving wages, have "all things common," as "at the day of Pentecost." According to Divine, speaking at Hope Farm at about the same time, cooperatives were to be run by their participants making "a complete self-denial," without "thought of monetary gains," for "the common good of all humanity." In the latter 1940s, when for followers to give both cooperatives and churches free labor continued to be the norm, Professor Charles S. Braden of Northwestern University, who studied the Divine movement at that time, regarded "free service" as "the secret of Father Divine's amazing achievements." But having the wealthy subsidize Divine's enterprises was also a "secret" of Divine's "achievements."

Besides the factors of voluntary labor and subsidies by the wealthy, another factor that significantly helped the Peace Mission to flourish was the frugality with which the cooperatives operated. Cooperatives saved by not borrowing money. They saved by not building new buildings, but instead using their own voluntary labor to repair old ones. They also saved by dividing spacious living quarters into smaller quarters; by declining to carry insurance; and by purchasing in quantity, and as much as possible from other cooperatives within the Peace Mission movement, at low prices.

As for Divine himself, he endlessly repeated that he owned no property and had no money, and that both he and his staff, including his secretaries and chauffeurs, gave their services free. How then did he and his staff survive? They survived the same as the workers in the cooperatives and churches did, by accepting support in kind. Divine and his staff, like members of cooperatives generally, ate meals provided by followers. They occupied living quarters provided by followers. They drove automobiles made available by followers. They accepted donations from followers of gasoline, clothes, office supplies, and other necessities. While some observers regarded accepting donations in kind as much the same as accepting them in money, in Divine's view, it was not the same; in his view, he and his staff gave voluntary, unpaid service, and he regarded their doing so as a model inviting his followers to do the same.

Many public officials were not convinced that Divine's financial system was legitimate. They suspected that Divine, despite his denials, must have milked his movement to provide him with personal income and a personal stash of funds. Several official investigators, including a Suffolk County District Attorney, an Ulster County Grand Jury, a Newark, New Jersey, Grand Jury, the FBI, as well as state and federal income tax officials, pried into Divine's financial system, but could not find evidence of fraud. They eventually dropped their investigations.[7] But Verinda Brown did not drop her suit, and Divine continued to feel its threat.

34. OUTSIDE EMPLOYMENT

MOST FOLLOWERS of Father Divine did not work regularly as volunteers within Divine's movement, in its cooperatives or churches. Instead, most of them worked regularly outside, in the conventional working world.

Divine insisted that his followers who did conventional work should be well paid. It was his intention, he said, that his followers be well paid to help them become financially independent, as everyone should be. This was true whether they were intending eventually to enter of one of his cooperatives or not. Divine promised that if his followers who were employed in conventional work were now determined to deny themselves, work hard, live righteously, and follow him, they would become financially independent, or, if they already were financially independent, they would become more so.

Divine followers who worked in the conventional world might be able to become financially independent more readily than many other workers could. This was so, even though large numbers of them worked only as domestics or handymen. Steeped in Divine's values as they were, they tended to be honest and willing to work hard, which helped them secure substantial pay. Moreover, in so far as they followed Divine's teachings, they did not spend their money on tobacco, drink, narcotics, cosmetics, or gambling. They did not borrow and thus did not pay interest. They did not buy insurance. If they found their entertainment within the Divine movement, it was often free, and if they slept and ate in Divine facilities, the cost was small.

The story of these followers raises the questions of how they found their outside work, where they worked, what service they gave, and what they did with their income. It also raises the question how Divine's unusual teachings relating to work affected them in practice—such teachings as against accepting gifts because they were corrupting and against participation in Social Security because doing so indicated lack of trust in God. Information is available to help answer some of these questions, if in part only obliquely.

EMPLOYMENT SERVICE

In 1937, a woman living in the Catskill Mountains in Tannersville, Greene County, wrote Father Divine, saying that she employed one of his followers as a houseworker. She found this houseworker patient and trustworthy, she wrote, and as a result, was recommending that someone else also employ a Divine follower. She asked Divine for an address in nearby Ulster County where she could inquire for such help. In reply, Father Divine wrote her that he believed all his followers in Ulster County were already busy, but that she could apply to his office in New York, where an

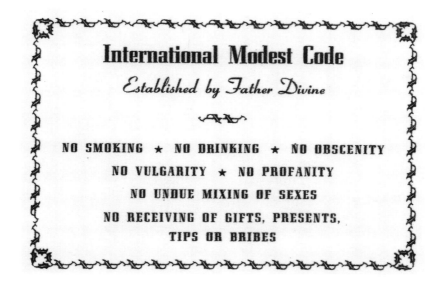

EMPLOYMENT SERVICE EXTENDED GRATIS TO ALL READERS OF THE NEW DAY

We secure and supply positions for the following types of help:
DOMESTIC:
$15.00 — $25.00 per week
DAY WORKERS:
40c to 50c per hour plus carfare
WINDOW WASHERS:
(Men) 15c — 25c per window and up.
MECHANICS — CHAUFFEURS — CHAUFFEUSES — STENOGRAPHERS and OTHER OFFICE HELP — MAIDS — BUTLERS — GOVERNESSES — GRADUATE NURSES — PRACTICAL NURSES — COMPANIONS — CATERERS — SOCIAL SECRETARIES — MILLINERS — TUTORS AND OTHER PROFESSIONALS.
Prices by no means limited to $25.00 per week as workers' receive wages according to experience and profession.
This courtesy is without discrimination as to race, creed or color — absolutely without charge or fee of any kind to either employer or employee.
LEhight 4-5894 LEhigh 4-3042 MOnument 2-2386
(These telephone numbers are for New York City readers.
Out-of-town readers call Peace Mission Extension nearest your community.)
THANK YOU, FATHER.

International Modest Code

Established by Father Divine

NO SMOKING ★ NO DRINKING ★ NO OBSCENITY
NO VULGARITY ★ NO PROFANITY
NO UNDUE MIXING OF SEXES
NO RECEIVING OF GIFTS, PRESENTS, TIPS OR BRIBES

DIVINE'S EMPLOYMENT SERVICE WAS AVAILABLE FREE, THROUGH ANY PEACE MISSION (*New Day*, March 13, 1941) **FATHER DIVINE PROMOTED THIS "MODEST CODE" LONG-TERM, making it basic in his movement. An effect of it was to help his followers find jobs.** (*New Day*, Ap. 28, 1956)

employment service was available. By 1939, however, the Peace Mission movement was making it known that its employment service could be reached through any of its missions. A notice in the *New Day*, said the Peace Mission's employment service had available such workers as day laborers, domestics, window washers, mechanics, chauffeurs, stenographers, butlers, nurses, caterers, and tutors. The service was available, the notice explained, without discrimination as to race, creed, or color. The service was available to anyone whether a follower of Divine or not, and the service was free to both employers and employees.

To Divine, it was important that this service be free. He did not oppose employment agencies charging fees to employers, but he opposed employment agencies charging fees to those seeking work– such agencies should be helping those looking for work, he argued, including the underprivileged. He urged any of his followers looking for work not to patronize any employment agency, which would charge them fees. Thus, it was often through the Peace Mission's free employment service that Divinites found jobs outside of Divine missions, whether in Ulster County or elsewhere.[1]

DIVINE'S TEACHING ABOUT WORK

While Divine asked that his followers employed outside of his missions be paid decent wages, he did not encourage them to be greedy, as the following example of Willing Heart suggests. Heart was a follower of Divine, formerly a resident of Harlem, who by the 1940s was employed as a domestic by a Kingston family, at their home on Wall Street. The father of the family found Heart "trustworthy to the highest degree," as he wrote Divine. When the parents were out of town, they would leave her "alone with the baby, knowing that our child would be cared for with the fullest consideration." But then when a grandmother in this family was dying, Heart did extra work, and for this work the father "tried to give her extra compensation," he wrote, "which she refused." She evidently refused it because she regarded it as a gift, "stating that she was doing nothing more than her duty." In reply, Divine honored Miss Heart for declining the extra pay, explaining that "no doubt" she felt that the extra work she did for him was "of a spiritual nature." She felt that declining the extra pay "was her duty as a Christian American, more than mere service as an employee."

Another follower came to Divine in 1947 in Philadelphia, saying she was considering seeking a government job, but was uneasy about it because Divine taught against participating in Social Security, which in such a job would be required. Divine responded by saying, yes, he taught against participating in insurance or pension systems, but explained that what followers decided to do about it was up to them. If she decided not to take a job because it would require payments into the Social Security system, that would be a "sacrifice" on her part; such a sacrifice should only be made, he said, if it grew not out of his teaching, but out of her own "internal conviction," in accord with her "highest intuition." Evidently the younger Divinites often did not follow Divine's teaching against participating in pension systems, however, because by 1955, Divine was saying that, as the education of those who had grown up in the movement improved, and as the government moved away from racial discrimination, the "majority" of his "younger" followers were in government "civil service work," where participation in pension systems was certainly required.[2]

THE NATURE AND QUALITY OF THE OUTSIDE WORK

Divine followers who worked in Ulster County outside of Divine's cooperative communities included both blacks and whites, but mostly blacks. They included both men and women, but a significant proportion of men. They made many different work arrangements.

In High Falls, a number of workmen lived in Divine missions but went out to work at odd jobs. Among these were several men who went out from the Divinite garage on Lucas Avenue to do roofing. They were said to be in demand especially because, unlike much of such help, they worked without drinking.

In Kingston, follower Sincere Meekness worked in a boarding house on Wall Street. The proprietor, M. E. Fessenden, wrote Divine that "her quiet, peaceful humility has been a benediction to us all." In reply, Divine wrote that "spiritual discipline in the lives of millions has cultivated good habits."

Considering Divine's teaching against family affection, it was unusual for an adult family pair to live at the same Divine community, but a black mother and son lived at Divine Farm, in the Saxton neighborhood of the town of Saugerties. They went out from there to work near the village of Saugerties, for the Herman Knausts, a family known for raising mushrooms. The mother, Lily Branch, worked as a cook, and the son, David Be Praised, as a handyman. They lived at the

Knausts' on the days they worked there, but on their days off they returned to Divine Farm. One of the Knaust family remembers that this pair had their own custom—not at all a general Divinite custom—of doing breathing exercises each morning, usually facing east, toward the sun, and in doing so, thanking Divine for his blessings.

A New Jersey follower, E. Redemption, worked as a nurse in the 1950s in Woodstock, in the Catskill Mountains, caring for a woman of nearly one hundred years who was mentally disturbed. Having found this work through the Divinite community, Redemption felt that Father and Mother Divine had blessed her "to handle her with love." When Redemption tried to wash her, as she wrote Father and Mother, she would "bite me and scratch me." Then Redemption would "roll the sheet over her arms and hold her with one hand and wash her with the other." The family gave Redemption a separate little three-room cottage to live in, near the main house, where she slept, took her own meals, and read the *New Day*. On days off, she returned by bus to a Divinite hotel in Newark, the Hotel Riviera, where she made her permanent home.

One spring, several men from Divine's Krum Elbow community worked out in nearby West Park at a boarding house, Donnidick Lodge, readying it for its new season. Afterwards Virginia Gordon, the manager of the lodge, wrote Divine that she could not "sing their praises too much." In reply, Divine said that his followers "reach beyond selfish gain and seek the good of others."[3]

Four Divinite women—at least two of them from New York City—worked at a hotel in Woodstock, the Willowbrook Lodge, on Highwood Road. In August, 1943, a group of the hotel's guests, understanding that these women workers were followers of Divine, wrote Divine, saying they were a "credit" to his teaching. Divine replied that these followers had the spirit of "brotherly love," which eradicates "prejudice" and "all the other evils exemplified by Hitlerism."

Among followers who worked for summer camps, Faithful Ada and Happy Joyful worked for Camp Woodcliff in Sawkill, just north of Kingston. The director there wrote Divine that they were "conscientious" and "everyone here liked them." Two Divinite men, Faith Determination and Joseph Simon, worked at a farm camp, Camp Bruce Lynn, near New Paltz. After the summer was over, the director of the camp attended a Divine meeting in New York, where he spoke, saying that his summer's success "was entirely due to their whole-hearted support."

In the early 1940s, Patrick Henry, a black school boy who lived at Divine's Krumville farm, worked about five miles away at a summer children's camp, Camp High Point, in Brodhead on the south side of Ashokan Reservoir. When he was not doing his usual work, such as washing dishes, he joined enthusiastically in the camp's sports. In the summer of 1945, this same camp employed at least six Divinites. Of these, Watchful Sarah and Peace Endurance came from the Krumville commune, Philip David from the Bronx, and Happy Alone from Manhattan. The Director of the camp, I. A. Greenberg, wrote Divine that they all were "conscientious" and there were certain ones among them, including Mr. David and Miss Alone, with whom he spent "many hours" in "discussing the problems of humanity," which led to his becoming "attached" to them.

In the summer of 1947, Greenberg employed still more Divinites at his camp, this time twelve of them, all males. Among them, two were Kingston High School students, George Braye and Alfonso McLenan, who regularly lived at Divine's Kingston Mansion. Most of the rest, including two chefs, came from the metropolitan areas of New York or Philadelphia. Two of them are believed to have served in World War II, one, Clifton Burton, as a conscientious objector, the other, Sun Beam, as a soldier. According to Greenberg, all these men were not only "efficient," but also were "the finest examples of manhood in the entire community."

Among followers who worked out as apple pickers were fourteen adults, both men and women who lived at the Divine community of Krum Elbow. The follower who served as foreman of this group, Mr. Green, had once owned a Long Island nursery, but when a leg infection had crippled him, and doctors had told him he should have his leg amputated, friends took him to Father

Divine who, he believed, healed him. At once Green, in gratitude, had become a follower.

The farmer who hired these apple pickers, Michael Nardone, owned an apple farm a few miles south of Krum Elbow, on Highland's North Road. To transport the apple pickers from where they lived at Krum Elbow to his farm, Nardone hired a local young man, Kenneth Erichsen. who, as Erichsen recalled long afterwards, drove them in an old army truck. Because the Peace Mission required it, he drove extra trips to drive the women apart from the men. The men picked standing on ladders. The women, a smaller group, picked up the dropped apples from the ground. Erichsen found that there was "no fighting" among the pickers. He heard them "sing and joke." He considered them "good workers."

As their foreman, Green kept records of the pickers' time, and at the end of the week, reported it to farmer Nardone for payment. While nearly all the followers who worked at outside jobs were paid as individuals, and kept the pay to do with as they wished, in this case, according to Erichsen's recollection, Nardone paid for all of the pickers in one envelope which he gave to Green, and Green turned over all this money not to the individual pickers, but to their Krum Elbow mission.[4]

WHERE TRUST IN DIVINE WORKERS COULD LEAD

Solomon Heart was a black follower of Divine who lived in High Falls and did odd jobs in the surrounding region. An elderly white resident of nearby Cottekill, Lloyd D. Prall, became acquainted with Heart by taking his car to him for repairs, and in doing so, Prall learned to respect Heart. With Heart's encouragement, Prall read Divine literature, and was impressed. Eventually Heart advised Prall to write Father Divine about his and his wife's health.

Prall would have preferred to talk with Father Divine in person. But Divine had moved his headquarters from Harlem to Philadelphia, and hardly ever came to Ulster County any longer. So Prall wrote Divine on August 21, 1945, as follows:

> My name is Lloyd D. Prall, age 80. Mrs. Prall is 77. We have lived at this place 14 years.
>
> When you first came in this vicinity I do not think there was anyone more opposed to your coming than myself. Time passed on. I saw conditions develop far different than what I expected. I began to think, what is this movement? I noticed your followers did not in any way interfere with anyone, and certainly were peaceful and law-abiding. I commenced to trade in a small way at your stores in High Falls, also your garage there, and Tailor Shop, and cannot but say I was always treated in every way right.
>
> Mr. Heart has done quite some work on my car and we have had quite a few conversations on conditions of the world in general, and I am proud to say I consider him as good a friend as I ever had. He is familiar with my condition, both my health and financial condition, so he advised me very strongly to write to you, and something inside me said the same.
>
> We have a comfortable home and an income enough (by using strict economy) for necessities. Mrs Prall has had 2-3 strokes and has arthritis. Her memory has been bad for 2-3 years. At present her mind has gone. She acts in most ways just like a child. I had her with me as long as I could keep up; now she is in Hacketts Sanitarium in Kingston.

Although Prall did not directly ask for any help, within a few days Divine replied, saying that because "you have confessed your attitude toward me and my mission when I first appeared among you," I "extend the spirit of compassion to you and yours." "By a change of heart and mind you bring yourself under the law of the spirit of life." Divine added, "So then, by faith both you and yours will regain your health and will come into the newness of life, even as millions under my teaching have prospered." Although Divine's promise was not conditional, but absolute, Mrs. Prall died about a year later, in September, 1946.

In a somewhat related story, several years later in 1951, when Jeanette Fineman, of the Bronx, was planning to construct a new casino building for her Ulster County hotel, the Elmar Lodge in High Falls, she asked the advice of Thankful Daylight, a Divinite workman who lived in High Falls. Daylight had worked for Fineman for six years, and had done so, she said, "very satisfactorily." She asked him to recommend Divine followers who could build a casino for her. When he recommended three Divinite workmen to do the job, she, believing that Divinite workmen were, as she said, "conscientious," asked them to do it.

As they constructed the building, however, Fineman came to believe that they were not reinforcing the roof sufficiently, and felt obliged to hire Solomon Heart, the High Falls Divinite workman who was Prall's friend, to redo the roof. But it was too late. After she had already spent more than $5,000 on the new building, when the first snow of the winter deposited its weight on its roof, in December, 1951, it collapsed.

Fineman did not blame Solomon Heart. She blamed the three workmen who had done the major portion of the job. "Since I acted in good faith with your people," she wrote Divine, " I feel that the responsibility for repairing the casino is theirs." She added, "My relations with all your people have always been most cordial," and she would "dislike very much taking this to a court action."

In response to Fineman's complaint, Divine allowed it to be published in the *New Day*, though without naming the three workmen except by giving their initials. However, Divine answered the complaint directly and he made his answer available for publication in the *New Day*. In his answer, Divine wrote that he did not have the authority to "force" the men to do anything, but if what Fineman said was true, the men should "make good for all damages." His publication of this correspondence in the *New Day* put significant pressure on these men to do just that.[5]

35. CHILDREN APART

PROBABLY MOST FOLLOWERS OF DIVINE raised their children within their own families, according to the usual American practice. But the more devoted followers of Divine, if they had children at all, were expected to separate themselves from them. In accordance with this expectation, many devoted followers, once their children had grown beyond infancy, allowed them to be sent away, to be raised in various Divine communities. Divine believed that many of these children would be better off if they were sent out of crowded metropolitan areas like Harlem to live in Peace Mission facilities in the Promised Land, in a quieter, more rural setting. Thus it was that a significant number of children were raised in Divine's Ulster County communities, apart from their parents.

Among the major questions that arise about this subject are the following. Since Divine taught against bringing more children into the world at all, how sympathetic to children was he? How much education did he encourage for them? In the long run, did the children who were brought up by his Ulster County communities apart from their parents become responsible, productive citizens? While information to answer such questions is limited, it is at least possible to approach answers.

At one time, as we have already seen, Divine followers planned to establish a private children's home somewhere in Ulster County, and at another time to establish a private school at Greenkill Park. Since neither of these proposals was carried out, the children living among Divinites in Ulster County were not concentrated in any one or two locations. While children did not live at all the Ulster County missions, they lived at many of them, as at Kingston Mansion, Kingston Junior, Hope Farm, High Falls, New Paltz, Krumville Farm, Olive Bridge Farm, Spot-in-the-Road, and Stone Ridge Farm.

Who paid for the care of these children? As we have already seen, if the parents were considered true followers, they would not be expected to pay for the care of their children within the movement. If, however, the parents of these children were not considered true followers, they would be expected to pay for their care.

When a state institution for delinquent boys proposed to place one of its boys as a foster child in a Divine residence in High Falls, Divine asked the state if it would pay for the boy, as the state normally did for foster children. But the state declined unless the residence applied for a state foster care license, which Divine refused to have it do. Divine wanted his mission homes to be independent, not subject to state "red tape." Because Divine consistently maintained this policy, no Divine missions anywhere were known to have been licensed as foster care homes.

In their Mission homes, Divinite children were assigned guardians. Under the care of their guardians, the children were taught the virtues of honesty, self-respect, and faith. They were taught to look up to Divine. They were not allowed to read comic books. They were not allowed to read ordinary newspapers or magazines. They were taught not to swear, drink, smoke, or attend theater. They were expected to prepare their school lessons and aim high.

Missions normally arranged for their children, when they reached the appropriate age, to attend public schools. Divine encouraged education for these children not only on the elementary and high school levels, but also, when appropriate, at higher levels, seemingly unafraid of the impact of such education on them. The Divine platform, as adopted in 1936, called for free universal education, at all levels, and opposed segregation in education, at any level. Simon Peter, when he was the proprietor of a Peace Mission grocery in High Falls, speaking at a Divine meeting, pointed out the need for "children to qualify themselves if they expect to perform tasks of a responsible nature." Divine himself advised his followers to educate their children so that they would be ready to meet the demands of life. He boasted that "practically all" of the "thousands" of children who were Rosebuds were promoted from grade to grade as expected. Holding up high standards, he often urged those in high school to achieve test scores not just of 100 percent, but 200 percent. He encouraged them to do it not for themselves but for the "glory of God."[1]

A century earlier, in the 1840s and 1850s, when public schools were first becoming significant in the state, segregated black public schools had become common in the Hudson River region, as in New York City, White Plains, Haverstraw, Newburgh, Poughkeepsie, Catskill, and Hudson. Such segregated schools were outlawed by the state by gradual steps, as in 1873, 1900, and 1938. In Ulster County, however, no known segregated public schools had ever existed, the concentration of blacks being too small to make them practical. So by the 1930s, it was clear that children living in the Divine communities in Ulster County were legally entitled to enter all public schools. But how they would be received was another question.

WHEN THIS BUILDING WAS THE ONE-ROOM KRUMVILLE SCHOOL, CHILDREN ATTENDED IT FROM TWO DIVINE FARMS, THE KRUMVILLE AND OLIVE BRIDGE FARMS. Later the building, no longer used as a school, became a Reformed Church. (Photo by Robert Tucker, July, 2004)

A New Paltz mission child, the dark-complexioned Sweet Peace, attended the New Paltz public elementary school, which at this time was the State Normal School's practice school, located in its own new building on the Normal School campus. According to the recollection of a local white boy who attended school with her, Sweet Peace was agreeable, polite, and smart. Another Divinite child who attended the same school, an Afro-American boy named Cleveland Hall, was conspicuous for his ability to run fast. A local white boy who attended school with Cleveland liked to run with him, that is, he did until once Cleveland showed him that he carried a straight razor—Cleveland seemed not to have absorbed Divine's teaching of nonviolence. Other children being raised at the New Paltz mission included two whites, Laura Brock and her brother by adoption, Robert Mace. Robert attended the New Paltz schools, but Laura, frightened by the other children, refused to attend, and was taught at home, at her mission.

In the Krumville neighborhood, children growing up there on both of the Divine-related farms, the Krumville and Olive Bridge Farms, were sent to the Krumville public elementary school. It was a one-room school, located on County Route 2, near its junction with a road to Olive Bridge. In the 1930s, when the white children of the neighborhood first encountered the Divinite black children at this Krumville School, as one of the white children, George Kruger, afterwards recalled, they looked at them with wonder, because they had never seen blacks before. When Kruger attended there, he recalled, it had perhaps thirteen children altogether, ten whites and three blacks, the three being from the two neighboring Divine farms. Later other children who attended the school from the Krumville Farm recalled the school as having perhaps twenty pupils, and in the recollection of one of them, the Afro-American Patrick Henry, the children accepted him easily, in school and out, because he was an agile baseball player.

George Kruger recalled that in his second or third grade, he inherited books which had been used by previous pupils, and noticed that where the books referred to non-whites by such terms as "Negro," the terms had been crossed out. He believed that Divine mission pupils had crossed them out, because, according to Divine's teaching, they were to avoid even reading terms that designated people by race.

Kruger remembered that in Krumville, when blacks were not present, whites, whether children or adult, would refer to blacks by derogatory terms. However, he recalled no other overt racial discrimination by the whites of the community, though it is a question if the blacks saw it the same way. Kruger did recall that one of the black boys, who attended the school, an older and stronger boy than he was, bullied him. When he recalled this bullying many years later, he chose to regard it as the way bigger boys typically treated littler ones, not as a racial matter.

After George Kruger's time, another white boy, Sheldon Boice, when he was visiting his grandparents in Krumville, would visit the Krumville school. In his recollection, two Divine mission girls, named Morning Star and Bright Star, attended the school. They were both older than he was, both blacks. Some sixty years later what he said that he especially recalled about these girls was their extreme Southern accent.[2]

In Kingston, the Peace Mission Mansion on Chapel Street housed a considerable number of children, especially children from the New York City region. When they were old enough, they walked downhill to the nearest public elementary school, which was close by, on Wilbur Avenue. There were sometimes four or five children from the Kingston Mansion in the school at a time.

In fact, Divine's standards for the children in his missions were at times painfully high. He seemed to want the black children to do extraordinarily well not as much to make them useful in his movement as to smooth their way to being integrated into American life. After the child named Free Will had moved out of Hope Farm to New York City, and had just graduated from Wadleigh High School, she took the flowers she had received at graduation to present to Divine, and Divine startled her by remarking that he knew she had failed the History Regents exam, a state-mandated achievement test. She felt so let down, she recalled many years later, that she "felt like a dog." Similarly, as June Peace was preparing to graduate from New Paltz High School, she received a grade of 100 percent on one of her Regents tests; when she sought out Father Divine to tell him about it, he told her he was not satisfied with only one such grade, and she went home and cried.

In response to high expectations, Divine mission pupils generally managed well in school. In the 1940s, when an Afro-American girl living at the Kingston Mansion, Melissa Williams, attended the Wilbur Avenue elementary school, she competed there with her white friend Margaret Naccarato for the top place in their grade. In 1950, when a probation officer representing a Brooklyn court checked on a child who lived at the Kingston mansion and attended the Wilbur School, school authorities told him that all the Mission children who had ever attended the Wilbur School were "better behaved and better trained and better kept" than most of the other children at the school. A child, Carmella Gardier, who lived at Kingston Junior, in the May Park neighborhood, wrote Divine in 1943 that she had succeeded in passing through fifth grade "with the highest marks in the class." The May Park one-room school having already been closed some years before, the school Carmella attended was probably Port Ewen's elementary school, a five-room school, on Broadway, which she could reach by bus. Years later, Carmella said she was grateful that Divine held out the standard of "perfection" because "it really makes you strive."[3]

TENSIONS FOR CHILDREN RAISED APART

If Peace Mission children were raised apart from their parents, there were inevitably tensions for them. What was Divine's attitude on his responsibility for such tensions? In a case in New York, in which a Divine follower was accused of neglecting her small child, she told a court that because of Divine's teaching, she felt "no responsibility" for the child. When the court asked Divine if he approved of her "leaving" the child, Divine answered that he did not. When the court asked him if he directed the woman to live with her child, Divine answered, "I do, if she so will," and explained that his followers should be "governed by their highest intuition."

Two psychiatrists, Lauretta Bender and M. A. Spalding, studied eight Divine-related children, all troubled, who had been sent to Bellevue Hospital, in New York, for observation. In 1940 they made sweeping charges in a medical journal that the parents of these children, having been taught by Divine to loosen their parental responsibility, had neglected them emotionally and physically, and consequently the children, when in school or elsewhere, were inclined to "asocial" acts. Two of these children had been living in Divine missions but were ousted for misbehavior. Two others were children whose father had taken them to live in a mission, but whose mother went to court to remove them, and then did not care for them.

In response to the psychiatrists Bender and Spalding, a Hope Farm resident, Sweet Inspiration, wrote an angry letter to them, denying that what they reported was typical of the treatment of Divine movement children, and citing in contrast what she considered to be Hope Farm's exemplary treatment of its children. As the farm's chef, Sweet Inspiration argued that the children were served milk three and four times a day. They were served "the freshest of choice vegetables from the well-kept gardens on the farm," "plenty of fruit" from the farm's orchards, and "fresh eggs" from prize chickens.

The children who lived at Hope Farm, all apparently apart from their parents, Miss Inspiration explained, lived in their own living quarters, the boys and girls separately, as Divine taught they should. "Their living quarters are the best, with every modern convenience; they have their own private dining room and a waitress-governess to serve them; they have the association of a trained matron who at one time was a high school teacher." They attend, she said, a nearby public school—she did not name the school, but it was the Blue Mountain School, a walk of less than a mile. They walk there when the weather permits, she explained, but "a good car is at their disposal with a licensed chauffeuress who takes them back and forth to school when the weather is bad. Everything is done to make them happy and they are well trained, clean-minded, generous hearted and trustworthy, peaceable and loving."

Divine seemed alert to the danger of cruelty to children. Speaking at Stone Ridge, he said he was aware that some residents of his own missions were "brutal" to them. He said he would not allow anyone to "beat" or otherwise "mistreat" children, pets, or farm animals. Care for them with "mercy and compassion," he urged," as you desire God to care for you." But if you cannot, he said, find someone else to care for them.

Divine also seemed alert to children mistreating each other. From the Spot-in-the-Road mission, outside of Stone Ridge, there was a report that three of its children, all girls, quarreled with each other as they walked back and forth from their mission to their one-room school, the Peak School on Peak Road. They were said to be "hitting and scratching each other." Their names were Mary Light, Sweet Love, and Miss Joy, ironical names for such scrappy girls. Providing an example of how Divine controlled his followers, he wrote them, "If you were in my mind and my spirit, you would not even say an unkind word to each other, much less resort to violence." Indicating he was concerned about his image, he warned them, your actions could "cause others to criticize and condemn my work." He threatened them severely: "If you are old enough to fight, you are old enough to know and understand what I am saying: if there is any more fighting among you, your guardians can put you in an institution or reformatory where you will not have the opportunity to fight." This was not entirely an idle threat on Divine's part, as Bender and Spalding cited cases of children who had been ousted from Divine missions in New York City for misbehavior and then sent to children's institutions. However, no such cases are known in Ulster County.[4]

CHILDREN WHO LIVED AT KINGSTON MANSION OFTEN ATTENDED THIS NEARBY WILBUR ELEMENTARY SCHOOL. Now the building, no longer used as a school, consists of apartments. (Photo by Rene F. Ramos, Aug., 2007)

OTHER TENSIONS

There were tensions over the relation of boys and girls to each other. As Divine said, in an interview at Krum Elbow, his teaching was that boys and girls should not play together, while teachers often encouraged them to do just that.

There were tensions if children called themselves by their religious names. When a child was ready to graduate from Kingston High School, she insisted on using her religious name to do so, but the school refused to allow it. In another case, a Divinite girl insisted on being called in school by her religious name, Bright Beautiful, but children often made sport over such names. When the school, disturbed by the name, brought it before a Kingston judge, the judge argued that using such an easily ridiculed name would create chaos, breaking down school discipline. The judge sought a ruling on the issue from the State Education Department, which decided in 1938 that in school, children must go by their original family names. Several years later, in a Kingston school, when a teacher asked a Divine mission boy who his father was, and he replied Father Divine, the teacher argued with him about it. The boy, however, persisted. As the boy recalled later, he would not "budge an inch."

There were also tensions over whether the Divine movement permitted its children to participate in certain school activities. When Edith McFarlane lived at Divine's Kingston Mansion, she attended a school, which had a gym class. When the gym teacher asked her to dance with boys, Edith explained that she could not do it because of her religious beliefs. She stopped attending the class, and her grades dropped as a result. Sunshine Love, who also lived at the Chapel Street mansion, attended Kingston High School, and was a member of its Dramatic Club. When she wrote Divine asking his permission to accompany the club on a one-day bus trip to New York, chaperoned by four teachers, "to see a play," he replied that he did not endorse "going to theaters, dances, and other such places." They would lead to "the lusts of the flesh." Anyone who wished to be a true follower, he said, "must be willing to make the sacrifices that are required." While as we have seen Divine could be tolerant of children like Laura Brock who scarcely warmed to his beliefs, he seemed firm in insisting that his followers adhere to certain standards of outward behavior.

According to what Divine heard, in the Krumville neighborhood a bus driver who was supposed to pick up two children from Divine's farms there to carry them to high school in Ellenville refused to pick them up because they were blacks. The driver, Divine heard, insisted he would give up his job first. If this report is true, Divine said, speaking in New York during World War II, it is like Hitler's treatment of the Jews. "We demand an immediate curb" to such behavior, he said, "Now is the time" for us as Americans "to fight Hitlerism up in Ulster County, but we must "fight it," he said, not with violence but with "love and with kindness and understanding." God does not want us to act "by violence but by righteousness." As Divine explained, the person at the Krumville mission who was especially affronted by the bus driver's refusal to pick up the children—evidently the Divine follower who was the guardian of these children—put the matter "in the hands of God." When you do that, Divine said, "God will fight your battle" for you. The driver was eventually persuaded to pick up the children after all, one of the children concerned later recalled, but in doing so, the driver "gave us a look as if we were dirt."

In another incident during the war, an Afro-American girl who lived at the Kingston Mansion, Wonderful Joy, wrote Divine complaining of the treatment that she and others of her color had "received at the hand of a prejudiced teacher." While the details of her complaint remain unknown, Divine was clear with his advice to the girl: "Hold your peace at all times," he told her. Meantime, "keep the faith," and "present perfect work." He added that for any teacher "to abuse an American citizen because of the color of his skin" is un-American, and encourages "Hitlerism."

Sunshine Flowers, a dark-complexioned resident of Divine's New Paltz mission, was disturbed by an incident in 1943 at the New Paltz High School. Sunshine was in a history class taught by Marie Bahnmuller when the class talked about "Negroes" in the South. As they did so, some of the class looked at Sunshine and laughed. Sunshine was hurt. She afterwards tried to explain to her teacher how she felt. She also tried to explain it to the adults in her Peace Mission.

One of the adults in her mission, the white nurse Mina Brock (Mighty Love), went to the school to discuss the incident with both the teacher and the principal, Ray G. Cunningham. According to Divine's understanding, Brock reported to them the usual Divine teaching that the term "Negro" was "vulgar" and was used to downgrade black people, and that while Divine preferred not using any racial terms at all, if any divisive expression was necessary, he recommended that a better term would be "Afro-American." In their conversation, Principal Cunningham asked, "Why not call them just Americans?" That, Divine wrote afterwards, "is exactly what every citizen of America should be called, regardless of his complexion."[5]

MANY CHILDREN BEING RAISED IN DIVINE COMMUNITIES ATTENDED KINGSTON HIGH SCHOOL, especially in the 1940s and 1950s. (Photo by the author, Aug., 2007)

HIGH SCHOOL

Some Divine mission children lived close enough to their high school to walk there, as did those who lived at the New Paltz Farm and the Kingston Mansion. Others attended high school by traveling on public busses, as did the children from High Falls who attended Kingston High School; they normally rode on a public bus, which took them via Route 209 through Stone Ridge, with the

Left: **NORMAL MITCHELL, WHO WAS RAISED AT THE KINGSTON MANSION, GRADUATED FROM KINGSTON HIGH SCHOOL in 1950. Afterwards he became a soldier in the Korean War, and then a New York City policeman.**

Center: **JOHN O. HENVILLE, UNDER PEACE MISSION GUIDANCE, FIRST ATTENDED THE KRUMVILLE SCHOOL, AND LATER KINGSTON HIGH SCHOOL. Afterwards he studied electrical engineering at New York University. He was warned that for a black to find an engineering job would be difficult. When he found one in Boston anyway, Divine spoke at a celebration for him.**

Right: **WHEN PAUL JEFFREY, WHO GREW UP AT KINGSTON MANSION, GRADUATED FROM KINGSTON HIGH SCHOOL IN 1950, HE WAS ALREADY A BAND LEADER. Afterwards he became well known as saxophonist, a promoter of jazz, and a Duke University music professor.** (All: Kingston High School Year Book, *Maroon*, 1950)

school system paying their fare. Still others attended high school by school bus, as we have seen the children from Krumville did who took a school bus to Ellenville High School.

When he was living at the Krumville farm, the black Patrick Henry, after he had graduated from the one-room Krumville school, took a school bus to Ellenville High School. Though few blacks attended that school, Patrick became comfortable enough there so that when his Krumville mission closed, and he moved to live at mission facilities in High Falls, he chose to continue attending the Ellenville High School, even though, since he was then living outside of its district, he was required to pay tuition. At Ellenville High, he was known for his participation in sports. When he graduated in 1946, his class year book reported he belonged to the Leader's Club, and teased him about his impressive "biceps."

Another child living at the Krumville farm, the white Peter Love, felt afterwards that he learned well while he was attending the one-room Krumville School. He believed so because he afterwards became an honor student in high school, first, when he attended Ellenville High School, later also, after he had moved to High Falls, when he attended Kingston High School.

Curtis Van Demark, a local boy who was not part of the Divine community, attended Kingston High School about 1946-48 with several of the children who lived at the Divine's Kingston Mansion; he recalled them all as Afro-American like himself. Especially on days when Curtis was out of school, he often visited them at the Kingston Mansion, on Chapel Street, reaching there by bicycle. In turn his friends at the mansion sometimes visited him, but not often, it seemed to him. They usually had to stay home to do chores such as caring for the lawn or house cleaning. But when they could get together, one of the mission children, Normal Mitchell, remembered playing basketball with Curtis, and having "lots of fun."

At the mansion, the children slept in a building separate from the main house, Curtis recalled. The children, including Curtis when he visited there, were expected to avoid being noisy. When adult guests were present, the children's were expected to avoid using the swimming pool. If adults asked the children to do something, Curtis recalled, the children who lived there "snapped" to do it, and Curtis did so too, believing that he would not be allowed to return if he did not. If he was at the mansion at meal time, he was invited to eat with the other children. They ate in the main mansion building, but at a special children's dining room, next to a kitchen. According to Normal Mitchell's recollection, the boys and girls were seated separately, the girls on one side of the table, the boys on the other side.

Curtis Van Demark does not recall ever seeing these children with their parents. It seemed to him as if the children did not have parents, and that the mansion served as an orphan asylum for them. The adults who especially watched and disciplined these children, as Curtis recalled them, were Satisfied Love, who was in charge of the mansion, and her assistant, Mary Lamb. Their discipline seemed to Curtis a little stricter than that of most families he knew.

Some of the boys living at the mansion also recalled an elderly male who helped discipline the boys. He was David Truth, known as Little David, who looked after the lawns, the furnace, and the chickens. One of the boys, Harold Maybanks, recalled that the mission raised many chickens, to serve in their dinners, and that Mr. Truth taught him, in bloody detail, how to wring their necks.

According to Curtis's recollection, he never attended a meeting at the mansion, never saw Father Divine there, and never asked the children about their religious beliefs. But he noticed that they were expected by their Divine mentors to be well mannered, not to participate in fights, and in school to complete their required studies. They usually did what they were expected to do, it seemed to him, including graduating from high school.

A considerable number of students were living at the Kingston Mansion when they graduated

IN 1950, THE KINGSTON HIGH SCHOOL SENIOR CLASS, IN A STRIKING GESTURE, CHOSE TWO RESIDENTS OF DIVINE'S KINGSTON MANSION AS CLASS OFFICERS. The two, both on the right, were Harvey Keyes, Treasurer, and Melissa Williams, Secretary. (Kingston High School Year Book, *Maroon*, 1950)

from Kingston High School. One was Juanita C. Otto, who graduated in 1938 and married a local boy, becoming Juanita Harris. Another was the black Melissa Williams, who graduated from Kingston High School along with her white friend Margaret Naccarato, in 1950. Other such blacks graduating about that same time included Alfonso McLennan (1949) who entered the Air Force; George Braye (1950) who entered the Army and long remained in it; Harvey Keyes (1950) who became a professional football player for the Los Angeles Rams; Normal Mitchell (1950) who entered armed forces and later became a New York City policeman; Harold Maybanks (1951), who became a soldier in Korea, worked in a Peace Mission grocery in Philadelphia, and later clerked in a variety of government offices; and Robert Hampton (1952) who became a military policeman in Korea. Maybanks recalled their Peace Mission upbringing as having produced "no major dysfunction," and Mitchell recalled that their upbringing "enabled most of us to be productive citizens."[6]

While the teachers in the Ulster County

schools seemed to be virtually all whites, some of them were known to be friendly to the mostly black Peace Mission children. A teacher of shorthand at Kingston High School, Marion A. Murray, visiting the Divine resort at Milton, said she had taught "many" Peace Mission girls in her classes, and "enjoyed them." A teacher of English at Kingston High, Joseph Block, speaking at Kingston Mansion, expressed his appreciation for "the kind of children" that Peace Missions sent to his school: "Although they vary in ability, they are uniformly well-mannered and well-behaved and are well-disciplined ladies and gentlemen," he said. "I wish I had a whole class of them."

According to Margaret Naccarato, who grew up in the Wilbur neighborhood near the Kingston mansion, she was not aware of bias against the Divinite children, whether in the Wilbur neighborhood or in the schools they attended. Her family being the first Italian family to live in the neighborhood, it is understandable that in her recollection, it was the Italians, not the blacks, who had to cope with having nasty epithets hurled at them.

In 1950, when Kingston High School's senior class elected their four class officers, two of them were blacks, and they were both from the Kingston Mansion. This was a striking sign of the increasing acceptance of Divine followers in the county. One of the two children thus honored was Melissa Williams, who sang in the school chorus, served as a cheerleader, and was called in her class yearbook "genuine." The other was Harvey Keyes, who also sang in the chorus, was a " spectacular" football player, and was reported in his class yearbook as having "friendly ways."[7]

COLLEGE

When June S. Peace was about to graduate from New Paltz High School in the early 1950s, she applied to be admitted to the New Paltz State Normal School. The school agreed to admit her, but warned her that when she graduated, they would not be able to place her in a teaching position because of her race. After deciding it would then be fruitless to attend the Normal School, she could have given up any ambition for the future, she recalled later, but because of Divine's support she kept pushing ahead. She moved to New York City, studied business, and eventually became one of Divine's secretaries.

While Divine churches helped to support some Divine-related youths to pursue higher education, such youths usually worked to help pay much of their own way. In 1953, a trustee of one of Divine's churches said that "most of us" Rosebuds, in keeping with Divine's advocating that we should be financially independent, "can see ourselves through college," especially if we stay in inexpensive Divine housing.

Carmella Gardier, after attending school near her Kingston Junior residence, eventually moved to Philadelphia where she worked her way through Temple University. When she graduated in 1955, followers gave her a graduation party, which Father and Mother Divine attended. Thereafter, Gardier became a teacher in the Philadelphia public schools.

Patrick Henry did well enough at Ellenville High School so that one of its staff helped him secure the offer of an athletic scholarship at a Vermont college, but he declined it. Henry's friend, Peter Love, however, after studying at both Ellenville and Kingston High Schools, worked to pay much of his own way for his higher education, and, with Divine Mission encouragement, eventually earning a Ph.D. in Chemistry from Pennsylvania State University, and became a college teacher.[8]

Among those who graduated from Kingston High School and went on to college were Paul Jeffrey and John Henville. Jeffrey, while still in school, led a school orchestra and then went on to study music at Ithaca College and later directed Duke University's Jazz Studies. Henville, who earlier had attended the Krumville School, after graduating from Kingston High School, went on to study electrical engineering at New York University and became an engineer in Boston.

Altogether, deliberately raising children apart from their parents was a practice not generally acceptable to Americans. However, this practice was so significant in Divine's Ulster County communities that it was inevitably a factor discouraging any replication of these communities in the outside world.

On the other hand, according to the limited evidence available, children raised in Divine's Ulster County communities often seemed grateful for being brought up in such communities even if they were apart from their parents. Despite their often living under tensions, many of them did well in school, and the Peace Mission often encouraged them to continue into higher levels of education, seemingly without fear that they would thereby be estranged from the Mission. Moreover, no matter what level of education they attained, many of them seemed to grow up to be disciplined, responsible citizens.

36. VISITORS

VISITORS to Ulster County's Divine sites varied in their expectations. Some came for the inexpensive, quality meals. Some came to vacation. Others came out of curiosity, as journalists or students. Some came to condemn. Still others came to learn what it was that led the Divine communities in such different directions from most of the world. Because their expectations differed, their reactions to their visits also differed.

When an associate editor of the *New Day* visited High Falls for the first time and saw its many Divine-controlled buildings, he was "astonished," he wrote, at Divine's "dominance" there. When a journalist from Philadelphia visited various Divine sites, he was impressed that men and woman were discouraged from sitting together at banquets or anywhere else. When the movie actress Elissa Landi (she starred in *Count of Monte Cristo*), visited a Divine site in High Falls, she saw "peace" in everyone there, she said, just as she saw it in the Divine follower whom she employed at her home.

While two evangelists were holding a revival in Saugerties, they attended a meeting at Greenkill Park where they heard testimony in praise of Divine. At the meeting, when the evangelists were themselves invited to speak, as visitors customarily were, they said it was blasphemous for Divine to allow his followers to claim that he was God, and he needed to be saved from his sin. In response, Divine followers, aroused, shouted, "Father Divine is God Almighty," until the visitors departed.

Gaius C. Bolin, Jr., who lived across the Hudson River in Poughkeepsie and served as an attorney for Divine followers, often visited nearby Divine sites. He was of an old family of public-spirited free blacks who just after the Civil War proposed the founding of an interracial college in Poughkeepsie, and recently included Jane Bolin who in 1939 had become the nation's first Afro-American woman judge, in New York City. In 1944, Gaius Bolin wrote Divine, "I have never seen the Christian attitude expressed in deeds more than I have observed it while with you and your followers."

W. E. B. DuBois, the radical black historian, after vsiting Krum Elbow in 1942, wrote that the Divine movement's publication, the *New Day*, was "not easily readable," probably being "intentionally obscure." But the movement itself, he conceded, was different from other "religious cults" in not being "noisy and obtrusive. It does do a great deal (just how much no one knows) of charity in feeding people and giving them work. It is (and this is most curious of all) interracial among people of the laboring and middle class." Considering what a natural skeptic DuBois was, he gave the movement significant praise when he concluded: "Of the various religious movements of our day, there is least in this that one may criticize."

A New York *Herald Tribune* writer, after visiting at least six Divine sites in Ulster County over several days in 1939, reported that opposition to the Divine movement's acquisition of property in Ulster County "has diminished steadily" as Divine's adherents have proved to be "hard working," and "quiet." Insisting that Divine followers did not bother their neighbors, he explained, "whatever revelry or song occurs on these hidden estates is almost invisible and absolutely noiseless

Facing page: **MAP SHOWING VISITORS SEVERAL "ROUTES TO THE PROMISED LAND."** (Often republished in the *New Day*, as on Sept. 26, 1940)

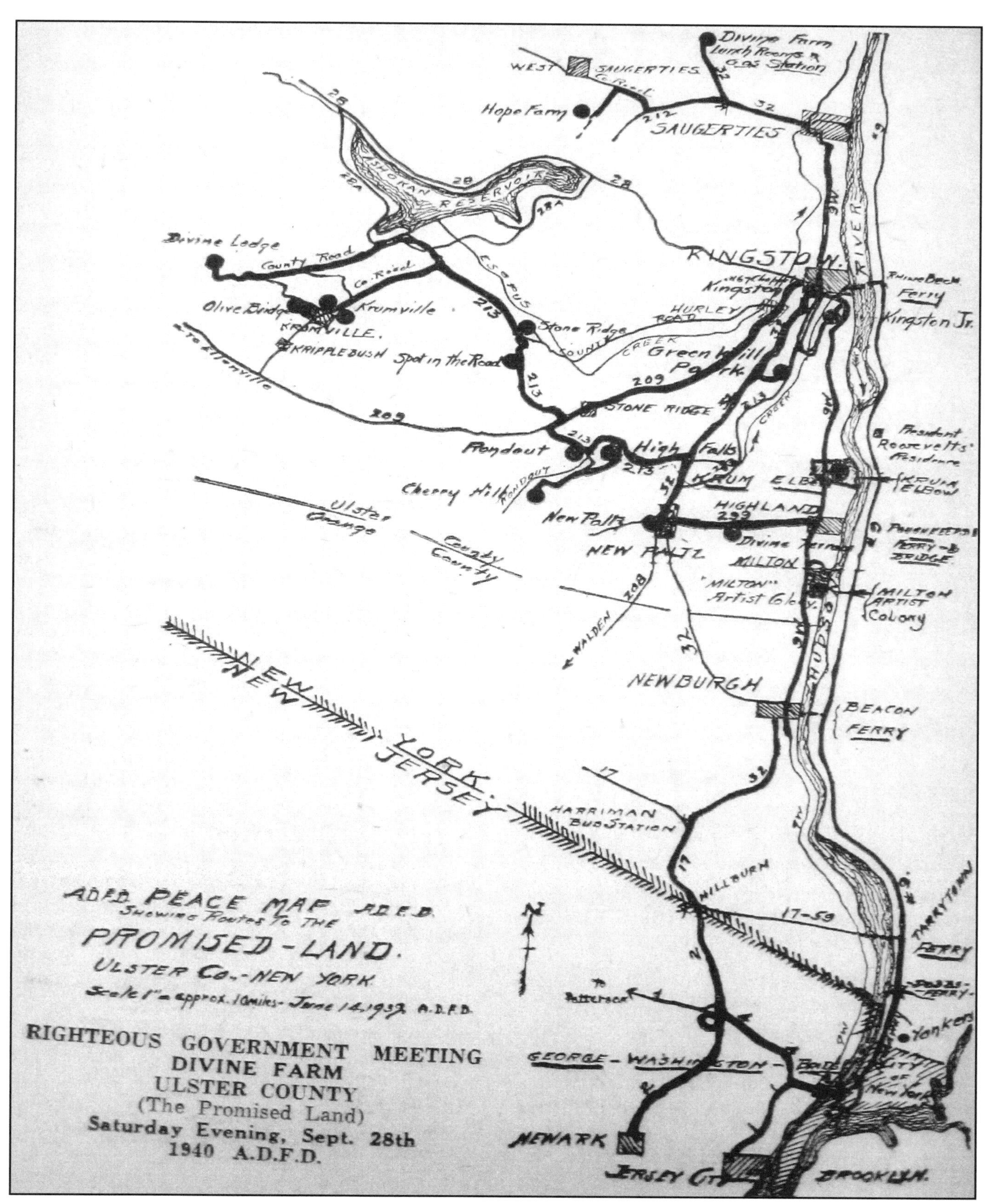
Divine Farm
Lunch Room &
Gas Station
WEST SAUGERTIES
Co. Road
Hope Farm
SAUGERTIES
ASHOKAN RESERVOIR
Divine Ledge
County Road
Co. Road
Olive Bridge
Kromville
KROMVILLE
KRIPPLEBUSH
Spot in the Road
Stone Ridge
ESOPUS
KINGSTON
Kingston
HURLEY ROAD
Rhine Beck
Ferry
Kingston Jr.
Greenkill Park
STONE RIDGE
To Ellenville
President Roosevelts' Residence
Rondout
High Falls
Cherry Hill
KRUM ELBOW
KRUM ELBOW
HIGHLAND
New Paltz
NEW PALTZ
Divine Terrace
MILTON
Ulster
Orange
County
County
POUGHKEEPSIE
FERRY & BRIDGE
"MILTON" Artist Colony
MILTON ARTIST Colony
WALDEN
HUDSON
RIVER
NEWBURGH
BEACON FERRY
NEW YORK
NEW JERSEY
HARRIMAN
BUS STATION
HILLBURN
TARRYTOWN
FERRY
DOBBS FERRY
Yonkers
GEORGE - WASHINGTON - BRIDGE
CITY OF New York
NEWARK
JERSEY CITY
BROOKLYN
A.D.F.D. PEACE MAP A.D.F.D.
Showing Routes To The
PROMISED-LAND.
ULSTER Co.-NEW YORK
Scale 1" = approx. 10 miles - June 14, 1937 A.D.F.D.
RIGHTEOUS GOVERNMENT MEETING
DIVINE FARM
ULSTER COUNTY
(The Promised Land)
Saturday Evening, Sept. 28th
1940 A.D.F.D.

VISITORS AT KINGSTON MANSION (*Spoken Word*, Aug. 22, 1936)

VISITORS VIEWING HOGS AT STONE RIDGE FARM, with Divine (center right). The visitors seem well dressed. (*New Day*, Sept. 5, 1940)

a short distance away." While Divine stores "undersell" neighboring stores, he said, they do not threaten them because "their stocks are meager." Nevertheless, he found that many followers, "white and colored," showed "ecstatic happiness verging on insanity." Divine "pulls" their "strings of emotion," he said, making them "dance." Divine, he decided, has "complete domination" over them.[1]

TEACHER EDWARD THORLAKSON

Vacationing in the Promised Land in the early 1940s was the academic Edward J. Thorlakson, a teacher of speech at Brooklyn College. A Canadian by origin, he had been a teacher in Alberta, had served as president of the Alberta Teachers Association, and had dabbled at being a playwright. What first caught his attention about Divine was his saying, "Where coercion begins, the work of God that moment ends." In regard to Divine's teaching against family connections, Thorlakson—who himself was married and stayed so—admitted that a family "ties us down," and may be selfish and domineering; we need to feel free from family "to consider all humanity as our brothers and our sisters." In regard to Divine's teaching sexual abstinence, Thorlakson cited Tolstoy and Gandhi as also teaching it.

While Thorlakson was visiting Krum Elbow, "a whole sweep of history" came before his eyes. He thought of the Pharaohs "building huge temples" by "grinding down" the common people. He thought of Romans "driving their slaves" to market. He thought of more recent slums "where many men have grown rich on the money of poor children with rickety limbs." He was thankful to find at last a place where all people, of any race, of any status, even if they had been slum dwellers, "can come and be happy and healthy."

Living as Thorlakson did among "intellectuals" and "cynics," he found it wrenching to try to follow Divine. He found himself saying with Shelley: "I fall upon the thorns of life, I bleed." However, it helped him, he said, that over time he learned to listen to what people said about Divine, no matter what it was, and not to "argue with them any more." By the mid-1940s, after someone had told his superiors at Brooklyn College that he was associated with Divine, the college told him, according to Thorlakson, that he was too "simple-minded" for college teaching, and dismissed him.

Thereafter Thorlakson scarcely tried to get back into college teaching, finding it "too restricted." He found he could be freer and make more money by teaching speech privately, and by doing radio work, writing, and lecturing. But he and his wife continued to maintain their loyalty to Divine so that his "power" would keep "flowing in." By 1955, Thorlakson had written the manuscript of a book on Divine's movement, and Divine, having read portions of it, considered it "very good." With Thorlakson saying that he had already been rewarded for writing it by his "enlightening" experience in the Peace Mission, he and Divine talked about publishing the book on a not-for-profit basis, so that, according to the spirit of Divine's teaching, it could be distributed free. But it is not known that the book was ever published.[2]

NEIGHBORING SCHOOL GIRL

Mildred Jerry grew up close to the Spot-in-the-Road farm, one of Divine's smaller Ulster County communities, near Stone Ridge. Long afterwards she recalled that by the time she was a teenager in the late 1930s, only four Divine followers usually occupied this farm: one black man, in his fifties, who lived above the garage, and three women who lived in the main house, two being middle aged blacks, and one being a young white, called Gentle Presence, who believed Divine had healed her.

Mildred and her parents, becoming well acquainted with their Peace Mission neighbors, found they welcomed being called by their first names. They found that they dressed much as other people did, and kept their buildings clean. They did not seem pushy, but rather friendly, and willing to help. Mildred did not recall hostility toward them from any of the neighbors, whites though they were, including Mildred's family.

Although Father Divine occasionally visited the farm, Mildred doubted that he ever stayed there overnight because, she believed, the house was too small. During his visits, however, he would sometimes call on the Jerry family. He was just being neighborly, Mildred Jerry explained. He would bless them, and wish them health, prosperity, and peace. Mildred felt Divine's charismatic power and was moved.

At this farm, followers enlarged a chicken house into a restaurant capable of seating twenty-five, Mildred recalled. The restaurant became popular, especially on weekends, partly because, in keeping with Divine's insistence, its dinners cost only 15 cents. When the young white woman served the meals, to Mildred she seemed pasty-faced because she was not allowed to use make-up.

Mildred and her parents were among those who occasionally went to the dining room for dinner. They were usually served boiled chicken, Mildred remembered, not fried chicken. It was served with rice and gravy and was delicious, it seemed to her. Besides, they were invited to have second helpings if they wished. At the dinners, Mildred remembered never hearing any singing and never hearing Father Divine speak. But Mildred found herself drawn to Divine and his teachings.

When Mildred was in her upper teens, about 1941, she was bothered by headaches. Aware of the healing powers attributed to Divine, she considered asking him to heal her. But she also had heard that it was not necessary for him to be present to heal anyone, since he taught that he healed not by saying any particular words or by any touch of his hands, but by his spirit reaching the faith of the person being healed. Finally, once when Mildred was at home and Divine was not present, she called out, "Thank you, Father," the same as she had heard the neighboring Divine followers call out many times. Instantly she felt healed.

Long afterwards, when asked if she had ever actually become a follower of Father Divine, her only answer was that after her healing, Divine, having moved out of New York State, seldom came to Spot-in-the-Road.[3]

COSMETICIAN SARA WASHINGTON

Sara S. Washington was the head of a prominent beauty culture business for blacks, the Apex Hair Company, of Atlantic City, New Jersey. A black herself, she became a follower of Father Divine, and as such she became one of the buyers for the Divine movement of the Brigantine Hotel, an ocean-front hotel just outside of Atlantic City. She tried to inject into her business such practical teachings of Divine as honesty, courtesy, paying substantial wages, selling at low prices, and paying bills promptly. Like Divine, she enjoyed talking "volitionally," without a prepared manuscript, and became a frequent speaker at Divine meetings, as in Ulster County.

Once Washington vacationed at Greenkill Park with a party of ten friends—some from Atlantic City, others from Philadelphia. She reported that most of the Park's visitors were not followers of Divine, but simply vacationers, seeking health, quiet, and safety for their children. She and others vacationers regularly went hiking. both morning and evening. One day, they made a side-visit to the Stone Ridge farm, where one of the farmers showed them their cows and crops; Washington, who owned a farm of her own, was pleased that the farmer did not complain about his work, as in her experience most farmers did. Altogether she reported that the Promised Land was suffused with "infinite love."

When Washington was visiting Krum Elbow, Father Divine asked to interview her about her soap products. He interviewed her at 3:30 one Sunday morning, with secretaries present as usual, to record the interview—he chose this time because he was expecting to leave soon for New York City. Divine told her that if some of her non-cosmetic products, like bath and laundry soap, were available in suitable quality at low prices, he would recommend that his followers buy them. Illustrating his effort to ally himself with those capable of significantly supporting his movement, he explained, "I would like to show my appreciation for your contact with me." Afterwards, when Washington advertised in the *New Day* certain non-cosmetic products including mouth wash, tooth powder, and several soaps, the periodical took care to explain editorially that these non-cosmetic products were the "maximum amount of beauty preparations endorsed by Father Divine," meaning that he did not endorse Apex cosmetic products such as rouge or hair straighteners.[4]

SARA WASHINGTON, PRESIDENT OF THE APEX COMPANY, often visited Divine sites in Ulster County. She was a follower. Nevertheless, because Divine regarded some of her company's products as cosmetic, he would not endorse them. (*New Day*, Sept. 11, 1941)

BENEFACTOR CALLOWAY

Once in 1936, Charles Calloway was riding in a truck of his in Ulster County, on business for Divine, when it was in a minor accident. Both Calloway and the driver were identified in a local newspaper as from "one of Father Divine's Ulster County 'heavens,'" without naming which one, at the same time that they were also identified as being from New York City. The truck was driving at night on the edge of the village of Saugerties, on Ulster Avenue, carrying, according to the Saugerties *Telegraph*, "several colored men." After the accident, owner Calloway and his driver were fined for the truck's not having appropriate reflectors. According to the newspaper, Divine, when he was notified of the fines, promptly paid them.

While it is a question whether Calloway, a man of dark complexion, ever lived any length of time in Ulster County, he was believed to be married to Mom Sarah of the New Paltz mission, and he clearly had a significant presence in the county. When Divinites ran a big excursion to open Greenkill Park in the summer of 1937, Divine's secretary, John Lamb, explained that "finances" for the excursion were provided by Charles Calloway. Later that year, after a fire at the Park burned down its hotel building, when reporters asked the long-time caretaker there if he knew of any plans to rebuild the hotel, the caretaker referred them "to Mr. Calloway in New York City."

Charles Calloway, a retired railroad worker, had been impressed with Divine ever since 1931 when he attended Divine's meetings at Sayville and became convinced that Divine was unselfishly assisting the poor and weak. Soon afterwards, when Divine was moving out of Sayville, Calloway, who leased several apartments on 135th Street in Harlem, and made his home in one of them, invited Divine to move into his home, which Divine did, making it his headquarters. In 1933, when Lena Brinson offered Divine a larger house, on West 115th Street, to occupy as his headquarters, Divine moved there instead, and Calloway moved there also, with his wife.

When the first Peace Mission church, the Palace Mission Church, was founded in 1940, Calloway was one of a small group who took the initiative to found it. From at least 1945, Calloway served as that church's president. In 1954, however, at a Palace Mission Church annual meeting, when Calloway was up for reelection as a church trustee, Divine reported, without giving any details, that Calloway had not been living according to the church's discipline, and asked that he be excommunicated. The members promptly voted to do so, with "thunderous applause."[5]

QUAKER LOVELL

A frequent visitor to Peace Mission sites was Malcom R. Lovell, of a Quaker family with a long history of concern for racial minorities. At first, in recognition of significant similarities between Quakers and the Peace Mission, the relation between Lovell and the Divine community was glowing.

Lovell, a vice president of the Title Guarantee and Trust Company, lived in New York on Riverside Drive. He had served on Quaker boards. He was the great-grandson of Quaker Arnold Buffum, who before the Civil War had been the president of the New England Anti-slavery Society and was such a radical abolitionist that conservative Quakers disowned him.

Lovell made his first visit to a Divine event, in February, 1939, attending a banquet in Harlem where Divine was presiding. When Divine asked as usual if any visitors wished to speak, Lovell did so, saying, as reported in the *New Day*, that he had never before seen such a "spirit of love" as he saw here, and he was "deeply moved." He said he hoped to share in the work they were doing.

During the next summer, Lovell was one of thirty Quakers who were dinner guests of Divine at his home in New York. Also that summer, Lovell, at a Divine meeting in New York City, supported Divine's campaign to persuade Congress to pass an anti-lynching bill, saying Americans are hypocrites to condemn Germany for its cruelty to Jews while it tolerates the lynching of blacks. Also that summer, Lovell visited several Ulster County extensions, with his wife and little son. At the Milton extension, Divine introduced the Lovell family at a meeting, saying, "the majority of you know them quite well." Divine explained that they were Quakers who according to their tradition, wait to speak "until the spirit moves," as he himself did also. Lovell spoke, attributing the abundant blessings Divine followers enjoyed to their "undeviating faith." After Germany had invaded Poland, Lovell, again visited Milton, in October, 1939, and again spoke, saying that the word "peace," with which the followers kept greeting him, was "the finest word that is said in the world."

The next month, Divine invited Lovell to the opening of a new Peace Mission mansion in New Rochelle. Reporting on Lovell's being there, the New York *Sun* declared that Lovell was a "follower" of Divine. This and similar exaggerated claims led some of Lovell's associates to shun him. Organizations he belonged to, including a Quaker board, asked him to resign. Lovell, appalled, pulled back. He wrote the *Sun*, "I am proud to include Father Divine among those of whom I think well." But if for "my wife and myself" to accept an invitation to dine with someone "constitutes following," then "we are followers" not only of Divine but also of "Catholic bishops, Baptist clergymen, and Shinto priests, for we have dined as guests of all of them." Then seeming to shift to a more rigorous meaning of the word "follower," he concluded bluntly, " but I and my family are Quakers and followers of George Fox and no one else."

Divine, apparently having little tolerance for

what seemed to him to be public disavowals of loyalty to himself, became upset by Lovell's statement. Hearing this, a few days later Lovell went to see Divine, hoping to repair any hurt. Divine reminded him that he had repeatedly assured Divine privately that he was "with me one hundred percent," but now you are "ashamed to own me." You are afraid "it might hurt you in your contact in Wall Street."

Lovell insisted that Divine had always known that he was a Quaker, and that he still believed in Divine's work. Divine in turn insisted that you could be a Quaker, Catholic, Jew, Buddhist, or Mohammedan and still be a "devout follower" of his, but not if you were ashamed to be identified with him.

Lovell asked if he could still help Divine with his work. Divine replied, as he customarily did to such offers, that he did not need any help. My "spirit," he said, "sustains me." When they parted, uneasy with each other, Lovell asked, "May I come again?" Divine replied, "Sure, you may." But thereafter Lovell seemed to drop out of sight in the Divine movement.[6]

E. TEACHING AGAINST WAR

37. RESISTING THE APPROACH OF WORLD WAR II

BEFORE THE OUTBREAK OF WORLD WAR II, Father Divine led his movement to be peace conscious. He called his movement, in Ulster County and elsewhere, the "Peace Mission Movement." His followers commonly used the word "peace" to greet one another. They said "peace" in answering the telephone. They used it on signs in parades.

Just as the term "peace" has many meanings in the Christian tradition generally, so it came to have many meanings in the Divine movement. In the movement, it could mean the desired condition of an individual's inner nature. It could also mean an individual's relation to God, to neighbors, and to the world. By the mid-1930s, one of its major meanings was anti-war.

By 1936 when Hitler was threatening Europe, in America the hope of keeping America out of war had encouraged the growth of pacifism. At that time, when the Divine movement held a big convention in New York, at St. Nicholas Palace on West 66th Street, it adopted, with considerable input from followers, a platform which the movement has continued to regard as its platform ever since. This platform opened by greeting "all mankind" with "peace." It called for the radical restructuring of society, including the abolition of tariffs between nations, the abolition of racial segregation, limiting the charging of interest, and making education at all levels free, and it called for doing all this by peaceful means, "by the ballot, and not by the bullet." It called on both individuals and nations to destroy "all fire-arms" except those "used for law enforcement." Of particular significance here, the platform declared forthrightly that "the true followers of Father Divine will refuse to fight their fellowman for any cause whatsoever."

This was an absolute anti-war platform. Divine and the convention, in adopting it, were scarcely trying to curry favor with the flag-waving public. It was a question if they were looking ahead as to what the consequences of such a radical peace platform might be.

In accord with such nonviolent teachings, however, the Divine movement had already persuaded a swaggering West Indian gangster of the New York metropolitan region, Job Patience, to throw his gun into the Hudson River, and eventually to say that he would not "even use a toothpick to defend myself." It was also in accord with such teachings, that Clarence V. Howell, a Methodist minister who had taken many students to visit Divine's missions, claimed in the *Christian Century* in 1936 that Divine's movement was "absolutely pacifist."[1]

Meanwhile, Divine was protesting both the persecution of the Jews in Germany and discrimination against Afro-Americans in the United States, often indicating that they were parallel. He kept emphasizing his familiar theme that all peoples and all religions are one, and that true Americanism was an amalgamation of them all.

In 1937, as Hitler became a growing threat in Europe, the Divine weekly *New Day* argued editorially for keeping America out of war. "All any war ever proved," it claimed, "was who was strongest and who was weakest; it never proved who was right and who was wrong." Similarly, the *New Day*, looking at the world's militaristic powers, advocated the use of the boycott as a means to "bog down" their "war machines." In particular, to slow Japan's military expansion in Asia, it encouraged the boycott of Japanese silk stockings, a move which was becoming popular in progressive circles.

Soon afterward, the *New Day* repeatedly advertised that it was selling a "peace sticker"—it could be affixed to correspondence—which quoted President F. D. Roosevelt as asking people to pray for peace. Also the *New Day*, looking back at the previous Great War, quoted a Foreign Policy Association report as saying that that war, for the allies, was "a great land grab."

Divine himself, speaking in 1937 at the Kingston Mansion, told the story—which he often retold—of a Harlem black who had refused to fight in the previous great war because of his religious conviction. When officials asked him what his religion was, he would not say that he was a Methodist, only that he belonged to the "Overcoming Church of Jesus Christ," and that he would not do any work in support of the war, even non-military work. He was imprisoned. He was put in straight jackets. His limbs were stretched. He was threatened with guns. His weight dropped to sixty-five pounds. Still he would not fight. Finally officials, convinced of the reality of his religious conviction, released him. If your conviction is "radical enough" commented Divine, "you will overcome every opposition."[2]

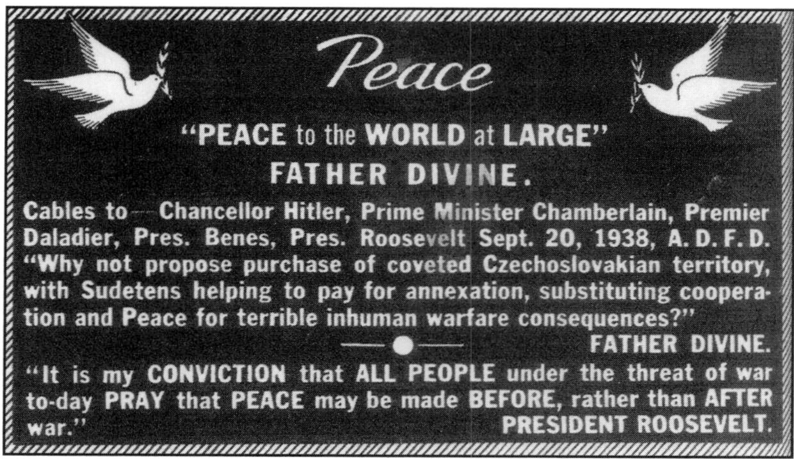

TO PREVENT GERMANY FROM VIOLENTLY SEIZING the German-speaking part of Czechoslovakia, Divine advocated that Czechoslovakia sell it to Germany. ("Peace Stamp," enlarged, *New Day*, Jan. 19, 1939)

In September, 1938, when Germany was threatening to seize part of Czechoslovakia—its German-speaking Sudetenland part—Father Divine cabled Hitler, President Roosevelt, and other heads of state, proposing that Germans be required to pay for the territory it coveted rather than being allowed to seize it violently. This would substitute "cooperation and peace for terrible inhuman warfare," Divine explained. When one of Divine's secretaries sent copies of the cablegrams to the press, he explained that Divine made his proposal in accordance with the same method he was using in purchasing "large tracts of land on the cooperative basis" in Ulster County, evidently taking pride that Divine and his followers had used peaceful rather than violent methods to obtain the land despite the county's customary racial suspicion. A few days later, after representatives of Germany, Italy, Britain, and France, meeting at Munich, had agreed to allow Germany to annex the disputed territory, Divine claimed, in a speech at the Kingston Mansion, that Czechoslovakia had made a "complete sacrifice" in ceding this territory without war, and that this was in keeping with Jesus's teaching that if any man sues you at law, and takes your coat, let him have your cloak also.

When Germany invaded Poland in September, 1939, marking what came to be regarded as the opening of World War II, Divine telegraphed President Roosevelt, asking him to save "civilization" by keeping America out of the war. About the same time, speaking at a banquet at the Divine's mission at Ulster County's Samsonville, Divine said that if people would stop stressing negatives like the differences between groups, races, and nations, and instead teach the positives like love and the unity of all people, they would end war. In October, speaking at Ulster County's Milton art colony, he said that Moses's teaching of "an eye for an eye" was "limited" religion, but Jesus's teaching of turning the other cheek was "advanced" religion, and if you follow Jesus, "you would not fight your brother for any cause." Restating his long-held pacifist position, Divine declared flatly, it is impossible "to be a Christian" and "make war."

During that same October of 1939, the Divine weekly *New Day* protested against America's policy of pretending to be neutral, but actually favoring Britain by making loans and leasing war materials to it. It argued instead for a real neutrality policy that would treat both sides in the war alike.

At about this time, someone who was hostile to Divinites burned a cross on their Krumville Farm. In response, followers there took turns patrolling the farm, carrying "shotguns." Perhaps these followers justified themselves by saying they were using firearms to enforce the law, as the Divine platform allowed.

In November, 1939, a group of youthful Divine followers who attended Kingston High School presented a play on how to serve your country in the time of war. They presented it at the Kingston Mansion, with some of their Kingston High School teachers present. The play argued that, while Europe was at war, a war that was more real was the war at home against anger, hate, and prejudice.[3]

By December, 1939, when Germany seemed to threaten to invade the Americas, Divine was advocating uniting all the Americas. Join all the Americas together, he proposed, including the United States, Canada, Central America, and South America. Join them into one democratic nation, with one language. Doing so would prevent invasion, he said, and reduce defense expenses. This would be "constructive" defense, he explained, rather than the usual "destructive" military defense. Later Rev. Ashton Jones, a peace advocate from Atlanta, goaded Divine about this proposal, insisting on asking him if his saying he was for defense of the Americas meant that he supported using physical force to defend them. Divine said no, he meant defense as in uniting the people without racial discrimination and as in helping people to become economically stronger. Divine and his followers pushed this unite-the-Americas concept, advocating it in a peace sticker and proposing it in writing to the heads of state of all the Americas.

In January, 1940, when big Russia had invaded its little neighbor Finland, and Finland seemed remarkably adept in resisting the invasion, a Finnish visitor to a Divine meeting at High Falls asked Divine to comment on the Finnish resistance. Divine said the Finns were "forced" to fight. "If they continue in the faith," he said, God "will give them the victory." But "we know fighting with the sword is not the keynote to salvation! It is not the standard I have lifted." The Finns have "not come to that place in consciousness where they can fight with the spirit of passiveness." They are not yet able to "fight with the sword of the spirit."

As 1940 advanced, Germany invaded Denmark and Norway (April); then it invaded the Low Countries (May); and then also France (June), leaving Britain, threatened with invasion herself, to fight on, among Western nations, almost alone. This increased pressure on the United States to come to her aid. It also whittled down many pacifist convictions, including Divine's. But in September, when Congress created a new conscription system, the first-ever American peacetime military conscription, Divine, while protesting that the military continued to be racially segregated, praised the new law for providing that conscientious objectors could perform alternative service.[4]

The new draft law treated conscientious objectors far more generously than they had been treated in World War I. It provided that objectors could perform alternative service outside of the military system, as had not been permitted in World War I. It also provided that, while the objectors anti-war views must be based on religious belief, the objector was not required to be a member of any church at all. As draft registration day approached, October 16, 1940, the day on which all males of draft age were required to register for service, whether military or non-miliary, Divine advised his followers to register as the law required.

TO HELP THE AMERICAS WARD OFF GERMAN OR JAPANESE INVASION, Divine proposed that all the Americas, including Central and South America, unite with the U. S. into one nation. ("Peace Stamp," *New Day*, Dec. 5, 1940)

Soon the *New Day* was reporting how conscientious objectors, including followers of Divine, were registering. Some were asking to be assigned to non-combatant service within the military system, with the customary army pay. Others were asking to be assigned outside of the military system to work of "national importance" under civilian direction, in units which came to be called Civilian Public Service, without pay. Gradually it became evident, according to *New Day* reports, that Civilian Public Service, unlike the Army, was racially unsegregated. It became evident that the conscientious objectors assigned to it were normally sent, especially at first, to camps, usually former Civilian Conservation Corps (CCC) camps, where they did rough outdoor work, like CCC men, as in forestry or soil conservation.

As Divine followers registered, some as soldiers and some as conscientious objectors, a New York City draft board appealed to Divine to clarify his teaching about participation in war. Divine replied that he himself had registered for the military draft in the First World War as a conscientious objector, but had not been called to serve, presumably because he was a clergyman. In this war, he said, if he were of draft age, he would again register as a conscientious objector, and he expected "practically all of his immediate staff" would do so too. But Divine did not insist directly on what his 1936 platform plainly said, that his "true followers" would "refuse to fight their fellowman for any cause whatsoever."

Under pressure to be patriotic and anti-Hitler, and to avoid any charge that he was advising anyone to refuse to comply with the draft law, he was beginning what was to be a long, gradual process of softening his anti-war teaching. He noted that his platform said that all persons and nations should destroy their firearms except those needed for law enforcement. Stretching that exception, he considered that the American military could be regarded as a "great law enforcement body." From this point of view, for his followers to serve in the American military was permissible, he explained, taking a position that seemed to differ from his earlier absolute pacifism. As to whether his followers should choose to do military service or be conscientious objectors, he emphasized at this time and afterwards again and again, that each follower should follow his own "individual religious conviction," or "highest intuition."

Before the adoption of the 1936 platform, Divine had only occasionally advised his followers not to follow his teaching merely because it was his teaching, but rather to follow their own "highest intuition." While this tolerant policy did not pervade the 1936 platform, after the military draft went into effect in 1940, urging followers to follow their "highest intuition" gradually became a major aspect of his teaching, and he applied it not only to war but to a broad variety of other complex concerns, including whether to stay married, be vaccinated, take on new work, or engage in civil disobedience.[5]

In early 1941, the *New Day* interpreted the government's actions relating to the war, such as lend-lease assistance to Britain and providing gas

— PEACE —
RIGHTEOUSNESS, TRUTH and JUSTICE
You Are Cordially Invited To
ATTEND A GREAT
Patriotic Outing, Demonstration and Mass Meeting
IN THE INTEREST OF WESTERN
HEMISPHERE DEFENSE
FATHER DIVINE Expected to Be Present in Person
AT
• Greenkill Auditorium •
DIVINE GREENKILL PARK
Near Kingston
THE PROMISED LAND, Ulster Co., N. Y.
Columbus Day
12 Noon to 5 P. M.
SUNDAY, OCTOBER 12th, 1941 A.D.F.D.
All Persons Interested in HOME DEFENSE are Welcome
Special invitation to all officials and representatives of Civil Defense Groups to Speak.
NO OFFERINGS — NO COLLECTIONS — NO SMOKING — NO DRINKING —
NO TIPPING NO PROFANE LANGUAGE — ON THE GROUNDS

ANNOUNCEMENT issued about two months before the attack on Pearl Harbor. (*New Day*, Oct. 9, 1941)

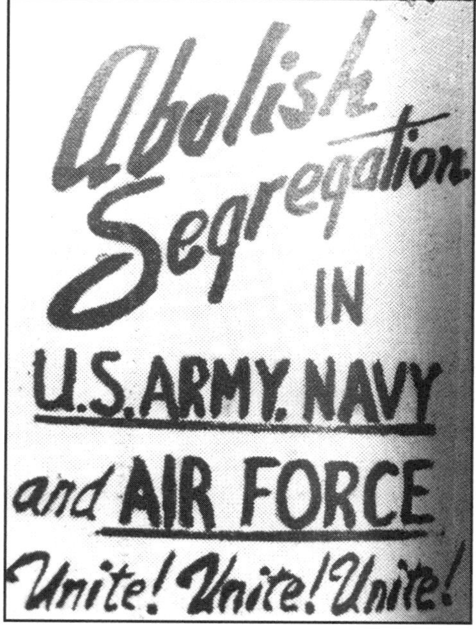

Above, left.: **POSTER DISPLAYED IN DIVINE COMMUNITIES, as at Greenkill Park.** (*New Day*, Sept. 11, Nov. 13, 1941) Above right: **POSTER DISPLAYED AT BOTH ROCKLAND PALACE AND GREENKILL PARK** (*New Day*, Sept. 11, Nov. 13, 1941) Below: **AT THIS CIVIL DEFENSE MEETING AT GREENKILL PARK, OCT. 12, 1941, DIVINE'S YOUNG WOMEN "ROSEBUDS," WEARING RED JACKETS, FORMED THE LETTER "P" FOR PEACE, and sang such songs as: "Give every nation a place in the sun; God's will, not ours be done." The four posters on the wall at the right say, from the left, "Enact the Bill of Rights" in every state, "Abolish Segregation" in the US military, "Unite the 3 Americas for Hemisphere Defense," and "Save Democracy: Pass the Anti-Lynch Bill."** (*New Day*, Nov. 13, 1941)

masks to the public, as devices to draw America into the war. In mid-1941, when a Los Angeles follower wrote Divine, reporting that he had registered for the draft as a conscientious objector, Divine replied to him, admitting that "all of my so-called followers may not be inspired to that degree," but insisting that each person should move according to his own "conviction," and asked to be kept informed of the outcome. At about the same time, when the FBI, trying to understand Divine followers who were registering as conscientious objectors, asked Divine about his teaching on participating in war, he replied that he taught his followers to be conscientious objectors, saying with Christ that we should "overcome evil with good," and "all they that take the sword shall perish with the sword." While he did not coerce his followers to be conscientious objectors, he explained, some were becoming so, and he included a list of thirty-three of his Northeastern followers who were conscientious objectors, including the *New Day* editor John DeVoute and a resident of Ulster County, Happy Mirth, of Saugerties.

At about the same time, Wisdom Kindness, one of Divine's New York City followers who had registered as a conscientious objector, was called by the FBI for a hearing. Before the hearing, Divine, in an interview with Kindness, told him that the government had a right to investigate him to find out whether he was a genuine conscientious objector rather than a draft dodger. He also told him that while the Peace Mission's 1936 platform said that "The true followers of Father Divine will not fight their brother for any cause whatsoever," nevertheless there are some of his followers who mean well, but "who have not lived exactly according to my teaching," and if they have a "fighting spirit in them," it is "justifiable" for them to use that spirit to fight for "national defense." Soon afterwards when two FBI agents interviewed Divine about Wisdom Kindness, Divine made it clear that he believed that Kindness was a legitimate conscientious objector. He has in him "the real seed of the Christ," Divine said. Wisdom Kindness, like "the majority of my followers," has reproduced the "characteristics of Jesus," Divine explained. Kindness would not use violence to "break in." He would not use violence "even for self-defense."

In October, 1941, only two months before the Japanese attacked Pearl Harbor, when the United States seemed close to being drawn into the war, and Divine followers were being pushed to show that they were patriotic, they arranged a bus excursion from New York City to Ulster County's Greenkill Park, where they held a civilian defense mass meeting. Thousands filled the auditorium and others spilled onto the grounds outside. Civilian defense officials both from Ulster County and New York City participated. By this time, many followers had already volunteered to serve in civilian defense posts, such as air raid wardens, and speakers at the meeting encouraged more of them to do so. Divine himself told the meeting that he and "a good many" of his followers "do not believe in taking up arms." But they could join in the civilian defense program because it tries, he said, using the words of a traditional hymn, to "rescue the perishing and care for the dying."[6]

Under the impact of Germany and Japan's brutal threat to civilization, Divine had gradually softened his pacifism. Although he continued to teach nonviolence as an ideal, he allowed his followers to apply the ideal in their own way.

38. WORLD WAR II: SOLDIERS AND CONSCIENTIOUS OBJECTORS

After the attack on Pearl Harbor on December 7, 1941, and the American entry into war, Father Divine continued to insist that his followers should follow the law by registering for the draft. To a youth who was about to become old enough to be required to register, but was questioning doing so for a nation that practiced racial segregation, Divine advised him to register anyway and not to let his resentment interfere. But on the question whether his followers should register as soldiers or as conscientious objectors, Divine said cautiously that there were no "binding laws" for his followers, and while he taught nonviolence, they should be "governed by their highest intuition."

Meantime, Divine encouraged cooperation with such war policies as the "mass production" of food. Speaking in New Paltz, Divine pointed out that while formerly the federal government, to raise prices for farmers, had encouraged the "mass destruction" of agricultural products, which Divine considered wrong, now he was glad to say that, for the sake of war production, the government was pushing for growing as much food as possible. Also Divine tolerated cooperation with the Red Cross. He did so despite its ties to the war effort and despite its refusal to accept Afro-American blood in its blood drives. Speaking at Krum Elbow, Divine told his followers, if they wished to give to the Red Cross, they were free to do so.

Moving further into cooperation with the war, when Divine heard that "several" followers were doing "very satisfactory" work as paid civilians at the Army's Camp Shanks, in Rockland County, and that officers there would be pleased to employ more followers as laborers, truck drivers, or firemen, Divine agreed to make this invitation known, and he did so without questioning the appropriateness of his followers thus serving the military. Similarly, when Divine heard that his follower True Jacob was working as a cook for a Navy mess hall at Cornell University in Ithaca, and that his follower Mary Joseph was working as a draftsman at the Brooklyn Navy Yard, Divine responded warmly, without questioning their thus supporting the military.[1]

Moreover, continuing to cooperate with civilian defense, by 1942 Divine himself was serving as a "chief" air-raid warden. Speaking to followers in New Paltz, he explained that participating in civilian defense was not "taking up arms to kill" contrary to "your religious conviction"; it was instead, as he often said, "rescuing the perishing and caring for the dying." Speaking in Kingston, not far from the Ashokan Dam which helped to store a large share of New York City's water supply, Divine said that he supported civilian defense against any enemy parachutists who might drop out of the sky to "blow up" the dam. He seemed to avoid the possibility that providing such civilian defense might call for violence.

In 1942, when the Coast Guard indicated that it would like to lease the Brigantine Hotel, a large Divine facility on the ocean near Atlantic City, New Jersey, Divine, in negotiating with the Coast Guard about it, seemed to side step his anti-war scruples. When the Coast Guard undertook to care for the building, Divine successfully persuaded his followers who owned the hotel—they included some of the same followers who owned Divine missions in Ulster County—to vote to lease it to the Coast Guard for the duration of the war, and even to lease it free. Leasing it in this manner, Divine explained to his followers, would be "our patriotic service to the government." We would not be "fighting," he insisted, much as he had when he was encouraging participation in civilian defense; the "Coast Guards," he explained, merely "guard the coast." Divine seemed to avoid the possibility that Coast Guardsmen in guarding the coast might be drawn into violence.

By about the middle of the war, when it had become clearer both to Divine and to the public at large that Hitler was a monster intent on exterminating Jews, and there was talk about establishing a homeland for them in Palestine, Divine was arguing that Jews belonged everywhere, the same as other religious groups did, and that it was just as wrong to advocate "Jerusalem for the Jews" as it was to advocate "Africa for the Africans." At about the same time, Divine was encouraging his followers to buy war bonds, which, not surprisingly, some critics saw as support of the war. Divine, however, seemingly elastic in his views, argued that buying bonds was not supporting the war. Applying his belief that mind controls matter, when his followers bought war bonds, he explained that if they had the "right mind," they would intend that the bonds would not be used to kill people but to build a peaceful postwar world, and if they so intended, it would happen. He promised he would make it happen. "I will cause" the bonds "to be used constructively," he declared. "The war bonds will be converted into peace bonds." As the war continued, Divine and the *New Day* kept promoting the sale of war bonds, and Divine took pleasure in the impressive amount his followers purchased.[2]

During the war, Divine did not teach as absolutely about refusing to fight as he did about other subjects. He continued to say firmly, no "true follower" of mine would lie, steal, drink, smoke, accept a tip, be on relief, or leave a bill unpaid. Although his platform continued to be published unchanged, he hardly any longer insisted, as his platform did, and as he himself often had earlier that not a "true follower" of his would "fight their fellowman for any cause whatsoever."

Still, Divine continued to teach pacifism as an ideal. Speaking in New Paltz shortly after the attack on Pearl Harbor, Divine said, "we do not believe in coercion." If you want "real security," he said, live "exactly" by "the teaching of Jesus," and then you can "put ten thousand to flight." Writing an Army officer who had asked him what his teaching was about war, he stated firmly in 1943 that his teaching was that the "use of military weapons of war is in violation to Christ's life and teaching." Moreover, Divine opposed children playing with toy guns. He opposed exposing children to war pictures. He opposed comic strips that taught hatred of Germans and Japanese. He quoted an anti-war poem which the *New Day* repeatedly republished, including these lines which followers made into placards and banners:

The child that was born in the manger
Was never a god of war.

He kept advocating means other than war to achieve lasting peace. Such means, he argued at various times, included living "exactly according to the Gospel," or living with a "fundamental change of heart and mind." Or when he was advocating more political means, he included "arbitration," living "democracy in its fullest," and uniting all the nations of the world into "one big universal sovereignty." But the effect of such anti-war teaching was diminished by Divine's increasing tolerance of participation in war, as when he said in 1943, "both the pacifists and military sympathizers are right according to their own understanding."[3]

DIVINITES AS REGULAR SOLDIERS

During the war, some Divinites served directly in the armed forces. Especially by searching for their names in the weekly Divine publication, the *New Day*, it is possible to state the names of twenty-six followers who were regular soldiers. Divine seemed proud of any followers who became soldiers. Since he wanted the United States and its allies to win the war, as he said, if a young man was willing to fight "for any cause whatsoever," then he "should," in order to help the allies win.[4]

Divine followers in the military often wrote Divine, and when Divine replied to them, he did not raise questions about why, as Divine followers, they were serving in the military. When one of them wrote Divine from an air field in Texas, Divine replied, advising him to "be the best," in whatever field he was serving. "Be a model patient, or a model prisoner, or a model soldier." When another wrote him from an air base in New Orleans, protesting against its segregated housing, Divine replied—without questioning either his being in the military or his cooperating with segregation—that if our nation does not overcome segregation, it will fail. When a mother asked Divine about the safety of her son who was fighting the Japanese in the Philippines, Divine told her—without raising the question of why he had become a soldier—if she prayed for her son through human affection for him, that would be "personal egotism," and her prayer would not work. But if she prayed for him as God's son, making "a complete self-denial," then God would protect him. When a Minnesota mother wrote Divine, saying that her son, whom she had brought up not to play with toy pistols, had been conscripted, Divine wrote her that if her son "carries the spirit of brotherhood in his heart, even as you taught him as a youth," then even in the military "he will not be subject to the spirit of hate." When a soldier stationed in Pennsylvania wrote Divine wondering if he should be a conscientious objector, Divine replied that he might seek to be transferred into a noncombatant unit in the military, but wherever he was, if he tried to live "the life of Christ," "my spirit" will be "your protection."[5]

DIVINITES AS CONSCIENTIOUS OBJECTORS IN THE MILITARY, DOING NON-COMBATANT WORK

While it is possible to name 26 followers who were regular soldiers, it is possible to name more than twice as many followers, 56, who were conscientious objectors. These conscientious objectors included three types: those classified as 1A-O who served within the military as noncombatants, those classified as IV-E who served outside of the military in Civilian Public Service, and those sent to prison.

Altogether in the United States, from 1940 to 1947, the number of men who asked for recognition as conscientious objectors is estimated to have been between 70,000 and 100,000, the number being uncertain because the records kept were imprecise. Of these, about 25,000 to 50,000 men were classified by draft boards as 1A-Os, that is, conscientious objectors willing to do non-combatant work within the military, with regular military pay. (The largest religious group among these 1A-Os were Seventh Day Adventists.) In addition, about 12,000 men were classified by their draft boards as IV-E, that is, as assigned to Civilian Public Service (CPS), which provided governmental work "of national importance," under civilian direction. (Most CPS men were from the three historic peace churches: Friends, Mennonites, and Brethren.) About 20,000 men were believed to have been refused classification as conscientious objectors, for a variety of reasons; of these, many went to prison. (Among the conscientious objectors in prison, the largest religious group, about 5,000, were Jehovah's Witnesses.)[6]

Among the followers of Divine who were classified 1A-Os, that is, as conscientious objectors willing to do non-combatant work within the military, many were assigned to medical work. Among these, one was assigned to an army hospital at Fort Huachuca, Arizona; another to naval medical service in Panama; another to a naval hospital in Puerto Rico. One Divinite classified as 1A-O asked for a different kind of non-combatant work. He was John Hunt. As we have seen, he had been associated with Ulster County in several ways: through his mother, who lived there; through serving there as a photographer of Divine mission sites (many of the photographs published in this book were undoubtedly taken by Hunt); and through hiding there when he was wanted for seducing an underage girl. By war time, Hunt, having served his prison term for his seduction, was forty, over-age for the draft. But when he learned that the Army was seeking photographers, under the name of Prodigal Son he volunteered to enlist as a conscientious objector with the understanding that he would serve as a photographer. His New York City draft board classified him 1A-O , as he wished. However, once in the Army, its officers sent him to serve at Camp Pickett, Virginia, in the Medical Corps. Hunt protested that this was religiously offensive to him because he did not believe in medical care. He kept reporting this to Divine, but Divine declined to tell him what to do about it, repeating the advice he often gave to both conscientious objectors and soldiers alike: be governed by your "highest intuition." After being an unhappy soldier for six weeks, Hunt asked that if he could not serve as a photographer, he be discharged. By September, 1943, he was offered a discharge if he was willing to accept it with the designation that he was "psychopathic." He was reluctant to accept it. By the next year, however, he had been discharged, with his designation unknown, and had soon set himself up in Philadelphia as a Divine-related news photographer.[7]

DIVINITES AS CONSCIENTIOUS OBJECTORS OUTSIDE OF THE MILITARY, DOING CIVILIAN WORK, IN CIVILIAN PUBLIC SERVICE (CPS)

Other Divine followers were classified as IV-Es, that is, as conscientious objectors not willing to serve in the military, even in non-combatant positions, but willing to do civilian government work, under civilian direction, in Civilian Public Service (CPS) units.[8] A favorable aspect of CPS from the Divine point of view was that, unlike the military, it was not racially segregated. However, to dis-

DRAWINGS BY CPS MEN OF THEIR WORK, including digging stock watering ponds, laying out terraces for contour plowing, and fighting forest fires. (From mimeographed bulletins produced by CPS men, at CPS #9, Petersham, Mass., Oct. 5, 1941, and CPS # 14, Merom, Ind., June 26, 1942)

courage men from entering CPS, the government, in effect, punished CPS men. It denied them any pay. It also denied them the benefits it gave soldiers, such as life insurance, medical care, or support for dependents. Besides, especially in the early years of the war, the government tended to place CPS men in remote, isolated locations, and to provide them work which, despite the legal requirement that it be of "importance," sometimes hardly seemed so.

Churches helped to administer CPS, especially the three historic peace churches: Quaker, Mennonite, and Brethren. Other religious groups also took part, through various agencies related to them, if not at first, and only on a small scale. These others included Baptists, Methodists, Episcopalians, Catholics, and Jews, but not Divinites. Although details varied, depending on the work, the site, and the government agencies involved, the government agencies that directed the CPS work usually supplied the men with housing, but not with pay, food or clothing. This meant that the men themselves, or their families, or their religious groups were pushed into supporting them. In turn, the cooperating religious groups, who worked through a joint board, the National Service Board for Religious Objectors (NSBRO) based in Washington, D. C., appealed for the funds to support them.

In 1943 the NSBRO wrote Divine, asking him, since a number of his followers were in the CPS units, if his Peace Mission could contribute funds to CPS. He answered that his Peace Mission movement does not take up collections, does not solicit donations from the public, and is not like "the average denominational church." Consequently, he said, "although I respect the work" of the churches, which have led in supporting CPS, the Quakers, Brethren, and Mennonites, "and commend them on their unselfish, patriotic endeavors," his mission movement had no funds for such a purpose.

A few months later, an NSBRO representative, Dr. E. Leroy Dakin, spoke at a Divinite meeting in Philadelphia. "We esteem" Divine followers who are in our CPS camps, Dr. Dakin said. We "esteem" all CPS men as a "minority" which is "trying to do the will of God faithfully," providing a "service which will register through all the days that are to be." It was his duty, he said, "to entreat you to have an interest" in the CPS men; "to maintain fellowship with them; to call your attention to the fact that the government does not pay them anything, neither does the government feed them—they are guests of the peace churches. They are being fed and clothed by them, except as anything may come to them from you, and they are doing this while yet they serve the government. We call your attention to this in the hope that your relationship to them as a group may be such that they will feel while they are thus isolated, a tiny minority, that you are caring for them—not just the peace churches—and in the days when the war is over they will come back to you, the folk who loved and cared for them, and thought for them when they were away."

A few Divine followers who were in CPS contributed to the churches' support of CPS by returning to these churches the meager allowance that they gave them as CPS men—$2.50 a month—or otherwise making direct donations. Beyond their minor individual contributions, there is no record available that Divine's Peace Mission contributed to the support of CPS.[9]

Divine is not even known to have done for CPS what he did for the Red Cross, that is, say to his followers that they were free to contribute to it if they wished. Divine is not known to have encouraged his followers to do for CPS anything comparable to what he did in encouraging his followers to buy war bonds. He is also not known to have personally visited conscientious objectors either in prison or in CPS, although many conscientious objectors were within easy reach of Divine, as in the many CPS units along the East Coast. At the time, as Divine was certainly aware, it was good public relations to give to the Red Cross and to buy war bonds, but it was not good public relations to encourage conscientious objectors. Nevertheless, Divine kept in friendly touch with individual CPS men, and publicized his correspondence with them, as he could have avoided doing.

Among the earliest CPS units, established in 1941, were three small ones, administered together by the American Friends Service Committee. They were located in a rural region of central Massachusetts, in Petersham, Royalston, Ashburnham, all housed in former Civilian Conservation Corps (CCC) camps. The men in these units worked for the United States Forest Service, especially cleaning up hurricane-damaged forests; they also fought forest fires, dug water holes for fire fighting, and maintained fire towers. Five Divine followers were sent to these camps, one of them being from a Divine community in Ulster County. He was Walking Jerusalem from the Samsonville mission. He was a former longshoreman who at Samsonville served as a farmer.

While another follower, Faith Somes, was at the Petersham CPS unit, Somes wrote Father Divine, saying he found those at his camp "harmonious." Divine replied, in a letter published in the *New Day*, saying that he was thankful that in this war, unlike in the First World War, thousands of Americans were not forced "to violate their religious convictions and take up arms." Aware that other of his followers were in other CPS camps nearby, Divine expressed the hope that Somes could "make contact" with them.

Another Divinite who was classified IV-E for service in CPS was Sigmund Michota, of Astoria, Long Island. When he first registered for the draft, he already knew he was opposed to participation in war, but felt unable to "explain my position." He therefore decided he could not register as a conscientious objector. It was only later, after he had encountered Divine "in Saugerties, N.Y.," he said, that, in Februrary, 1943, he appealed to his local draft board, in Long Island City, for a change in his classification from 1-A to IV-E.

In his appeal, Michota made a long, articulate statement about himself. Michota said he was a musician who had taught music as at the Hunter-Tannersville Central Schools in the Catskills; it was probably while there that he became familiar with Divine, as he said, in nearby Saugerties. Michota explained that he had two degrees from New York University, a BS and MA. He said he had grown up a Catholic, but had drifted away from his church. About ten years before, he said, he had begun to study religious thought as a means to deepen his "understanding of all artistic creation." He studied the Bible, Theosophy, Rosicrucianism, and Yoga. He read the writings of Dr. Emmet Fox and attended his non-denominational preaching in New York. He "used to meditate in the Church of the Ascension," an Episcopal church, on Fifth Avenue at 9th Street. He studied Mary Baker Eddy. He studied William James. He studied Far Eastern masters. He studied Tolstoy and Gandhi. He came to believe that God inspired a variety of "prophets and thinkers," including Moses, Jesus, Gautama, Mohammed, Confucius, George Fox, Walt Whitman, and "thousands of others" who were "receptive" to God "in various degrees," but that Divine was more than just another prophet; he was God come to dwell on the earth. He believed, he said, that to be a Christian means to live what Jesus taught. This meant, he believed, that the brotherhood of man could be attained only "through understanding, love, and sacrifice," which in turn meant he could not participate in war. In response, Divine was accepting of Michota's statement, saying it exemplified "all humanity's search for God."

Another Divinite who was classified IV-E was a major figure in Divine's movement, John

DeVoute. The long-time editor of the principal Divinite publication, the *New Day*, DeVoute was a brother of John Hunt, and a son of Mary Bird Tree who lived at Divine's Kingston Mansion. After being classified IV-E by his Harlem draft board, DeVoute was first sent to a CPS forestry unit, at Kane, Pennsylvania.

Early in 1944, when DeVoute was on leave from his CPS duty, he spoke about his CPS experience at a meeting at Rockland Palace in Harlem. He praised the CPS men as working "quite hard" at their usual duty of cutting and splitting "large timber," and boasted that his camp, unlike the military, was not racially segregated. At the camp, he said, "There are brothers from the South, from the North, from the East and West, and we work together and sleep together and are happy together."[10]

QUESTIONING CIVILIAN PUBLIC SERVICE (CPS)

A significant portion of followers who were CPS men, however, including DeVoute, eventually came to question their position in CPS. Were they right to thus cooperate in conscription? Was their unpaid work in fact slave labor? After all, Divine taught that it was wrong to work and not be appropriately paid for it. Were the religious agencies, which helped to administer CPS right to give the men allowances and food and similar support because the government did not do it? Was their work of sufficient "importance" relative to the cataclysm of war?

In response to such questioning, a Divine follower, Felix G. Xavier, of Tacoma, Washington, chose to leave CPS and instead enter the Army to do non-combatant work for which he would be paid. Also in response to such questioning, later in the war Selective Service created CPS units in mental hospitals, to allow CPS men to work in what many of them considered more immediately important work, and with the hospitals providing not only housing but also food. One of the Divine CPS men, David Elihu, of New York City, who had originally done forestry work at Ashburnham, Massachusetts, chose to transfer to a mental hospital unit in Concord, New Hampshire. Also in response to such questioning, later in the war, Selective Service created CPS units which churches took no part in administering, but which were administered directly by Selective Service itself. Several Divine's followers in CPS chose to serve in such units, John DeVoute being one of them.

Eventually John DeVoute became a serious protester against CPS. He protested that the men at the first camp he was assigned to, in Kane, Pennsylvania, like CPS men generally, were not given any pay by the government for which they worked, but were given a meager allowance by the religious group which administered their camp, the Brethren Service Committee, for which they did not work. DeVoute returned his allowance to the Brethren Service Committee. As the Brethren camp director explained to Divine, DeVoute "feels that it is not proper for him to accept such an allowance since he is not working for the Brethren Service Committee but for the Forestry Service." In reply, Divine identified with DeVoute. He is acting according to "his religious conviction," Divine wrote, which is "not to accept anything such as money, or gifts, or tips from any individual or from any firm or organization to which he has not given practical service. He believes it is the duty of the government to pay the men for the service they give." Divine acknowledged the good intentions of the religious groups which, since the government refused to pay the men, provided them an allowance, and also provided much of their basic support in food and clothing. "Such organizations that have come forward, and shouldered the responsibility of the government proper," wrote Divine, "are to be commended for their help in the time of this great emergency; yet, it should be the duty of every man to earn his own living."

DeVoute, having become unhappy in CPS, and eager to return to his regular work as editor of the *New Day*, looked for possible ways to get out of CPS. Eventually, he decided to try reclassification as I-A-O, the classification his brother, John Hunt, had secured, to see if this would work for him. He asked for such a reclassification. But then, as he had expected, when he was almost ready for induction into the Army, he was pronounced over age (he was 38), and let go. By this route he thought he was freed from any further required service, and in June and July, 1944, returned to his usual work editing the *New Day*. As he left CPS, he spoke at a Divinite meeting, saying that while CPS was unjust, it was still "a blessing," because through it, "many" have lived out "their religious conviction" without being "subject to the armed forces."

However, DeVoute soon found that he was not free after all. He was notified that if he was not to be in the Army, he was due back at CPS, and this time he chose to be assigned to CPS 135, at Germfask, Michigan, a fish-and-wildlife camp, which was not administered, like most CPS camps, by a religious agency, but directly by Selective Service itself. There, however, he continued to be dissatisfied, considering the men were "doing just enough work to maintain our own self-existence." From there he wrote President Roosevelt, asking if he could be assigned as an individual to work that "the government would consider essential," as in a hospital. Not being granted his request, however, DeVoute remained in Selective Service-administered camps, first at Germfask, later at another such camp, in Minersville, California, and stayed there until after the war was over.[11]

A REFUSER IN PRISON

Among Divinite conscientious objectors who were imprisoned, at least one, Unison Heart, had lived in an Ulster County Divinite community. Heart, a white, had worked at Hope Farm as a farmer, and according to Divine, had been cooperative. By July, 1942, Heart had been classified as a conscientious objector and assigned to a CPS camp, but he refused to go. He was held in a jail on West Street, New York, while awaiting trial. From jail, Heart wrote Divine, saying that he liked to think of himself as "willing to go anywhere in your blessed name, regardless of the penalty." In reply, Divine seemed anxious to dissociate himself from Heart, as if not wanting to seem to encourage him to defy the law. Divine wrote him, "Your conviction should be your own." You should "not necessarily be influenced even by what I may or may not believe as a person, but allow the spirit and mind of Christ to lead you and guide you into all righteousness." Then "no hurt nor harm that can come nigh you." Heart was tried for disobeying the draft law. He pleaded guilty, and was sentenced to three years in prison. He was sent to the federal prison in Springfield, Missouri, which was understood to be a prison primarily for the mentally unsound. Many conscientious objectors were sent there.

More than a year later, when Heart was being considered for parole, Divine wrote his parole board. This time, when his support for Heart could scarcely be interpreted as defiance of the law, Divine asked the parole board to return Heart to Hope Farm. He was "badly needed" there, Divine wrote, because the government has "taken off" many men from the Ulster County Divinite farms—as draftees or to work in defense industries—at the same time that during the war emergency, national policy calls for increasing farm production. Heart was, however, not paroled.[12]

AS THE WAR APPROACHED ITS END

In the spring of 1944, when Italy had already been defeated, the Soviet Union was pushing the invading Germans out, and the allied invasion of Germany from the west was near, Rev. Albert Gaeddert, a Mennonite representative on the National Service Board for Religious Objectors (NSBRO), interviewed Divine in Philadelphia. Gaeddert came especially in order to understand a follower of Divine, a conscientious objector, who was in one of the Mennonite-administered CPS camps. Gaeddert made it clear that he knew that Divine had led some of his followers to become conscientious objectors, but Gaeddert, himself a pacifist in accord with the tradition of his church, wanted to know to what extent Divine, complex as he was, was really a pacifist. Divine allowed this interview to be published in his movement's periodical, *New Day*, as if he was satisfied with what he said.

When Divine said he endorsed the allies' asking for "unconditional surrender," Gaeddert challenged him, "I thought you didn't believe in coercion?"

Divine: "Well, I do not. This is not coercion."

Gaeddert: "Unconditional surrender coerces someone else to surrender."

Divine: "Since they do not understand the language of God, of love and mercy, when they find out that there is enough force to overcome them, they will unconditionally surrender."

Gaeddert: "Do you think that is God's way, that the strongest man make the weakest surrender?"

Divine: "If some men did not know a policeman had something besides his fist, they would do anything they wanted to do and would not try to obey the law; so it is with those madmen who are running the war."

Gaeddert: "I suppose you endorse the teaching of Jesus concerning turning the other cheek."

Divine: "That's right."

Gaeddert: "That is not quite in accord when a group gangs up to press unconditional surrender on another group."

Divine: "It has been proven distinctly that wickedness will try to engulf righteousness. "

Gaeddert: "I don't like to see you endorse the buying of war bonds. What would you say if people, instead of having any contact with the war through bonds, would use their money to buy food and feed the hungry?"

Divine:"When we buy bonds, it is not with the thought of the money being used for destruction, but it is for the post war days, for construction."

Gaeddert: "But the actual money will go for guns, battleships, tanks."

Divine: "Some of it will."

Gaeddert: "Don't you think the larger part will?"

Divine: "I do not. I direct my thoughts to that end."

As the war approached its end, Divine was claiming that he had helped to build the spirit which made it possible for the allies to create the United Nations. In fact, Divine wanted the United Nations to be stronger than it was created to be; it should have the same powers, he said, that the American Constitution gave the American federal government.

After the war had closed, in early 1946 while de-mobilization was underway, Dr. E. Leroy Dakin, the same NSBRO representative who had earlier appealed to Divinites to take an interest in their CPS men, wrote Divine summarizing what it had cost the cooperating churches to support the followers of Divine who were in CPS, because the government did not support them or pay them for their work. He said he hoped Divine "will give each one of them the benefit of your counsel," and hoped that these CPS men "will want to reimburse the Peace Churches."

Divine seemed aroused by this letter. He replied to Dr. Dakin, both in writing and in an interview with him, taking the view of some of his more radical followers in CPS that the churches, by participating in the administration of CPS, had unfortunately joined the government in coercing CPS men to work without pay, as "slave laborers." The churches having done this, they could hardly expect the CPS men to feel "morally obligated" to reimburse the churches for their costs. In fact, he insisted, the obligation was the other way around: the churches were obligated to pay the men for their work.

After the war, how did the Divine movement treat its followers who had been soldiers compared to how it treated those who had been conscientious objectors? Evidence is not available that Divine, despite his long continued teaching against war, scolded any of his followers for serving in the military, whether during or after the war. Moreover, two followers who had served as regular soldiers, on leaving service, were given positions of trust within the Divine movement. George Stewart, who before the war had served as a waiter at Divine's table in Philadelphia, and served during the war as a soldier in Europe and Africa, after his discharge again became a waiter at Divine's table in Philadelphia. Job Paul, who had served in the Army at Camp Breckinridge, Kentucky, after the war became a trustee of Divine's Unity Mission Church, and for ten years taught gymnastics in one of Divine's Free Schools.

However, far more examples are available of followers who had been conscientious objectors during the war being given positions of trust within the Divine movement after the war. Examples of conscientious objectors who were related to Ulster County being given such positions in the movement included John DeVoute who after the war continued as editor of the *New Day*, and besides became president of the Divine-related Palace Mission Church. They also included Radical Love who became not only a trustee of Palace Mission Church (both DeVoute and Love were officers of this church when it owned property for the Divine movement in Ulster County, at Krum Elbow), but also head of the Divine order for men, the Crusaders. They also included Happy Mirth, of Saugerties, New York, who taught gymnastics for the Peace Mission in Philadelphia, and John Hunt who became a press photographer much patronized by Divinites. Others who had served as conscientious objectors, but were not known as related to Ulster County, included David Elihu who became a chauffeur for Divine; Paul Delap who became the manager of a major Divinite hotel; two who became Divine movement youth leaders, Philip Life and David H. Praise; and seven who became trustees of Divine-related churches: Chris Hansen, James Johnson, Robert Jones, Wisdom Kindness, Paul Revere, Blessed Thomas, and Faith Victory. Clearly Divine's movement respected its conscientious objectors.[13]

Altogether, during World War II, in response to the fierce pressures of the times, Divine's support for absolute pacifism declined, and he developed a more fluid, pragmatic approach to war. This both allowed him to respond more freely to the overwhelming public support for the war, and also helped him to avoid public scandal as unpatriotic. By emphasizing that each person must follow his own "highest intuition," he was able to support individually both those followers who became soldiers and those who became conscientious objectors.

During the war, Divine cooperated with the draft. He facilitated the Coast Guard. He participated in Civilian Defense. He encouraged buying war bonds, but he seemed to need to camouflage his doing it by claiming he was converting them into peace bonds. Divine continued to maintain that his ideal was not to participate in war. His inclination to pacifism, though far less absolute, survived into the post-war period.

IN WORLD WAR II, PHILIP L. LIFE SERVED AS A CONSCIENTIOUS OBJECTOR in the military, doing medical work in Panama. In recent years he has been a major figure at Woodmont, as archivist, webmaster, and secretary to Mother Divine. (Photo, May, 2007, by the author)

E. SLOWING DOWN

39. MOVE TO PHILADELPHIA

JUST BEFORE THE UNITED STATES entered World War II, the Verinda Brown suit continued to disturb Divine. In early 1940, as we have seen, a judge of the New York State Supreme Court ruled against Divine, giving Brown a judgment against him of about $6,000. Thereafter Divine appealed to higher courts, eventually asking for permission to appeal to the state's highest court, but was denied, and no higher appeal was possible. However, Divine kept insisting that he possessed no money, and refused to pay the $6,000.

When Divine had been living in Sayville and was under a court's judgment, he seemed to consider that, being little known, he had little to lose, and so took the matter lightly. But under this court judgment, since he had become better known, and his movement had grown impressively, he seemed to feel that more was at stake, and he took the matter more seriously.

Meantime, lawyers on both sides tried to settle the case out of court. Meeting in a judge's chambers, with both Divine and Verinda Brown present, they agreed to exonerate Divine of any charges of fraud, if Divine or someone for him would pay the judgment. When the person expected to pay the judgment failed to show up as arranged, Divine's lawyers advised Divine to ask others to pay it instead, and put the whole matter to rest, but he refused. The courts then continued to insist that Divine pay the judgment, while Divine clung to the proposed out-of-court agreement as if it had legally exonerated him from any wrongdoing.

In early 1941, Verinda Brown asked a court for a ruling to hold the body of Father Divine, hoping that this would force him to pay the judgment. Responding to Brown's request, in March, 1941, the court required the New York County sheriff to hold Divine in the county for six months. Divine cooperated by turning himself in to the sheriff and allowing his lawyers to provide a bond to guarantee he would stay in the county as ordered.

His lawyers reminded Divine of his teaching that citizens should respect the law and pay their debts, and they again advised him to pay the judgment, or allow someone to pay it for him, so that he could continue his activities as usual. Divine's pride, however, seemed hurt. He seemed to regard Brown's charges as a personal affront. Moreover, he seemed to believe that if he caved in to Brown's demand, other opponents—"legal bandits" he called them—might make similar demands on him, which could cause his whole financial system to collapse. Although he had allowed his lawyers to provide a bond for him, as his six months confinement began, he announced to the press that he not only had no money with which he could pay the unjust judgment against him, but that he would rather "go to the electric chair" than consent for anyone else to pay it for him. In fact, during the six months period, no one paid the money, and his inability to visit Ulster County deprived his followers there of his direct guidance, on which they heavily depended.[1]

THE MOVE

As early as 1936, Divine felt that New York City had not treated him and his movement well, as by over-assessing the property of his followers and making it difficult for them to register to vote. At that time, he threatened to leave the city, taking his followers with him, and move upstate to Ulster County. Later Divine felt that not only New York City but also the whole of New York State had mistreated him and his followers. This was so, he said, despite his taking many New Yorkers off the relief rolls, despite his reducing vice and crime, despite his having provided free food to thousands of the hungry, despite his having energized followers to invest in property and to improve it and to pay taxes on it, and despite his having encouraged thousands of followers to pay off old debts and to pay back charity they had received. Officials of both the city and state had often harassed him, he claimed. They had turned down his Peace Mission's application to create a children's home in Ulster County. They unfairly raised his followers' tax assessments. They made difficulties for his followers in registering to vote and in securing

IN 1948, DIVINE FOLLOWERS ACQUIRED THE LORRAINE HOTEL, on Broad St. at Fairmont Ave., Philadelphia. It had 300 rooms and a penthouse banquet hall. (*New Day*, Sept. 15, 1956)

THIS STATE HISTORIC MARKER WAS PLACED AT THE LORRAINE HOTEL in Philadelphia in 1994. So far, no similar historic makers have been placed at any Divine site in Ulster County, New York. (*New Day*, Ap. 29, 1996)

licenses under their religious names. In early 1942, when the city denied a permit to Divinites to operate a restaurant on West 126th Street, Divine threatened to move out of the city, and take at least "one hundred thousand" followers with him." Was Divine reasonable to expect the world to treat his movement impartially when it defied public opinion? Was Divine sophisticated about how the world works?

Soon afterwards, a New York court issued a summons for Divine to return to court for not having paid the Verinda Brown judgment. He decided that if the summons was personally delivered to him, as it had to be to make it effective, he would decline to return to court, and he believed if he thus declined, the court would have the power to imprison him for doing so.

The threat that this court summons, if personally delivered to him, could send him to prison was finally enough to lead him, in July, 1942, to move out of New York City. He moved to another state, Pennsylvania, where the summons could not be delivered to him, and to a city, Philadelphia, which he had already felt for several years was more friendly to him.

Whether the decision to move was wise was problematic. In making the decision, Divine seemed to be paying little attention to the disturbing impact his moving away would inevitably have on the huge numbers of his followers in New York State, especially in New York City and Ulster County.

His move to Philadelphia meant that if he visited New York State during the week, the court summons could still be delivered to him, and, if he did not pay the judgment, he might well be jailed. But since the summons could not legally be delivered to him in New York State on Sundays or holidays, at least he was still free to make short visits to the state.[2]

IN 1949, DIVINE FOLLOWERS ACQUIRED HOTEL TRACY. Located near the University of Pennsylvania, its low prices attracted students. (Postcard, no date, Woodmont)

APPEAL TO GOVERNOR DEWEY

Six months after Divine had moved to Philadelphia, in January, 1943, he wrote New York's governor, Thomas E. Dewey, appealing for his help. Divine summarized for the governor some of the advantages New York State had received from his presence there. His followers had paid off old debts, Divine said, and paid cash for new purchases, and so remained out of debt. His followers had stayed off relief. Followers who had been criminals had become law abiding, and had aided the police in law enforcement. Followers had "such a high standard of honesty and morality" that they were "in great demand as employees." Cooperative enterprises owned and operated by his followers had been led "to give the best for the least," as by offering good meals at fifteen cents each. Properties bought had been improved and taxes on them had been paid. Further withdrawal of his activities from the state, Divine warned, would mean a loss "that cannot be estimated."

Divine explained to the governor that in his view the rulings against him in the Verinda Brown case had been affected by false publicity, especially as the result of Faithful Mary's charges against him which she had since confessed were lies. Because of the judgment in the Brown case, Divine wrote, he was "subject to arrest and incarceration" if he came to New York State, and that this "has greatly impeded the activities of my followers. . .by no means the least of them" being "in Ulster County." His movement's holdings there, he explained, included "good farmland" which he desired to keep "under cultivation," in accordance with the President Roosevelt's war-time call for "mass production." But because he lacked "free access" to this farmland, "little or no progress" on it has recently been made. He appealed to the governor to "take what steps you deem just." The governor's counsel, however, replying on behalf of the governor, wrote that according to the state constitution's separation of powers, the governor had no power to intervene in such a court matter.[3]

CONSEQUENCES

Eight months after Divine had moved to Philadelphia, a Poughkeepsie newspaper wrote Divine's secretary John Lamb, asking him, since Divine had moved out of the state, what would happen to the Divine properties in Ulster County. In April, 1943, Lamb answered, in his usual direct style, that an exodus of Divine's followers from the state had begun as soon as Divine moved out of it, in mid-1942. "There has been a continual drain of followers and co-workers from the farms and properties in Ulster County to other occupations where they can be near Father Divine personally and at the same time be gainfully employed," he wrote, "and no doubt this will continue." He explained, "such a result was inevitable, as Father is an irresistible magnet, and wherever he is personally, the masses are drawn." But as to what will happen to the Divine movement properties in Ulster County, "I cannot give you a great deal of information, as the decision will be with the owners of the various places." Some of the owners "may wish to live on the properties and others may desire to lease or sell them." As Lamb expected, the owners made a

WOODMONT

HAS BEEN DESIGNATED A

NATIONAL HISTORIC LANDMARK

THIS ESTATE POSSESSES NATIONAL SIGNIFICANCE IN COMMEMORATING THE HISTORY OF THE UNITED STATES OF AMERICA

DESIGNED BY WILLIAM L. PRICE IN 1892 FOR INDUSTRIALIST ALAN WOOD, JR., THIS IS ONE OF THE FINEST EXAMPLES OF RESIDENTIAL DESIGN IN THE NATION. SINCE 1952 IT HAS SERVED AS THE HEADQUARTERS OF THE PEACE MISSION MOVEMENT, AN INTERNATIONAL SOCIAL AND RELIGIOUS MOVEMENT FOUNDED BY REV. M.J. "FATHER" DIVINE.

1998

NATIONAL PARK SERVICE
UNITED STATES DEPARTMENT OF THE INTERIOR

IN 1952, A DIVINE CHURCH ACQUIRED THE WOODMONT ESTATE, INCLUDING THIS FRENCH-STYLE STONE CHATEAU. It was located near Philadelphia, on a height above the Schuylkill River, in Gladwyn, Montgomery County, Penn. (Postcard, no date, Woodmont) Right: **THIS NATIONAL HISTORIC MARKER WAS PLACED AT WOODMONT in 1998.** (*New Day* Digest, Sept., 1999)

variety of decisions. They sold their property off only gradually, stretching out their sales over many years.

After moving to Philadelphia, Divine encouraged his followers to buy real estate there. Among their purchases were two splendid hotels, the Lorraine in 1948 and the Tracy in 1949. In 1952, especially with funds donated by Editor John DeVoute, they also purchased in the Philadelphia Main Line suburbs a grand estate called Woodmont, with a magnificent French Gothic mansion on it for Father and Mother Divine to live in. Altogether the buildings his followers acquired in the Philadelphia region were probably of better quality than the buildings they had occupied in Ulster County or New York City. However, Divine's being based in Philadelphia, along with the court's limitation on his visiting New York State, as well as his increasing age, tended to isolate him from his large number of followers who remained at a distance in New York State.

As a result of Divine's move out of New York City, there was a decline in his movement's activities in the city, but it was a gradual decline. While many of his New York City admirers followed him by moving to Philadelphia, as late as 1950, eight years after his move to Philadelphia, a census official was saying Divine still had many more followers in New York City than in Philadelphia.[4]

Ulster County was especially affected by Divine's move. It was about a hundred miles farther from Philadelphia than New York City was, and its missions were spread out in the county. As a result of Divine's move out of the state, his visits to Ulster County sharply declined. While in 1940, Divine spoke in Ulster County 112 times; in 1941, 49 times; and even in 1942, 26 times; in the next ten years, as far as is known, he spoke in Ulster County only five times. The effect of this drastic decline in Divine's visits was devastating for his followers who still remained in the Promised Land.

AN OPPORTUNITY TO RETURN FREELY TO NEW YORK STATE

In 1952, ten years after Divine had moved to Philadelphia, an opportunity was presented to him once again to settle the Verinda Brown suit, and free him to come into New York State whenever he chose. By this time, New York City itself had legally taken over responsibility for Verinda Brown's suit, by assignment. It had done so because two or three years before, Verinda Brown, when she had inadequate means of support, had applied to the city for relief, which the city gave her, and the city was trying, as it usually did, to recover any assets available to repay itself for the relief. William W. Lowell, a lawyer who had been representing Brown ever since her suit began, was by this time representing New York City on behalf of Brown, and Lowell proposed to Divine a settlement out of court. By this time, the judgment against Divine had risen, Lowell explained, to about $10,000 because of the added legal fees and interest.

In the meantime, attorney Lowell had been attending Divine meetings for several years, and he now said that by doing so, he had become convinced that Divine's Peace Mission was doing New York City much good, and the city would benefit more if Divine could freely come to it again. Acting on behalf of the city, Lowell, in an interview with Divine, offered to settle if Divine, or anyone for him, would pay only a reduced amount, $4,000. In proposing this reduction, Lowell explained that he was abandoning his own claim to be paid most of his legal fees, but was retaining his claim to be paid his legal expenses.

Lowell knew very well, he said, that if Divine only said the word, the reduced amount required would be quickly paid by his followers. Paying this amount, as Lowell told Divine, would allow Divine to return New York freely. "Everybody in New York wants you to," Lowell said, adding, "You are needed in New York." In saying this, while Lowell could be interpreted as trying to flatter Divine into agreeing to a settlement, he could also have genuinely meant it, as his years of attending Divine meetings suggest.

Divine could have seized on Lowell's saying New York needed him as sufficient excuse to settle. Or he could have seized on Lowell's having reduced the amount of the judgment as sufficient excuse to settle. Or, since the courts, acting in the Brown case, had dropped all charges of fraud against Divine, he could have seized on that as sufficient excuse to settle. Moreover, since in the years since the Brown suit began, Divine had tightened his financial system, any likelihood that the Brown case would lead to other similar legal action against his financial system appeared to have declined. But Divine seemed fiercely committed not to give in to any settlement. He chose to continue to regard requiring him to pay any judgment, even a reduced judgment, as a personal "outrage." He seemed to be allowing his pride to play a greater role in his decision than concern for his movement in New York State. By refusing a settlement, he virtually abandoned his model communities in Ulster County. He was willing to deprive them almost entirely of his charismatic presence, thus limiting the effectiveness of their example of unpaid, cooperative, interracial living.

With Divine still refusing to agree to a settlement, Lowell, feeling sadly defeated, said he would withdraw entirely from the case. Divine himself, however, seemed to explode in anger, insisting it was "immaterial" to him if the case was never settled, for "the cosmic forces of nature usually avenge my enemies." In a cruel thrust, he said, as his movement's periodical reported, that if New York City goes down "like Sodom and Gomorrah did, it will be immaterial to me." He seemed to care more about a public exoneration of himself than he cared about the whole city, not to mention his followers, whether in the city, or in Ulster County, or anywhere in the nation. I may "turn the United States upside down!" he explained. "It is absolutely immaterial."[5]

In fact, there never was a settlement. Divine was never again free to visit New York State whenever he chose.

A PROVOCATIVE QUESTION
What if Divine had settled the Verinda Brown suit by early 1942, as he easily could have by allowing someone to pay the court judgment for him?
Then he would probably have kept his residence in NY City, and not have moved to Philadelphia. **Then he would probably have continued his frequent visits to his communities in Ulster County, fostering them.** **Then would his Ulster County communities have been more effective models for the world, better fulfilling his intentions?**

40. MARY BIRD TREE: WAS SHE DIVINE'S PRISONER?

BY THE LATTER 1940s, Florence Hunt, otherwise known as Mary Bird Tree, had moved from the Kingston mansion, in Ulster County, to Philadelphia. She was living there in a mission residence, at North 41st Street and Westminster, where, being elderly and frail, she was being cared for by several Divine followers, especially Miss Jonah.

Mary Bird Tree's two talented sons were also living in Philadelphia, all three of them having been drawn there by Divine's having moved there first. Her son Warner Hunt, known in the movement as John DeVoute, was still editing the Divine movement's principal publication, the weekly *New Day*, which by this time was being published in Philadelphia. Her other son, the volatile John Hunt, had established himself as a press photographer in Philadelphia, and was crediting Divine for having made him successful.

In Philadelphia, John Hunt became influential in the Divine movement, as he had been earlier, first in California, later in New York. On behalf of the movement, he reached out. He persuaded people to visit Divine activities, such people as an army chaplain, who found ideal Americanism "materialized" there, and as a former member of the Pennsylvania legislature, Crystal Bird Fauset, who appreciated the "inner strength" she found in Divine followers. Hunt thanked Divine for not coercing him, instead leaving him free to make his own choices, but changing his heart, so that he held back from his usual addictions to drink and chasing women.[1]

However, after Divine's first wife had died and Divine had remarried, John Hunt, unsteady as usual, underwent another change. He came to resent Divine's remarrying at the same time that he continued to teach celibacy.

AN UNOPENED LETTER

About June 1, 1949, a registered letter arrived for John Hunt's mother, Mary Bird Tree, at her Philadelphia home. It was addressed to her in both her conventional name, Florence Hunt, and her Peace Mission name, Mary Bird Tree. Miss Jonah woke her up to give her the letter.

Just looking at the envelope without opening it, Tree became upset. The envelope indicated it came from her son John Hunt. Tree knew that despite Divine's teaching against marriage, her son had recently married Carol Sweet, one of Divine's followers, and had openly rebelled against Divine.

Being upset, Mary Bird Tree wanted to see Divine. With Tree's consent, Miss Jonah and her associates telephoned Divine, to arrange for her to see him. They brought her for an interview to Divine's "private study" at 764-772 Broad Street. The course of the interview raises questions as to the effect of a person's being dependent on a charismatic figure. Does it strengthen an individual in some ways? Does it weaken that individual in other ways?

Beginning the interview, Tree took the still unopened letter out of her bag, and handed it to Divine, saying, "I wanted you to see this, Father."

Divine replied, "I don't open anyone's mail." He said she herself should decide whether to open it.

She explained, the letter "really upset me."

Divine said, "Whatsoever you want to do about it, it would be up to you."

She replied, "I would just like to have you quiet me down a little bit."

Divine said, "Maybe you will get quieted down after a while." But, he added, "you may be aroused again when you read what it says." John Hunt "is so malicious he is liable to do anything."

"I have been through these things so many times," Tree said. "I should be used to it by now."

Divine continued, "My spirit will take care of everything."

"I wanted you to take care of it, Father," Tree responded. "I just can't get myself together." She said it was difficult for her when she saw the woman her son had married. "It was a long time before I could ever say 'Peace' to her."

You are "free to be governed by your highest

intuition, " Divine said, "so long as it is something that would not be directly destructive."

Tree was still focused on her letter. She said she was "surprised to see that I was so upset to get it." She added, "I just want to do your will, Father."

"The main thing, " Divine said, " is to give me your heart, and stay self-denied, and stay in my mind and spirit, and then you are doing that which is my will."

"That is so wonderful," Tree responded. "That is an answer, Father."

John Hunt's difficult behavior, Divine explained, "was not because you did not try to raise him the same as you did the other one [the other son, DeVoute], but it was because of his own rebelliousness. He rebelled against you, against God, and against the law."

"That is an answer!" Tree exclaimed. "I am so glad for it, Father. It is wonderful!"

By later that same month, John Hunt was publicly campaigning against Divine. Hunt charged in an article he wrote for *Our World*, a New York periodical intended for blacks, that Divine was a hypnotist and con man. He charged Divine was a "smart cookie who has surrounded himself with every possible legal protection," and his movement was a "hoax." Hunt also charged that his own mother, Mary Bird Tree, was, as an elderly "invalid," a "virtual prisoner" of Divine. She had given all her money away to Divine's movement, so that now, he claimed, she did not even have money enough to "buy herself a bottle of milk."

Editor DeVoute, in his *New Day* weekly, replied to his brother's charges. DeVoute wrote that Hunt had turned against the Peace Mission because he "could not live the clean, wholesome life that Divine advocates." As for Hunt's claim that their mother was a "prisoner" of Divine and without funds, DeVoute said, "she has not given Father Divine one cent." She is in "good health." She has the privilege of staying at any Peace Mission she chooses, has the use of a car any time she chooses, and now has, what she did not at all have before coming to Divine, "that precious boon, peace of mind." DeVoute did not raise any question as to what her peace of mind had cost her, whether psychologically or otherwise.[2]

A NOTARIZED REFUTATION

The next month, July, 1949, Mary Bird Tree herself replied to her son John Hunt's charges. She did so in a careful, notarized statement, probably prepared with help. Her statement may be variously interpreted.

In her statement, Tree said Father Divine "does not know" and has never "asked me about my personal business," such as "my financial status." She added, "I have never given Father Divine any money" and he "has never asked me for any money."

"Upon my own free will and volition I came to Father Divine because no doctor, no practitioner or anybody else could heal me of my condition, but Father Divine did. Now I would like to have paid Father Divine if I could, because for medical treatment I had paid thousands of dollars, not only to Battle Creek Sanitarium, but also to Christian Science practitioners and to other physicians, but they could not heal me. Father Divine came as a free gift and he healed me without [asking] one cent.

"It was my sincere wish to participate in his activities, for they were a blessing to all the people. In order to do this I endeavored to co-operate with many others in the purchase of different properties which I did of my own free will, and at all times was amply secured in my investments. Father Divine at no time persuaded or coerced me in this respect. It was a heart-felt desire on my part to see that others without regard to race, creed, or color had the same privilege of enjoying beautiful homes, cars and all the other necessities of life because of the reality of the Christian life which he had caused them to live, as well as the healings of mind and spirit and body which he has brought to all those who sincerely sought his assistance."

John Hunt stated in his *Our World* article "that I was an invalid and a virtual prisoner in Father Divine's Kingdom. I am not a prisoner and I am in excellent health. All of the followers who own and operate properties, homes and estates under the Peace Mission movement agree to have me live at any of their places if I so desire, and enjoy the same privileges, freedom and comfort that Mother Divine has. How can I be a virtual prisoner" while

MARY BIRD TREE INTERVIEWED DIVINE AT THIS CIRCLE MISSION, at 764-772 South Broad St., Philadelphia. The mission, purchased by Divine followers in 1939, provided accommodations for Divine, his wife, and his staff. It included both major buildings shown, the one in the center, where, from 1942, Divine's main offices were, and also the taller one to the right, which contained an auditorium. (Postcard, ca. 1950, Woodmont).

living "in an atmosphere of purity, holiness, love and real Christianity?"

"Regarding John Hunt's statement that I couldn't even afford a bottle of milk, I have a-full and a-plenty of everything that life demands. I am independent and free financially, physically, and in every other way. I have enough money to buy anything I desire.

"In particular one of the properties in which I co-operated with a number of individuals [in buying] was in High Falls known as 'Rondout' [the garage and accompanying residence on Lucas Turnpike]. The title and deed to this property was made out to all of us who had participated in the purchasing of the property. Later on [in 1946] this property was sold and the total money was divided among the owners. The property was sold at a gain."

She also recalled she had given "thousands and thousands of dollars" to her son John Hunt for an advertising business venture, but he preferred to be "out gallivanting, chasing around with women," so his business "went into bankruptcy." She had also given him money to "help support his children." But as she looked back at it now, "it seems to have been done in vain."

Certainly Mary Bird Tree was not Divine's physical prisoner. According to her perception, her involvement with the Divine movement was voluntary. Yet questions remain as to how much freedom of mind and spirit she retained. Having such freedom may not have seemed significant to her, however. After all, as her son DeVoute said, she had found "peace of mind," and as she herself said, she had found "real Christianity."[3]

41. DECLINE AND SUCCESSION

IT was a question how well Divine's movement would survive. It was little organized. It depended heavily on one person. It made promises it could scarcely carry out. As it aged, while it tended to become more conciliatory, it still defied public opinion on some issues.

The peak years of the movement as a whole may be said to be 1938 to 1943. From the later years of World War II, the movement declined, but only slowly. According to lists of Peace Missions in the United States published in the *New Day*, in 1938 there were 130, but by 1950 they were down to 73.

In the New York City region, several years after Divine's 1942 move from there to Philadelphia, Divine's associate, attorney Arthur Madison, complained that the services the Divine movement offered the public were decreasing. By 1949 the movement no longer leased Rockland Palace, which had been their major meeting place in Harlem. While in 1938 they had run two Peace Mission Free Schools in New York City, by 1958 they ran only one.[1]

FACTORS IN THE BROAD DECLINE

The movement's general decline began in significant part because World War II, as its impact accumulated, provided substantial jobs to many people who had previously been distressed by the Great Depression, so that they needed the Divine movement less. The decline also occurred in part because of Divine's emphasis on chastity for his followers, so that the natural increase of children growing up in the movement was curtailed.

Moreover, in the 1930s, at the same time that Divine was working against segregation by creating multi-racial communities in Ulster County, he was also leading his followers at large to participate in broad coalitions for racial equality. By the mid-1940s, however, after having built a big campaign to urge Congress to pass an anti-lynching bill and not succeeding, Divine, deeply disappointed, moved away from such methods. He became more reluctant to cooperate with others working for racial equality, thereby tending to isolate his movement. In 1948, when several young men who wished to desegregate the military by civil disobedience came to Divine for help, he advised against it. He now emphasized fighting discrimination, he said, not by either civil disobedience or political struggle, but through individual hearts.

From the late 1940s into the early 1960s, Divine and his followers were aware of the striking progress being made toward desegregation, as by legal measures taken by President Lyndon Johnson, and as by the marches and sit-ins led by Martin Luther King. In 1965, the civil rights activist Leon Sullivan, looking back, saw Divine not as a leader in the civil rights movement, but as having

EVENTS IN THE DIVINE MOVEMENT'S DECLINE

DATE	EVENT
1941-1945	World War II drew support away from Divine
1942	Divine moved from NY City to Philadelphia, reducing his ability to inspire his followers in NY State
1946	Divine married a second time, to a young white Canadian, disturbing some of his followers, but providing a likely successor to him
1949	The movement ceased to lease Rockland Palace, a major meeting place in Harlem
1952	Divine's last known visit to Ulster County
1960	Divine, in declining health, stopped speaking in public
1965	Divine died, or, as his followers preferred to say, "laid his body down"
1971	Jim Jones, with 200 of his followers, visited Divine's movement in Philadelphia, hoping to take control of it
1985	Divine's movement sold off its last remaining property in Ulster County, the Kingston Mansion
1992	The major Divine periodical, the *New Day*, ceased regular publication
2000-2006	Divine's movement sold off two major hotels in Philadelphia for lack of volunteers to run them

significantly prepared the way for it. According to Sullivan, "While many people were yet talking about what religion could do about integration and self-determination and human dignity, he was practicing it." Divine himself, especially in the 1950s and early 1960s, concentrating as he was on inward readiness for racial integration, seemed to keep his movement aloof from major organized efforts toward integration, leading historians of the civil rights movement to indicate scarcely any significant contribution by Divine.[2]

Left: **GEORGE W. BRAYE. WHO GREW UP IN DIVINE'S KINGSTON MANSION, became a soldier in the Korean War.** (Kingston High School Year Book, *Maroon*, 1950)

Right: **PATRICK HENRY, WHO GREW UP IN DIVINE FACILITIES in Krumville and High Falls, became a conscientious objector in the Korean War** (Ellenville High School Year Book, *Blue and Gold*, 1946)

THE KOREAN WAR

After World War II, when the Western world was deeply alarmed by the threat of Communist aggression, Divine continued to teach non-violence as an ideal. Violence was limited in its effect, Divine said. It did not work to bring about fundamental change. He had always taught, he said, that you must "conquer with love." In 1949, when his followers purchased the Hotel Riviera in Newark, New Jersey, they carried over half million dollars in cash in suitcases to a bank to pay for it, and they did so, as Divine proudly pointed out afterwards, without carrying guns.

In June, 1950, when Communist North Korea invaded non-Communist South Korea, the United Nations quickly supported South Korea, and in cooperation with it, the United States sent troops. Divine believed that one cause of North Korea's invasion was the continuing racial division in America and elsewhere which had helped to convert millions around the world to Communism. He believed that the fundamental strength of a nation was not its military, he said, but its social and economic justice.

Nevertheless, Divine, a month after the Korean War began, stretching his nonviolence thin, urged his followers to support the United States even if it built a million atomic bombs. He did so, he said, not with the intention of using such bombs, but merely with the intention; of being ready to use them when "necessary."

Meanwhile, in 1948 President Truman officially ordered the desegregation of American military forces, and Divine claimed that it was his own spirit, working through President Truman, that was responsible for it. While the implementation of Truman's order was slow, it led to a marked increase in the numbers of blacks going into the armed forces.

In the same year, 1948, Truman led Congress to reinstate a military draft. While in World War II, the percent of draftees who were conscientious objectors was estimated to be only 0.15 percent, under this new draft, by 1952 during the Korean War the percent was estimated to have risen to 1.6 percent, and by 1956 as the war wound down but the draft survived, to have risen to 9.2 percent.

One reason for the increased proportion of conscientious objectors was that the draft law became more tolerant of them. As revised during the Korean War, while the law still provided that conscientious objectors could serve in non-combatant work within the military, it also provided that if they declined to go into the military system altogether, they were no longer required to do alternate service, as in World War II, in a government-controlled work system, without pay. Rather they were allowed to do any essential civilian work that the objectors' draft board and the objectors themselves could mutually agree on, with pay.[3]

Early in the Korean War, as a Divine follower who became a regular soldier recalled, Divine called together a group of his draft-age male followers, to talk to them about the draft. He told them that if they were conscientious objectors, they knew it in their hearts and should act accordingly, but if they were willing to fight, and knew that in their hearts, they should join the military. As in World War II, Divine declined to push them to decide one way or the other.

During the Korean War, although for the United States as a whole the proportion of conscientious objectors went up, for Divine followers it seemed to go down. More names are available of followers becoming soldiers than becoming conscientious objectors, just the reverse of their proportions in World War II, suggesting a decline in the intensity of Divine's teaching of nonviolence. While the names are available of twenty-four Divine followers who became Korean War soldiers, by contrast, the names are available of only four followers who became Korean War conscientious objectors. Of those who became soldiers, four grew up in Ulster County, all at the Kingston Mansion, these being George Braye. Harold Maybanks, Normal Mitchell, and Daniel Love. Of those who became conscientious objectors, two of them grew up in Ulster County, both of them at Krumville and High Falls, these being Peter Love and Patrick Henry.[4]

DECLINE IN ULSTER COUNTY

In Ulster County, the Divine movement may be said to have reached its peak of strength from about 1937 to 1942, and then to have gradually declined. Under the impact of Divine's inability to visit New York State freely, the number of significant Peace Missions in the county dropped significantly from twenty-five in 1942, when Divine moved to Philadelphia, to nine in 1950, and then for several decades continued to drop, but slowly.

If Ulster County's poor had taken advantage of the opportunities offered by Peace Mission communities, as Divine had hoped they would, the mission's decline there might have been slowed. Some of Kingston's poor lived in appalling conditions, and they did so, as Kingston resident Jacob Butler, a mechanic for a car dealer, complained to Divine, even in 1943 during the World War when opportunities for jobs improved. Seven poor Kingston families lived, Butler said, in one five-room house.

Divine replied to Butler that it was difficult for him to sympathize with these families because they could easily have taken advantage of such Peace Mission sites as Greenkill Park. At the park, Divine wrote, my followers "were willing to spend their own money, time and labor to make it a comfortable, convenient and fit place for all to dwell in who would be willing to live the life of Christ." But, Divine asked Butler, "Have they taken advantage of the sacrifice my followers have made to better their condition? You know they have not." The underprivileged of Kingston, Divine grieved, "would rather be tools and slaves of an unjust system in order to have the freedom to get a bottle of rum. They would rather live in squalor than live the life of Christ."

From the late forties, not only was the Peace Mission movement as a whole shrinking, but within the movement, the importance of Ulster County markedly declined. A sign of this was that the *New Day* published few advertisements from Ulster County, or letters from Ulster County, or notices of meetings in Ulster County.

Meantime, the use of Ulster County missions as vacation sites, already declining during World War II, continued to decline. By 1945, Divine already said that such major resorts in Ulster County as Greenkill Park, Milton, and Krum Elbow were "somewhat idle." By about 1950, Greenkill Park was no longer significantly used by vacationists; huge resort though it was, it was often occupied only by a single caretaker, who kept a few cows there. In the summer of 1952, when a party from New York City vacationed at Kingston Mansion, they found, according to their report to Divine, that the staff there, Miss Satisfied Love and her assistant Miss Lamb, under the pressure of insufficient help and insufficient funds, were not only serving inadequate quantities of food, but were also charging more than expected, and were unwilling to refund anything when the visitors decided to leave early. In 1953, Divine told someone who had once visited Krum Elbow that it was hardly open as a vacation site anymore,

BANQUET AT WOODMONT, October, 2006, in the Chapel Dining Room, with Mother Divine, left, at the head of a long table which extended into the next room (upper right), altogether seating perhaps fifty persons. Shown in the back row, from left, were: Edna Mae Claybrook, author Mabee, Peter Love, Robert Tucker (face obscured by microphone), two guests from Eritrea, Richard Menn, Sally Edwards Menn (the author's niece), and Judy Edwards Forbes (also the author's niece). On the other side of the table, the woman in the foreground wearing a tam is Meekness Faith. (Photo by Roger Klaus)

because we have so many such sites that "we don't know what to do with them."

At about this same time, it is likely that the Ulster County farms, which were still owned by Divine followers—including such substantial ones as Krum Elbow, Hope Farm, and Divine Farm—were not producing much. In 1952 when a visitor asked Divine if such sites shipped out much of their produce to Divine sites elsewhere, he said no. When the visitor then asked if these farms sold their produce commercially, Divine answered no to that also, suggesting they scarcely grew enough produce, beyond their own needs, to ship out.[5]

DIVINE'S LAST KNOWN VISIT TO ULSTER COUNTY

To celebrate the "Sixth Anniversary" of his second marriage, Divine, his wife, and his staff motored to the Promised Land on Labor Day weekend, in 1952, on what turned out to be Divine's last known visit to Ulster County. They drove in a "caravan" including "hundreds" of followers from the Philadelphia area. Many others traveled from New York, by bus, ship, or car, according to the *New Day*, making a crowd altogether of "thousands." Divine and his immediate party expected to stay at Krum Elbow, on the Hudson River, but

Left: **MOTHER DIVINE, SPEAKING AT A BANQUET AT WOODMONT, Oct., 2006.** (Roger Klaus) Right: **EDNA MAE CLAYBROOK, A SECRETARY TO MOTHER DIVINE.** (Photo by Robert Tucker, May, 2007)

the need for space there became so pressing that they stayed instead in the less crowded Kingston Mansion, in the city of Kingston.

At the Kingston Mansion during the day, the guests "frolicked" about the swimming pool; during the evening, they watched outdoor movies "on the rolling lawn." At Krum Elbow, the guests swam and boated in the Hudson River; dinner included fresh fish caught in the Hudson off Krum Elbow's own dock. Followers distributed a Sixth Anniversary souvenir they had prepared, which included a photo of Father and Mother Divine and a copy of the Sermon on the Mount.

The celebration occasioned a Kingston radio commentator, Bob Browning, to say in a broadcast that, in his experience, Divine's followers in the county, "without exception," had "set us an example of honesty and integrity and good Christian living." As the movement declined, it seemed less of a threat to the people of Ulster County, and resistance to it eased.

As the guests moved around the Promised Land, however, a group of Rosebuds—that is, members of the Divine order for young women—rode in a truck, and they did so "with a man." When Divine heard of it, he wrote the Rosebuds riders that they had ignored his teaching that women do not converse with men except "strictly on business," "much less" ride with them. Unlike his stance on such other topics as nonviolence, Divine's stance in this matter was absolute. He did not say that whatever these women did was acceptable if they were following their highest intuition. He just said what these women did was plain wrong. To punish these women, he promptly required them to turn in their red Rosebud suits.

Soon afterward, Mother Divine reminded a meeting of Rosebuds that, when any Rosebuds have their suits taken away, the other Rosebuds, to indicate their support for the punishment, did not "socialize" with them. She also told them, however, that Divine was being merciful to the offenders by allowing them to hope that if they repented, they could be "reinstated."[6]

THE PROBLEM OF SUCCESSION AND SURVIVAL

In the short term, Divine's early operating strategies seemed to work. That is, such strategies as his receiving no pay and owning no property, and his movement's not keeping financial records or membership lists seemed workable in a growing movement, helping to protect its assets and give it flexibility. In the long run, however, such strategies seemed not only inefficient, but also invited suspicion, and limited the independent responsibility of followers. Moreover, though Divine seemed little concerned about it, any movement that heavily depended on one charismatic leader was inherently impermanent.

Such factors may have persuaded Divine and his associates, as they looked into the future, that it would be wise to give the movement more institutional structure, as by creating churches. Such factors may also to have helped to convince Divine that he should marry again, as a means of providing a wife who might succeed him as the leader of his movement. In 1946, after he married a young white Canadian, his followers learned to thank both him and the new Mother Divine, for their blessings, and she, often called—as by followers at Krum Elbow—a "Spotless Virgin Bride," became almost co-equal in status with him. There were claims that others hoped to become Divine's successor. One other such was Simon Peter, who had successfully managed cooperative groceries first in High Falls and later in Philadelphia, and became president of the Unity Mission Church. Another such was Tommy Garcia, the son of a Hispanic father and a Greek mother, who seemed to be specially raised at the Woodmont estate. Despite such claims, the new Mother Divine gradually took on the role of Divine's expected successor.

As Divine's movement aged, it seemed to become more eager to identify with the American main stream. In the 1930s when Divine had been establishing his communities in Ulster County, he had been creative, adventurous, and willing to take risks. He had created interracial communities. He had taught absolute pacifism. He had cooperated with Communists on matters on which he agreed with them. But later, especially during the Cold War, Divine, when he had more to lose, had grown more conservative. He relaxed his pacifism. Like most Americans, he came to regard Communists as dangerously subversive. While Divine followers had long identified themselves with America, they now seemed to do so more intensely, as when President Simon Peter said in 1958, "We are proud to be Americans because Father Divine is truly the American of Americans"; he teaches that "true Americanism, true Christianity, true Judaism, and true democracy" are "synonymous." Once churches had been created within the Divine movement, the movement tended to use the Bible more, in meetings, speeches, and correspondence, often citing it by chapter and verse. Similarly, the *New Day*, which had been calling Divine's speeches merely "messages" or "lectures," learned to call them "sermons," and it published a new Bible study column. Divine's churches, gradually becoming more conventional, reduced the movement's spontaneity. While they did not repudiate the movement's 1936 platform, they tended to ignore its more radical features.

In addition, Divine seemed to become increasingly devoted to threatening his critics. By the late 1940s, retribution had become a common theme for Divine, and the *New Day* was packed with reports of events which followers interpreted as Divine's retribution. At that time, Divine said, "all who have risen in opposition to me," are "getting just what is rightfully due them." In 1954, after a woman talked against him, her daughter died, and Divine commented, as he often did in such cases, "retribution is sure." Individuals themselves should not carry out acts of retribution, Divine explained. Retribution should be left in the hands of God.

Still, as long as Divine himself led his movement, he retained the power to elicit fervent support. As an Afro-American who was growing up in West Philadelphia in the latter 1950s recalled, he was "mesmerized" when Divine and his entourage passed through the streets. "Universal energy was all over the place," he remembered, "and it was free for the taking."

In the 1950s, as Divine aged, he became less active, and because of his movement's heavy dependence on him, it slowed. In 1960 he was sent to a hospital in a diabetic coma. Thereafter, he ceased to speak in public, and the second Mother Divine often substituted for him. By 1964, while he continued to see his secretaries daily, he was no longer strong enough to see visitors. On September 10, 1965, when he was in his eighties, or nineties, or, as some claimed, hundreds, he died. As his followers chose to say, he laid his body down. His movement no longer had the stimulus of his direct presence.

More than a dozen years after Divine's death, however, the Divine movement was still proving to be organized enough, enthusiastic enough, and wealthy enough to hold on. In 1979, it seemed to Kenneth E. Burnham, a Temple University Sociology professor who had studied the Divine movement at length, that with the problem of succession having been met by "a charismatic Mother Divine," the Divine movement was not "likely to fade out" in the "foreseeable future."[7]

JIM JONES ADOPTS DIVINE'S PROMISED LAND AS A MODEL

In 1957, Jim Jones, an earthy, frustrated Pentecostal pastor in Indianapolis, first visited Divine in Philadelphia. While Jones himself was white, he had dared, like Divine, to make his congregation multiracial, resulting in shots being fired at him, the windows of his church being broken, and his home devastated. When Jones visited Divine again in 1958, Jones' persistence in trying to overcome racism encouraged Divine's followers to receive him warmly. At that time, Divinite leader Peter Simon introduced Jones and his associates to Divine as "successful in their endeavor to follow your teaching." Also at that time, the still youthful Jones, perceiving Divine and his mission as illustrating what he had been "yearning for," was identifying with Divine and ready to learn more from him. He had "wasted" years of his life, he said, looking for what he now found in Divine's movement. Jones recognized, he explained, "the spirit of God" in Divine. He said he felt Divine's "energy" being "transmitted" to him. He said Divine's followers were living "the reality of the Kingdom of Heaven." He said he felt he was "at home" in Divine meetings. He admitted his language sometimes differed from Divine's, but he told a Divine meeting, that he and his followers had adopted "some" of "your principles," and promised to work in the future with "you in our minds."

Adapting Divine practices to his own situation, Jones stopped taking a salary, instead working like Divine as a volunteer. Like Divine, Jones avoided referring to races by name. Like Divine, Jones conceived of his movement as being an extended family led by a God-like father. Divine's emphasis on social service encouraged Jones to lead his followers to provide more help for the destitute and the aged, and Divine's emphasis on the international character of his movement encouraged Jones to lead his followers to adopt foreign children.

Particularly significant here is that, according to sociologist John Hall, Jones adopted Divine's communities in Ulster County—Divine's Promised Land—as a model for his own movement, providing an impressive example of the Promised Land's impact. In fact, soon after the Communist take over of Cuba in 1959, Jones tried to create a rural Promised Land, like Divine's, for Cuban refugee families in the United States, but failed. By 1967, however, he succeeded in establishing a Promised Land farm community in California, in a permissive neighborhood north of San Fransisco, in Redwood Valley. This new community, which became the Jones's movement headquarters, followed Divine's Ulster County model not only in being rural, interracial, and frugal, but also in promising both spiritual and material salvation.

As Jones observed Divine aging, Jones

dreamed that since Divine's movement had much in common with his, he might be declared Divine's successor, so he could absorb Divine's movement into his. Divine, however, had not only prepared his wife, Mother Divine, to be his successor, but also the differences between the Divine and Jones movements had become significant. After all, Jones believed that the end justifies the means, as Divine did not. Jones did not embrace abstention from violence, sex, and drugs, as Divine did. Compared to Divine, Jones was more committed to mixing Christianity and socialism, and was more pessimistic about the possibility of remaking America into a just society. Jones' continued, however, to visit the Peace Mission in Philadelphia. In 1971, six years after Divine's death, Jones visited there with over 200 of his followers. They stayed several days, during which his followers pressed their views on Divine followers enough so that their impact grew disturbing. Later that same year, the Jones movement sent a fleet of buses to Philadelphia's Divine sites, inviting Divine followers to visit the Jones communities in California free of charge, with the hope that once there, they would wish to stay. While Jones hardly succeeded in pulling any significant number of followers away from the Divine movement, in 1972 Mother Divine, finding Jones' attempts to take over the Divine movement growing brazen, and his hostility to American society intensifying, told Jones that he was no longer welcome to visit.

Meanwhile, Jones felt hounded by his critics, including tax investigators, racial segregationists, and defectors who charged that his movement was holding followers against their will. Such hostility, built up over a long time, seemed to make Jones distraught. Deeply alienated from American society as Jones had become, it was increasingly difficult for him to be satisfied with Divine's model of a Promised Land in the United States, so that he turned away from it more nearly to Marcus Garvey's model of a Promised Land outside the United States, where he could hope to escape his fiercest critics. In 1974 Jones began to establish a settlement in the jungle of Guyana, a predominantly black South American nation, with leftist leanings that suited Jones. In the next few years, he sent substantial numbers of his followers from California to settle at the new jungle site.

By 1978, Jones himself was at the Guyana settlement, but physically sick. As some of those close to him knew, he had become a drug abuser, it was doubtful that he would live long, and his sanity was in question. When California Congressman Leo Ryan, egged on by defectors from Jones' movement, planned to visit Guyana to investigate charges that the settlement was holding followers there against their will, Jones asked him not to come, but he came anyway. After his visit, as the Congressman was preparing to leave, a group of Jones's followers, with Jones's consent, killed the Congressman and others of his party. Soon afterwards, Jones, at the settlement, told his followers that it was hopeless to escape their enemies. "They invaded our privacy," he said. Then, declaring that they were committing "an act of revolutionary suicide protesting the conditions of an inhumane world," he persuaded more than 900 of his followers to join him in a mass suicide.[8]

Jones's experience is a reminder both of the profound influence that Divine's movement could have, and also of the dangers inherent in charismatic figures exercising almost unchecked power. While Jones allowed his movement's early benevolence to become conspicuously perverted, Divine's movement, despite such lapses as Divine's threatening retribution to his critics and virtually abandoning his Ulster County followers, continued its essential benevolence.

42. SELLING OFF, MOVING OUT, LINGERING ON

BY THE LATTER PART OF 1942, with Divine having moved to Philadelphia, and the war pulling workers away from the Divine communities in Ulster County, it became evident that Divine properties there might soon be for sale. At that time the New York Urban League asked Divine if it would be possible for it to buy any of his Ulster County property for a convalescent home for blacks. Divine replied that the property was owned by his followers, not by him, and that he doubted any of his followers would consent to the sale of their property for "any such limited purpose" as a home "for any especial so-called race." Divine seemed to be more driven by his opposition to segregation than by any desire to secure money for his followers.

The next year, Divine himself, aware that only modest use was being made of his movement's property in the county, proposed that it be made available to the federal government for the duration of the war. The land, he said, about 2,000 acres, much of it "good tillable land," could be used to increase food production, and the buildings, capable of accommodating as many as 3,000 people, could be used for military or housing purposes. The government did not accept the offer.

As World War II came to a close, however, with Divine's visits to Ulster County having become rare and likely to stay that way, Divine's followers began to sell off some of their Ulster County property. In 1944-1945, followers sold off their Stone Ridge Farm, their New Paltz Farm, and their Samsonville resort.

Naturally owners sometimes differed among themselves about whether they wanted to sell. In 1946, when one of the owners of Greenkill Park, Blessed Faithful Heart, wanted to sell but other owners did not, she arranged to sell her share to the other owners, so Greenkill Park remained owned entirely by Divine followers.

When followers sold their property, most of them were governed by a provision which the Divine movement had inserted into their deeds, that the owners were "joint tenants," so that if any of the owners died, their share of ownership passed not to their heirs, but to the remaining owners. In the case of the Samsonville resort, when Divine followers originally bought it, there were five buyers who bought it as joint tenants, but when they sold this property in 1945, one of them having died, it was the surviving four owners who sold it and shared the proceeds. In the case of the Kingston Mansion, however, of the four original buyers of the property, by 1961 only one remained living, she being Heavenly Rest, who was one of Divine's secretaries in Philadelphia. Since she did not wish to sell the property away from Divinites, but they considered it unwise to leave the property in one name alone, it was arranged for Heavenly Rest to sell the property to herself and three other followers, so that again it was owned by multiple followers.[1]

NUMBER OF MAJOR DIVINE MISSIONS REMAINING IN ULSTER COUNTY

YEAR	NUMBER OF MISSIONS
1942	25
1950	9
1960	3
1970	2
1980	1

Followers sold off their Ulster County property gradually, over many years. In 1947, they sold off one of their impressive resort properties, Milton. Originally it had fifteen buyers, and one having died, fourteen remained to sell it. In 1950, followers sold their Krumville Farm, and in 1958 their Hope Farm. In 1960, they sold their magnificent Krum Elbow estate on the Hudson River. There had been twenty-one original Krum Elbow buyers, most of them living in New York, but when they sold it, only eighteen of them were still alive, most of them by this time living in Philadelphia, where they could be near Divine.[2]

By 1965, when Father Divine died, the only Ulster County properties still owned by Divine followers were two major ones, Kingston Mansion and Greenkill Park. As the Divine movement declined, and Ulster County seemed far from the

PEACE

THE DIVINE HOTEL'S POLICY—RULES AND REGULATIONS

All hotel's owned by the followers of FATHER DIVINE are operated on a non-profit basis for the upliftment of mankind in general.

It is our desire to be a blessing to everyone who avails themselves of the facilities we offer. This can only be made effective to you by your willingness to cooperate in maintaining the standard of Americanism, Brotherhood, Christianity and True Judaism that FATHER DIVINE dedicated these hotels to exemplify.

The following rules and regulations you are required to adhere to in accord with this standard that promotes modesty, independence, honesty and righteousness. Upon violation of any of these rules the management, at their discretion, may check you out.

We recognize only one race, the human race. We appreciate your willingness to share a room with another. This is not required but promoted in the interest of the Brotherhood of man.

Ladies and gentlemen are accommodated on separate floors and may see each other only in the hotel lobby or dining room.

No smoking on hotel premises.

No drinking of alcoholic beverages.

No vulgarity, obscenity or blasphemy.

Attire must be evangelical at all times.

Check-out time — 1:00 P.M.

Charge for additional day is automatically in effect after this hour.

Rooms must be available no later than this hour for proper servicing, unless permission is granted for necessary exceptions.

Rent

Must be paid in advance on day due.

If not paid on day due occupant is then charged at daily rate for delinquent period.

If rent becomes three days in arrears, the occupant will be checked out.

If occupant is away and cannot be notified that their rent is in arrears, they will be checked out and their belongings stored until a satisfactory adjustment is made.

Anyone is privileged to volitionally donate more than the required price for their accommodations if their appreciation impels them to.

Key to be left at the desk when you leave the building.

Lights and all other electrical appliances should be turned off upon leaving the room.

Door should be locked when room is not occupied. The hotel accepts no responsibility for any loss of personal effects.

Visitors are not allowed in rooms. Guests of the hotel are only allowed in rooms to which they are assigned.

Food is not to be kept in the room. Candy, fruit and nuts are permissible.

Laundry is not to be done in the room.

A NOTICE FOUND POSTED AT KINGSTON MANSION when Divine followers sold it away in 1985. (Joanne Bush)

movement's new center in Philadelphia, followers maintained the considerably used Kingston Mansion, but neglected the little-used Greenkill Park, scarcely doing even the most necessary repairs to its large number of houses. Some of the park's owners had long been willing to sell it, but any proposed sale was complicated by its deteriorated condition, and by its having many owners—originally, when it was bought in 1937, twenty-seven of them—who needed to be traced and their consent obtained. Finally in 1967, the remaining owners who could be located, only seven of them, sold the property to a Divine church, the Unity Mission Church, which secured a clear title for it. Then in 1971, the church sold it away from the Divine movement to a lumber company, which allowed much of what had been the Greenkill Park to become a gigantic sand mine.

In 1967, after Divine's death, Mother Divine and a party of Divine followers from the Philadelphia region visited Ulster County, renewing the Peace Mission's ties to it. They stayed at the Kingston Mansion, which was still being used as a resort, and still boasted of its outdoor swimming pool. Among those in the party were Patrick Henry, who had grown up at the Krumville farm, and had been a conscientious objector in the Korean War, and Roger Klaus, originally of Colorado, who at about this time was becoming a conscientious objector in the Vietnam War.

On this trip, Klaus and Henry stayed in the men's dormitory building, which Divine followers had built as an attachment to the old kitchen building, so that in the morning when Klaus and Henry woke up, as Klaus recalled later, they smelled the preparations for breakfast from the kitchen below. During the day, their party visited many sites in the county where Divine missions had once been. As they drove up the twisting Catskill Mountain roads on their way to visit what had been Divine's Samsonville resort, they passed a newer resort, which had followed the Divine movement into the neighborhood, the resort of Peg Leg Bates, the black entertainer, where Mother Divine stopped briefly to greet Bates. Later Klaus and other followers visited Ulster County several times again, sometimes taking bicycles with them, and bicycling to Greenkill Park.

SELLING OFF MAJOR PEACE MISSION PROPERTIES IN ULSTER COUNTY,
1950s to 1980s

PROPERTIES	SOLD
Olive Bridge Farm (Krumville)	1950
Divine Farm (Saxton)	1955
Department Store (High Falls)	1956
Hope Farm	1958
Divine Terrace (Elting Corners)	1959
Krum Elbow	1960
Greenkill Park	1971
Kingston Mansion	1985

In 1978, when the town of Marbletown was celebrating its 200th anniversary, a group of followers from Philadelphia, who themselves had lived in Ulster County, drove to High Falls to take part in the celebration. Included in the group were Sunshine Flowers and June S. Peace, both of whom had grown up at the New Paltz mission. As part of the celebration, Marjorie Hasbrouck, of the Stone Ridge Library, showed slides of Divine movement activities, suggesting the county's increasing tolerance of the movement in its decline. Afterwards Mother Divine wrote Hasbrouck saying that Ulster County had "played a very important role" in Divine's work to create "brotherhood."

Continuing its long, drawn-out withdrawal from New York State, the Divine movement sold its last remaining property in Harlem in 1984. Then the next year, 1985, it also sold its last remaining property in Ulster County, the Kingston Mansion.[3]

DID DIVINE'S FOLLOWERS DESERT HIM OR REMAIN LOYAL?

As the Divine followers who originally bought properties in Ulster County gradually sold them off, were they deserting Divine? According to the available addresses of those who bought property in Ulster County from 1935 to 1942, as listed in their deeds of purchase at that time, thirty-one of them lived in Ulster County, ninety-five in New York City, and none in Philadelphia. After Divine moved to Philadelphia, however, as these owners gradually sold off their property in Ulster County, of those whose addresses are available for the years 1943 through 1960, those living in Ulster County had dropped to nine, and those living in New York City had dropped to thirty-seven, while those living in Philadelphia had risen from nothing to thirty-six. Altogether this suggests that a significant number of these property owners were selling their property not because they were disillusioned by their experience with the Divine movement, but because, after Divine moved to Philadelphia, they wanted to follow him there, to be closer to him.

Did other Ulster County followers—those who

had not been owners of Divine communities in the county, but had been related in some meaningful way to Divine's activities there—desert Divine or stay loyal to him? Two such persons, both prominent in the Divine movement, can be cited as deserting Divine. They were John Hunt, who turned against Divine conspicuously, as already noted, and Secretary John Lamb, who, after Divine's marriage to his second wife, left the movement quietly, without publically criticizing Divine, and became a manager for a New York hospital.

However, many other non-property owners who had been significantly related to Divine missions in Ulster County in some way, continued to be actively engaged in the Divine movement elsewhere, suggesting their Ulster County experience helped bond them to the movement. Among them, Greta B. Love, who had lived at the Stone Ridge Mansion, became a member of Divine's secretarial staff. Magnetic Love, who had solicited advertisements for the *New Day* in Kingston, became the secretary of the Peace Center Church. Deborah Newmind, who had been articulate as a resident of Hope Farm, moved to Philadelphia, and continued to speak for the movement. Simon Peter, who had been the manager of a Divine grocery in High Falls, became the president of one of the major Divine churches. Vida Victoria, who had run a gas station at the Krumville farm, afterwards moved to Philadelphia, lived in a Divine facility, and worked as a registered nurse. Holy Love Dove, who had often been a companion for the first Mother Divine in High Falls, reading and singing with her, later moved to Philadelphia to a Divine facility, the Circle Mission Church on Broad Street, and became one of Divine's inner circle. Editor John DeVoute, who had often been in Ulster County reporting on Divine's activities there, afterwards moved to Philadelphia and continued to edit the *New Day* there.

FOLLOWERS WHO LINGERED ON

Other followers who lived in Ulster County stayed on there, even as Divine missions were sold off around them. In the 1950s in High Falls, after some of its Peace Mission properties had already been sold off, several men, calling themselves "the Brothers at the Divine Residence, High Falls," remained there. Among these men were black electricians who worked out in the neighborhood, as by installing electric wiring in the barn of Louis Crepet, on Mohonk Avenue at the edge of town, as well as in a house in Krumville.

At about the same time, however, when it was apparent that the Divine movement's future in High Falls seemed unpromising, another such High Falls workman, the black Solomon Heart, a carpenter, bought seven acres in a mountain region a few miles southwest of High Falls. It was along Coxing Creek in the town of Rochester, on Clove Valley Road, in the neighborhood of two black resorts. Heart was soon living there, supporting himself by doing handiwork for neighbors. By the 1960s, when the white Bob Larsen became a researcher for the nearby Mohonk Preserve and moved into Heart's neighborhood, as Larsen recalls, Heart introduced Larsen and his wife to the neighboring black resorts, Smitty's and Wicki Wackie.

As the Divine movement's use of its Krum Elbow estate declined, Miss Noah Endurance, who had long been in charge of it, sometimes went out to work from there, with other followers, as at a nearby resort, Donnidick Lodge, in West Park. In 1960, when Divine followers sold their Krum Elbow estate to Walter Seaman, a hardware merchant in nearby Highland, Endurance stayed on at Krum Elbow for some time to help the Seaman family orient themselves to their new estate.[4]

At the Kingston mansion, its long-time manager, Satisfied Love, as she became older in the 1950s, clung to her conspicuous name, even though by listing it in telephone books she was inviting teenagers to call her, anonymously, to tease her about it. In Love's last years, when she was said to be like Aunt Jemima, large, warm, and nurturing, if she was not busy enough at the mansion, Love sometimes supported herself by working outside as a housekeeper. After her death, in the early 1980s the mansion still continued to be operated as a vacation site, under the care of a white follower, Anita Lea, originally from Minneapolis. Lea kept the outdoor pool operating till near the end. Finally, when the mansion was sold away, Divine followers had held it for fifty years.

The couple who bought the Kingston mansion—Richard and Joanne Bush—came upon the site accidentally. They were looking for property to buy, and were being shown around the neighborhood by a realtor, who, having mixed up the street numbers, took them to the mansion by mistake. Attracted to the site, they met Anita Lea at the mansion door, and she invited them in. She told them the mansion might be for sale, and they were quickly intrigued by its relation to the Divine movement. As they sat down to talk with Miss Lea, she pulled up a chair for Father Divine, so that in spirit he could join the talk. At the time, besides Lea, probably only one other follower was then living in the house, but the huge table in the dining hall was still set. Divine's office was still furnished as it was when he died. Later Richard Bush, wanting to understand the Divine movement better, traveled to Woodmont to discuss a possible purchase with Mother Divine and others. As they eventually arranged the purchase, it included both the original main mansion and the two new separate buildings Divine followers had added—the men's residence hall and the cottage built by Mary Sheldon Lyon. At the sale's closing, held around a table at a bank, among those present were several Divine followers, including representatives of the Unity Mission Church, which then owned the property. At that time, the Bushes recalled, followers kept an empty chair at the table, for Father Divine.[5]

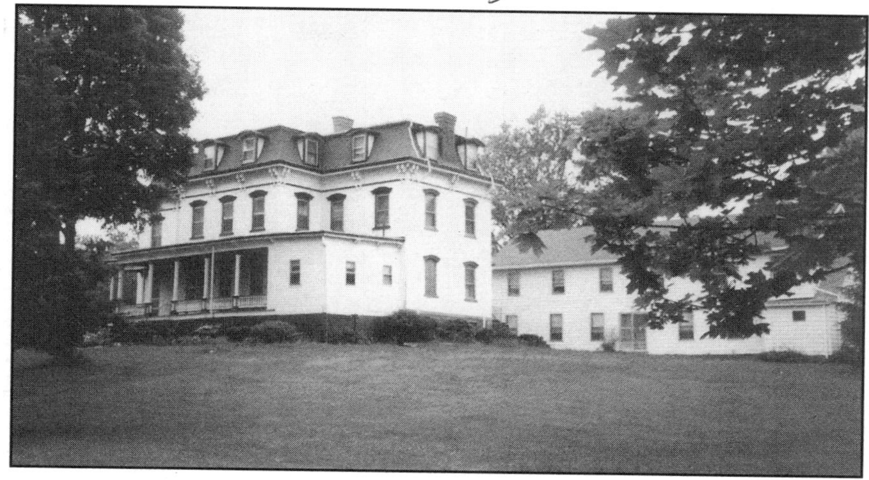

KINGSTON MANSION, AFTER IT WAS SOLD TO THE BUSH FAMILY. Showing at the rear right is a separate dining hall and dormitory, built by Divine followers, which several years later, neglected, collapsed. The Bushes removed it. (Photo about 1988, Joanne Bush)

Best Wishes to Father & Mother Divine
from Peace Cooperative Express

247 Lenox Ave. New York 27, N.Y.

Phone: Riverside 9-5437

FREDERIC N. CRABB, SR.
HENRI STEPHEN

ANNOUNCEMENT:

I am thanking FATHER and MOTHER DIVINE for blessing me to a transfer to P.S. 615 Manhattan, at my own request, effective September 1, 1955 A.D.F.D. The school is known as The Wiltwyck School for Boys, Esopus, N.Y. a few miles above Krum Elbow.

My residence and phone: Frederic N. Crabb, Sr., Divine Terrace, R.F.D. 2, Box 61, Highland, N.Y. Tel.: Clintondale 7-3427 (two rings).

ACCORDING TO THIS ADVERTISEMENT, IN 1955 FREDERIC CRABB ALREADY LIVED AT THE DIVINE TERRACE SITE. (*New Day*, Sept. 10, 1955)

At Elting Corners, in the town of Lloyd, long after the main Peace Mission building there had burned, a few Divine followers hung on, eventually including the black Frederic N. Crabb, who was a long-time New York City public school teacher and a trustee of one of Divine's churches. Crabb held strong beliefs. Inspired by Divine's teachings, he warmly supported the United Nations. He encouraged everyone to follow Divine disciples not only in making the world less race conscious

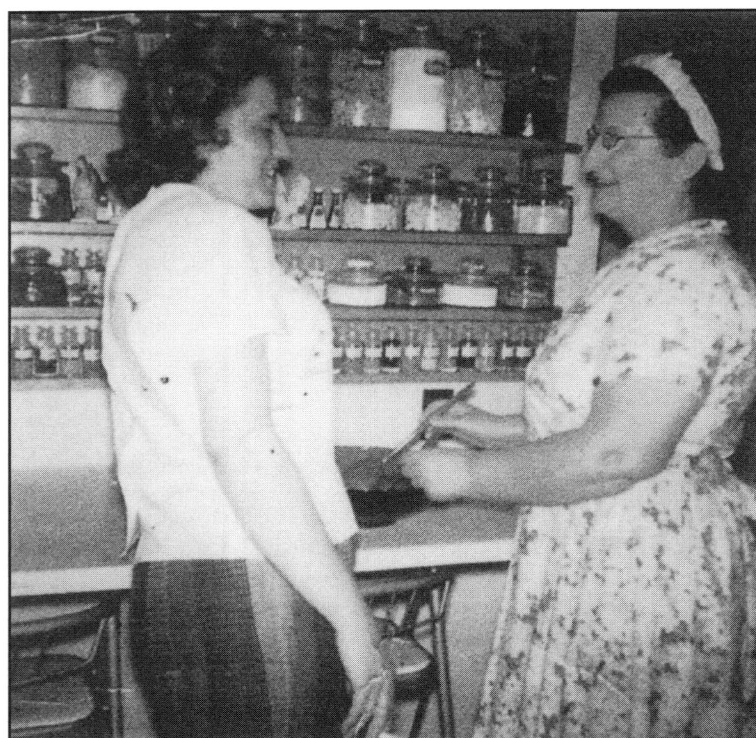

Left: **LAURA BROCK MILLER (left) WITH HER MOTHER, THE FORMER MINA BROCK, but remarried as Mina Crabb, in the kitchen of their new house at the Divine Terrace site, 1970s?** (Laura Brock Miller) Right: **FREDERIC CRABB, SHOWN AT A PIANO, at first lived in a barn at the Divine Terrace site. Then he bought the site, and by 1960 built a house on it, for himself and his new wife, the long-time Divine follower Mina Brock.** (Laura Brock Miller)

by no longer referring to races by name, but also in making world more peace-conscious by using the word "peace" as a greeting.

By 1955, when Crabb was transferred, at his own request, to teach in a special New York City public school located in Ulster County in the town of Esopus, a residential school for troubled boys called Wiltwyck School, he found it convenient to live about ten miles from the school, at the Peace Mission's Divine Terrace site, at Elting Corners. Crabb lived there in a big barn which still stood on the site, with at least two other men, both Afro-Americans like himself, who did a little farming on the spot. They were all Divine followers, though it was a question how fervent they were by this time. But in 1959, when Crabb was about at retirement age, he decided to buy the Divine Terrace site, including its barns. To buy it, which Crabb was financially able to do in part because he had defied Divine's teaching against participating in pension systems, Crabb conducted a long search for the four Divine followers who had originally bought it in 1936. He found only one surviving, Wonderful Peace, of Passaic, New Jersey, and bought Divine Terrace from her.

By the late 1950s, despite Divine's teaching that marriage interfered with spiritual development, Crabb, who had been divorced, decided to marry again. This time he married a long-time Divine follower, the white nurse Mina Brock, who had once lived at the New Paltz mission, and had been the wife of the long-deceased Arthur Brock. In about 1960, Crabb and his new wife Mina built a brick house on the Divine Terrace site, just south of where the Terrace Inn had burned down long before. The Crabbs allowed the other two men who lived in the big barn to continue to live there and keep a cow.

In the 1960s, Mina's daughter, Laura Brock Miller, having herself been divorced, came to this

DIVINE TERRACE SITE, SIXTY YEARS AFTER ITS INN BURNED, showing the inn's two barns (right), one large and one small, which did not burn, and were occupied by Divinite men, one of them being Frederic Crabb. Also showing the brick house (left) which Crabb built in 1960, and which was long occupied by his stepdaughter, Laura Brock Miller. (Photo by Rene F. Ramos, Feb., 2007)

new house with her children to live with her mother Mina Brock and her stepfather Frederic Crabb, thus returning to live near where she had spent much of her childhood in the Divine community at New Paltz. Crabb and his new wife continued to live at Divine Terrace until they died and their house passed to Mina's daughter, Laura Miller.

Recently, as Miller, who at this writing still lives in the house, has looked back at her upbringing in the Divine movement, she has been uneasy that she was considerably separated from her parents, but grateful she was brought up under Divine's guidance to be open to a variety of religious experiences. She has often visited Peace Mission friends in the Philadelphia region and participated in Peace Mission celebrations there, sharing her memories. She has found it sad that as the remaining followers age, fewer and fewer people attend these celebrations. Less aggressive than she used to be, however, if any of her friends there bring out differences in religious views, she prefers not to focus on those differences, but to brush lightly over them. She likes to say that she believes, as Divine did, in the "allness of God." That means to her that since all life, including all human life, is God, that includes Father Divine. In this sense, she says, she recognizes Divine as God.[6]

THE PRESENT AND FUTURE

More than seventy years after the first Divine communities were established in Ulster County, while none of these communities survives, Divine's Peace Mission movement itself survives, still centered in the Philadelphia region. It is, however, not flourishing. In 1992, Divine followers ceased to publish the *New Day* regularly. In 2000, they sold their huge Lorraine Hotel in Philadelphia, on Broad Street north of City Hall, and in 2006, they sold their impressive Tracy Hotel, in the University of Pennsylvania neighborhood. They sold these hotels, they explain, not as much because of financial need as because they could not find enough of their own volunteers to run them, and they did not want to hire outsiders, as doing so, they felt, would destroy the hotels' Peace Mission character. Other Philadelphia properties still remain in the hands of Divine followers, including the Circle Mission on South Broad Street, where Divine once had his central office, but it no longer either holds free classes or serves inexpensive meals to the public because, followers explain, it lacks the necessary volunteers. The movement is seriously aging and shrinking.

Divine's early house at Sayville, Long Island, remains in his followers' hands, and Divine's estate in the Philadelphia suburbs, Woodmont, still serves as Mother Divine's residence, and both sites continue to be beautifully maintained. Divine's Peace Mission serves Sunday evening communion banquets regularly in the Philadelphia area, often at Woodmont. Following tradition, the banquets are elaborate, usually last three hours, and feature Mother Divine presiding, participants singing and giving testimonies, the food being abundant, and platters passing continually along the long tables. The banqueters, many of them having glowing faces, still represent a variety of races, but they tend to be elderly, their numbers are dropping, and they are hoping for a miracle to revive their movement.

Devotion to Father Divine still persists, however, more than forty years after his death. With his followers believing he still lives in spirit, even now it is the custom to set a place for Divine at banquets, and to serve his plates with food. Even now recorded speeches by Divine, including speeches he gave in Ulster County, are played at banquets. Even now Rita Free Will, who often wrote to Divine while she was growing up in Ulster County's Hope Farm, treasures his replies. Even now Laura Miller, who grew up at Ulster County's New Paltz Farm, regards Divine as a heroic figure who hovered over her early life.

Looking back, in some ways Divine was like Marcus Garvey, Divine's rival of the 1920s, many of whose followers eventually gave their support to Divine. Both Garvey and Divine were black, charismatic, short in stature, and had roots in evangelical Christianity. Both worked to empower their followers, underprivileged as many of them were, to run businesses. In other ways, however, they were opposites. Garvey taught that women should be subordinate to men, while Divine taught sexual equality. Garvey encouraged families, while Divine discouraged families. Garvey emphasized accepting blackness, while Divine emphasized ignoring blackness or any racial affiliation. Garvey promoted racial separateness, while Divine promoted the races coming together. Garvey held out the ideal of going back to Africa, while Divine identified with America, and called on it to live up to its ideals.

In certain ways, Divine was more like Martin Luther King, who rose to leadership in the civil rights movement in the 1950s when Divine's movement was already declining. Like Garvey, both Divine and King were black, charismatic, and rooted in evangelical Christianity. Both Divine and King worked for racial integration, not separation, and considered themselves patriotic Americans, challenging Americans to live more in accord with their own ideals. Both Divine and King promoted nonviolent action on behalf of civil rights partly because, while violent action would be likely to arouse opposition, nonviolent action would be more likely to reach hearts. But King deliberately invited experienced practitioners of nonviolence to assist him, and went to India to study Gandhi's practice of nonviolence, as Divine did not. While Divine claimed he was God, and worked outside of the conventional church, departing radically from it, King did not claim he was God, and stayed within the conventional church, invigorating it as an instrument in the civil rights struggle. While both encouraged protest marches, King emphasized them more than Divine. On the other hand, Divine led in creating intentional, interracial communities, while King, although he brought blacks and whites together in civil rights activities, did not create such communities.

In retrospect, Divine seemed to launch his career as a visionary, offering alternative answers to life's major problems. Central to his early vision was his advocacy of the brotherhood of all mankind, to be achieved through racial integration, gender equality, absolute pacifism, food and jobs for the hungry, and healing for the sick, addicted, and criminal. On an individual level, he advocated a life of self-denial, honesty, hard work, and financial independence, as well as avoidance of family ties, sex, drugs, alcohol, gambling, and violence.

As his movement grew, Divine seemed to become more pragmatic, more willing to revise his beliefs in response to public pressure and the need to protect himself and his movement. He shifted from the absolute nonviolence of his 1936 platform to encouraging the buying of war bonds and supporting his followers who became soldiers. While at first he urged his followers to pay back their debts, including relief payments or charity received, later, as a means of retaliation against governments and private institutions, he asked them to stop doing so. He moved from giving little attention to reincarnation to teaching that for his followers it was to be expected. For the most part, however, his followers retained such faith in him that they seemed untroubled by any shifts in position.

Divine's exerting of his charisma inevitably had costs, as in fostering psychological dependence. Nevertheless, Divine avoided many of the potential excesses of exerting charisma. As far as available evidence indicates, he did not retain followers against their will. He did not personally take advantage of his position to exploit others sexually. While Divine personally lived the luxurious life style which his followers made available to him, he did not take advantage of it to accumulate personal wealth. While he moved away from advocating absolute nonviolence, he did not personally act violently, and his opposition to alcohol, drugs, gambling, and sex, helped his followers to become more healthy and frugal, as well as to avoid addiction and violence. While Jim Jones modeled his movement significantly after Divine's, Jones lost hope for the world, and led many of his followers into deliberate self-destruction, but Divine, despite such significant lapses as virtually abandoning his New York State followers, remained essentially beneficent toward both his followers and the world.

Looking back, Divine's interracial communities in Ulster County had less impact as models for the world than he and his followers had hoped they would. One reason was that these communities were permeated with practices which the public generally found difficult to tolerate, such as raising children apart from their parents, calling Divine God, promising that those who lived righteously would be prosperous, healthy, and never die, and calling for retribution for those who opposed him. Another reason was that these communities were so dependent on Divine's charismatic presence, that once he had he moved out of the state and could rarely visit, his communities had little opportunity to flourish.

However, the Divine movement's creation of interracial communities, notably in the Promised Land, was an extraordinary achievement for its time when racial integration was virtually absent in American society. These communities were outstanding for providing proof that harmonious interracial living was possible. As the minister and Congressman Adam Clayton Powell, Jr. said of the Divine movement in the 1940s, "This is probably the only place in the world where democracy and brotherhood are actually practiced in everyday living."[7] Father Divine's communities in Ulster County, particularly from the 1930s into the 1950s, were a significant contribution to preparing the way for the revolutionary civil rights movement to come.

NOTES

In the text, quotations have occasionally been condensed or otherwise edited for brevity and clarity, with care not to alter their meaning. Also in the text, while Divinites were uneasy with using any racial designations at all, sometimes racial designations have been used that Divine recommended when they seemed necessary, such as "light complexioned," "dark complexioned," and "Afro-American." (*New Day*, Dec. 8, 1945, 24; Ap. 15, 1950, 26)

In the notes, abbreviations used include *ND* for *New Day* and *SW* for *Spoken Word*. Also in the notes, because certain books are cited often, they are sometimes cited in abbreviated form, as, for example, Weisbrot, *Father Divine*, and Watts, *God, Harlem,* but they are fully cited in the Sources.

Preface

1: "Opposition": *New Day* (hereinafter abbreviated as *ND*), Oct. 22, 1949, 12. Sokolsky, "Giants in These Days," *Atlantic Monthly*, June, 1936, 699. Pittsburgh *Courier*, July 2, 1949, in *ND*, July 16, 1949, 15. Rosten, *People I Have Loved*, 1970, 201.

2: "Book": *Spoken Word* (hereinafter abbreviated as *SW*), Feb. 20, 1937, 9

Ch. 1. Divine and the Rise of his Movement

1: General sources for this chapter: Braden, *These Also Believe*, 1949; Burnham, *God Comes to America*, 1979; Weisbrot, *Father Divine*, 1983; Kephart and Zellner, *Extraordinary Groups*, 1991; Watts, *God, Harlem*, 1992. While Watts, 12, suspected that Divine grew up embarrassed by his mother's obesity, Griffith, "Body Salvation," *Religion and American Culture*, v. 2, no. 2, 2001, 133-134, argues that Divine's later encouragement of heavy eating makes any such embarrassment unlikely.

2: By 1899: Watts, 16. On New Thought: Braden, *Spirits in Rebellion, The Rise and Development of New Thought*, 1963; Belstrom; *Rediscovering God*, 2005, 57-87.

3: Divine's recollection: *ND*, July 24, 1941, 60; Sept. 11, 1948, 8

4: Divine recalled already using the name "Major J. Divine" on his draft card in WWI (*ND*, Dec. 3, 1949, 24).

5: Hadley's written report: Sayville *Suffolk County News*, Ap. 25, 1930

6: Before this, some called him God; overflow crowds: NY *Age*, Dec. 5, 1931-Jan. 9, 1932. List of those arrested: Watts, 206n21.

7: Lena Brinson was also known as Blessed Pure in Heart. By the latter name, she later became a purchaser of an Ulster County site, Kingston Jr.

8: Communists: NY *Times*, Aug. 5, 1934

9: List of communities: *SW*, July 6, 1935, 24

Ch. 2. Establishing the First Ulster County Mission: New Paltz

1: "Just why": *SW*, Nov. 16, 1935, 24. Deed: George Sachs to Clara Budds, July 27, 1935, liber 577, p. 12. "Diligence," "actual value": *ND*, Jan. 3, 1948, 26; Sept. 30, 1937, 26. $5,500: NY *Herald Tribune*, June 26, 1939. "Richest": *SW*, Nov. 24, 1936, 11.

2: "Blot": New Paltz *Independent* , Aug. 29, 1946. "Lavish": New Paltz *News*, Sept. 13, 1935.

3: Three persons: New Paltz *Independent*, Aug. 22, 1935. One black youth: R. Francis Hasbrouck, interv., Aug. 7, 2004. Thousands: New Paltz *Independent*, Oct. 3, 1935; *SW*, Oct. 5, 1935, 3-4, 15-16, 18. "Resent": New Paltz *News*, Sept. 13, 1935.

4: "Quibble": Wallkill *Wallkill Valley World*, Nov. 9, 1935. "Did shove," "ridiculous": *SW*, Nov. 16, 1935, 24-25. "Wax," "mannered": New Paltz *Independent*, Jan. 18, 1940; Aug. 29, 1946. Perhaps 20 children: June S. Peace, interv., Oct. 24, 2006.

5: "Aroma," "fluttering": *SW*, Nov. 24, 1936, 11. Victory: Stanley Newkirk to CM, Nov. 5, 2004. Twenty men, "proportioned", supervised: Wallkill *Wallkill Valley World*, Oct. 26, 1935.

6: New names: *ND*, Dec. 8, 1945, 22; Dec. 9, 1950, 35;

May 29, 1954, 14-16. Stone, "spacious," attitudes: *SW*, Nov. 30, 1935, 3; Jan. 2, 1937, 26; July 13, 1937, 3-4. Bricks: Wallkill *Wallkill Valley World*, Oct. 26, 1935. Fireproof: *ND*, Feb. 20, 1941, 32-33. Le Fevre family: Jay A. Le Fevre, interv., Nov. 4, 2004.

Ch. 3. Stone Ridge Farm

1: Payment: NY *Times*, Dec. 18, 1936. "Satchel": Parker, *Incredible Messiah*, 1937, 280. Augustus' affidavit: *SW*, June 22, 1937, 59-60. Hasbrouck wanted to back out: *SW*, Dec. 7, 1935, 24. Stone Ridge Farm deed: Arthur Hasbrouck and wife to Abraham Augustus, Nov. 22, 1935, liber 579, p. 26. The house is still standing. The farm, larger now, is a horse breeding farm owned by Donald Schupak, and is reached from Tongore Rd.

2: "Improvements": *SW*, Nov. 2, 1935, 19. "Windows": comment on a Divine speech of 1935 at Stone Ridge, in *ND*, Nov. 19, 1955, 3. Daily, pushcarts: Mitchell, *My Ears Are Bent*, 2001, 95-96. Cabbage, porches, "love": *SW*, Oct. 30, 1936, 2; Nov. 10, 1936, 20; Feb. 2, 1937, 6.

3: Spot-in-the-Road deed: Carmelo Calcagno and wife to Ernest P. Vaughn et al, May 29, 1936, liber 581, p. 479. The house is now occupied by the Balogh family.

4: "Hot": *ND*, July 16, 1942, 69. Treat: George Walden, interv., Dec. 3, 2004. "Practicality": *SW*, July 17, 1937, 22. "Squabble": *ND*, Sept. 30, 1937, 9.

Ch. 4. Kingston Mansion

1: Sweeneys: Rhoads, *Kingston, New York: The Architectural Guide*, 2003, 149. Formerly a hotel: NY *Herald Tribune*, Ap. 6, 1936. "Lofty": *SW*, July 18, 1936, 10. "Pool": ND, Aug. 27, 1936, 10. Kingston deed: Katherine Rusch to Esther Grace et al, Dec. 21, 1935, liber 580, p. 375.

2: Tour: *SW*, July 18, 1936, 10. On Divine's land plan: NY *Post*, Ap. 17, 1936; Mrs. M. J. Divine, *Peace Mission Movement*, 1982, 40. Weisbrot, *Father Divine*, 126, indicates that Divine's land plan was carried out, and on a large scale, saying "thousands" individually received "small tracts of land," but evidence is not available to support any such claim. A few years after Richard and Joanne Bush bought the mansion in 1985, the separate banquet hall and men's building, neglected, collapsed, and the Bushes removed it. Lyons' little "cottage" is not known to have been owned separately from the main mansion until 2001, when Judy Pfaff bought the main mansion from the Bushes (she still owns it), while the Bushes continued to own the "cottage" (they still own it). (Judy Pfaff, interv., Oct. 23, 2005; Joanne and Richard Bush, intervs., Feb. 10, 17, 2008).

3: Observer: Wilson Tinney, interv., July 21, 2006. Excursion, parade: Boston *Traveler*, Aug. 21, 1936; *ND*, Aug. 27, 1936, 10. Glorious Illumination: *SW*, Aug. 15, 1936, 19. Almost 1,000: NY *Times*, Aug. 21, 1936. If work found: New Paltz *Independent*, Aug. 27, 1936.

4: Kingston Junior deed: Anne V. Sammon to Sincere Determination et al, Nov. 21, 1936, Liber 585, p. 84-86. When Divinites sold this Kingston Junior farm in 1943, they sold it to the John E. Schultz family who gave their name to the lane. (Alan and Pamela Larkin, the present owners of this farm's house, interv., Dec. 19, 2004)

5: Schoolboy: Curtis Van Demark, interv., Dec. 5, 2004. Rumored might move: *SW*, July 18, 1936, 10. "Mumbling", "authority", "rushing," "stay": *ND*, Sept. 28, 1939, 80, 84. "Mortal minded": *ND*, Sept. 13, 1952, 5. "Impractical": *ND*, Ap. 6, 1939, 13. "True Americanism": *ND*, Jan. 22, 1942, 38.

Ch. 5. Divine Farm, Restaurants, and Gas Stations in Saugerties

1: Inspecting sites in Saugerties village: Saugerties *Telegraph*, May 15, 1936; Sept. 18, 1936. Purchase and use of the Quarryville site: Saugerties *Telegraph*, May 29, June 5, 1936; *ND*, July 20, 27, 1939, cover. Quarryville deed: Lillian Burden to Ernest P. Vaughn et al, May 29, 1936, liber 581, p. 478.

2: Divine Farm deed: John Decker and wife to John Fountain et al, Aug. 31, 1936, liber 583, p. 295. According to Sue Wick to CM, March 28, 2008, who traced the deed through recent assessor records, the farm extended along Rt. 32 from number 3691 to 3746. Additional farm of 23 acres deed: James Flanagan to Celester Grace et al, Aug. 4, 1936, liber 582, p. 583. Much of this site, including Vinnie's Farm Market. at 3689 Route 32, has long been owned by the family of Vincent Neglia, whose forebears, the Mattera family, bought it from Divine followers. "System," "garden": *ND*, Aug. 3, 1939, cover. Resident recalled, sign: Karlyn Elia and Amanda Jones, interv., Oct. 21, 2004. The rock sign is about the distance of two or three city blocks north of Vinnie's Market. Tradition: Vernon Benjamin, interv., March 28, 2008.

3: Purchase and use of the Veteran site: Kingston *Ulster County Press*, Sept. 17, 1937; *ND*, Oct. 28, 1937, 23; July 21, 1938, 22, 57; Oct. 6, 1938, 74, 81; June 15, 1939, 16. Song: *ND*, July 18, 1940, 11-12. Divinites not voting: *ND*, Sept. 23, 1944, 29; Oct. 8, 1949, 9; Dec. 6, 1952, 29. Bill not passed: *ND*, Sept. 11, 1948, 8.

Ch. 6. Buy a Whole Factory Village? Chichester

1: General source for chapter: Bennett, *The Mountains Look Down: A History of Chichester*, 1999. All quotes are from Bennett unless otherwise noted.

2: "Manor": NY *Times*, Oct. 29, 1939. Bennett, 138, dates Divine's first Chichester visit as summer, 1935, but 1936 seems more likely. In 1935, Divine had hardly begun to establish himself in Ulster County. Moreover, reports that Divine was considering buying upstate furniture factories, such as Chichester, appeared in 1936: NY *Post*, Ap. 17, 1936; NY *Times*, Ap. 30, 1936; McKelway and Liebling, "Who Is This King of Glary?" *New Yorker*, June 27, 1936, 26; NY *World-Telegram*, Sept. 10, 1936.

3: Auction: NY *Times*, Feb. 12, Oct. 15, 29, 1939; Margaretville, NY, *Catskill Mountain News*, Feb. 24, Oct. 20, Nov. 3, 1939; Bennett, 144-151

Ch. 7. Neighboring Farms: Olive Bridge and Krumville

1: "Delightful": NY *Herald Tribune*, Ap. 6, 1936. "Invested": *SW*, June 22, 1937, 59. Main Olive Bridge Farm deed: Benjamin O. Davis and wife to Hannah James et al, Dec. 12, 1935, liber 579, p. 234. Additional deed that included another house, a wooden one: Frank Anderson to Lettie Vaughn et al, Ap. 4, 1936, liber 580, p. 529. The present owner of the old stone house is Michael Ratner, a civil liberties lawyer, and the owner of the additional wooden house is Deborah Trager, an artist. "Cozy": *ND*, Nov. 3, 1938, 61.

2: Cars: George Kruger and Richard Rydant, interv., July 1, 2004. "Brother Joseph": *SW*, Nov. 24, 1936, 11. Children found: *SW*, Jan. 9, 1937, 30. More pigs: Sheldon Boice, interv., Aug. 21, 2005. "More hale": *ND*, March 14, 1940, 39-41. Sheldon Boice, intervs., Aug. 17, 21, 2005.

3: Krumville Farm description: NY *Herald Tribune*, June 26, 1939; *ND*, March 2, 1939, cover. Krumville Farm deed: Florence S. Donohue to Lettie Vaughn et al, Ap. 11, 1936, liber 581, p. 35. Part of this Krumville farm is now occupied by Seward R. Osborne, a Civil War historian. Sister: Donald C. Donohue to CM, Nov. 22, 24, 2004, explained that it was his grandmother, Florence Donohue, who sold Divinites the Krumville Farm, located on County Route 2, and she was the sister of Benjamin O. Davis who sold Divinites the main part of the Olive Bridge Farm, located on Lower Sahler Mill Road.

4: Off relief: *SW*, Sept. 15, 1936, 3. Prices: *ND*, Oct. 21, 1937, 7, 14-15. Secretaries: *ND*, Ap. 6, 1939, 77; March 14, 1940, 29. Peter Love, interv., Oct. 22, 2006.

5: Children found: *SW*, Jan. 9, 1937, 30. Specialize, manager: Sheldon Boice, interv., Aug. 21, 2005; Patrick Henry and Peter Love, interv., Oct 22, 2006. Arrested: unidentified clipping, marked June 2, 1938, at Elting Memorial Library. Life-long resident: George Kruger, interv., Dec. 2, 2004.

6: Boice recalls: Boice, intervs., Aug. 17, 21, 2005. Store: George Kruger, intervs., July 1, Dec. 2, 2004. The foundation of the gas pump is still visible. After Divinites stopped using the store building, Kruger bought it and moved it to his own yard, southeast on County Route 2, where it still is.

7: Owen farm: Donald C. Donohue to CM, Nov. 22, 24, 2004. Melons: George Kruger and Richard Rydant, intervs, July 1, 2004; Kruger, interv., Dec. 2, 2004. "Doodle bug": Boice, interv., Aug. 21, 2005.

Ch. 8. Elting Corners: The Inn that Burned

1: Deed, Adolph J. Trimborn to Charlotte Becker et al, Oct. 31, 1936, liber 584, p. 555. Buyers especially women: *ND*, Sept. 16, 1943, 17. On Divine and women: Satter, "Marcus Garvey, Father Divine and the Gender Politics," *American Quarterly*, v. 48, no. 1, 1996, 43-76. Sign: *SW*, Nov. 24, 1936, 11.

2: Fire: NY *Times*, Ap. 25, 26, 27, 1937; New Paltz *Independent*, Ap. 29, 1937. Tax policy: Kingston *Sunday Press*, May 22, 1938.

3: Lived in barns: Laura Miller, intervs., Dec. 17, 2004, Feb. 21, 2005. Handyman: William A. Coy, interv., May 9, 2007.

Ch. 9. Create a Children's Home in Saugerties or New Paltz?

1: General sources for chapter, including all quotes (some condensed): New Paltz *Independent*, Nov. 12, 19, Dec. 17, 1936. On the State Board's action: NY *Times*, Nov. 18, Dec. 16, 1936.

2: Poughkeepsie *Sunday Courier*, Dec. 13, 1936

Ch. 10. Hope Farm, West Saugerties

1: Located "on the Pine Grove road": Stone Ridge *Ulster County Press*, Ap. 9, 1937. "Degradation": *ND*, Nov. 16, 1939, 9. Deed: Herman A. Bennink and wife to Charlotte Becker et al, Oct. 31, 1936, liber 584, p. 550. "Outstanding": *SW*, Nov. 14, 1936, 24-25. The farm was mostly on the west side of what is now Band Camp Road, between numbers 485 and 541. Today the central part of the farm can be accessed by taking Hide-Away Lane south from Rt. 33. (Sue Wick to CM, March 28, 20008; Vernon Benjamin, interv, March 28, 2008). Contrary to rumor, Divine's Hope Farm had no relation to the present Hope Farm Press and Bookshop in the village of Saugerties.

2: Liked it, "antiquated," "glorious": *ND*, June 16, 1938, 19, 22. Twenty workmen: Stone Ridge *Ulster County Press*, Ap. 9, 1937. Thirty rooms: New Paltz *Independent*, Jan. 21, 1937. Laundry: *ND*, Nov. 21, 1940, 14-15.

3: Lovely Sweet(ness): NY *Herald Tribune*, June 26, 1939. Chef, Newmind: *ND*, June 6, 1940, 64; June 30, 1938, 54.

4: Free Will's story: Free Will, interv., Oct. 24, 2006. "Gave up," "surrender": *ND*, March 30, 1939, 6; Aug. 10, 1939, 63.

Ch. 11. "In the Cup of the Mountains": Resort at Samsonville

1: "Cup": *ND*, Nov. 30, 1939, 94; Nov. 2, 1939, 71."Fragrant," trails: *ND*, Ap. 28, 1938, 25; Sept. 26, 1940, cover caption. Today driving toward the Divine Lodge site, you pass the site of what was the "Peg Leg Bates Country Club," at 121 Rocky Mountain Rd., operated 1951-1987 by Clayton "Peg Leg" Bates, a well-known black tap dancer. This site, now called Mountain Valley Resort, has been mistaken for Divine Lodge, but the latter was about half a mile farther northwest. Doubtless the earlier predominantly black Divine resort helped prepare the way for the later also predominantly black Bates resort.

2: Catherine Lackey, of Baylis, Ill., gave a power of attorney, to her son Reath B. Lackey, a.k.a. Barry Townley, of the town of Rochester, NY, on March 11, 1936, liber 580, p. 378. Samsonville deed: Catherine Lackey, through her son Reath Lackey as her attorney, to Julia B. Shelton et al, Oct. 7, 1936, liber 584, p. 145. Teenager: Winston Van Kleek, interv., July 8, 2004.

3: "Lamps," "spiritual": *SW*, Oct. 20, 1936, 23. "Gracious": *ND*, Nov. 2, 1939, 71, 74. Winter: Wallkill *Wallkill Valley World*, Feb. 11, 1937. Hay, customarily went: Winston Van Kleek, interv., July 8, 2004. Barley: *ND*, Sept. 26, 1940, back cover, photo caption. Pigs: *SW*, Jan. 9, 1937, 30. Fifteen cents: *ND*, Nov. 30, 1939, 94.

4: Duesenberg, got the word: *ND*, May 11, 1939, 27, 83. "Mahogany": *SW*, Nov. 24, 1936, 11. "Twists," "reckless": *ND*, Sept. 29, 1938, 45; May 12, 1938, 41. Suitable sites, "nothingness": *ND*, Sept. 8, 1938, 5; Nov. 17, 1938, 77.

Ch. 12. "The Choicest Spots": High Falls

1: Cherry Hill Farm deed: Henry Burkhard and wife to St. Mary Bloom, Oct. 1, 1935, liber 578, p. 152. The house on this property is now numbered 517 Cherry Hill Rd. "Modern": *SW*, Nov. 2, 1935, 19. Hotel deed: Isidore Pekarsky and wife to Faithful Mary, Aug. 3, 1936, liber 582, p. 563. Signs, meals, gas: *SW*, Sept. 22, 1936, 10-11.

2: Department store deed: Samuel Rosen and wife to Victory Luke et al, Aug. 27, 1936, liber 583, p. 254. Had been a shoe store: Saugerties *Telegraph*, Sept. 4, 1936. "God's Children": unidentified newspaper clipping, marked Aug. 30, 1936, at Elting Library. Candy factory deed: Anna L. O'Neil to Charlotte Becker et al, Oct. 27, 1936, liber 584, p. 548. Candy quality: *SW*, Jan. 5, 1937, 26-27. "Tea-room": *ND*, Sept. 23, 1937, 30.

3: "Choicest": *SW*, Feb. 27, 1937, 3. Tailor shop deed: Max Kneitel and wife to Julia H. Shelton et al, March 2, 1937, liber 587, p. 11. Blacksmith: Stone Ridge *Ulster County Press*, Ap. 16, 1937. Garage and residence deed: John E. Gibbons and wife to Rachel Whitfield et al, Ap. 13, 1937, liber 587, p. 434. Dress Shop: NY *Post*, Ap. 22, 1937; *ND*, Sept. 23, 1937, 30; Sept. 4, 1941, 50. Mother's cottage: *SW*, Sept. 22, 1936, 11; Saugerties *Telegraph*, Aug. 28, 1936. Mother's cottage deed: Cinderella Depuy to Eva Barbee et al, Aug. 14, 1936, liber 583, p. 91.

4: Threw brick: *ND*, March 9, 1939, 74. Cross, pooling assets: Stone Ridge *Ulster County Press*, March 12, Ap.

16, 1937. Loudspeakers: Saugerties *Telegraph*, Sept. 11, 1936. "Wreck": New Paltz *Independent*, March 18, 1937.

5: Simon Peter: *ND*, Sept. 23, 1937, 30. "Source of food": Stone Ridge *Ulster County Press*, Ap. 9, 1937. Customers: *ND*, Dec. 23, 1937, 18. Area residents: Sonia Gittens, interv., Ap. 7, 2006; Wilson Tinney, interv., Aug. 11, 2006.

6: Advertised: *ND*, March 16, 1939, 99; May 25, 1939, 102. Paint: *SW*, Nov. 24, 1936, 11; *ND*, July 29, 1937, 3; Mitchell, *My Ears Are Bent*, 1938, 96. Whites: Shirley and Don Briggs, interv., Dec. 9, 2004. "Wild dogs": *ND*, March 9, 1939, 54-56. "Cheerful": *ND*, March 2, 1939, 42. "Lovely": *ND*, Ap. 21, 1938, 27. "Matter of time," *ND*, Nov. 17, 1938, 25-26.

7: "Like a million": Shirley and Don Briggs, interv., Dec. 9, 2004. Barnett's recollections: Barnett, *Summer Song*, 2000, 27-31.

Ch. 13. Buy Kingston Airport?

1: "Aroused": Wallkill, NY, *Wallkill Valley World*, Oct. 26, 1935. "Bought": *Newsweek*, Aug. 29, 1936, 34. "Bellanca": McKelway and Liebling, "Who Is This King of Glory?" *New Yorker*, June 27, 1936, 28.

2: Julian: *SW*, July 28, 1936, 6; *ND*, Nov. 16, 1939, 10. Angel: *SW*, Sept. 26, 1936, 13; Jan. 9, 1937, 9; NY *World-Telegram*, Ap. 27, 1937. "Own planes": NY *Times*, Ap. 30, 1936. "Bumpy": *SW*, May 2, 1936, 3, 14.

3: Possible site: *SW*, Ap. 25, 1936, 18. Acreage, lighting, talked to Walker: NY *Times*, Ap. 30, 1936. Two planes: New Paltz *Independent*, Aug. 27, 1936. Dellay: NY *Times*, Aug. 21, 1936. Diminish: *ND*, Sept. 20, 1952, 10.

Ch. 14. Risk Taker: John Dellay, Rosendale Realtor

1: General source for chapter: John Joseph Dellay (the realtor's son), intervs., March 14, 17, 2005. "Run out of town": Wallkill, NY, *Wallkill Valley World*, Oct. 26, 1935. "Deposit back," "Divine City": *SW*, Dec. 7, 1935, 24.

2: "Exclusive": Kingston *Freeman*, March 19, 1937. Photo, "abuse": Stone Ridge *Ulster County Press*, March 26, Ap. 2, 1937.

3: "Investment," investigation, rumored: Stone Ridge *Ulster County Press*, March 12, 19, 26, Ap. 30, 1937; NY *World-Telegram*, Sept. 10, 1936. "Respect of officials," "no fear": Stone Ridge *Ulster County Press*, Ap. 2, 1937.

4: Operating a still: Saugerties *Telegraph*, July 3, 1936; Stone Ridge *Ulster County Press*, Ap. 23, 30, 1937. House burned in Rosendale, Dellay wrote to the *Press*: Kingston (note change in place of publ.) *Ulster County Press*, Aug. 6, 1937, Nov. 16, 1937.

5: Advertisements: *ND*, Feb. 24, 1938, 2; Aug. 10, 1939, 75; Oct. 24, 1940, 102. Continued to serve: Deed, Seth Noah et al, property on North Ohioville Rd., New Paltz, to Dellay Realty Co., Oct. 1, 1942, liber 630, p. 377. "Wheeler-dealer": Raymond F. Le Fever, interv., Feb. 11, 2004.

Ch. 15. Resort on Rondout Creek: Greenkill Park

1: Description: *Green Kill Park*, 1917, 1-32. Schmeling: Stone Ridge *Ulster County Press*, Ap. 23, 1937; NY *Times*, July 11, 1937. Sale: Kingston *Freeman*, March 6, 19, 20, 1937; NY *Times*, March 20, 1937. Deeds: Kingston Trust Co. to Charlotte Becker, March 13, 1937, liber 586, p. 567; Charlotte Becker to Anna Reed, March 16, 1937, liber 587, p. 436; Anna Reed to Joy Love et al, March 18, 1937, liber 587, p. 12. Headquarters: Kingston *Ulster County Press*, June 25, 1937.

2: Music pupil and plumbing supplies assistant: Wilson Tinney, intervs., July 21, Aug. 11, 2006. "Hitler": Kingston *Freeman*, Ap. 9, 1937. Madison: *SW*, July 27, 1937, 13; *ND*, Feb. 19, 1949, 21.

3: Excursion plans: *SW*, June 15, 1937, 9; Kingston *Freeman*, June 30, 1937. "Evangelical," cricket: NY *Times*, July 9, 10, 1937. Calloway to pay: Kingston *Ulster County Press*, June 25, 1937. Excursion celebration: *SW*, July 13, 1937, 3, 18; July 17, 1937, 3, 5, 14; July 27, 1937, 18; Kingston *Freeman*, July 7, 8, 9, 1937. Keyser: Kingston *Freeman*, July 7, 1937; *SW*, July 13, 1937, 19. Danced: *ND*, July 29, 1937, 3.

4: "Weaklings": *SW*, July 27, 1937, 13. "Healing," "waiting": *SW*, July 17, 1937, 3, 5. "Watch," "renovation": *SW*, July 13, 1937, 18, 19. Settle: NY *Times*, July 10, 1937. Invited: Kingston *Freeman*, July 6, 1937; *SW*, July 24, 1937, 6-14. Fire, pipe story: NY *Times*, Nov. 8, 1937; Kingston *Ulster County Press*, Nov. 9, 1937; Wilson Tinney, interv., July 21, 2006.

5: "Losers," "blessed assurance," "over-assessed," "better": *ND*, March 9, 1939, 73; Nov. 18, 1937, 27, Jan. 22,

1942, 12-13; Sept. 28, 1939, 75-76; Kingston *Ulster County Press*, Nov. 16, 22, 1937. Intended to rebuild: Kingston *Freeman*, Nov. 9, 1937. Big chair: Raymond F. Le Fever, interv., Feb. 11, 2004.

Ch. 16. Art Colony on the Hudson: Milton

1: General source for chapter: file on Elverhoj art colony, at Marlboro Free Library. Negotiating: Kingston *Ulster County Press*, Nov. 22, 1937. "Valuable," "power","much less": *ND*, May 12, 1938, 37. "Porcelain plaques": *ND*, Aug. 11, 1938, 50.

2: Price: Wallkill, NY, *Wallkill Valley World*, Ap. 29, 1938; NY *Herald Tribune*, June 26, 1939. "Adherent," "moment": *ND*, Jan. 19, 1939, 37. Deed: Attorney Michael Nardone, referee, to Esther Anderson et al, Ap. 25, 1938, liber 594, p. 443. Current owners of the site are Bruce and Bill Weiss.

3: Remodeling, description: NY *Times*, Aug. 9, 1938; *ND*, Aug. 11, 1938, 42; March 9, 1939, 75; Petersen, *Stories*, 1960(?), 8-10. Pennants: *ND*, Aug. 11, 1938, 50. "Paradise," sign of blessing: NY *Times*, Aug. 9, 1938.

4: "Owns": NY *Evening Journal*, Ap. 15, 1937. "Communal": NY *Times*, Aug. 7, 1938. "Rest": *ND*, Sept. 4, 1941, 52. "Expensive": NY *Herald Tribune*, June 26, 1939. Grapes: Wallkill, NY, *Wallkill Valley World*, Aug. 12, 1938.

Ch. 17. Becoming a Neighbor of President F. D. Roosevelt: Krum Elbow

1: General source for this and the following chapter: Casey, "F. D. R., Father Divine and the 'Krum Elbow' Flurry," *Hudson Valley Regional Review*, March, 1991, 44-56. Relative, threatened: Wallkill, NY, *Wallkill Valley World*, July 28, 1938. Sister: Poughkeepsie *Evening Star*, May 14, 1938.

2: Spencer: NY *Times*, July 29, 30, Aug. 6, 1938; June 20, 1939; *Time*, Aug. 8, 1938. "Wanted us": *ND*, Dec. 7, 1946, 25. Tree and Harmony: NY *Times*, July 30, 1938; NY *Amsterdam News*, Aug. 6, 1938. Deed: Crum (sp. sic.) Elbow Holding Corp., Howland Spencer, pres., to Rebecca Good et al, July 28, 1938, liber 596, p. 368.

3: "Annoy," "pleasant to feel": *Time*, Aug. 8, 1938, 8. "Finer," "good neighbors": NY *Times*, Aug. 10, 28, 1938. Rose, Carr: Poughkeepsie *Evening Star*, July 29, 1938. "Nearly every": NY *Times*, Aug. 7, 1938. It has been rumored persistently that Divinites painted a sign on a rock along the Krum Elbow shore saying, "FDR," which could be interpreted as meaning the President's initials, or "Father Divine's Residence," or "Father Divine Redeemer." Jean Seaman Roumelis (intervs. Aug.23, Sept, 30, 2007), who is the present owner of much of the Krum Elbow estate, reports she is familiar with the rumor but is unable either to affirm or deny it.

4: Sixty: Poughkeepsie *Evening Star*, Sept. 18, 1939. Cows, grapes: *ND*, Sept. 19, 1940, 116. "Cross": Kenneth Erichsen, interv., Nov. 12, 2004. "Efficient and charming": *ND*, Nov. 2, 1939, 74. Knows: NY *Herald Tribune*, June 26, 1939. William A. Coy, interv., May 9, 2007. Kenneth Erichsen, interv., Nov. 12, 2004. "Milk": *ND*, July 24, 1941, 111. "Neat": *ND*, Dec. 28, 1939, 40-41.

5: "Almost a follower": Poughkeepsie *Evening Star*, Sept. 18, 1939. "Veritable": Poughkeepsie *Sunday New Yorker*, Oct. 12, 1947. "Relaxation": *ND*, Oct. 13, 1951, 13. In 1939 and 1952, Spencer sold Divinites additional parcels of Krum Elbow land, deed: Crum Elbow Holding Corp., Howland Spencer, pres., to Rebecca Good et al, Sept. 18, 1939, liber 605, p. 11; deed: Howland Spencer to Palace Mission, July 14, 1952, liber 832, p. 437. "Lay down," "detestable": *ND*, Nov. 27, 1941, 105; Jan. 26, 1939, 69-71.

Ch. 18. Buy the Vanderbilt Estate, Across the Hudson, in Hyde Park?

1: "Magnificent": Poughkeepsie *Evening Star*, Aug. 16, 1939. Acreage: NY *Times*, Aug. 20, 1939. Designed by White: Poughkeepsie *Eagle-News*, Aug. 18, 1939. "Perhaps 10,000": NY *Times*, July 2, 1939. Fully utilizing: *ND*, Oct. 5, 1939, 23. Secretly, "embarrass": *ND*, Aug. 17, 1939, 94.

2: Roosevelt-Divine correspondence: *ND*, Aug. 17, 1939, 96-101

3: "Models," "parked," "earmarks": Poughkeepsie *Eagle-News*, Aug. 18, 1939. "Neighbors": Poughkeepsie *Evening Star*, Aug. 16, 1939. Not sell: NY *Times*, Aug. 17, 1939; NY *Herald Tribune*, Aug. 17, 1939. President announced: NY *Times*, Feb. 6, 1940.

Ch. 19. Divine's Personal Traits

1: Day and night: *ND*, Sept. 20, 1952, 12. Wore out: Mrs. M. J. Divine, *Peace Mission Movement*, 1982, 102. Sleep: *ND*, Nov. 16, 1939, 10; Jan., 30, 1941, 36; Oct. 17, 1953, 14. Height: Stone Ridge *Ulster County Press*, Ap. 23, 1937; NY *Times*, Sept. 11, 1965; *Time*, Sept. 17, 1965, 41. "Out of the way," "Custom," "stick": *ND*, Aug. 1, 1953, 18; Sept. 4, 1948, 39; July 8, 1943, 6.

2: Jewelry, "smart": *ND*, Jan. 4, 1958, 34; Sept. 13, 1952, 32. Knife, towel: *ND*, Nov. 21, 1940, 15. "Mixed drink," "purity": *ND*, March 10, 1951, 21; Dec. 17, 1966, 54. "Lighter": *ND*, June 10, 1950, 6-7. Phone company: *SW*, Aug. 15, 1936, 19-20. Reporters: Stone Ridge *Ulster County Press*, Ap. 16, 1937. Persecuted: *ND*, June 15, 1991 (sic), 9. Competitive games: *ND*, Jan. 25, 1975, 18.

3: Turnpike: NY *Times*, Feb. 26, 1953; *ND*, March 7, 1953, 3-4. Harris' book, *Father Divine*, 1953: in NY *Times*, Oct. 25, Nov. 19, 1953; *ND*, Jan. 16, 1954, 3. Victory: *ND*, June 30, 1945, 3. "Inspirationally": *ND*, Aug. 18, 1938, 8, 14. Eisenhower: NY *Times*, June 8, 1952.

4: "Vibrations": *ND*, Oct. 12, 1939, 98. The sense of the term "vibration" as an intuitive, inner response to a person or situation was a sense which had a history reaching back at least to Oscar Wilde, but which, often abbreviated as "vibe," did not come into American colloquial use until the 1960s. "Allness": *SW*, July 28, 1936, 6."Heaven," preferred to call: *ND*, Aug. 18, 1938, 14; Oct. 27, 1938, 76. "Humanly," "chop": *ND*, Jan. 11, 1940, 5; Dec. 12, 1940, 49. "Plane": *ND*, Aug. 18, 1938, 7. "Sample": *ND*, March 2, 1939, 75. "Tangibilating": *SW*, July 17, 1937, 15. "Extremiation": *ND*, Nov. 14, 1940, 55. Woods: her review of Parker, *Incredible Messiah*, in NY *Times*, May 16, 1937. "Virtually": NY *Times*, Sept. 11, 1965.

5: Quakers: *ND*, Oct. 11, 1947, 12; March 22, 1958, 34. Shakers: *SW*, Nov. 21, 1936, 8; Feb. 20, 1937, 3, 9. "Geographically,""stressed": *SW*, Ap. 7, 1936, 4. In 1994, a group of Divine's followers from the Philadelphia area, including Mother Divine, Yvette Calm, Meekness Faith, Philip Life, Roger Klaus, Aaron Enaharo, and Leon Jeter, visited the Shaker community near Poland Springs, Maine, and soon afterwards, a group of Shakers from there visited the Peace Mission in Philadelphia. Since then, they have kept in touch with each other by phone. (Belstrom, *Rediscovering God*, 2005, 151; Aaron Enaharo to CM, March 1, 2007; Roger Klaus, interv., Aug. 22-24, 2007). Truth: Mabee, *Sojourner Truth*, 1993.

6: Joy Love: *ND*, March 18, 1944, 11-13. Not re-elected: *ND*, March 11, 1944, 9. Elected to lesser office: *ND*, March 15, 1947, 22; March 19, 1949, 7; March 17, 1956, 23. Grace Quietness: *ND*, March 4, 1944, 12-13.

Ch. 20. Divine's Duesenberg

1: General sources for chapter: Elbert, *Duesenberg*, 1951; Burness, *Cars of the Early Thirties*, 1970; Adler, *Duesenberg*, 2004. Reporter: *ND*, Nov. 16, 1939, 10; Dec. 7, 1939, 105. Cost $28,000: Kingston *Ulster County Press*, Nov. 30, 1937; *ND*, Jan. 30, 1941, 36-37. "Duesie": *Dictionary of American Slang*, 1995, entry for "doozie."

2: "Raised," without his knowledge: Elbert, 58, 114. "Wanted to install": Alexander, "All Father's Chillun," *Saturday Evening Post*, Nov. 18, 1939, 69. "Beaming," "palace": Kingston *Ulster County Press*, Nov. 30, 1937.

3: Manufacture of candy: John Wuest, pres., Wuest-Mackenzie Co., listed in Cleveland City *Directory*, 1900. "Proofreading": *ND*, Sept. 29, 1938, 50-51. Divine's 1948 letter: Elbert, 114. John Hunt's claim his mother hardly managed her own money: Hunt, "Father Divine," *Our World*, Aug., 1949, 15. Auburn Cord Duesenberg Museum to CM, March 31, 2005. "Throne Car": Adler, 276.

Ch. 21. Scarcely Organized

1: General source for chapter: Burnham, *God*, 1979, 61-96. "Servant": *ND*, May 18, 1939, 37."Organized as": *ND*, March 9, 1939, 68. "No officers": *ND*, Feb. 16, 1939, 19. "Is the organization": Fauset, *Black Gods*, 1944, 56. Critic: Katherine Woods, reviewing Parker, *Incredible Messiah*: NY *Times*, May 16, 1937.

2: Initiative in founding: *ND*, Ap. 2, 1949, 17. Assistant pastor was a woman, did not know if belonged: *ND*, March 22, 1947, 20, 22.

3: "Excommunicated": *ND*, Dec. 30, 1950, 36. Nothing to do: *ND*, Oct. 20, 1951, 18. Sing Happy: Fauset, 55. Retribution should be by God, is inevitable: *ND*, Nov. 16, 1939, 5-9; Aug. 11, 1945, 27-28; June 10, 1950, 7-8. Madison: *ND*, Oct. 14, 1950, 11. "Coercion": *ND*, Feb. 19, 1942, 78.

4: Seats reserved: *ND*, Sept. 30, 1943, 15; June 30, 1945, 13; Feb. 16, 1946, 21

5: Spontaneous: *ND*, March 19, 1942, 32. Two members, Miss Matthew: *SW*, Jan. 2, 1937, 13. Happy Heaven: *SW*: July 13, 1937, 18. Literacy tests: *SW*, Sept. 19, 1936, 3, 23. Preferred, "bring programs back": *SW*, May 11, 1937, 18. Quakers: *ND*, Oct 13, 1951, 13. Major distinction: *ND*, Aug. 23, 1958, 10. Orders: Burnham, 84-96.

6: Secretaries: *ND*, Sept. 4, 1941, 51; Burnham, 62-63, 84. "Occult": *ND*, Oct. 3, 1940, 57. "Complexion": *ND*, May 11, 1939, 7-8."Scum": *SW*, Jan. 11, 1936, 23. "Grandest": *ND*, Jan. 25, 1940, 89.

Ch. 22. Calling Divine *God*

1: "New creature": *ND*, Aug. 18, 1938, 13-14."Gaze upon": Divine, speaking probably in 1932, in *ND*, Feb. 22, 1975. 19. Hearing in 1933, "God has the right": Parker, *Incredible Messiah*, 1937, 74. Hearing in 1935, "God dwells": *SW*, Ap. 13, 1935, 5. British reporter in 1937: *ND*, Oct. 27, 1951, 19.

2: Lamb and Gabriel: Divine speaking about 1931, in *ND*, Jan. 25, 1975, 18. "Fruition": *ND*, Aug. 10, 1939, 41. "Take on": *ND*, Oct. 10, 1940, 32. "Likeness": *ND*, March 15, 1952, 8. "Millions": *ND*, Ap. 26, 1958, 4. "Jesus": *ND*, Jan. 6, 1938, 29. "Peace": *ND*, Ap. 30, 1942, 17. "Unadulterated": *ND*, March 1, 1947, 42. "My deity": *ND*, June 23, 1951, 3. "Proof": *ND*, July 12, 1952, 29.

3: Adam: *ND*, Oct. 31, 1940, 43. Running: Mary, *God*, 1937, 39. "Recognize": *ND*, Jan. 14, 1950, 20. Sullivan: *ND*, Aug. 25, 1945, 27. Humble: *ND*, Oct. 13, 1945, 21. Howell: *SW*, Aug. 4, 1936, 8. McKelway and Liebling, "Who is this King of Glory?" *New Yorker*, June 20, 1936, 22. Harkness, "Father Divine's Righteous Government," *Christian Century*, Oct. 13, 1965, 1259.

Ch. 23. A Jew Reflects.

1: "Rabbis": *ND*, Oct. 30, 1954, 7. "Pounded": *ND*, Aug. 9, 1952, 17. "Obligations": *ND*, Nov. 15, 1958, 21. Invited to move, telling "lies": *ND*, June 7, 1947, 33. In 1935 the Peace Mission protested the "mistreatment" of Jews in Germany: *SW*, July 13, 1935, 18. By 1939 Divine was trying to persuade Congress to allow Jewish refugees to enter the US more freely: *ND*, Jan. 26, 1939, 24-26.

2: *ND*, June 30, 1938, 54 (condensed)

3: Correct name: *ND*, Oct. 14, 1944, 31. "Peculiar people": *ND*, Jan. 20, 1945, 33. "Nothingness": *ND*, Ap. 28, 1945, 25. Working, speaking: *ND*, Oct. 8, 1955, 14-15.

Ch. 24. Healing

1: General sources for chapter: Braden, *These Also Believe*, 1949, 65-71; Burnham, *God*, 1979, 56-57. "Victory": *ND*, Oct. 28, 1937, 20. "Ache": *ND*, Oct. 26, 1939, 45. "Love God": *ND*, Ap. 27, 1939, 82. Spencer: *ND*, Oct. 18, 1947, 16. Shey: *ND*, Oct. 12, 1939, 96-98.

2: "Guarantee a cure": platform, in *SW*, Jan. 14, 1936, 9. (When the platform was republished, as in *ND*, Ap 21, 1945, 45, and in Mrs. M. J. Divine, *Peace Mission Movement*, 1982, 160, it still said any physicians called in "must guarantee a cure.") Assumed names: NY *Post*, Ap. 22, 1937. Care "not necessary": *ND*, June 6, 1940, 64. Medical advertisements: *ND*, Jan. 9, 1941, 98; Feb. 6, 1941, 98. Apple pickers: Highland *Southern Ulster Pioneer*, Feb. 24, 1999. Glasses: *ND*, Aug. 20, 1949, 15.

3: Star at Stone Ridge: *SW*, May 22, 1937, 3-6. Possible confirmation that Star and friends were planning to create a new cooperative farm is that, according to the Stone Ridge *Ulster County Press*, May 21, 1937, Divine follower Helen Young, an associate of the Stars, was reported to have bought, through John Dellay, property in Marbletown. Surrendered, charges dismissed: NY *Times*, May 4, 16, 19, 1937. Paid to hospital: *ND*, Feb. 19, 1942, 74. Divine encouraged working as nurse: *ND*, Aug. 16, 1947, 41-42.

Ch. 25. Divine's Two Marriages

1: "Cohabitation": *ND*, Aug. 19, 1944, 24. Followed teaching, Mary's claims: Mary, *God*, 1937, 61, 93. "Rather live," in hospital: NY *Post*, Ap. 22, 1937. Stayed New Paltz: New Paltz *Independent*, Aug. 22, 1935. Stayed Stone Ridge: NY *World-Telegram*, Sept. 10, 1936. Stayed High Falls: *SW*, Sept. 22, 1936, 11.

2: "Overcome": *ND*, March 9, 1939, 41. "Selfishly": *ND*, Dec. 15, 1938, 17. "We have heaven": *ND*, Aug. 26, 1937, 10. "Save our bodies": *ND*, Sept. 10, 1955, page S. 69. "Deserted": Stone Ridge *Ulster County Press*, Ap. 23, 1937. "Almost daily," paid bills, would decide: NY *Post*, Ap. 22, 1937.

3: High Falls youth: *ND*, Ap. 14, 1938, 39-40. Kingston: *ND*, Sept. 22, 1938, 5. Listed: *ND*, Oct. 24, 1940, 96. "Cottage": *ND*, Sept. 4, 1941, 50. Banquet in NY: *ND* July 2,

1942, 35. Weisbrot, 213, mistakenly claimed Mother Divine died in 1937. Died 1942: Hunt, "Father Divine," *Our World*, Aug., 1949, 9. Died 1943: Watts, 167.

4: On the second marriage, Divine's recollection: *ND*, Nov. 1, 1952, 4-5; Mother Divine's recollection: her intervs., Oct. 22-24, 2006. Without cohabitation, fish bowl: *ND*, June 25, 1949, 23; Aug. 7, 1954, 10. "Knocked": *ND*, May 20, 1950, 9. "Retribution": Article of 1950, reprinted New Day, Ap 28, 1956, S. 5. "Rosebud's body": *ND*, Oct. 5, 1946, 35. "Will never die": Fauset, *Black Gods*, 1944, 63.

5: "Hearts and lives": *SW*, May 4, 1937, 4. "If not in": *ND*, Nov. 27, 1941, 55. "Purged": interv. of 1942, republished *ND*, Feb 8, 1958, 14. "As it pleases": *ND*, Nov. 1, 1952, 5. Rejected: *ND*, Ap 25, 1953, 32.

6: Madison: *ND*, Jan. 14, 1950, 20; Dec. 23, 1950, 61. Moses marrying Ethiopian: 1950 article, reprinted in ND, Ap 28, 1956, S. 5. "Inter-raciality": *ND*, Ap. 28, 1956, page S101. "Exemplifying": *ND*, Oct. 5, 1946, 35. "Example of the virginity": talk 1946, reprinted in ND, Ap 29, 1996, 8. "Marriage of Christ": *ND*, Sept. 15, 1951, 5-6.

Ch. 26. Faithful Mary: From Gutter to Throne and Back

1: General sources for chapter: Mary, *God*, 1937; McKay, "Father Divine's Rebel Angel," *American Mercury*, Sept., 1940, 73-80. Quotes from "fast crowd" through " are possible": Mary, *God*, 7-19.

2: Quotes from "finance" through "remunerative": Mary, *God*, 96. Contributions, businesses: *SW*, Oct. 12, 1935, 10; June 22, 1937, 56-57; Weisbrot, 123. Hotel deed: Isidore Pekarsky and wife to Faithful Mary, Aug. 3, 1936, liber 582, p. 563.

3: Gottlieb: NY *World-Telegram*, May 27, 1937; NY *Evening Journal*, May 27, 1937. Divine's memory: *ND*, Ap. 16, 1949, 12-13, Ap. 23, 1949, 7. Demote, Search, Mary's revolt: New Paltz *Independent*, Ap. 22, 1937; Stone Ridge *Ulster County Press*, Ap. 23, 1937; NY *Times*, Ap. 22-25, 1937; Mary, *God*, 89-91; 111.

4: "Smash," " curse": *SW*, Ap. 27, 1937, 3-4. "Crazy": *ND*, Jan. 5, 1939, 12-14. Deed publicized as surprise, investigation "appeared" to close: Stone Ridge (or later Kingston) *Ulster County Press*, Ap. 30, May 7, 21, 28, Oct. 5, 1937. Deeds: Faithful Mary to Farm Owners Corp., Jan. 14, 1937, liber 586, p. 149; Farm Owners Corp, "Nat N. Kranzler, Pres.," to Sonia Zwick et al, May 24, 1937, liber 588, p 244. In recent years the hotel's site has been an empty lot.

5: From "pleasure" through "sex-crazed": Mary, *God*, 18, 21, 23-26, 66. Mary's ghost writer, Cheves Richardson, later claimed that soon after Mary's book had been published, but before it "hit the market," the publishers, having learned that Mary had deceived them, stopped its publication (*ND*, Dec. 12, 1953, 6-8).

6: Continuing her movement: Kingston *Ulster County Press*, Aug. 27, Sept. 3, 1937; NY *Times*, Aug. 27, 30, 1937. "Fold," "lower," "throne," "assured": *ND*, Jan. 5, 1939, 15; Dec. 29, 1938, A3-A6, 35-36; Ap. 16, 1949, 27-28.

Ch. 27. Son Peter: A Doubter at Hope Farm

1: Quotes "bodily punishment" to "suitcase": NY *Amsterdam News*, July 10, 1937. Comment by Faithful Mary: Faithful Mary, *God*, 1937, 80-81.

2: Visit to Ulster County: Kingston *Ulster County Press*, July 30, 1937. Confession, in touch: *ND*, Jan. 19, 1939, 4; Sept. 23, 1944, 29.

Ch. 28. John W. Hunt, Habitual Seducer

1: Open letter, quotes "loose" to "internationally famous": *SW*, Feb. 8, 1936, 26-30; Feb. 15, 1936, 3, 29. Arrested: *SW*, March 7, 1936, 3. While the present author calls John Hunt's brother and mother by their religious names, for clarity he calls John Hunt by his family name especially because at various times he chose different religious names: John the Revelator, Jesus, St. John the Divine, and Prodigal Son.

2: Hunt as photographer: *SW*, Sept. 5, 1936, 15. Devotion's license: *SW*, Aug. 18, 1936, 23-24; Saugerties *Telegraph*, Aug. 28, 1936. Newmind's and Hunt's licenses: *SW*, Sept. 1, 1936, 23; July 18, 1936, 15. "Unfoldment," "evangelical": *SW*, Dec. 19, 1936, 4; Dec. 29, 1936, 4. "Perfection": *ND*, June 15, 1939, 47.

3: "Tragedy," "badness": Stone Ridge *Ulster County Press*, Ap. 2, 1937. Hunt, Smith, and the Jewetts: Kingston *Freeman*, Ap. 3, 1937; NY *Evening Journal*, Ap. 5, 1937; NY *Post*, Ap. 22, 1937; NY *Times*, Ap. 22, 29, July 2, 1937.

4: Divine's letter: *SW*, July 17, 1937, 11 (condensed).

Ch. 29. Jean Becker, Hiding at Hope Farm

1: "Struck," "proselytizing," "doing a service": Kingston *Ulster County Press*, Nov. 2, 9, 1937.

2: Letter to Divine, jailed, released: Kingston *Ulster County Press*, Nov. 9, 12, 1937; NY *Times*, Nov. 9, 1937. "Know it": Kingston *Freeman*, Nov. 9, 1937.

Ch. 30. The Brocks: A Family with a Questioning Daughter

1: General source for chapter: Laura Brock Miller, intervs., 2004-2008. Brock's letter: *SW*, Aug. 1, 1936, 29 (condensed).

2: Recollections of Arthur Brock in *SW*, Feb. 20, 1937, 10-11; of Mina Brock ("Miss Mighty Love") in *ND*, March 26, 1949, 17. Opened their own school of nursing: *ND*, Ap. 9, 1949, 19; Oct. 22, 1949, 16. The Peace Mission's Employment Service often announced, as in *ND*, June 1, 1939, 110, that it could provide nurses, both practical and graduate. Divine asked nurses to reach "perfection" in their "medical skill": *ND*, March 29, 1958, 25.

3: Divinite concern for "minor" children: Fauset, *Black Gods*, 1944, 66. "Mom Sarah" seems not identical with "Sarah Love" who was in charge of the New Paltz house. Eventually Sarah Love in her old age moved from New Paltz back home to Hendersonville, NC, where she died among her kin (New Paltz *News*, June 4, 1986). By contrast, Mom Sarah in her old age moved to Divinite housing in Phila., where Laura Brock Miller visited her, as about 1960. According to Miller's understanding, Mom Sarah was Charles Calloway's wife.

Ch. 31. Mary Sheldon Lyon, Frustrated Philanthropist

1: General source for chapter: Mary S. Lyon Probate File 2815, 1946, Surrogate Court, New York County, NY City. Residence rented out, lived Italy: NY *Times*, Feb. 18, 1947, Dec. 21, 1946. Refused offer, "inexhaustible": Examination of Major J. Divine, held Newark, NJ, Ap. 17, 1947, 11-12, in Lyon Probate File.

2: "Happily": *SW*, July 18, 1936, 10. Lyon's will, Dec. 28, 1943, Lyon Probate File, does not say she left the house to anyone, which suggests she did not own it legally. In 1951, five years after Lyon's death, Divine and his wife dedicated this house "for the evangelical service of humanity" (*ND*, June 23, 1951, cover).

3: Paintings: NY *Times*, Dec. 18, 1946. Patience Budd recalled that the bulk of Lyon's paintings were kept at her apartment in NYC (Budd, interv., Nov. 15, 2006). Since the state courts apparently did not allow Lyon's will to go into effect as written, her intention of donating paintings to the Metropolitan may not have been carried out. The Metropolitan Museum to CM, Ap. 5, 2005, reported having no paintings donated by Lyon.

4: "More so," "serving,": *SW*, Aug. 22, 1936, 27-28. Created church, named church: *ND*, Ap. 2, 1949, 17; Ap. 22, 1950, 27. Rent, hotel buyer: Examination of Major J. Divine, held Newark, NJ, Ap. 17, 1947, 19, 29, 31, 40-41, 111, in Lyon Probate File.

5: Budd and Bloom: NY *Times*, Dec. 18, 1946; *ND*, March 29, 1947, 36. Will: NY *Times*, Dec. 18, 19, 21, 1946. Divine on the will: *ND*, May 10, 1947, 35. Contest the will, "undue influence": NY *Times*, Feb. 18, March 28, Ap. 18, 20, 27, 29, 1947.

6: "Scandalous," "heartache": David Diamond, Proponents' Supplemental Brief, ca. March 1, 1947, 2-3, in Lyon Probate File. Proposed settlement: NY *Times*, May 6, 1947; *ND*, May 17, 1947, 6-7; May 24, 1947, 31.

7: "Kill"" Lucy Latham et al v. Father Divine et al, NY Court of Appeals Reports, March 3, 1949, 1-2, in Lyon Probate File. "Least", "long": *ND*, Ap. 22, 1950, 27. "Shadowy": Lucy Latham et al v. Father Divine et al., *New York Appellate Division Reports*, July 8, 1948, 3; Application of Palace Mission Church, Brigantine, NJ, for an order directing payment, and the order, Sept. 3, 1948, in Lyon Probate File.

8: Court voted: NY *Times*, March 4, 1949. Appeal dismissed: Lucy Latham et al v. Divine et al, NY Court of Appeals, Ap. 6, 1950, in Lyon Probate File. Neither the Surrogate Court, NY City, nor the Law Library, Ulster County Court House, Kingston, NY, appear to have any records of the case after the 1950 Court of Appeals's dismissal of Divine's appeal.

Ch. 32. Paying What You Owe

1: Highest: Pittsburgh *Courier*, July 2, 1949, in *ND*, July 16, 1949, 15. Paying old debts was established practice by 1936: SW, March 24, 1936, 9. Paul: *ND*, Oct. 7, 1950,

24. "Cover the earth": *ND*, Aug. 5, 1943, 19. "Ashamed": *ND*, June 10, 1943, 37-38.

2: Welfare, Grace Love: *ND*, Aug. 12, 1950, 29; Sept. 9, 1943, 30-31

3: Wollenberg: *ND*, Oct. 22, 1942, 100-102 (letter condensed). "Conquers": Proverbs 16:32.

4: Gas station find: *ND*, Ap. 15, 1943, 37

5: "Nature to grace": *ND*, Feb. 16, 1946, 9. Hasting and Hirsch: *SW*, Ap. 10, 1937, 14. Stop voluntary donations: *ND*, March 16, 1946, 3-6.

6: Bullock: *ND*, June 25, 1955, 9-11, 14; Aug. 27, 1955, 20 (quotes condensed)

Ch. 33. The Mystery of Financing

1: "Automatically," "presence": *ND*, Aug. 1, 1953, 18

2: "Banks," into purchasing, "chief witness": Verinda Brown v. Father Divine, NY State Supreme Court, Special Term, NY County, *New York Miscellaneous Reports*, June 28, 1937, 799-802. "Decent, honest": McElway and Liebling, "Who is This King of Glory?" *New Yorker*, June 20, 1936, 22-28. Verinda Brown's testimony: NY *Times*, Dec. 19-20, 1939. Faithful Mary's influence on the suit: *ND*, Jan. 7, 1943, 70-71. Followers testified: *SW*. June 22, 1937, 10- 60.

3: "Legal bandits," other Divine comment on Brown case: *ND*, Jan. 25, 1940, 61-65, 67; March 13, 1941, 114; Baltimore *Sun*, March 19, 1940. Contempt of court, further appeal denied: NY *Times*, Aug. 14, Dec. 11, 1942.

4: Offer of island: *ND*, Aug. 11, 1951, 36. Cost of meals: Braden, *These Also Believe*, 1949, 28. Schools free: *ND*, Sept. 8, 1945, 29; July 5, 1958, 14-18. Employment service free: *ND*, Jan. 14, 1936, 12; Oct. 25, 1947, 47. Humble: *ND*, May 6, 1944, 35. Boasted: *ND*, Aug. 9, 1952, 21.

5: Such principles, not required, Jesus' saying "except" [Luke 14:33], "surprising" to find themselves owners: *ND*, March 19, 1955, 7-8. According to John Lamb, it was permitted for one person "to contribute the major portion of the purchase price" of a cooperative property," but the cooperative would still give all donors "equal shares in the title."(*SW*, June 22, 1937, 47)

6: Most Divinite property in Philadelphia was still in cooperatives, not churches: *ND*, May 31, 1852, 9. Churches were not cooperatives: *ND*, Oct. 14, 1950, 17. Loophole: *ND*, Oct. 22, 1949, 15; March 8, 1952, 14.

7: "All things," "self-denial": *ND*, Nov. 17, 1938, 21, 30-31. "Secret": Braden, 38-39. Investigations: Braden, 29; Hunt, "Father Divine," *Our World*, Aug., 1949, 9; Watts, 217n18, 224n62.

Ch. 34. Outside Employment

1: Independent, low costs: *ND*, June 10, 1943, 37-38; Sept. 20, 1952, 3. Tannersville woman: *ND*, Aug. 12, 1937, [7-8]. Employment Service: *ND*, May 11, 1939, 106; May 18, 1939, 35-38. From at least 1953, the Employment Service required workers who used it to sign a pledge that they would not accept tips or gifts, and not drink or smoke, a pledge which would tend to limit its prospective employees to followers (*ND*, Dec. 26, 1953, 34; Feb. 12, 1955, 27).

2: Willing Heart: *ND*, July 8, 1944, 24. Social Security: *ND*, Ap. 5, 1947, 19-20. While at the time of this interview in 1947, domestics were not required to pay into Social Security, by 1951 they were. Nevertheless Divine continued to teach against participating in it (NY *Times*, Jan. 7, July 28, 1951). Government service: *ND*, March 19, 1955, 8.

3: Roofing: Richard Rydant, interv., May 12, 2004. Meekness: *ND*, July 1, 1943, 39. Knausts: Karlyn Knaust Elia, intervs., Oct. 21, 2004; March 17, 2006. Redemption: *ND*, Jan. 8, 1955, 22, 27. Donnidick Lodge: *ND*, June 17, 1944, 24.

4: Willowbrook Lodge: *ND*, Aug. 26, 1943, 23. Camp Woodcliff: *ND*, Sept. 30, 1944, 29-30. Camp Lynn: *ND*, Aug. 7, 1941, page A-4; Sept. 18, 1941, 7. Camp High Point: Patrick Henry, interv., Oct. 22, 2006; *ND*, Sept. 22, 1945, 35; July 26, 1947, 41-42. Apple Pickers: Kenneth Erichsen, interv., Nov. 12, 2004; Highland *Southern Ulster Pioneer*, Feb. 24, 1999.

5: Prall's letter: *ND*, Sept. 1, 1945, 39 (condensed). Mrs. Prall's death: Kingston City Registrar, interv., Jan. 16, 2008. (While Prall gave no first name for Heart, the author knows of no male follower named Heart living in High Falls at about this time other than Solomon Heart.) Elmar Lodge: *ND*, Jan. 12, 1952, 25-26.

Ch. 35. Children Apart

1: Plan for school at Greenkill Park: NY *Times*, March 20, 1937; Kingston *Freeman*, March 20, 1937 (Weisbrot, 97, mistakenly seemed to assume the plan was carried out). "Red tape": *ND*, Feb. 9, 1939, 10. Assigned guardians, taught the virtues: June S. Peace, interv., Oct. 24, 2006; Peter Love, interv., Oct. 22, 2006; *ND*, May 15, 1954, 21. Peter: *ND*, March 3, 1938, page C. Promoted, 200%, "glory": *ND*, Feb. 5, 1949, 5-6; March 6, 1954, 29.

2: Segregated schools: Mabee, *Black Education in New York State*, 1979, 158, 263, 290-291. New Paltz School: R. Francis Hasbrouk, interv., Aug. 17, 2004; Richard Hasbrouck, interv., Oct. 24, 2004. Sweet Peace, when she graduated from New Paltz High School, was called "modest" in its Yearbook, *Huguenot*, 1940. She afterwards married locally, and long lived in Ulster County. Krumville School: George Kruger, intervs., July 1, Dec. 2, 2004; Patrick Henry, interv., Oct. 22, 2006; June S. Peace, interv., Oct. 24, 2006; Sheldon Boice, interv., Aug. 17, 2005 (After the school closed, its building became a little Reformed Church, and still stands).

3: Kingston: Margaret Naccarato Ahl, interv., Oct. 18, 2005. Painfully high: Free Will, interv., Oct. 24, 2006; June S. Peace, interv., Oct. 24, 2006. Recollections: Margaret Naccarato Ahl, interv., Nov. 7, 2004. "Better behaved": *ND*, Oct. 14, 1950, 29. Gardier (also Gardia): *ND*, July 1, 1943, 38; Sept. 6, 1958, 19.

4: Court testimony: *SW*, Ap. 13, 1935, 4-5. Bender and Spalding, "Behavior Problems in Children from the Homes of Followers of Father Divine," *Journal of Nervous and Mental Disease*, Ap., 1940, 460-472. Inspiration's response: *ND*, June 6, 1940, 63-65. Divine seemed alert: *ND*, March 28, 1940, 41; Oct. 21, 1943, 41-42.

5: Not to play together: *ND*, Sept. 5, 1940, 58. Ready to graduate: Sweet Praise (Jacqueline Baker). interv., May 13, 2007. Made sport, Education Dept. ruling: Doris Phillips, interv., Aug. 31, 2003; NY *Times*, June 1, 1938. "Budge": *ND*, May 15, 1954, 21. Gym class, one-day bus trip, refused to pick up: *ND*, Feb. 23, 1952, 29-30; Feb. 14, 1948, 23-24; Sept. 24, 1942, 19-22. "Dirt": Patrick Henry, interv., Oct. 22, 2006.Wonderful Joy: *ND*, Sept. 30, 1943, 37. Sunshine Flowers: *ND*, March 4, 1943, 30-31.

6: Became comfortable: Patrick Henry, interv., Oct. 22, 2006; Ellenville High School Yearbook, *Blue and Gold*, 1946, 17, 33, 50. Felt afterwards: Peter Love, interv. May 13, 2007. Recollections: Curtis Van Demark, interv., Dec. 5, 2004; Normal Mitchell to CM, Dec. 14, 2005; Harold Maybanks, interv., Aug. 27, 2007. Harold Maybanks, List of Kingston High School Students living at Kingston Mansion, received Aug., 2007.

7: "Enjoyed": *ND*, May 2, 1940, 27. "Well-mannered": *ND*, Nov. 16, 1939, 21. No bias: Margaret Naccarato Ahl, interv., Oct. 18, 2005. "Genuine," "friendly": Kingston High School Yearbook, *Maroon*, 1950, 16, 34, 53.

8: June S. Peace, interv., Oct. 24, 2006. Churches helped: Mother Divine, interv., May 13, 2007; *ND*, Aug. 30, 1958, 26. "Through college": *ND*, Dec. 5, 1953, 11. Gardier: *ND*, Feb. 26, 1955, 7. Patrick Henry, interv., Oct. 22, 2006. Peter Love, interv., Oct. 22, 2006.

Ch. 36. Visitors

1 :
Associate editor: *SW*, Oct. 20, 1936, 23. Phila. journalist: *ND*, Nov. 30, 1939, 96. Landi: *ND*, Jan. 11, 1940, 5-7. Evangelists: Kingston *Ulster County Press*, Aug. 20, 1937. Bolin family: Mabee, *Black Education in New York State*, 1979, 177-178, 271-272. Gaius Bolin, Sr., obit.: NY *Times*, Ap. 17, 1946. "Attitude": *ND*, Jan. 13, 1945, 39. DuBois: NY *Amsterdam News*, May 23, 1942. Writer: NY *Herald Tribune*, June 26, 1939.

2: Thorlakson: *ND*, Feb. 26, 1942, 93; Ap. 9, 1942, 54; July 23, 1942, 27; Ap. 14, 1945, 23; June 11, 1955, 18-20

3: Mildred Jerry, interv., Oct. 20, 2004; Richard Rydant, interv., May 12, Oct. 20, 2004. Advertised dining: *ND*, Aug. 31, 1939, 84.

4: SaraWashington: *ND*, Aug. 28, 1941, 27-30: Jan. 30, 1941, 57-61; June 25, 1942, 131

5: Calloway: Saugerties *Telegraph*, June 12, 1936; Kingston *Ulster County Press*, June 25, 1937; Nov. 9, 1937; *SW*, June 22, 1937, 50-51; *ND*, Ap. 2, 1949, 14, 17; Ap. 3, 1954, 11

6: Buffum: Mabee, *Black Freedom*, 1970, 225. Lovell: NY *Sun*, Nov. 28, 1939; *ND*, Feb. 23, 1939, 51-52; July 27, 1939, 81-82; Aug. 24, 1939, 28; Oct. 19, 1939, 25-27; Nov. 14, 1940, 31-38.

Ch. 37. Resisting the Approach of World War II

1: Convention: NY *Times*, Jan. 13, 1936; Watts, 132-136.

Platform text: *SW*, Jan. 14, 1936, 7-18. The movement has never held another such convention, but still regards this convention's platform as its own. Job Patience: *ND*, Sept. 30, 1944, 20. Howell: *Christian Century*, Oct. 7, 1936, 1332-1333.

2: Parallel: *SW*, July 13, 1935, 18; *ND*, Oct. 19, 1939, 29-30. Theme: *SW*, Jan. 14, 1936, 7-8. "Proved": *ND*, Nov. 25, 1937, 26. Boycott: *ND*, Nov. 11, 1937, 20."Sticker": *ND*, Nov. 3, 1938, 88; March 23, 1939, 94. "Grab": *ND*, July 27, 1939, 3. A black Methodist refused to fight: *ND*, Nov. 25, 1937, 7-8; *ND*, Nov. 28, 1940, 41, 43; July 17, 1948, 21.

3: Cabled, "tracts," "sacrifice": *ND*, Sept. 22, 1938, 61; Oct. 6, 1938, 31-32. "Civilization," negatives: *ND*, Sept. 28, 1939, 110; Sept. 21, 1939, 49-50. "Limited," "make war": *ND*, Oct. 19, 1939, 6-10. Neutrality: *ND*, Oct. 26, 1939, 102. Burned cross: Patrick Henry, interv., Oct. 22, 2006. Play: *ND*, Nov. 16, 1939, 43, 75-79.

4: "Constructive," Rev. Jones interview: *ND*, Dec. 7, 1939, 38; July 10, 1941, 22. To Roosevelt, sticker: *ND*, Dec. 14, 1939, 83; Dec. 28, 1939,79. Finns: *ND*, Jan. 11, 1940, 7-8. Protested military segregation: *ND*, Oct. 24, 1940, 5-6.

5: "Staff," "enforcement body," "intuition": *ND*, Nov. 28, 1940, 37-45, 94. Before 1936, Divine rarely used the term "highest intuition," but did use it when, under pressure from a court, he was advising a follower whether she should live with her child: *SW*, Ap 13, 1935, 5.

6: Lend-Lease: *ND*, March 6, 1941, 3. "Inspired": *ND*, June 12, 1941, 71-72. List: *ND*, June 12, 1941, 70. "Justifiable": *ND*, June 19, 1941, 61-63. "Real seed": *ND*, June 26, 1941, 26-27. "Arms," "rescue": *ND*, Oct. 23, 1941, 11-22. While Divinites might sing such traditional evangelical hymns as Rescue the Perishing and Wonderful Words of Life, they were more likely to adapt popular tunes, including non-religious tunes, to original words of their own, words which concentrated on Father Divine.

Ch. 38. World War II: Soldiers and Conscientious Objectors

1: Resentment: *ND*, May 7, 1942, 86-87. "Intuition": *ND*, May 14, 1942, 29-30; Feb. 3, 1944, 8. Food: *ND*, Jan. 22, 1942, 43-44. Red Cross: *ND*, Jan. 22, 1942, 11; June 17, 1944, 2. Camp Shanks: *ND*, Aug. 5, 1943, 35-36. True Jacob: *ND*, Feb. 25, 1943, 20; Oct. 28, 1944, 40-41. Mary Joseph: *ND*, Feb. 24, 1945, 30.

2: Warden, "rescuing," dam: *ND*, June 18, 1942, 53; Jan. 22, 1942, 33, 42. Coast Guard: *ND*, June 18, 1942, 51-56; Nov. 26, 1942, 21-22. Jews: *ND*, March 4, 1943, 30. War bonds: *ND*, March 18, 1943, 2; July 15, 1944, cover.

3: Platform: *ND*, Feb. 3, 1944, 8-9; June 2, 1945, 43. "Coercion," "flight": *ND*, Jan. 1, 1942, 42, 45. "Violation": *ND*, Sept. 2, 1943, 29. Children playing: *ND*, May 6, 1943, 49. Poem, republished: *ND*, Jan. 15, 1942, 105; Feb. 10, 1944, 31 May 27, 1950, 25; Jan. 30, 1954, 33. "Gospel," "heart and mind": *ND*, Sept. 3, 1942, 22; Nov. 26, 1942, 58. "Arbitration," "universal sovereignty": *ND*, July 23, 1942, 8; June 10, 1944, 30; Feb. 26, 1944, 24-25. "Own understanding": *ND*, Feb. 18, 1943, 46.

4: "Should": *ND*, Ap. 15, 1943, 45. The 26 known followers who became regular US soldiers: Sun Beam, C. Beresford, Theodore R. Bowen, Justin V. Bray, Milo Brown, Julian Caplain, Naaman O. Cole, Robert Collier, Jr., Jeremiah Craig, George Driscoll, Wallace M. Evans, Isaac L. Ford, Cleveland Gober, Mack Grady, Clarence M. Heath, Jr., William Henry, George Honesty, Aaron Keith, Clinton B. Keys, Calvin Makell, Paul Matthew(s), Job Paul, Son Peter, John G. Post, George Steward(t), James Allen Watson. (A source for these 26 is the list of soldiers whom Divine asked to boycott the 1944 Presidential election: *ND*, Sept. 23, 1944, 29.)

5: "Model": *ND*, July 22, 1943, 41. Fail: *ND*, June 4, 1942, 92. "Egotism": *ND*, Ap. 16, 1942, 55. "Brotherhood": *ND*, May 6, 1943, 49. "Protection": *ND*, Feb. 11, 1943, 45.

6: Sibley and Jacob, *Conscription of Conscience*, 1952, 83-90; Anderson, *Peace Was in Their Hearts*, 1994, 1-2. The 56 known followers of Divine who became US conscientious objectors, including those who served as non-combatants in the military, or as civilians assigned to work (CPS), or in prison: Floyd J. Baldwin, John R. Bayard, Otis Brodie, Peaceful Brother, Clifton Burton, John Wesley Carter, Enos Clark, Charles E. Coles, Paul Delap, John DeVoute, Calvin Eddington, Jr., David Elihu (Henry L. Stovall), Elijah Faithful, Peaceful Faithful, Cephas Gabriel, Chris R. Hansen, Unison Heart, John W. Hunt, [Rayfield?] Israel, Walking Jerusalem, James Johnson, Second Jonas, Cornelius Jones, Robert Jones, Wisdom Kindness, Curtis Lagrone, Philip Love Life, John Love, Radical Love, John Mark, David Marsh,

Sigmund Michota, Happy Mirth, Zephaniah Patience, David Praise, John Pressley, Charles Rabb, Paul Revere, Reynold A. Russell, Faithful Servant, Rudolph Simmons, Blessed Simon, Henry Small, Faith Somes, John Son, Clifton Stafford, Alexander Stevens, Ed. Fraser St. John, Roscoe Strother, Grady Taylor, Jon Taylor, Blessed Thomas, John Eunuch Tree, Faith Victory, Love Victory, Felix Garth Xavier. (Sources for these 56 include Divine's list of his followers who were war objectors, *ND*, June 12, 1941,70, and a list of Divinite objectors provided by the Center on Conscience & War, Washington, D. C., Sept. 20, 2004.)

7: Hunt enlisted: *ND*, Aug. 5, 1943, 21-25; Aug. 12, 1943, 39. "Psychopathic": *ND*, Sept. 2, 1943, 9. Advertised as photographer: *ND*, Sept. 30, 1944, 3.

8: A total of 14 Divine followers whose names are available were in CPS, nine of them being from NY State, one, Walking Jerusalem, from Ulster County. These 14 were: Floyd Baldwin, Jack R. Bayard, Peaceful Brother, Charles Coles, John DeVoute, David Elihu, Walking Jerusalem, John Love, Radical Love, John Mark, David H. Praise, Reynold A. Russell, Faith Somes, and Felix Garth Xavier. Of these, 12 were listed as in CPS according to Center on Conscience & War, Washington, D. C., to CM, Sept. 20, 2004. Additions to the 12 were Faith Somes, of NY City, who is named in *ND*, Aug. 13, 1942, 108, as at CPS, Petersham, MA; and Charles Coles, of Newark, NJ, who is listed in *Directory of Civilian Public Service,* 1988, as Moslem, but was a Divine follower according to *ND*, June 3, 1944, 50, and July 1, 1944, 27.

9: NSBRO: *ND*, Oct. 28, 1943, 43-44; Feb. 3, 1944, 24. Returning allowances: *ND*, Ap. 15, 1944, 38; Dec. 23, 1944, 32; Aug. 11, 1945, 42. Outright donation: *ND*, July 1, 1944, 27.

10: Walking Jerusalem: William D. Foye, intervs., letter, Sept. 12, 2004, Ap. 5, 2005; Ap. 30, 2005. Faith Somes: *ND*, Aug. 13, 1942, 108-109. Michota: *ND*, Oct. 7, 1943, 31-33. Evidence that Michota served in CPS is not available. Working "hard": *ND*, May 27, 1944, 13.

11: DeVoute protested, asked reclassification: *ND*, Ap. 15, 1944, 38-39; June 10, 1944, 11. Wrote Roosevelt: *ND*, Jan. 27, 1945, 28.

12: Heart was "willing": *ND*, July 16, 1942, 100-101. Sentenced: NY *Times*, July 15, 29, 1942. Punished: Sibley and Wardlaw, *Conscientious Objectors in Prison*, 1945, 30, 48-56."Needed," still in prison: *ND*, Oct. 7, 1943, 31; Jan. 6, 1944, 35

13: Gaeddert interview: *ND*, Ap. 1, 1944, 9-12. UN: *ND*, March 3, 1945, 5; March 31, 1945, 3; May 26, 1945, 1, 3. Dr. Dakin: *ND*, Jan. 26, 1946, 28, 36; Feb. 23, 1946, 32-33. Stewart: *ND*, Jan. 6, 1945, 19. Paul: *ND*, March 15, 1947, 11. DeVoute as president: *ND*, March 24, 1956, 35. Love as Crusader: *ND*, June 1, 1946, 13. Mirth: *ND*, June 22, 1946, 40. Hunt: *ND*, Aug. 11, 1945, 33; July 3, 1948, cover photo. Several such objectors could fit into more than one category.

Ch. 39. Move to Philadelphia

1: Recollections of proposed settlement by Divine and attorney Lowell: *ND*, Jan. 7, 1943, 69-71; June 7, 1952, 10. Hold the body: Verinda Brown v. Father Divine, NY State Supreme Court, Special Term, NY County, *New York Miscellaneous Reports*, Feb. 28, 1941. "Legal bandits": *ND*, Jan. 25, 1940, 65. "Electric chair": *ND*, March 13, 1941, 114.

2: Threatened: *SW*, Oct. 13, 1936, 3; *ND*, March 5, 1942, 66-67; March 26, 1942, 23. Move: *ND*, July 16, 1942, 88-89.

3: Appeal to governor: *ND*, Jan. 7, 1943, 66-71; Jan. 21, 1943, 44-46. Governor's reply: *ND*, Feb. 4, 1943, 21.

4: Lamb: *ND*, Ap. 8, 1943, 25-26. Census official: *ND*, Ap. 22, 1950, 10.

5: Lowell's proposed settlement, "will be immaterial": *ND*, June 7, 1952, 10-13

Ch. 40. Mary Bird Tree: Was She Divine's Prisoner?

1: Tree was already living on N. 41 St., Phila., according to her deed: Mary Bird Tree et al to AT&T (for the right to construct communication lines at Greenkill Park), Ap. 2, 1947, liber 683, p. 259. Was crediting: *ND*, Dec. 21, 1946, 27. Chaplain: *ND*, Feb. 23, 1946, 21. Fauset: *ND*, July 22, 1944, 6. Hunt thanked: *ND*, Oct. 26, 1946, 27; Dec. 21, 1946, 27.

2: Divine-Tree interview: *ND*, June 11, 1949, 9-10 (condensed). John Hunt's charges against Divine: Hunt, "Father Divine," *Our World*, Aug., 1949, 8-15. Although Hunt's article was prepared to be published in August, DeVoute already had a copy of in June when he wrote his reply to it: *ND*, June 25, 1949, 12.

3: Tree's reply to John Hunt's charges: *ND*, July 9, 1949,20 (condensed)

Ch. 41. Decline and Succession

1: Missions listed: *ND*, Oct. 27, 1938, 76; Aug. 19, 1950, 34. Madison complained: *ND*, Nov. 9, 1946, 29. Rockland Palace: *ND*, Oct. 22, 1949, 17. Schools: *ND*, June 30, 1938, 49; Sept. 6, 1958, 28.

2: Sullivan: Phila. *Inquirer*, Sept. 11, 1965. Aloof: NY *Times*, May 10, 1964.

3: Divine taught love: *ND*, Dec. 18, 1948, 17-18; Dec. 25, 1948, 29. Without guns: *ND*, Aug. 1, 1953, 19. Convert millions, strength of a nation, "necessary": *ND*, Feb. 10, 1951, 3; July 14, 1951, 26; Aug. 5, 1950, 3. Responsible for military desegregation: *ND*, Oct. 13, 1951, cover. Percentages of objectors: Kohn, *Jailed for Peace*, 1987, 70. Law more tolerant: Flynn, *The Draft*, 1993, 128-129.

4: Called together: Leon Jeter, interv., Oct. 22-23, 2006 (Divine's view confirmed in *ND*, Jan. 27, 1951, 29). In the Korean War (understood for this purpose as 1950-1954), Divine followers who were soldiers included: Emanuel Biera, Alcorn Bonds, George Braye, Joseph Brown, Mr. Butterfly, Capt. Craigswell, Sterling J. Evans, Solomon Gilbert, Edward B. Hammond (Bunch Love), Robert Hampton, Rudolph Hill, Leon Jeter, Stanley L. Larkins, Daniel Leon, Harold Maybanks, S. A. McLenon, Fred Miles, Normal Mitchell, Charles Newman, Jake Overstreet, John M. Poole, Jr., Mr. Rawlins, Josh Roper, Shadrach Royful. Divine followers who were conscientious objectors included: Herbert Buffington, Patrick Henry, Peter Love, Happy Love.

5: Butler: *ND*, Jan. 28, 1943, 32. Resorts "idle": *ND*, July 7, 1945, 13. Greenkill caretaker: Harold Maybanks, interv., Aug. 27, 2007. Vacationing at Kingston: *ND*, Aug. 30, 1952, 27. "Don't know": *ND*, Aug. 22, 1953, 9. Produce: *ND*, Nov. 1, 1952, 7.

6: "Caravan," "exception": *ND*, Sept. 13, 1952, 5, 12, 19, 32. Souvenir: Joanne and Richard Bush, intervs., Feb. 10, 17, 2008. Rosebuds: *ND*, Oct. 4, 1952, 15-16.

7: "Bride": *ND*, Ap. 28, 1956, 22. Peter as successor: Boaz, "My Thirty Years," *Ebony*, May, 1965, 96, 98. Garcia as successor: Las Vegas *Sun*, Ap. 21, 1998. "Proud": *ND*, March 8, 1958, 20."Due them": ND, Ap. 23, 1949, 7."Sure": ND, Aug. 7, 1954, 27. "Energy": Gibson Hall, statement, sent by Judy Edwards Forbes, Jan. 8, 2007. Coma, not see visitors: NY *Times*, May 14, 1960; Sept. 13, 1964. Died: Kingston *Freeman*, Sept. 10, 1965; NY *Times*, Sept. 11, 1965; Phila. *Inquirer*, Sept. 11, 1965. "Fade out": Burnham, *God*, 1979, 112.

8: "Successful," "wasted," "principles": *ND*, July 26, 1958, 16-17; Aug. 2, 1958, 18-21; Aug. 30, 1958, 10-11. Model, Redwood Valley, end justifies means, violence, socialism : Hall, *Gone from the Promised Land*, 1987, 50-53, 72-73,79-80, 162, 205; Maaga, *Hearing the Voices of Jonestown*, 1998, 56, 65, 107-108, 110-111. Continuing visits: Hall, 70; Mrs. M. J. Divine, *Peace Mission Movement*, 1982, 137-141. Drug abuse, "suicide": Maaga, 101, 107, 164. "Privacy": Hall, 284-285.

Ch. 42. Selling Off, Moving Out, Lingering On

1: "Especial": *ND*, Nov. 26, 1942, 71. "Tillable": *ND*, Nov. 25, 1943, 19. Greenkill deed: Martha B. F. Hart (Blessed Faithful Heart) to Joy Love et al, Nov. 18, 1946, liber 1269, p. 521. Samsonville deed: Eliza N. Shelton et al to Gerhard Hahn and wife, Feb. 5, 1945, liber 648, p. 377. Kingston deed: Heavenly Rest to Heavenly Rest et al, March 6, 1961, liber 1104, p. 816.

2: Milton deed: Esther Anderson et al to Emilio Guarino et al, June 18, 1947, liber 684, p. 571. In turn, the Guarinos resold in 1952 to black Seventh Day Adventists. Krum Elbow major deed: Rebecca Good et al to Walter R. Seaman, Ap. 11, 1960, liber 1091, p. 276. An additional minor Krum Elbow deed indicated that a State Supreme Court had authorized the Palace Mission, Inc, of New York City, of whose board of trustees John DeVoute was chairman, to sell 15 acres more of the estate to the same Walter R. Seaman, Ap. 18, 1960, liber 1091, page 271.

3: Neglected Greenkill, willing to sell but complicated: Raymond F. Le Fever, interv., Feb. 11, 2004; Philip Life and Roger Klaus, intervs., Oct. 22-24, 2006; Wilson Tinney, interv., July 21, 2006; *ND*, July 7, 1945, 13. Greenkill deeds: Joy Love et al to Unity Mission, May 12, 1967, Liber 1197, p. 1008; Unity Mission to Ramapo Lumber Corp., Nov. 3, 1971, liber 1269, p. 71. Sand mine: John Jamiolkowski, interv., Jan. 21, 2005. Recently a construction supply firm has built an office on the former Greenkill site. Visit of 1967: Roger Klaus, intervs., Feb. 6-7, 2007. Visit of 1978: correspondence at Stone Ridge Library. Harlem: *Wall Street Journal*, May 8, 1985.

4: "Brothers": *ND*, Dec. 24, 1955, 44. Installed wiring: Tom and Jean Crepet, intervs., Nov. 7, 8, 2004; Aug. 16, 2006; Kenneth Oakley, interv., May 15, 2004. Heart deed: J. Sanford Cross and wife to Solomon Heart, Aug. 24, 1954, Liber 901, p.1; Robert Larsen, intervs., Oct. 12, 15, 2004. Heart lived there until he died in 1975. Endurance: Jean Seaman Roumelis, interv., Sept. 20, 2004.

5: Kingston: Wilson Tinney, intervs., July 21, Aug. 11, 2006; Anita Lea, interv., Oct. 23, 2006, Roger Klaus, interv., Aug. 22-24, 2007. It was only in 1960 that Satisfied Love stopped listing her name as such in Kingston phone books, relying thereafter on the mansion's listing as "Father Divine's Peace Mission," 67 Chapel St.. Sale of the Kingston mansion: Joanne Bush, papers, correspondence, and interv., Feb., 2008. By the time of the sale, two of the other owners of the mansion, Redeemed Love and Jewel Lamb had died, and the third, H. Rest, had signed a quit claim. Deed: Unity Mission to Richard and Joanne Bush, Oct. 16, 1985, liber 1547, p. 155.

6: Crabb encouraged: *ND*, June 3, 1944, 53; July 14, 1945, 4-5. Deed for Crabb's house lot: Wonderful Peace to Frederic N. Crabb, Nov. 11, 1959, liber 1081, p. 348. Miller's recollections: Laura Brock Miller, intervs., 2004-2007. By 2008, Miller had sold her house to a commercial development being built nearby, and moved, not surprisingly, to Philadelphia.

7: Powell: *ND*, May 25, 1946, 17.

ACKNOWLEDGMENTS

WHILE MANY PERSONS who have assisted in this study have been acknowledged in the Sources or in photo captions, it is a pleasure to acknowledge others.

For computer assistance I thank Karen Vassell. For computer and photography assistance I thank Rene F. Ramos. For travel, interviewing, and film reading assistance, I thank Robert Tucker. For preparing maps, I thank Colin Mills. For guiding me to sources, interviews, the location of Divine sites, and the like, I thank especially Vivian Wadlin, Judy Forbes, Charles Cullen, Richard Rydant, David Krikun, Ralph Neaderland, John Jacobs, Linda Tantillo (Rosendale Library), and Dietrich Werner (Century House Historical Society, Rosendale). Especially for their advice and encouragement, I thank Shirley Anson, Sister Adrian Hofstetter, Donald Roper, and my publisher Wray Rominger. For local help, I thank town historians, especially Saugerties Town Historian Karlyn Elia and Lloyd Town Historian Terry Scott, and for help on property records, Sue Wicks. For interpretation of legal issues, I thank attorney Paul Newhouse.

For giving the entire manuscript a broader, more balanced point of view, in repeated readings, I thank my daughter, Susan Mabee Newhouse. For detailed work on my style of writing, I thank Richard Menn and John Noffsinger. For endless patience with my requests for help, I thank especially my home library, the Sojourner Truth Library, of the State University College at New Paltz, and especially there Corinne Nyquist and Joseph Stoeckert. Also I thank many other libraries, such as Elting Memorial Library, New Paltz; Ulster County Community College Library, Stone Ridge; Kingston Area Library, Kingston; Vassar College Library, Poughkeepsie; the NY State Library, Albany; the Enoch Pratt Free Library, Baltimore, Md.; and the New York Public Library, both its main library and its Schomburg Research Center. For many courtesies, including identifications of persons, providing documents, and providing opportunities to interview followers and to visit current Divinite sites, I thank Mother Divine, Philip Life, Roger Klaus, and others of Divine's Peace Mission headquarters, Woodmont, Gladwyne, Pa.

For stories, hints, and prods, I thank a vast number of others as well, including friends, family, colleagues, historians, librarians, followers, non-followers, and many others who at various times in their lives came in touch with the Divine movement.

SOURCES CITED

in both Notes and Photo Captions

A. BOOKS, PAMPHLETS, AND ARTICLES CITED

Adler, Dennis, *Duesenberg*, no place, Krause Publications, 2004

Alexander, Jack, "All Father's Chillun Got Heavens," *Saturday Evening Post*, Nov. 18, 1939, 69

Anderson, Richard C., *Peace Was in Their Hearts: Conscientious Objectors in World War II*, Watsonville, Calif.: Correlan Publications, 1994.

Barnett, Charles R., *Summer Song: Growing up along the Rondout*, Rosendale, NY: Century House Historical Society, 2000

Belstrom, LaVere Eliot, *Rediscovering God, Our International Treasure*, on the web: www.libertynet.org/fdipmm/rediscov.html, 2005. A review of historical writing about Divine, by a follower.

Bender, Lauretta, and M. A. Spalding, "Behavior Problems in Children from the Homes of Followers of Father Divine," *Journal of Nervous and Mental Disease*, April, 1940, 460-472. By respected psychiatrists, but the sample they studied was limited.

Bennett, Reginald, *The Mountains Look Down: A History of Chichester, A Company Town*, Fleischmanns, NY: Purple Mountain Press, 1999.

Boaz, Ruth, "My Thirty Years with Father Divine," *Ebony*, May, 1965, 88-98. A sour view by a former Divine secretary.

Braden, Charles S., *Spirits in Rebellion: The Rise and Development of New Thought*, Dallas: Southern Methodist University, 1963

Braden, Charles S., *These Also Believe: A Study of American Cults*, NY: Macmillan, 1949. Even-handed on Divine.

Burness, Tad, *Cars of the Early Thirties*, Philadelphia: Chilton, 1970

Burnham, Kenneth E., *God Comes to America: Father Divine and the Peace Mission Movement*, Boston: Lambeth Press, 1979. Restrained.

Casey, Thomas W., "F. D. R., Father Divine and the 'Krum Elbow' Flurry," *Hudson Valley Regional Review*, March, 1991, 44-56

"Come Ye...to Woodmont," pamphlet, 1950s?

Directory of Civilian Public Service, May, 1941 to March, 1947, Middlefield, Ohio: Dan E. Miller, 1988

Dictionary of American Slang, NY: Harper Collins, 1995

Divine, Mrs. M. J. (the second Mother Divine), *Peace Mission Movement*, Phila.: Imperial Press, 1982

Elbert, J. L., *Duesenberg, The Mightiest American Motor Car*, Arcadia, Calif.: Motor Classic, 1951

Elverhoj Lectures, Milton, NY, 1920s?

Fauset, Arthur Huff, *Black Gods of the Metropolis: Negro Religious Cults of the Urban North*, Phila.: University of Pennsylvania, 1944, 2002

Flynn, George Q., *The Draft, 1940-1973*, Lawrence, Kas.: University Press of Kansas, 1993

Green Kill Park. Kingston, NY: Freeman Publishing, 1917

Griffith, R. Marie, "Body Salvation: New Thought, Father Divine, and the Feast of Material Pleasures," *Religion and American Culture*, v.2, no. 2, 2001, 119-153

Hall, John R., *Gone from the Promised Land: Jonestown in American Cultural History*, New Brunswick, NJ: Transaction Books, 1987

Harkness, Georgia, "Father Divine's Righteous Government," *Christian Century*, Oct. 13, 1965, 1259-1260

Harris, Sara, *Father Divine, Holy Husband*, NY: Doubleday, 1953. Divine cursed this book.

Hunt, John, "Father Divine: Man or God?" *Our World*, Aug., 1949, 8-15. By a follower who rebelled.

Kephart, William M., and William W. Zellner, *Extraordinary Groups*, NY: St. Martin's Press, 1991

Kohn, Stephen M., *Jailed for Peace: The History of American Draft Law Violators*, 1658-1985, NY: Praeger, 1987

Maaga, Mary McCormick, *Hearing the Voices of Jonestown*, Syracuse, NY: Syracuse University Press, 1998

Mabee, Carleton, *Black Education in New York State: From Colonial to Modern Times*, Syracuse, NY: Syracuse University Press, 1979

Mabee, Carleton, *Black Freedom: The Nonviolent Abolitionists from 1830 through the Civil War*, NY: Macmillan, 1970

Mabee, Carleton, with Susan Mabee Newhouse, *Sojourner Truth: Slave, Prophet, Legend*, NY: New York University Press, 1993

Mary, Faithful, *God: He's Just a Natural Man*, NY: Universal Light Publishing, 1937. By a follower who rebelled. Ghost written.

McKay, Claude, "Father Divine's Rebel Angel," *American Mercury*, Sept., 1940, 73-80

McKelway, St. Clair, and A. J. Liebling, "Who Is This King of Glory?" *New Yorker*, June 20, 1936, 22-28; June 27, 1936, 22-32

Mitchell, Joseph, *My Ears Are Bent*, NY: Pantheon, 1938, 2001, 95-99

Parker, Robert Allerton, *Incredible Messiah: The Deification of Father Divine*, Boston: Little, Brown, 1937

Petersen, Sorens K., *Stories*, no place, no publ., 1960(?), 7-10. Background on the Milton mission.

Rhoads, William B., *Kingston, New York: The Architectural Guide*, Hensonville, NY: Black Dome Press, 2003

Rosten, Leo, *People I Have Loved, Known or Admired*, NY: McGraw-Hill, 1970

Satter, Beryl, "Marcus Garvey, Father Divine and the Gender Politics of Race Difference and Race Neutrality," *American Quarterly*, v. 48, no. 1, 1996, 43-76

Sibley, Mulford Q., and Philip E. Jacob, *Conscription of Conscience, The American State and the Conscientious Objector, 1940-1947*, Ithaca, NY: Cornell University Press, 1952

Sibley, Mulford, and Ada Wardlaw, *Conscientious Objectors in Prison, 1940-1945*, Phila.: Pacifist Research Bureau, 1945

Sokolsky, George, "Giants in These Days," *Atlantic Monthly*, June, 1936, 699-700.

Watts, Jill, *God, Harlem U. S. A.: The Father Divine Story*, Berkeley, Calif.: University of California Press, 1992. Substantial.

Weisbrot, Robert, *Father Divine and the Struggle for Racial Equality*, Urbana, Ill.: University of Illinois Press, 1983. Seriously researched; helped to establish Divine as a progressive figure.

B. PERIODICALS CITED

Baltimore, Md., *Sun*
Boston, Mass., *Traveler*
Christian Century
Cleveland, O., *Directory*
Ellenville, NY, High School Yearbook, *Blue and Gold*
Highland, NY, *Southern Ulster Pioneer*
Kingston, NY, *Freeman*
✓Kingston, NY, High School Yearbook, *Maroon*
Kingston, NY, *Sunday Press*
Kingston, NY, *Ulster County Press.* Earlier publ. in Stone Ridge.
Las Vegas, Nev., *Sun*
Margaretville, NY, *Catskill Mountain News*
New Day (abbreviated as *ND*). A Divine movement-related periodical.
New Day Digest. After the New Day itself ceased regular publication, the Divine movement occasionally published this substitute.
New Paltz, NY, High School Yearbook, *Huguenot*
New Paltz, NY, *Independent.* Title varies.
New Paltz, NY, *News*
Newsweek
New York *Age*
New York *Amsterdam News*
New York Appellate Division Reports (NY State Supreme Court, Appellate Division)
New York *Evening Journal*
New York *Herald Tribune*
New York Miscellaneous Reports (NY State Supreme Court, NY County)
New York *Post*
New York *Sun*
New York *Times*
New York *World-Telegram*
Our World
Philadelphia, Pa., *Inquirer*
Pittsburgh, Pa., *Courier*
Poughkeepsie, NY, *Eagle-News*
Poughkeepsie, NY, *Evening Star*
Poughkeepsie, NY, *Sunday Courier*
Poughkeepsie, NY, *Sunday New Yorker*
Saugerties , NY, *Telegraph*
Sayville, NY, *Suffolk County News*
Spoken Word (abbreviated as *SW*). A Divine-related periodical.
Stone Ridge, NY, *Ulster County Press.* Later publ. in Kingston.
Time
Wallkill, NY, *Wallkill Valley World*. Available as clippings, as at Elting Library, New Paltz.
Wall Street Journal

C. INTERVIEWS AND CORRESPONDENCE CITED

(All took place from 2003 to 2008)

Ahl, Margaret Naccarato, Kingston, NY
Auburn Cord Duesenberg Museum, Auburn, Ind.
Benjamin, Vernon, Saugerties, NY
Boice, H. Sheldon, Krumville, NY
Briggs, Shirley (dec.) and Donald, Hurley, NY
Budd, Patience, Howell, NJ

Bush, Joanne and Richard, Kingston, NY
Center on Conscience & War, Washington, DC
Coy, William A., Clintondale, NY
Crepet, Tom and Jean, Gardiner, NY
Dellay, John Joseph, Southern Pines, NC
Divine, Mrs. M. J. , (second Mother Divine), Gladwyne, Pa.
Donohue, Donald C., Woodstock, NY
Elia, Karlyn Knaust, Saugerties, NY
Enaharo, Aaron H.. Gladwyne, Pa.
Erichsen, Kenneth, Highland, NY
Forbes, Judy Edwards, Westtown, Pa.
Foye, William D., Middletown, Conn.
Gittens, Sonia, High Falls, NY
Hall, Gibson, Smyrna, Del.
Hasbrouck, R. Francis, New Paltz, NY
Hasbrouck, Richard, New Paltz, NY
Henry, Patrick, Philadelphia, Pa.
Jamiolkowski, John, Rosendale, NY
Jeter, Leon, Gladwyne, Pa.
Jerry, Mildred, Stone Ridge, NY
Jones, Amanda, Palenville, NY
Kingston City Registrar, Kingston, NY
Klaus, Roger, Gladwyne, Pa.
Kruger, George, Accord, NY
Larkin, Alan and Pamela, Kingston, NY
Larsen, Robert, High Falls, NY
Lea, Anita, Gladwyne, Pa.
Le Fever, Raymond F., Bloomington, NY
Le Fevre, Jay A., Gardiner, NY
Life, Philip L., Gladwyne, Pa.
Love, Peter, Stamford, Conn.
Maybanks, Harold, Elkins Park, Pa.
Metropolitan Museum of Art, New York, NY
Miller, Laura Brock, Highland, NY; later Philadelphia, Pa.
Mitchell, Normal, Graham, NC
Newkirk, Stanley, Ulster Park, NY
Oakley, Kenneth, Krumville, NY
Peace, June S., Philadelphia, Pa.
Pfaff, Judy, Kingston, NY
Phillips, Doris, New Paltz, NY
Praise, Sweet (Jacqueline Baker), New Brunswick, NJ
Roumelis, Jean Seaman, Highland, NY
Rydant, Richard, High Falls, NY
Tinney,Wilson, Watertown, NY
Van Demark, Curtis, Kingston, NY (dec.)
Van Kleek, Winston, Kerhonkson, NY (dec.)
Walden, George, Lomontville, NY
Wick, Sue, St. Remy, NY
Will, Free, Philadelphia, Pa.

D. COLLECTIONS CITED, INCLUDING MANUSCRIPTS, LEGAL DOCUMENTS, CLIPPINGS, PHOTOS

Auburn Cord Duesenberg Museum, Auburn, Ind.: photo
Bush, Joanne and Richard, Kingston, NY: souvenirs, letters, clippings, photos
Century House Historical Society, Rosendale, NY: photos
Deeds, in Deeds Vault, Ulster County Office Building, Kingston, NY: deeds and similar legal documents
Elting Memorial Library, New Paltz, NY: clippings, photos
Franklin D. Roosevelt Library, Hyde Park, NY: photo
Klaus, Roger, Woodmont, Gladwyne, Pa.: photos
Law Library, Ulster County Court House, Kingston, NY: Mary Lyon's case records
Mabee, Carleton, Gardiner, NY: photos; Civilian Public Service bulletins
Marlboro Free Library, Marlboro, NY: file on Elverhoj Art Colony, photo
Miller, Dolores A., Woodstock, NY: photos
Miller, Laura Brock, Highland, NY: photos, clippings
Ramos, Rene F., Forest Hills, Queens, NY: photos
Rhoads, William B., New Paltz, NY: photo
Rydant, Richard, High Falls, NY: photo
Stone Ridge Public Library, Stone Ridge, NY: file on 1978 visit of Divinites to Marbletown; file on local schools.
Surrogate Court, New York County, 31 Chambers St., New York City: Mary S. LyonProbate File 2815, 1946
Taylor Street Studio, Portland, Ore.: photo
Tucker, Robert, Los Angeles, Calif.: photos
Ulster County Clerk's Office, Kingston: legal records
Woodmont, Peace Mission headquarters, Gladwyne, Pa.: files, videos, photos

INDEX